Fountas & Pinnell

Word Study Lessons

Phonics, Spelling, and Vocabulary

GRADE 3

Heinemann
361 Hanover Street
Portsmouth, NH 03801-3912
www.heinemann.com

Offices and agents throughout the world

Grateful acknowledgment to the following school for generously allowing Heinemann to photograph its students, teachers, and classrooms: The Channing Elementary School, Hyde Park, MA.

Cataloging-in-Publication Data is on file at the Library of Congress
ISBN: 978-0-325-10507-9

Editorial: David Pence, Jeff Byrd, Alana Jeralds
Production: Joseph Hinckley
Cover design: Suzanne Heiser, Ellery Harvey
Interior design: Monica Ann Crigler
Typesetter: Technologies 'N Typography, Inc.
Manufacturing: Erin St. Hilaire

Printed in the United States of America on acid-free paper
22 21 20 19 18 VP 1 2 3 4 5

PWS Contents

PWS Lessons

PWS Lessons *(continued)*

PWS Lessons *(continued)*

WORD-SOLVING ACTIONS (*continued*)

Introduction

When you teach this collection of one hundred phonics, spelling, and vocabulary lessons, you invite children to join you in exploring an exciting subject— language and how it works. We often think that phonics applies only to using letters and sounds in reading; in fact, knowledge of the building blocks of words is useful to readers and writers across all literacy learning. And, in turn, engaging in reading, writing, and talking propels learning in phonics and word study.

In this book, you will find guides for the explicit, systematic teaching of aspects of language through lessons outside of continuous text; but you will also find suggestions for explicit systematic teaching as students read and write texts. The goal of these lessons is to help your students expand and refine their reading and writing powers; but, we hope that they will also become enthusiastic explorers of words—investigating their meanings, seeing patterns, puzzling out simple and more complex letter-sound relationships, taking words apart to notice base words and affixes, and connecting them in an active way. In this way, they learn *how to learn* aspects of words and develop efficient and powerful word-solving strategies.

We believe that it is essential for all readers and writers to have a wide range of word-solving strategies—possibly hundreds—that they can use rapidly, flexibly, and in a largely unconscious way as they read and write. This flexible range of strategic actions enables them to keep their attention focused on the meaning as they process text. Third graders will have a repertoire of known words, and they will recognize many word parts; they are likely to need experience in looking closely at words, noticing parts, and solving words with ease and fluency "on the run" while reading for meaning. Also, children in third grade need to develop highly efficient systems for adding to their repertoire of known words because problem solving should take place against a backdrop of accurate reading.

What Is Phonics?

Phonics is more than relating a letter to a sound. Learning phonics is complex. According to Clay (1991), a competent reader "uses not just the sounds of letters but phonological information from several levels of language. He can provide phonological identities for letters, digraphs, clusters, syllables, prefixes and suffixes, root words, phrases, and non-language strings. He will select a larger rather than a smaller unit for efficiency and may check one source of information against another" (290).

Let's look at the term *phonics,* which we often use as a kind of "shorthand" for everything Clay described above. But there are more precise definitions for the understandings children are developing. Here are some relevant terms:

▶ The **phonological system** is the sound system of oral language.

▶ A **phoneme** is a unit of sound that makes it possible to distinguish one word from another. For example, a single sound can make the difference, as in *pat* and *bat*.

▶ **Phonological awareness** refers to an individual's sense of the phonological structure of words, for example, rhymes, onsets (beginning part of a one-syllable word) and rimes (the rest of the word), syllables, and individual phonemes. It refers to awareness of *sound*, not letters.

- **Phonemic awareness** is an individual's ability to hear, identify, and manipulate the individual sounds—or phonemes in a word. Phonemic awareness (or **phoneme awareness**) is a subset of phonological awareness and has to do with sounds (not letters) in oral language.
- A letter, or **grapheme**, is a written character in an alphabetic system of writing. The **alphabetic principle** is the understanding that sounds and letters are related.
- A **phonogram** is a common word ending that appears in many words or syllables (-*am* in *Pam, ham, jam*).
- **Phonics** is a method for teaching that involves developing learners' ability to hear and manipulate sounds and to learn the correspondence—both simple and complex—between sounds and letters as well as between sounds and larger units.

So, when we identify our one hundred lessons (including many that are generative because they are used over and over to teach a variety of letters, sounds, phonogram patterns, and word parts), we are referring to specific areas of learning about phonics, spelling, and vocabulary—all of which are important for children to understand as they explore language and how it works.

What Do Third Graders Need to Know?

Third graders have the need to consistently increase stamina and efficiency as readers and writers. They read both "chapter books" and shorter pieces—fiction and nonfiction. They have full control of the early reading behaviors and automatically process print with all of its conventions. Also, they will have internalized simple and more complex letter-sound relationships. They understand vowels and consonants, as well as phonogram patterns, and they have automatic recognition of many word parts. Through the third grade year, they need to develop ease and flexibility in solving words and to learn more about base words and affixes. Most importantly, they will have developed beginning systems for learning new words and adding them to the repertoire of known words. But we cannot take it for granted that all of this learning has taken place for every student. So, assessment is important.

The Fountas & Pinnell Comprehensive Phonics, Spelling, and Word Study Guide (2017) is the key to the effective use of word study lessons. This comprehensive volume is a meticulously constructed picture of the linguistic and language knowledge students develop on their journey to become highly expert and flexible word solvers. Most important for teaching third graders are the areas identified as "in process" and "under control" during this year of school. Complex learning takes time over many examples, and few concepts are simply "taught" in one lesson and do not need further development. Nevertheless, the period of time from beginning to the end of third grade represents a massive acquisition of knowledge about the building blocks of words.

We know that as teachers we simultaneously help children expand their oral language capabilities while we work with them on the understandings needed for literacy. At the heart of literacy is a language process in which children use what they know about the language they speak and connect it to print (Clay 1991). The semantic (meaning), syntactic (structure or grammar), phonological (sound), and graphemic (letters) systems all work together as children are becoming literate. Decades of research have shown that when they are meaningfully engaged with print, children develop early awareness of the relationships between these systems (Read 1971; Treiman 1985). Most children, however, need explicit teaching that focuses their attention to the use of letters, sounds, and word parts to solve words (Adams 1990; Armbruster, Lehr, and Osborn 2001; Clay 1991, 1998, 2001; Juel 1988; Juel, Griffith, and Gough 1986; Moats 2000; National Institute of Child Health and Human Development 2001; Pressley 1998; Snow, Burns, and Griffin 1998). The challenge for teachers is to organize their own knowledge and design systematic ways to engage the children in constructing their understandings and help them use them effectively and efficiently in their reading and writing.

We have identified nine areas of learning about phonics, spelling, and word study. For third graders, we have provided a bank of lessons for the last six of those nine areas. The continuum is based on research in language and literacy learning; we have asked linguists, researchers on literacy education, and many teachers to provide feedback on the phonics and word study section. We found surprising agreement on the knowledge needed to become an expert word solver.

Let's look at the nine areas of learning in more detail.

Nine Areas of Learning About Phonics, Spelling, and Word Study

Early Literacy Concepts Early literacy concepts include distinguishing between print and pictures, understanding the concepts of letters and words and sentences, and learning that print has directionality. It will be rare for third graders to need instruction in early literacy concepts, so we do not include them here.

Phonological Awareness We recommend extensive work in reading aloud and shared reading to develop phonological and phonemic awareness. Songs, rhymes, and poetry give students the background and examples to participate fully in your lessons in this area. The development of phonemic awareness is basic to other learning about literacy, but third graders should have a good understanding of how to hear sounds in words. If you need guidance in this area, see the grade 1 lessons.

Letter Knowledge Children need many different experiences with letters in order to learn "what to look for" when distinguishing one letter from another. They learn that there are many different letters in the set called the alphabet, that each letter has a different name, and that each letter is just a little different from every other letter. We have not included Letter Knowledge lessons in this book because, typically, third graders know the letters and use this knowledge automatically. But if you have students who still need help, consult the grade 1 lessons.

Letter-Sound Relationships Understanding of more sophisticated letter-sound relationships is a foundation that all third graders need to use in further learning. Your lessons in this area will help students develop an organized view of the tools of literacy. Most third graders have good control of sounds associated with vowels, consonants, blends, and digraphs; but they are still learning more complex letter-sound relationships.

Spelling Patterns The patterns in regularly spelled words are helpful to third graders as they learn more complex strategic actions. As they explore more complex phonograms and words that have both reliable and irregular letter-sound correspondence, they learn strategies for decoding. Solving larger parts of words helps them read and write more efficiently and also gives them access to many words.

High-Frequency Words High-frequency words are also learned in many other components of effective and coherent design for literacy teaching. Lessons on high-frequency words help children develop a useful core of known words that they can use as resources to solve new words, check on their reading, and read and write fluently. We would expect that by the end of third grade, children have a repertoire of hundreds of words that they can read quickly and easily. You may wish to have them work toward control of the 500 most frequently used words. In addition, they will add many known words from their oral vocabulary.

Word Meaning/Vocabulary Children need to know the meaning of the words they are learning to read and write. It is important for them constantly to expand their vocabulary as well as develop a more complex understanding of words they already know. This area of learning describes understandings related to the development of vocabulary—concept words that have sets and subsets, words related by category, synonyms and antonyms, compound words, and words with literal and figurative meanings.

Word Structure Word structure deals with the underlying rules for understanding contractions, plurals and affixes. Third graders will be learning more about contractions, suffixes, the spelling of plurals, compound words, syllables, prefixes, possessives, and abbreviations. Work in this area will greatly expand word knowledge.

Word-Solving Actions Readers and writers use a variety of word-solving strategies to decode words when reading or writing continuous text. They also use parts of words and search for patterns they can connect. These strategies are invisible, "in-the-head" actions, although we can sometimes infer them from overt behavior. For example, children will sometimes make several attempts at words, revealing their hypotheses. Or they may work left to right on a word (traditionally called "sounding out"). Or they may make connections with other words. Proficient readers tend to use these in-the-head word-solving actions to read more smoothly, more sensibly, and more accurately. They orchestrate systems of information, always searching for a "fit." Most third graders have established a beginning version of this sophisticated system, and they are able to rapidly employ a wide range of actions.

While all areas are important, some are of critical significance in your teaching of phonics, spelling, and word study in third grade. A guiding question in the selection of lessons is: What are the essential literacy concepts my students need to understand to become accomplished readers and writers by the end of third grade? There is little disagreement on these essential areas:

Essential Literacy Concepts Every Third Grader Should Know

Third graders have learned:

▶ to fully control early and foundational aspects of print and how it works;
▶ a fully developed sense of the phonology of the language, including rhymes; initial, ending, and medial sounds in words; onsets and rimes;
▶ to separate words into sounds or to make words by putting sounds together;
▶ to identify phonemes in words;
▶ the alphabet and its uses and relationships to sounds, including consonants, vowels, consonant blends and digraphs;
▶ a core of words that they read and write quickly and automatically;
▶ to solve words using letters and sounds and word parts;
▶ an oral vocabulary that they can use to solve words;
▶ understanding of the structure of oral and written language;
▶ to read words that have long vowel sounds and short vowel sounds in words with silent *e*;
▶ to understand the use of *y* as a vowel;
▶ to recognize and use vowel clusters;
▶ to recognize and use phonogram patterns (VC, VC*e*, VCC, VVC) in one- and two-syllable words;
▶ to recognize and use phonogram patterns with /u/ and with /o/, as well as phonogram patterns with *r*; and
▶ to expand understanding of a wide range of concept words.

Third graders are learning to:

▶ expand understanding and use of more complex syntax in both oral and written language;
▶ expand understanding of letters that may be connected to more than one sound, and expand understanding of sounds that may be connected to more than one letter;
▶ expand understanding of consonant clusters that blend two or three sounds;
▶ expand understanding of consonant clusters that make one sound at the beginning of words or at the end of words;
▶ expand understanding of the use of double consonants;
▶ extend skill in using knowledge of patterns and word parts to read with efficiency and to spell accurately;
▶ continuously add to a repertoire of words they understand and can read and spell;
▶ expand understanding of special categories of words (homophones, synonyms, antonyms, and compound words);
▶ expand understanding of the use of words with multiple meanings;
▶ extend skill and precision in taking words apart by syllables to solve them;
▶ expand knowledge of contractions and how they work;
▶ expand knowledge of plurals and how they work;
▶ expand knowledge of possessives and how they work;
▶ develop understandings of verb, adverb, adjective, and noun suffixes and how they change words, including inflectional endings and comparatives;
▶ develop an understanding of prefixes and how they change words;
▶ understand simple abbreviations and their purpose; and
▶ use all knowledge of the oral and written language system to solve words while reading continuous text with fluency and understanding.

Phonics and word study lessons have an inquiry element that builds on the natural curiosity of human beings. Students become pattern seekers and discoverers of words. This activity is in itself satisfying; but the important goal of word study is to put it into action within the acts of reading and writing. The daily active processing of continuous print helps readers and writers use everything they know about sounds, letters, and words and to learn more in the process. They are, as Clay (2001) has said, assembling "working systems" for constructing meaning from print. These young readers and writers expect written language to make sense, be enjoyable, and give them the pleasure of acquiring knowledge and thinking deeply. Through reading (both paper and electronic), they learn more about life, and they build the content knowledge they need to succeed in school and life.

Where Does Phonics and Word Study Instruction Fit in the Design for Literacy Learning?

Phonics and word study instruction means explicitly teaching children about the relationships between letters and sounds; for us, it includes the nine areas previously mentioned because they are all interrelated and important in children's learning to read and write. We further distinguish between phonics and word study instruction within the context of continuous text and phonics and word study instruction that is out of the context of continuous text (see Figure 1). Both can be systematic; both can be explicit; both are essential. The lessons in this book provide explicit phonics and word study instruction *out of text*; but each lesson provides many suggestions for extending the learning through explicit instruction *in text*. For example, they include specific suggestions to use in interactive read-aloud, shared reading, guided reading, modeled writing, shared writing, interactive writing, and independent reading and writing. The list below provides the framework for Phonics/Word Study out of text.

Each lesson includes a series of elements:

1. **Teach** whole-class lesson based on a principle related to phonics and word study. Each principle is listed and explained in *The Comprehensive Phonics, Spelling and Word Study Guide*; and most incorporate an element of inquiry so students engage in constructing their understanding. The inclusion of inquiry, where possible, rivets students' attention to discovering and constructing the understanding for themselves; it makes the lesson enjoyable, even exciting. Students become pattern seekers and word discoverers, which we hope will be a lifelong habit.

2. **Apply** the principle through hands-on practice. Through this hands-on and often kinesthetic practice, students learn a great deal more. Each hands-on activity provides an experience in constructing their own knowledge. You may have the whole class, partners, or individuals engage

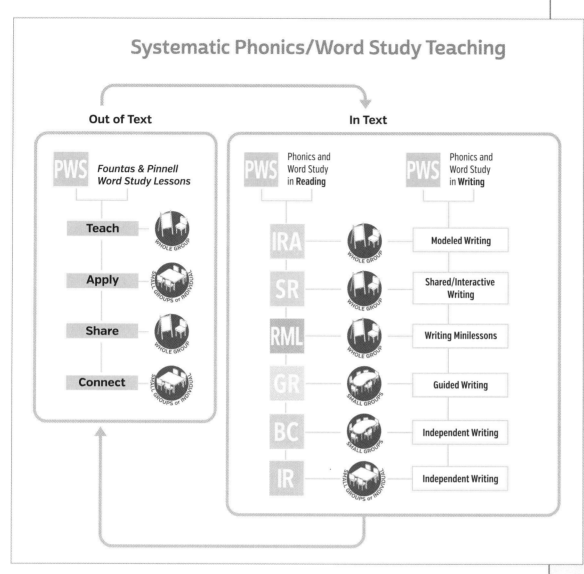

Systematic Phonics/Word Study Teaching

Out of Text

PWS *Fountas & Pinnell Word Study Lessons*

- **Teach** — WHOLE GROUP
- **Apply** — SMALL GROUPS or INDIVIDUAL
- **Share** — WHOLE GROUP
- **Connect** — SMALL GROUPS or INDIVIDUAL

In Text

PWS Phonics and Word Study in **Reading**

- **IRA** — WHOLE GROUP
- **SR** — WHOLE GROUP
- **RML** — WHOLE GROUP
- **GR** — SMALL GROUPS
- **BC** — SMALL GROUPS
- **IR** — SMALL GROUPS or INDIVIDUAL

PWS Phonics and Word Study in **Writing**

- Modeled Writing
- Shared/Interactive Writing
- Writing Minilessons
- Guided Writing
- Independent Writing
- Independent Writing

FIGURE 1 *Systematic Phonics/Word Study Teaching*

in the activity. You might use this application activity as part of students' independent work and it takes place while you are working with small groups in guided reading lessons.

3. **Share**, as students meet briefly in a whole-class meeting, to talk about the discoveries they made. This brief sharing time gives you a chance to assess the effectiveness of your lesson, return to the principle and summarize the learning, and link to reading and writing so students know how to use what they have learned.

In any part of the lesson above, you can choose to engage students in using a word study notebook. Each student has a notebook in which she can record her discoveries. He can write the principle of the lesson and one or two examples to remember. Notebooks can have sections for collecting words such as homonyms, synonyms, and antonyms, or for making words with common base words and affixes.

Your explicit phonics and word study lessons are ideally embedded in a design for responsive literacy teaching that offers a coherent, organized combination of experiences, each of which contributes uniquely to children's literacy development. Look carefully at the key and look along the right-side of the diagram A Design for Responsive Literacy Teaching (see inside back cover). Notice how this design also includes the teaching of systematic phonics and word study lessons that focus directly on the specific aspects of sounds, letters, and words that are appropriate for children to learn at the particular grade level. The chain of blocks to the right represents these short and direct lessons, and that is what the lessons in this book offer. These lessons provide systematic opportunities for explicit instruction out of the text. They are not embedded in other instructional contexts. But you will also notice yellow circles in the lower right corner of many other blocks, showing that phonics, spelling, vocabulary, and word study teaching is also embedded in many instructional contexts across the day. This phonics and word study instruction is also explicit and offers opportunities to teach children how to apply letter-sound/word vocabulary in continuous text.

Each of these instructional contexts is explicitly related to *The Fountas & Pinnell Literacy Continuum: A Tool for Assessment, Planning, and Teaching,* Expanded Edition (2017). Here you will find Characteristics of Texts and detailed Goals (behaviors and understandings to notice, teach, and support) for each context. The phonics lessons in this book are linked to these goals in each of the nine areas. Let's move briefly through each instructional context to understand the comprehensive literacy design.

Reading Contexts in the Third-Grade Classroom

Interactive Read-Aloud In interactive read-aloud, the teacher selects and reads a fiction or nonfiction text to the group (usually in a whole-class setting); students have the opportunity to discuss the story and often to extend it through inquiry, art, science, vocabulary study, or writing about reading. The syntax of the language is more complex than the syntax of the language students read independently or use in their own writing. By hearing it read aloud, they expand understanding of complex language. Through interactive read-aloud, third graders learn vocabulary as well as how to use academic vocabulary to talk about books. They build their background content knowledge and a body of shared literary knowledge that will support all learning.

Many read-aloud books in the *Fountas & Pinnell Classroom™ Interactive Read-Aloud Collection, Grade 3* (2019) include poetry and poetic language that will delight listeners. And certainly, you can choose books from your favorites in the classroom or school library that also have these features. You will find books with rhyme and alliteration and books with onomatopoetic words. The text sets in the grade 3 collection will expand students' content knowledge and also help them think and talk about "big ideas" that they connect across texts. Listening to written language read aloud is a pleasurable experience and provides the foundation for reading with deep comprehension.

You will notice that every word study lesson has specific connections to the texts that you read aloud to students. You can identify these texts quickly by noticing the IRA tiles in the Connect Learning Across Contexts section of each lesson in this book.

Shared Reading Closely related to interactive read-aloud, shared reading offers strong support for students' growing awareness of the qualities of written language, including syntax, vocabulary, letters, and sounds in words. Shared reading has the additional benefit of an enlarged text that students can see. The teacher reads the books to the students, but the books are designed for repeated reading that allows the class to join in on the reading and follow the print. In this way, students have the opportunity to participate in a powerful demonstration of reading. They can see and analyze the details in the illustrations. They can attend to print. Shared reading is usually used with the whole class but may also be used in a small group.

With the support of the group, students read a more complex text than they do in guided or independent reading. They acquire vocabulary and add to their repertoire of known words in reading. Also, they attend to the text features of nonfiction (see Holdaway 1984; Hundley and Powell 1999). Shared reading *leads* reading development so that students develop many strategic actions before they are expected to use them independently (see our book *Guided Reading: Responsive Teaching Across the Grades*, Second Edition 2017).

Our *Fountas & Pinnell Classroom™ Shared Reading Collection, Grade 3* (2019) includes carefully constructed original texts that offer students opportunities to try themselves out as readers. Small individual versions of each big book give students a chance to read again and again these familiar texts or listen to the audible version, each time noticing more about print. The books in the shared reading collection are nonfiction and include features such as maps, sidebars, timelines, charts, and other graphic elements. The books offer an ideal context for helping students learn to use such features.

Reading Minilesson Notice in A Design for Responsive Literacy Teaching (see inside back cover) that interactive read-aloud contributes directly to the four hexagons below it. The reading minilesson is a brief, specific lesson on anything related to reading—genre, characters, setting, problem and solution, text organization, writer's craft, nonfiction features like graphics, and so on. The minilesson emerges from the connected text sets that children have heard, discussed, and responded to in interactive read-aloud.

The reading minilesson forms the first part of a structure: (1) minilesson; (2) independent literacy work, guided reading or book club; (3) group share. You will want to use minilessons across the year, beginning after students are accustomed to the routines of interactive read-aloud and have a repertoire of text knowledge on which to build. The first minilessons might have to do with routines for just about everything related to working together and engaging in literacy learning—from choosing and returning books to tubs to engaging in productive discussion with a partner and then with a small group. Our professional book, *The Reading Minilessons Book, Grade 3* (2019) includes a complete set of reading minilessons for third grade, organized into categories such as Management, Literary Analysis, Strategies and Skills, and Writing About Reading.

Guided Reading You will want to begin guided reading as early as possible in the year, after you have completed an assessment for reading level. Many students will be reading level N or above in instructional groups, but some may need to start at earlier levels. As soon as students have learned the routines that will enable them to work independently for short periods of time, you can begin to form groups. The reading minilessons on management will be helpful here.

Guided reading is small-group instruction (generally about four, five, or six students). Teachers provide specific teaching for effective strategies (word solving, for example) that support comprehension. Guided reading groups consist of individuals who are alike enough that it makes sense to teach them together, which is necessary for efficiency. Because you know the reader's instructional level, you can select books that are more challenging than they can process independently and can provide the skilled teaching that enables them to read the new book with proficiency. All students read the same book, which the teacher selects from a leveled text set. A part of *The Literacy Continuum* provides text characteristics and goals for each level, A to Z. The *Fountas & Pinnell Classroom™ Guided Reading Collection, Grade 3* (2019) provides a collection of original fiction and nonfiction texts, with lessons. You can also use books from many other sources (see the *Fountas & Pinnell Leveled Books Website*, www.fandpleveledbooks.com).

The structure of guided reading is: (1) book selection by teacher; (2) book introduction; (3) book reading by individual students; (4) book discussion; (5) teaching point by the teacher; and (6) word work. The word work is preplanned and correlated with the word-solving demands of texts at the particular level. While students are reading individually, you may sample some oral reading and interact briefly. Sometimes, students may extend their responses to the book through writing or art.

As you work with students, you have many opportunities to look for effective reading behaviors (including but not limited to the application of phonics and word study principles). You can help them apply the principles they are learning by using lessons throughout this book.

Book Club [Small-Group Instruction] Third graders enjoy discussing books with others in a book club. For some, this year may be the first opportunity to participate in a book club. Like other instructional settings, having a good book club requires teaching and practice. *The Reading Minilessons Book, Grade 3* includes lessons in the conventions of choosing books and turn taking, as well as listening to and looking at others. Also, there are minilessons on what you can talk about, on preparing for the discussion, and for self-assessment afterward. After students are comfortable with the routines of interactive read-aloud, can work independently, and can choose books, you can begin some book clubs. Meetings do not have to be long. They may take about the same amount of time as do guided reading sessions, but the whole period is devoted to discussion of one text.

An effective book club might use this structure: (1) the teacher selects four books; (2) students choose the book they want to talk about; (3) students read and prepare for the book club; (4) students meet and talk about the book; (5) students self-assess how the book club went. Each student holds and refers to a copy of the book. The teacher guides and supports the group by supporting the process and encouraging them to engage in a line of discussion.

Books for book club are selected by the teacher for their potential to engage students and for appropriateness to the age group—NOT by level. In fact, these books are not identified by level at all (although the teacher has a good idea of their complexity). Students choose (from the limited set), and they can either read it themselves or listen to an audio recording. Book clubs enable you to work with a small group of diverse children to help them learn how to think and talk about age-appropriate, grade-appropriate fiction and nonfiction books regardless of their reading level.

Our book club collection includes texts that are organized in groups of four, most of which are related by theme to the text sets in Interactive Read-Aloud. For each title, the teacher has a Book Club card to support the process.

Independent Reading and Conferring Independent reading involves students reading books of their choice individually and independently. Of course, students in third grade may read several short books and respond to them in writing. We encourage the use of a reader's notebook to keep a record of texts and response. Reading minilessons will help you teach students how to use this tool.

The books for the classroom library and student choice should be chosen for appeal and accessibility to third graders. These books should accommodate a range of readers, from those substantially below grade level to more advanced. Independent reading helps children build a repertoire of high-frequency words that they can recognize quickly and without effort, reserving more attention for challenging solving of new words.

You can confer with readers while the other students are engaged either in independent reading, in writing or drawing about reading, or in other independent literacy activities. Conferring is your chance to do some quick individual teaching and also to gather some valuable assessment data.

In reading conferences, the teacher and student sit side by side at a desk or table and have a meaningful conversation about the student's book or his reader's notebook. In the *Fountas & Pinnell Classroom™ Independent Reading Collection Grade 3* (2019), we have provided one short "conferring card" for each book that will give you ideas for engaging the student in discussion even if you are not completely familiar with the book. In addition, we have included some generic conferring cards that you can use with any title to focus on literary elements, genre, or other area.

You may want to listen to a little oral reading to see how it is going and whether the student has chosen an appropriate text, but it is not always necessary to do this. You are really using the time to gather information about the student's thinking regarding his reading and also to do some quick teaching if the opportunity arises. You may reinforce the reading minilesson by helping the student apply the principle to this book (for example, animal characters that act like people). You may reinforce the phonics and word study lesson by pointing out an example. Often, you will find out something that you can invite the student to say in group share.

Group Share (Reading) For the reading, writing, and word study elements shown in A Design for Responsive Literacy Teaching (see inside back cover), it is useful to engage in a short group share to bring closure to the instructional period. For each, you will want to return to the minilesson principle to extend the learning and add to an anchor chart or as a reminder to students. You invite students to share something they noticed or discovered in the book they are reading, in their writing, or in the word study application. The group share for word study might be held immediately afterward if students participated in the application activity as a whole group. Group share for reading comes at the end of guided reading or independent reading; for writing, it comes at the end of independent writing. Sometimes you can have the group share about two areas of learning

Group share takes only two or three minutes. Not every student needs to share something every day. Also, you can have students share with a partner or in threes. Students can also self-assess how the period of time went.

Writing Contexts in the Third-Grade Classroom

Modeled Writing In modeled writing, the teacher demonstrates the process of writing for a variety of purposes and audiences. Students learn how a writer gets ideas down on paper and makes decisions.

Shared Writing In shared writing, the teacher is able to demonstrate the writing process, from (1) thinking of what to write, to (2) writing it word by word (composing), to (3) rereading it. In shared writing, a group of students participate in composing a common text. Together, the teacher and students develop a meaningful text, and then, with input from the students, the teacher writes the text on a chart, which is reread many times. Often, students contribute illustrations. This cooperatively constructed text becomes a classroom resource. Students can use it for independent reading or as a reference for their own writing. The writing can take many forms—"news of the day," a note or letter, response to a book from interactive read-aloud, steps of a science experiment, an argument related to social studies or finding from a math project. Charts are a resource for reviewing principles related to the ways words work. Shared writing is often used in reading minilessons, as a response in interactive read-aloud, guided reading, and shared reading.

Writing Minilesson The writing minilesson is a short lesson on some aspect of writing—craft, conventions, or process. The writing minilesson forms the first part of a structure that is similar to the reading minilesson: (1) minilesson; (2) independent writing with conferring or guided writing; (3) group share. The writing minilesson gives you the opportunity to demonstrate principles related to the conventions and craft of writing. The first minilessons may involve management, showing students procedures for getting and using writing materials, for example, or how to share computers. If students have had rich experiences in earlier grades, they may not need many of the management lessons, but you will need some at the beginning of the year to establish routines. The lesson may focus on any aspect of the writing process or the craft of writing. Students then apply the lesson principle to their own pieces of writing and then tell about it in group share.

Independent Writing and Writing Conferences In independent writing, students work individually on their own pieces of writing, usually on a topic of choice. Writing helps students build a repertoire of high-frequency words they can write quickly. They also get a great deal of practice saying words slowly and thinking about how they are spelled. As they learn spelling rules, they can apply them as they write about topics that interest them. In fact, everything you teach in these word study lessons will be applied as students write for their own purposes. Remember that many other contexts provide for writing about reading and offer models that influence independent writing.

When students are drawing and writing independently, you can take the opportunity to hold short conferences with students. Writing conferences involve the teacher and student sitting side by side at a desk or table with the student's current work in progress and writing folder in front of him. The conference can focus on anything related to writing—conventions like punctuation and spelling, craft such as using sound words and illustrations, or the process of writing. Many third graders will write expressive pieces and illustrate them, then go on to another piece without extensive revision. They may write books or reports about their experiences or topics that interest them. (They may choose some pieces to put into a writing folder.) As they gain experience, they can engage in the writing process, of drafting, revising, and producing a final copy. But in grade 3, you will not want to make this an unnecessarily tedious process by too much work on one piece. Or, they may want to display it, and this may require reconsideration of a piece. The writing conference helps you know where the student is in writing and this will give you information about what she knows about spelling and the conventions of written language.

Guided Writing Sometimes, during independent writing time, you may choose to bring together a small group of students, all of whom need to learn something in common about writing. It could be anything to do with writing—conventions, craft, or process. This grouping has nothing to do with reading level. It emerges from your observations of your students as writers. The students are all working on their own pieces of independent drawing and writing, but they can apply your small group minilesson to what they are doing. This is an efficient way to support several writers. Sometimes, it might be reminding students to use word parts they know or it might be using interesting words, so it may be directly linked to what the students are learning about letters or words in *Word Study Lessons.*

Group Share (Writing) At the end of a writing period, it is useful to engage in a short group share to bring closure to the instructional period. Group share takes only two or three minutes. Students can talk about something they learned about writing today, or they can share part of what they wrote. You can take the opportunity to reinforce the writing minilesson. Students can also self-assess how the period of time went.

Independent Literacy Work

Independent work takes place *while* you are working with small groups in guided reading or guided writing or conferring with individual students. It is necessary for students to be engaged in productive and purposeful independent work for a part of the day. This gives you a chance to zoom in more closely with small group instruction while working with the whole group. In addition, it builds self-management and self-determination as students begin to realize that they can make choices and be responsible for their own behavior. Each of these independent settings, however, takes careful organization and teaching.

We have provided procedural minilessons in *The Reading Minilessons Book, Grade 3,* as well as for writing about reading to support meaningful independent work. Students will engage in reading and writing in their reader's notebooks.

What Are Some Effective Ways to Engage Students in Phonics Learning?

The first priority is to find an effective way for you and your students to work together. Too much time can be lost when you have to constantly "direct traffic." Also, one of your goals for your students is independent, self-directed behavior. Below we describe two "systems": one is a simple system for children to complete a series of meaningful tasks that includes time for application of the word study principle during independent work time, and the other is a separate focused time for word study that includes the phonics lesson, application, and group share. For detailed descriptions of classroom organization and management see *Guided Reading.*

Literacy Tasks Within Independent Work Time For application activities and other independent work, you may engage students in the same three or four activities every day. Of course, there is change for the student because the books change and they draw and write on different topics. As mentioned before, you may want to engage students in working as partners to try out the word study application activity, but you may also have them do it as independent activity (after they have overlearned the routine and know exactly what to do). Independent work could include two to three of the following:

1. **Read a book.** Students have their own choice books from the classroom library, or they read from a tub of books that have been read before in guided or shared reading.

2. **Write/draw in a reader's notebook.** Many teachers have students write one thoughtful letter a week to the teacher to share their thinking about any of the books they have read or heard read. See *Reading Minilessons* and other F&P publications.

3. **Listen to a book.** It's quick and easy to record a book on a device, and children can listen to it play softly while they look at the book.

4. **Word Study.** Here students can engage in the application activity for today's word study lesson or one that they have participated in recently. The routine may also include using routines for studying spelling words.

5. Occasionally, students may **work on a personal poetry collection**. They copy a poem in a personal notebook of poetry and illustrate it. Small typed versions of poems you've read to the group make it easier.

Putting this system into practice requires organized supplies and teaching of routines. *The Reading Minilessons Book, Grade 3* provides 200 minilessons, some of which are "management" in that they show how to teach students routines for how to work independently. In addition, each word study lesson in this book has a section advising on how to teach the routines of the Apply activity.

A Separate Word Study Time You may decide to schedule a block of time— e.g., 30 minutes—for teaching the lesson followed by application and group share.

Organizing and Using Materials for Efficient Word Study Learning

Think about the materials needed for the independent work and the routines students will need to use them. If you can teach your students to use materials independently, share them with others, and return them, they will learn something valuable about self-regulation that will serve them well in school and other settings. Here are some suggestions for organizing materials for independent learning.

▶ Clearly organize supplies so that only one kind of material is in a single container.

▶ Label supplies with both words and pictures, especially if you have English language learners.

▶ Using words and pictures or outlines of the container shape, label the place on the shelf where the container is stored. Have all supplies that students will need for a given activity organized and available.

FIGURE 2 *Reading Time Activities*

- Teach them routines for getting and returning materials.

- Establish and explicitly teach the routines that will be needed for a word study learning activity. Post simple directions using both words and (where appropriate) pictures. In our lessons we recommend single words (tags) that describe the series of actions.

- We have limited the number of routines students are expected to follow— a few essential activities can be varied to explore different principles (for example, sorting).

- Introduce routines slowly, teaching as a lesson.

- Place needed resources (such as charts) on the wall to help students work with independence.

- "Walk through" the activity so that you can accurately estimate the time it will take.

- Ideally, students working independently will use a "0 voice," reading or writing silently. They may speak softly if working with a partner on a work study application.

Designing an Environment to Support Letter, Sound, and Word Learning

You can make your teaching more efficient and effective by making sure you have a rich array of tools available. That includes the materials students need to work independently as well as displays that serve as resources. It pays to think analytically about materials and tools and to organize them for maximum student independence. With good organization and careful teaching of routines, third graders can get, use, and put away supplies such as notebooks, books, reference materials, crayons, pencils, markers, scissors, and glue. They can select books and return them to the appropriate bins. They can use resources such as big books, the classroom library, individual book and supply boxes, and notebooks. Many routines are described in these lessons. You can also find detailed descriptions of classroom organization and suggestions for classroom management in *Guided Reading*. Following are some suggestions.

A Meeting Area Establish a meeting area for whole-class teaching. The meeting area should be a clearly defined space that is large enough for students to sit comfortably in a circle or in rows without touching each other. All students should be able to see and hear when you read aloud or engage them in shared reading. If possible, have a carpet for students to sit or use carpet squares that they can stack and retrieve.

In the meeting area you will need an easel with chart paper, a whiteboard (preferably magnetic so that you can demonstrate using magnetic letters), and references like a name chart, poetry charts, Consonant Clusters and Digraphs charts, and charts you have created with students. You will also need a pocket chart on which you can post words and word parts on cards large enough for the whole group to see. Shared reading books should be handy, as well as the books you are planning to read aloud for a week or two-week period. Here you can also store any word study lessons charts that you have made with the students.

A Print-Rich Environment A classroom that is alive with print is a rich resource for teaching and learning. Of course, you want your classroom to look beautiful, comfortable, and inviting with calming colors, but you can also be aware that everything you put on your walls can be a teaching tool or a resource for students. You will want

- charts of several kinds that show more complex letter-sound relationships;
- anchor charts from reading and writing minilessons;
- minilesson charts with word study principles;
- the class schedule of the day;
- a list of "Books We Have Shared";
- word charts of various kinds;
- a class name chart with first and last names;
- stories, messages, lists, letters, records of science experiments, and other written materials produced through shared writing;
- word study charts with principles;
- a rack of personal poetry books where each child's book can be kept and displayed;
- whiteboards to which magnetic letters and magnetic word cards will stick;
- the classroom library with a variety of tubs labeled with categories (for example, by author, illustration, genre, topic, special type).

You may have some basic, clear posters, such as a consonant cluster chart or beautifully illustrated poems, but in general, it is not necessary to spend money on commercially produced posters or other decorative elements. Nor should you be working every night to preprint and decorate charts. The best resources are those you and the students make together. And almost everything on the list above can be an "in process" document.

Elsewhere we have said:

> Teachers don't preplan and make attractive charts to decorate the room; our word walls and charts are *working documents* created by the teacher and children together. While the general plan and the principles repeat year after year {in *Phonics Lessons*}, the charts reflect the unique thinking of any one group of children; the examples they discover, the order in which they produce them, the way they organize them…When we recognize our word walls and charts as working documents that change and develop over time, we realize that they are also a living record of the teaching and learning that has taken place in our classroom program.
>
> —Fountas and Pinnell (1998, 52-53)

Books add to the quality of the environment. For example, the fiction and nonfiction big books with colorful and interesting colors can be displayed face out on a rack. The classroom library can have colorful tubs and books with covers facing out.

Vital Print Resources for the Classroom

Below are a few print resources that we think are very important and are referred to in the word study lessons.

While third graders will know how to read and write their names, it will build community to begin the year with a chart showing children's first and last names with small pictures of each child. The chart will be a useful "connector" to phonics and word study principles and will provide extra support to new English language learners; for example,

▶ "Whose name starts or ends with that consonant cluster (or digraph)?"

▶ "Whose name has those same two vowels together?"

▶ "Can you see a name that has a vowel or *v*?"

Consonant Clusters and Digraphs Charts These posters—one for initial and one for final clusters—are large enough for children to see in the meeting area. On the posters, you will see each consonant cluster, a picture that shows a key word, and the label attached to the picture.

In *Ready Resources*, we provide charts to post in the meeting area, as well as smaller versions that can be duplicated for every student to use.

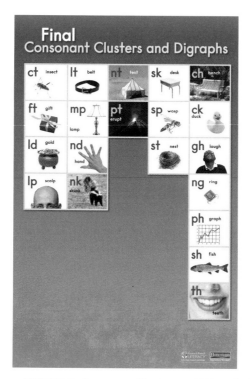

FIGURE 3 *Consonant Clusters and Digraphs Charts*

Word References In grade 3 students are able to use word lists in their writing folders or use simple dictionaries or digital tools. They are learning how to use reference tools that they will need for the rest of their writing lives.

We have described a comprehensive approach to authentic literacy learning. In this design, students spend their time thinking about books, reading books, talking about books, writing about books and learning how letters and words work. It is important to engage every child in learning successfully. Next we provide some general suggestions for working effectively with children who are building a literacy system in English as a new language.

What Are Some Ways of Working Effectively with English Language Learners?

You are likely to have many students in your class who not only can speak one language but are learning a second or even a third language. And that is a great thing. If English is an additional language for the student, then it will be important that you understand and value his expansion of both home and school language. Usually, it takes several years for children to learn English as a second language and to read, write, and think consistently in their new language.

It's important to remember that you need to work differently with English learners. You need to adjust your teaching to make sure that English language learners have access to your teaching of phonics and word study. Many of these adjustments will help all of the students in your classroom because they help to make instruction more explicit and clear. But we should make it clear that meeting the needs of English language learners doesn't simply mean "teaching more." It means teaching (and even thinking) in a different way about your teaching. Put yourself in the position of someone who is learning another language. What could be confusing about concepts and directions? What should be demonstrated instead of simply "told"? Where are pictures needed?

For each lesson in this book, look for a section on the first page labeled Working with English Language Learners. In this section, you will see suggestions specifically related to the implementation of that lesson. On the following pages, we have placed some general suggestions for oral language, for reading, for writing, and for phonics and word study. It is obvious that these four areas overlap and are inter-connected. Work in one area will tend to support learning in all other areas as well.

Oral Language

▶ Show students what you mean when you give directions. You may need to act out certain sequences of action and have students do it while you coach them. Have them repeat directions to each other or say them aloud as they engage in the activity. Support them during their first attempts rather than expecting independence immediately.

▶ Give English language learners more "wait and think" time. You could say, "Let's think about that for a minute" before calling for an answer. Demonstrate to students how you think about what you are going to say.

▶ Paraphrase and summarize for students. Repeat the directions or instructions several different ways, watching for feedback that they understand you. Paraphrase until you can see that they understand.

▶ Use pictures and objects that students understand and that connect to their homes and neighborhoods. At the same time, avoid examples that may be completely strange to students and to which they have difficulty bringing meaning.

▶ Use short, simple sentences in shared reading, interactive writing, and oral conversations. Avoid complex, embedded sentences that students will find hard to follow if they are just learning English. When a complex sentence is used (for example, in read-aloud or shared reading), watch for evidence of confusion on the part of students, and paraphrase with simpler sentences when necessary.

▶ Bring student's familiar world into the classroom through family photos, holiday souvenirs, and objects from home. Expand student's world by bringing in other objects that will give them new experiences.

▶ Demonstrate using sentence frames while talking about familiar topics. Provide oral sentence frames when needed. Involve students in games that require repeating these simple language structures, for example: "My name is _____." "_____ has two brothers and one sister." "I like _____ better than _____." "I like to eat _____." "Josiah likes to _____ (verb)."

▶ Make instruction highly interactive, with a great deal of oral language surrounding everything students are learning.

▶ Expand the activities using student's names. Be sure that you are pronouncing all student's names correctly and clearly as you draw their attention to the particular word that is a student's name. They can help you with your pronunciation. Help students learn the names of other children in the class by using them in sentences and placing them on charts.

▶ Engage English language learners in repeating and enjoying songs, rhymes, and repetitive chants. Incorporate body movements to enhance student's enjoyment of songs, rhymes, and chants and help them remember and understand the language better.

Reading

▶ Read aloud often to students; in general, it is wise to increase the amount of time that you read aloud and discuss books with them. Be sure that the material you are reading is comprehensible, that is, within their power to understand with your support.

▶ Watch for signs of enjoyment and reread some favorites. Rereading books to students will help them acquire and make use of language and content that goes beyond their current understandings.

- Be sure that students' own cultures are reflected in the material that you read aloud to them and that they read for themselves. They should see illustrations with people like themselves in books. They should see their own culture reflected in food, family, dress, customs, everyday events, and so on. (It's essential for all students to become familiar with many cultures.)

- Understand that shared reading involves students in repetition of language, often language that is different from or more complex than they can currently use in speech. Borrow some books from the second grade shared reading collection if you find that repeated reading of language is beneficial. This experience gives students a chance to practice language, learn the meaning of the words, and use the sentence structure of English. (Repetition gives students maximum experience with the syntax of English and will help them to develop an implicit understanding of noun-verb agreement, plurals, and other concepts. Once a text is well known in shared reading, it can serve as a resource to students. Revisit shared reading texts for examples of language structure and for specific words and their meaning.)

- Try to involve students in guided reading as soon as possible after the beginning of the year. Guided reading is a very valuable context for working with English language learners because you can scaffold their reading and their language through an introduction that clears up confusion, and you can observe them closely to gain information as to the accuracy and ease of their reading. Through observation and discussion, you can find what is confusing to them and respond to their questions.

- Be sure to use oral language, pictures, concrete objects, and demonstration when you introduce stories to help students untangle any tricky vocabulary or concepts they encounter in guided and independent reading. They may encounter words that they can "read" (which really means decode) but do not understand.

FIGURE 4 *A Digraphs Chart in a Third-Grade Classroom*

- Help them in guided reading to relate new words to words they already know. During and after reading, check with students to be sure they understand vocabulary and concepts; build into lessons a time when they can bring up any words they did not know.

- Include word work on a regular basis in the guided reading lessons for English language learners. Make strong connections to what they have been learning in phonics and word study.

Writing

- Value and encourage student's drawing, as it represents thinking and connects their ideas to writing.

- Have students repeat the sentence they are going to write several times so that they will be able to remember it. If the sentence is difficult for students to remember, that may be a sign that it is too complex for their present level of language knowledge; consider simplifying the structure or rephrasing the sentence so that it is easier for them.

Children write and illustrate words in a third-grade classroom.

- Focus on familiar topics and everyday experiences in interactive writing so that students can generate meaningful sentences and longer texts. Reread the piece of shared writing many times, encouraging fluency as students gain control over the language.

- Guide students to produce some repetitive texts that use the same sentence structure and phrases over and over again, so that students can internalize them.

- Know that once a text has been successfully produced in shared writing and students can easily read it, this text is a resource for talking about language—locating specific words, noticing beginning sounds and ending sounds, noticing rhymes, new content words, affixes, and so on.

- Encourage English language learners to write for themselves. Demonstrate how to think of something to write, and repeat it so that you remember it. Demonstrate how to say words slowly, providing more individual help and demonstration if needed. Provide some oral sentence frames where needed so students can use them in writing.

- Surround students' independent writing with a great deal of oral language. Talk with them and help them put their ideas into words before they write. Encourage them to tell their stories and share their writing with others and extend their meanings through talk.

- Provide a great many models of writing for English language learners—shared writing, shared reading, charts about people in the room or their experiences. Encourage students to reread and revisit these models to help them in their writing. In the beginning, they may use phrases or sentences from charts around the room, varying their own sentences slightly. Gradually, they will go beyond these resources, but models will be a helpful support for a time.

- For some students, small-group interactive writing is a powerful way to scaffold their transition to independent writing. They also find the text more accessible to read because they co-created it.

- Learn something about the sound system of the students' first language. That knowledge will give you valuable insights into the way they approximate spellings. For example, notice whether they are using letter-sound associations from the first language or whether they are actually thinking of a word in the first language and attempting to spell it. Notice whether they are using consonant clusters, vowel pairs, base words, and affixes.

- Accept spellings that reflect the student's own pronunciation of words, even if it varies from standard pronunciation. Notice the strengths in the student's attempts to relate letters and sounds. Show that you value attempts rather than correcting everything the student writes.

Phonics and Word Study

▶ Use many hands-on activities so that students have the chance to manipulate magnetic letters and tiles, move pictures around, and work with word cards and word parts.

▶ Be sure that the print for all charts (ABC charts, name charts, shared writing, picture and word charts, etc.) is clear and consistent so that students who are working in another language do not have to deal with varying forms of letters.

▶ Make sure that English language learners are not sitting in an area that is peripheral to the instruction (for example, in the back or to the side). It is especially important for these learners to be able to see and hear all instruction clearly.

▶ Provide a "rehearsal" by working with your English language learners in a small group before you provide the lesson to the entire group. Sometimes they may find it more difficult than other students to come up with words as examples; however, only a few minutes (for example, thinking of *s* words) will help these learners come up with responses in whole-group settings. It will not hurt them to think about the concepts twice, because that will provide greater support.

▶ Use real objects to represent pictures and build concepts in students' minds. For example, bring in a real lemon that students can touch and smell rather than just a picture of a lemon. When it is not possible to use real objects to build concepts, use clear pictures that will have meaning for students. Picture support should be included whenever possible.

▶ Be sure to enunciate clearly yourself and accept students' approximations. If they are feeling their own mouths say (or approximate) the sounds, they will be able to make the connections. Sounds and letters are abstract concepts, and the relationships are arbitrary. It will be especially complex for students whose sound systems do not exactly match that of English. They may have trouble saying the sounds that are related to letters and letter clusters.

▶ Accept alternative pronunciations of words with the hard-to-say sounds and present the written form to help learners distinguish between them. Over time, you will notice movement toward more standard English pronunciation. Minimal pairs (sounds that are like each other, have similar tongue positions, and are easily confused, such as /s/ and /sh/, /r/ and /l/, /sh/ and /ch/, /f/ and /v/) are often quite difficult for English language learners to differentiate. English language learners often have difficulty with inflected endings (-s, -ed).

A class-made chart of words with r-controlled vowels

▶ Speak clearly and slowly when working with students on distinguishing phonemes and hearing sounds in words, but do not distort the word so much that it is unrecognizable. Distortion may confuse English language learners in that it may sound like another word that they do not know.

▶ Use word cards and word part cards often so that students have the experience of working with words in a hands-on way. You may want to add pictures so that the meaning of words becomes clearer.

▶ Work with a small group of English language learners to help them in the application activity and make your instruction more explicit. Notice concepts that they find particularly difficult, and make note to revisit them during word work.

Using the *Fountas & Pinnell Word Study System* in the Third-Grade Classroom

Materials and Resources in the System

The *Fountas & Pinnell Word Study System* includes a range of materials and resources designed to help you plan and implement effective literacy instruction. At the core of the system are the one hundred lessons found in *Word Study Lessons*. The lessons are organized in six areas of learning for phonics, spelling, and word study. Each lesson is constructed on one principle detailed in *The Comprehensive Phonics, Spelling, and Word Study Guide*, which is also included in the system. A wide range of materials for teaching the lesson content, connecting learning across contexts, and extending learning are included in *Ready Resources*. Additionally, lesson-specific materials for application activities, extending learning, and formal assessment are included in Online Resources. (To access Online Resources, refer to the instructions on the inside front cover of this book. After you are logged in, click the image of *Word Study Lessons* to access the necessary forms.) A number of organizational ideas outlined in the next few pages of this book (such as the Master Lesson Guide and the Nine Areas of Learning Across the Year) can be implemented in a variety of ways using the labeled folders and dividers provided with the system.

Fountas & Pinnell Word Study Lessons, Grade 3, containing 100 brief lessons for whole-group instruction that help students attend to, learn about, and efficiently use sounds, letters, and words.

The Fountas & Pinnell Comprehensive Phonics, Spelling, and Word Study Guide

Fountas & Pinnell Word Study Ready Resources

Online Resources

Lesson Folders

An Annotated Lesson and Its Features

Over the next several pages you will learn more about how to use an array of features of a lesson.

What do your students already know, and what do they need to learn next? Your insights about your own students will guide your choice of lessons and help you plan instruction that targets your students' learning needs.

Each lesson title reflects the content of the lesson using precise language taken from *The Fountas & Pinnell Comprehensive Phonics, Spelling, and Word Study Guide.*

Recognize and Use Vowel Sounds with *r*

LETTER-SOUND RELATIONSHIPS 14

EARLY **MIDDLE** LATE

Plan

▶ **Consider Your Students**

This lesson will be most effective if students are familiar with a number of common words that have *r*-influenced vowels, such as *her, first, learn, corn,* and *farm.* In this lesson, students consider the different spellings for the same *r*-controlled sound. If students are more experienced with *r*-controlled vowels, you may wish to include several more vowel sounds or multisyllabic words. You may also wish to analyze how students represent *r*-influenced vowels in their writing. You can adapt the lesson to focus on letter-sound relationships with which students need more experience in order to understand and control.

▶ **Working with English Language Learners**

Depending on their first languages, English language learners may find it difficult to pronounce words with *r*-influenced vowels. Accept approximate pronunciations. Draw students' attention to the visual features of words. Then help them form categories of words for the different vowel sounds.

YOU WILL NEED

Online Resources
▶ LSR 14 Action Tags
▶ LSR 14 Word Cards
▶ LSR 14 Two-Way Sorts

Other Materials
▶ chart paper

Generative Lesson
A generative lesson has a simple structure that you can use to present similar content or concepts. Use this lesson structure to teach students a variety of vowel sounds influenced by the letter *r.*

All materials needed for the Teach, Apply, and Assess sections of the lesson are listed. Lesson-specific materials are provided as reproducibles in Online Resources. If studentss are working individually, as partners, or in simultaneous small groups, you will need additional copies.

Generative lessons provide a recurring structure you can use with similar items with a knowledge set. As students acquire knowledge, they build systems for similar learning that accelerate the learning.

Typically, it takes several years for young students to learn English as a second language and to learn to read, write, and think consistently in their new language. As you adjust the lesson for English language learners, your instruction becomes clearer and more explicit in ways that help all of your students.

We help you understand the language principle underlying each lesson so you can teach with clarity and a well-defined purpose.

UNDERSTAND THE PRINCIPLE

When the consonant sound /r/ follows a vowel sound in a syllable, the sounds blend in a way that modifies the vowel sound. These modified sounds are known as *r*-influenced, or *r*-controlled, vowels. The letter-sound relationships among *r*-influenced vowels are complex. The same letter combination may represent more than one vowel sound, e.g., *-ear* in the words *bear, dear,* and *learn.* Conversely, several different letter combinations may represent the same vowel sound, e.g., *-er, -ear, -ir,* and *-ur* in the words *her, learn, bird,* and *hurt.* To solve increasingly complex words efficiently, students need many opportunities to explore these relationships and learn common patterns.

EXPLAIN THE PRINCIPLE

When the letter r *follows a vowel or vowel combination, blend the vowel sound with* r.

Comprehensive Phonics, Spelling, and Word Study Guide

Refer to: page **30**, row **31**

Each lesson highlights a key principle from *The Comprehensive Phonics, Spelling, and Word Study Guide.*

Concise, clear language "rings inside students' heads." Avoid jargon and technical labels; use a common language that enables you to reach your readers and writers simply and easily. Sometimes you will show students examples and invite them to think of the principle; other times, you will state the principle, give a few examples, and invite the students to add examples.

14 LETTER-SOUND RELATIONSHIPS

EARLY **MIDDLE** LATE

ACTIVITY: WORD LISTS

INSTRUCTIONAL PROCEDURE

NOTICE PARTS

See page 36 for detailed descriptions of Instructional Procedures.

EXPLAIN THE PRINCIPLE

When the letter r follows a vowel or vowel combination, blend the vowel sound with r.

Comprehensive Phonics, Spelling, and Word Study Guide

Refer to: page **30**, row **31**

```
he
her
first   purr   worm   fern

do
door
soar   fork   four
```

Teach

1. On chart paper, write the word *he,* and read the word with students. *What vowel sound do you hear in this word?* • *The word* he *has the long e sound, /ē/.*

2. Write the word *her* beneath *he.* Read the word with students. *What do you notice about both of these word*s? *What is different?* • *The last letter is different. Is there anything else different about the words?* • *The letter* r *changes the vowel sound to /er/.*

3. Write the words *first, purr, worm,* and *fern* on chart paper. *What do you notice about all of these words?* • *They all have the vowel sound /er/. What do you notice about the spelling of all of these words?* • *The sound is spelled differently in each word.* Have volunteers underline the letters that stand for the /er/ sound in each word.

4. Draw attention to the word *worm. Sometimes* or *can stand for the /or/ sound, and sometimes it can stand for the /er/ sound. If you're not sure which sound to use, try saying the word both ways to see which pronunciation sounds like a word you know.*

5. If students have good control over the /er/ words, repeat the procedure for the /or/ sound using the words *do* and *door* to emphasize the change in the vowel sound caused by adding *r.* Then add the words *soar, fork,* and *four.*

6. Read both lists of words again with students. Invite them to talk about what they notice. Some comments students might have are:

   "The letter *r* changes long vowel sounds to /er/ or /or/."

   "If the letter *r* were another letter, the vowel sound would be regular."

   "There are different vowel combinations that can stand for the /or/ sound."

   Build on students' comments as you guide students to understand the principle: *When the letter r follows a vowel or vowel combination, the vowel sound changes to /er/ or /or/.*

7. Tell students that they are going to practice sorting words by thinking about the two vowel sounds /er/ and /or/. If the sound in the word sounds like the vowel sound in *store,* they will write the word under the column for *store.* If the sound in the word sounds like the vowel sound in *earn,* they will write the word under the column for *earn.*

Fountas & Pinnell Word Study Lessons, Grade 3

In each Apply section, we show an example of the product or process students will engage in as they practice and apply what they've learned.

Each Apply activity is based on a specific activity that is sometimes the same as—but sometimes different from—the Teach activity.

Students work independently (individually, with partners, in small groups) to apply and practice what they've learned in the lesson.

LETTER-SOUND RELATIONSHIPS 14

EARLY **MIDDLE** LATE

ACTIVITY: TWO-WAY SORT

INSTRUCTIONAL PROCEDURE

SAY AND SORT

See page 36 for detailed descriptions of Instructional Procedures.

ACTION TAGS

read words

say word

sort word

write word

Each Teach activity and each Apply activity is built around one of ten instructional procedures to develop students' knowledge of words and how they work.

The lesson routines are identified in concise words on tags that remind students of what to do. Post the tags where everyone can refer to them as they work. Tags help your students become independent learners.

Apply

Have students sort words with /er/ and /or/ vowel sounds using a two-way sort and word cards. They should first sort the word cards on their desks, and then write the words in the sort.

Share

- Have students share a word that they found difficult to sort with a classmate. The students can help each other as needed. You may wish to add new words to the pocket chart using blank pocket-chart cards.
- Review the principle and remind students to notice vowel sounds with *r* when they read and write.

Assess

- During shared reading and guided reading, notice whether students can quickly locate and read words with vowels followed by the letter *r*.
- Examine students' writing for evidence that they are beginning to represent *r*-influenced vowels accurately.
- You may wish to use Letter-Sound Relationships Assessment E, I, or J.

Use the guidelines to reinforce the principles and help students share their learning. In many lessons, we suggest behaviors to notice and support.

Assess the impact of the lesson and application in ways that are informal and integral to the work students are doing. For some lessons, we suggest using the more formal and systematic procedures in Online Resources to help you determine students' needs for further lessons.

For each lesson, we provide read-aloud titles from *Fountas & Pinnell Classroom™* chosen specifically to support the principle and work of each lesson.

If students need more experience, you can repeat the lesson format using these suggestions for variations, different examples, or more challenging activities.

These are not homework assignments; rather, they are ways you can help family members and caregivers make connections between home and school.

Connect learning across an effective and coherent design for responsive literacy teaching through interactive read-aloud, shared reading, interactive writing, and independent writing. Your observations across learning contexts will help you think of specific connections you can bring to your students' attention; add your own notes to enhance the lesson.

14 LETTER-SOUND RELATIONSHIPS

EARLY **MIDDLE** LATE

Connect Learning Across Contexts

Shared Reading During shared reading, you may wish to use the following title from *Fountas & Pinnell Classroom™* to locate a few words that blend the vowel sound with *r* after reading.

Exploring Underground by Louis Petrone

Guided Reading When students come to an unknown word with vowel sounds with *r*, prompt them by asking, "Do you know another word that looks like that?"

Shared Writing Model and check the spelling of a word with a vowel sound with *r*.

Independent Writing When students are attempting to write a longer word with an *r*-influenced vowel, remind them that there are usually a few possible spellings for the sound. Encourage them to try a letter pattern, see if it looks correct, and then confirm or revise their spelling.

Extend Learning

- Repeat the lesson with two-syllable examples of words containing *r*-influenced vowels, such as *barber, carpet, alarm, garbage, market, partner, sparkle, prepare, careful, repair, dairy, merry, alert, perfect, gerbil, learner, nearby, yearly, cheerful, sincere, dirty, birthday, admire, coral, florist, ignore, curtain, turkey, surely, person, squirrel, normal, important, purple, urgent,* and *surprise.*

- Distribute blank Follow the Path game boards (found in Online Resources), and have students work together to create boards with new sets of words with *r*-influenced vowels. Students can then play Follow the Path in groups.

▶ **Connect with Home**

Send word cards home so that students can practice sorting with family members.

Planning and Implementing Effective Word Study Lessons

While the Teach section of the word study lesson is explicit and structured, it also involves students in inquiry and encourages them to become "noticers" of the features of words. What they discover is memorable and results in deeper learning. They are always learning an important principle they can apply to their reading and writing.

Lessons should be conversational. In most lessons it is appropriate for students to derive the principle through inquiry and example, and you can state it at the end. Be sure to say the principle the same way each time. Your tone should be that of *I'm going to show you something interesting about how words work* or *What do you notice about these words?* Invite students to make connections to their names and words they know. Invite them to contribute further examples, and recognize their thinking even if the examples don't quite fit. Always try to understand their thinking and build on a partially correct response.

Remember that a lesson is brief. Don't let it go on too long. Depending on the particular principle, you'll need only a few examples to make an understanding clear. Your goal is for students to integrate some of these examples into their own thinking so they can connect them to new learning when they are working on their own. At the end of the lesson, summarize the understanding you are trying to instill and take another moment to restate the principle. If appropriate, place an example on a chart or a word wall. Then explain and demonstrate the application activity.

You may choose to have students do the Apply activity simultaneously immediately after the lesson. They can work individually or with partners. Here are some varied options for incorporating application activities.

▶ Present the lesson to the entire class, and then involve all children simultaneously in the Apply activity. They can work individually, with partners, or in a small group as you circulate around the room. Immediately follow the activity with sharing.

▶ Present the lesson to the entire class but involve students in application activities in small groups that you supervise. Have the rest of the children involved in independent reading/writing about reading activities. Follow the activity with sharing as soon as all groups have completed it.

▶ Present the lesson to the entire class and explain the application activity. Over several days, have assigned students complete the activity. Have a brief sharing at the end of each day. Ask the students who participated to talk about what they learned.

At the end of an Apply activity, students meet for a brief group share of something they have learned about letters, sounds, and words.

Routines and Instructional Procedures
for Effective Teaching

In the lessons we have designed for third grade, there are ten instructional procedures to develop students' knowledge of words and how they work.

Most procedures engage students in inquiry to generate an important principle. For example, students might be shown a group of words and asked to notice a common feature (e.g., all words ending with silent *e*). However, in some lessons inquiry is not included because it is not effective.

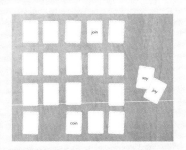

Students can use *see and say* to read a word and identify the silent letter in the word.

Students can use *find and match* to recognize spelling patterns for /oi/.

SEE AND SAY Efficient word solvers look for and find visual patterns in the way words are constructed. Recognizing familiar patterns helps students notice and use larger parts of words, which makes word solving faster and easier. The See and Say procedure described below helps students examine and identify familiar patterns in words and syllables—for example, CVC and CVCe patterns—and learn to make new words by putting a letter or letter cluster before the familiar pattern. Used in lessons in the area of Letter-Sound Relationships, Word Meaning/Vocabulary, and Word Structure, the See and Say procedure generally follows this sequence:

1. Show words that have a common feature. [*lamb, crumb, thumb*]
2. Students search for visual patterns. [They all have a silent letter–*b*–at the end.]
3. Help students articulate the principle. [*Some words have consonant letters that are silent.*]
4. Students work with words to apply the principle. [Students read the words and tell the silent letters.]
5. Summarize the learning by restating the principle.

FIND AND MATCH You will use Find and Match to help students discover connections between sounds, between letters, and between sounds and letters. The example provided below focuses on ending consonant sounds, but you'll also use Find and Match to support students in matching sounds or letters at the beginning or end of words, or pairing words and their abbreviations.

1. Show words that go together. [*coin, join; joy, soy*]
2. Students look for the connection between the words. [They all have the vowel sound /oi/.]
3. Help students articulate the principle. [*Several patterns of letters can stand for the /oi/ sound.*]
4. Students work with words to apply the principle. [Students match words that have the same pattern of letters to represent the /oi/ vowel sound.]
5. Summarize the learning by restating the principle.

SAY AND SORT Sorting helps students look closely at features of letters or words and make connections between them. Using Say and Sort, students form categories of pictures, letters, or words that are similar by sound, feature, word pattern, or word part. In the following example, students sort words by phonogram pattern, but across the lessons students will sort by other features as well, such as words with vowel sounds and *r*; words with ending consonant clusters, and compound words with common parts.

1. Show and say words that have a common feature. [*escape, complete, polite, became, amuse*]

2. Students search for the common feature. [The words have a vowel, a consonant, and silent *e*.]

3. Help students articulate the principle. [*Some words have a vowel, a consonant, and silent e. The vowel sound is usually the name of the first vowel.*]

4. Students work with words to apply the principle. [Students sort the words with the VC*e* pattern.]

5. Summarize the learning by restating the principle.

HEAR AND SAY You will use Hear and Say to help students hear the sounds in words and eventually connect those sounds to letters, a key process in building literacy. As children develop their understandings of how words work, they may be asked to represent the sounds they hear by constructing words with magnetic letters or in writing. Although the example given below centers on onomatopoetic words, you also will use Hear and Say to support children's work with homophones and homographs. Hear and Say typically employs the following sequence:

1. Show students words that are connected by the way they sound. [*splish, splash, ping, whoosh, hiss, buzz*]

2. Students say the words and notice features having to do with spelling, meaning, and sound. [The words imitate the sounds of the thing or action being named.]

3. Help students articulate the principle. [*Some words imitate the sound of a thing or an action. They are onomatopoetic words.*]

4. Students work with words to apply the principle. [Students read texts and identify onomatopoetic words.]

5. Summarize the learning by restating the principle.

Students can use *say and sort* to recognize and use words with the VC*e* pattern.

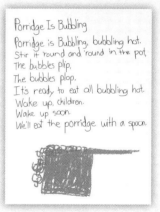

Students can use *hear and say* with onomatopoetic words.

Students can use *sound and letter boxes* to understand that some letters represent vowel sounds.

Students can use *words to know* to recognize and use high-frequency words.

HEAR, SAY, AND WRITE: SOUND AND LETTER BOXES D. B. Elkonin, a Russian psychologist, developed sound and letter boxes to help children become more aware of the sounds and letters in words. The technique has also been used by Marie Clay and by other researchers and educators. You can use the structure of sound boxes to help children listen for and identify each sound in a word. You can model by drawing the boxes and then support students in using them. Younger children who are still learning to hear sounds in words say words slowly and use *sound* boxes to write the letters for the sounds they hear (one box for each phoneme). In grade 3 you will be using *letter* boxes (one box for each letter in a word). The goal is for students to learn how to use the boxes to say words and think about the letters they would expect to see. When using letter boxes, they will notice the discrepancy between the number of sounds and the number of letters (digraphs, vowel pairs, silent letters, etc.). Using the procedures below, you'll make one box for each sound (not each letter) in each word. Students may need to learn these a step at a time. Sometimes you can divide boxes by syllables.

Letter Boxes

1. Make a row of boxes with one box for each letter in a word.
2. Model saying the word and running your finger under the boxes.
3. Ask, "What letter do you expect to see first?" Continue until all of the letters are filled in.
4. Students say words and write one letter in each box independently.
5. Summarize the learning by restating the principle: "You can say words and think how they look."

WORDS TO KNOW You will use this procedure to help students build and work with a collection of high-frequency words. Students need to be able to recognize high-frequency words quickly and easily. These words are enormously beneficial to readers, who can use them to monitor accuracy, to self-correct, to notice letter-sound relationships or word parts, to notice connections between words to solve words, to begin to write words correctly, and to read and write at a good rate. In many of the lessons that feature high-frequency words, you'll use the following procedure:

1. Show a group of high-frequency words, reading each one while running your pointer finger under it, left to right. [*ahead, caught, finish, matter, neither*]
2. Students look at each word to see if they recognize it.
3. Help students understand the principle. *You see some words many times when you read. You need to learn words that you see many times because they help you read and write.*
4. Students work with high-frequency words to apply the principle. [Students read, say, and write high-frequency words.]
5. Summarize the learning by restating the principle.

NOTICE PARTS Efficient word solvers notice particular features of words, including visual patterns in the way words are constructed. Recognizing common features and familiar patterns helps students notice and use larger parts of words, which makes word solving faster and easier. Notice Parts helps students examine and identify consonant sounds and letters, consonant clusters, and vowel sounds and letters in words. It is used frequently in lessons in the area of Letter-Sound Relationships. The Notice Parts procedure generally follows this sequence:

1. Show a group of words with a common feature. [*gnat, knot, wrist*]

2. Students search for the common feature. [consonant letters that represent no sound]

3. Help students articulate the principle. *Some words have consonant letters that are silent.*

4. Students work with words to apply the principle. [Students build and write words with consonant letters that are silent.]

5. Summarize the learning by restating the principle.

MAKE WORDS This procedure can help students build and/or break apart words through the use of discrete tactile materials such as magnetic letters, letter tiles, letter cards, or word cards. Make Words appears in lessons in Letter-Sound Relationships, Spelling Patterns, Word Meaning/Vocabulary, Word Structure, and Word-Solving Actions and may follow this sequence:

1. Show and say a two-syllable word with a double consonant in the middle. [*ladder*]

2. Students say and clap the syllables, and move the letters to divide the syllables. [*lad der*]

3. Help them articulate the principle. [*When a word has double consonants in the middle, divide the syllables between the consonants.*]

4. They work with letters and words to apply the principle. [Children break apart and put together syllables.]

5. Summarize the learning by restating the principle.

MAP WORDS Students need to know the meaning of the words they are learning to read and write. Map Words can help children read and write the names of concept words, synonyms, antonyms, words with multiple meanings, and compound words. This procedure, which appears in lessons in the area of Word Meaning/Vocabulary, may follow this sequence:

1. Show a word map with a concept word that stands for a big idea in the center. [*ocean*]

2. Students think of words that stand for smaller ideas or items related to the concept word. [*blanket, coral, clam, swim*]

3. Help them articulate the principle. [*Some words stand for big ideas or items. You can find words that stand for smaller ideas or items related to the big ideas.*]

4. Students work to apply the principle. [Students identify and write related words to fill in the word map.]

5. Summarize the learning by restating the principle.

Students can use *notice parts* to recognize consonant letters that represent no sound.

Students can use *make words* to recognize and use syllables in words with double consonants.

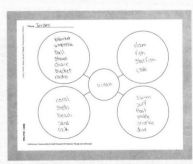

Students can use *map words* to recognize concept words that can have sets and subsets.

A Few Further Suggestions

We recommend using black or dark-colored markers on white chart paper for constructing the charts. You can alternate colors to make charts more attractive, but avoid light colors. The print should be very easy to see. You may want to use colored transparent highlighter tape to emphasize certain words or letters. You don't want a standardized color-coding, which confuses students because they will start to use the color as a cue (for example, nouns in red). If students work at their own desks or tables, arrange materials in a central area or on each table. If the activity is new or difficult, place a model in clear view so that students can check their results. Below are more suggestions.

▶ Focus on one principle that is appropriate and useful for your students at a particular point in time.

▶ Be sure that all students can see and hear as you demonstrate the principle or write examples on a chart.

▶ Engage the students in inquiry—getting them to notice important aspects of words and construct an important principle.

▶ Share examples and add examples from students (if students are unable to provide some examples, then either the principle is not clearly stated or it is too difficult).

▶ Place an example on the wall as a reference for the students. They may record examples in a word study notebook.

▶ Check for understanding by asking students to locate and talk about examples. Summarize the lesson by returning to the principle and stating it again.

▶ Use a conversational rather than a lecture style. Promote interaction so students can be active, engaged learners.

▶ Invite interaction so that students bring their own knowledge to bear on the application of the principle.

▶ Use a few good examples that you select in advance so that you have them ready to show the students.

▶ Clearly state the principle at the end as students come to their own conclusions from examples, or make a clear statement of the principle as you begin the lesson.

▶ Provide an Apply activity that students can do independently (after being taught routines) and that will be productive in their learning.

▶ Demonstrate the Apply activity explicitly so that you know students can perform it independently.

▶ Provide all necessary materials for the Apply activity in one place—for example, a clearly defined and organized materials center.

▶ Provide Apply activities with potential multilevel learning that permits advanced students to apply the principle to more sophisticated examples and to make more discoveries and allow students who are less experienced to develop the understandings with simple examples. You can add more complex examples to the Apply in the lesson if needed.

- Convene students for a brief sharing period so that they can comment on what they have learned and you can reinforce the principle again.

- Make connections to previous word study lessons or understandings and discoveries made in any other component of an effective, coherent design for responsive literacy teaching.

- Keep lessons brief; use just enough examples to make the principle clear.

The Assessment Guide

There is a time to use systematic, planned tasks that are designed to gather information about particular aspects of students' growing word knowledge. Performance-based assessment may involve observation, but it also represents more formal structured experiences in which the tasks are standardized. Standardization of the procedure creates a reliable assessment situation that is more objective than daily ongoing observation. The goal is to get a picture of what each student can do independently. Usually you do not actively teach during a performance-based assessment, but you may make teaching points after the neutral observation.

The Assessment Guide (found in Online Resources) includes more formal, performance-based assessment tasks across six of the nine areas of learning. You can use these tasks in multiple ways: as diagnostic tools to determine what your students know and need to know; as monitoring tools to help you keep track of your teaching and your students' learning; and as documentation of the teaching and learning you and your students have accomplished. You and your colleagues may even decide to place some of the summary sheets in your students' permanent cumulative folders as a way to create a school-wide record of the phonics and word study program.

As noted, the opportunities for informal assessment are embedded in each lesson in the Assess feature.

Word Study Lessons in the Daily Schedule

There are many ways to organize your schedule. It depends on your school schedule and the times you must reserve for special areas like music or library.

Remember that word study lessons are short—often, five minutes is enough time. Application also will take no more than five to ten minutes and after students become proficient and know routines, they can perform them independently or with a partner. The extent to which you use the suggestions for extending word study lessons is a teaching decision; and most of these involve integrating word study with other classroom work that you are doing anyway.

Schedules are tight. You have to plan carefully to include everything you want to do and everything that is required. And every third grader needs plenty of time to play and to choose some of her own activities.

Take a look at an example of the contexts that you may want to "fit together" in the management of your schedule for literacy learning (Figure 5).

Make a frame for your day with the times that school begins and ends, a space for lunch and recess, and then begin to "slot in" what you want to do. If you have very limited time, you may not be able to do everything every day. When you have created what you think will be a workable schedule try it. You can make adjustments, but once you find an excellent schedule, stick to it! Having a predictable schedule is very important for students' development of independence and self-regulation. There will always be some interruptions (special events, assemblies, field trips, and so on), but try to keep them to a minimum. Students should walk in the door with a good idea of what their work and play will be.

In the pages that follow, you will see two different tools for planning and organizing lessons across the year. These two organizational tools are Nine Areas of Learning Across the Year and the Master Lesson Guide: Suggested Sequence for Word Study Lessons.

Third Grade

FITTING IT ALL TOGETHER
Start with this suggested framework, or design your own

INSTRUCTIONAL CONTEXT	ACTIVITY OPTIONS	MINUTES EACH DAY
GROUP MEETING	• Bring the classroom community together to introduce/discuss the day and set goals.	5
INTERACTIVE READ-ALOUD LESSON **IRA**	• Teacher reads aloud a book from a text set, and students share their thinking. The text experience often leads to writing about reading in the *Reader's Notebook*.	15
SHARED READING **SR**	• Teacher engages students in shared reading using enlarged print books and often leads to shared writing across the curriculum.	10
BREAK		
READING MINILESSON **RML**	• Teacher provides an explicit minilesson for students to apply to their independent reading and writing about reading.	5
SMALL-GROUP INSTRUCTION **GR** **BC**	• Teacher meets with 3 Guided Reading groups each day. • Teacher initiates Book Clubs as appropriate, and they meet about once per month.	60
INDEPENDENT LITERACY WORK **IR**	• Students engage in: ◦ Independent reading ◦ Writing about reading in the *Reader's Notebook* *OR* engage in four tasks: 1. Read a choice book 2. Write about reading in a reader's notebook 3. Work on words (application from *Word Study* lesson) 4. Work on projects (poetry, content area research, etc.)	
GROUP SHARE	• Gather students together to reflect on and share learning.	5
BREAK		
PHONICS, SPELLING, AND WORD STUDY LESSON **PWS**	• Teacher provides an explicit, inquiry-based lesson on a word study principle to the class. Students apply the principle to reading and writing individually, with partners, or in small groups, then share their learning.	30
BREAK		
WRITERS' WORKSHOP	• Teacher provides an explicit minilesson, supports individual students as they work on their own writing, or convenes a guided writing group, and brings them together for group share.	50

Suggested time allotments shown are for utilizing the instructional contexts of *Fountas & Pinnell Classroom*™ within your grade 3 classroom.

TOTAL: 3 HOURS

FIGURE 5 *Fitting It All Together: A Sample Schedule*

Nine Areas of Learning Across the Year:
Early, Middle, Late

We have organized the third-grade lessons by six of the nine areas of learning (see *The Fountas & Pinnell Comprehensive Phonics, Spelling, and Word Study Guide*) and by suggested time of year (early, middle, or late).

EARLY THIRD GRADE If your third graders were engaged in *Word Study Lessons* regularly in grade 3, they will already understand many of the routines and will have a good foundation on which to build. If not, then you may need to spend a little more time on the management of the word-work component of the curriculum. In any case, it is a good idea to firmly establish the management system at the beginning of the year because there will be children new to the school and/or new to *Word Study Lessons*. You want third graders to share the spirit of inquiry and become interested in how words work. You will be reviewing some concepts (for example, consonant blends and digraphs) with more complex examples. You will be reviewing the concept of phonogram patterns and taking on more patterns. Students will be consolidating previous learning and expanding it.

MIDDLE THIRD GRADE During the middle three or four months, children can work to sustain independent activity so that the classroom will work more efficiently. They will delve more deeply into the functioning of vowels in complex patterns. A big expansion will involve working with multisyllable words. They consciously add to the body of words they know how to read, and they explore routines that will help them learn how to spell new words. Your young students will become more flexible in using everything they know to solve new words while reading.

LATE THIRD GRADE Third graders will continue to make connections between words in a variety of ways (spelling patterns, meaning) and will enjoy word sorting. They gain power over words as they learn how to change them to make new words. They continue to add more words to the body of known words they can read and write. They take on the "rules" for using inflectional endings and making words plural. Of course, the parts o the year are not precisely divided. We are talking here about continuous learning over time as children build on what they know already. They step to solving multisyllable words, for example, is made easier as children recognize and use phonogram patterns with the word.

In creating this overview or map (see pages 42–44), we considered how students' experiences are likely to build across the year as a result not only of the direct teaching of principles related to sounds, letters, and words but also of their daily experiences hearing written language read aloud and participating in shared, independent, and guided reading and interactive and independent writing.

This map shows a continuum of easier to harder principles. It will help you think in broad strokes about the program you are providing for the students in your classroom, which must always be considered in light of your observations and assessments of what your students know and can do at any given point. If students are very knowledgeable and experienced, you may decide that some lessons can be abbreviated or omitted. If students are very inexperienced in a given area, lessons may need to be repeated using different examples.

Reflecting on the map will help you be aware of the entire body of knowledge that is important for third graders to acquire as a foundation for literacy learning. The overview contains two kinds of information.

> ▶ Using the rows, you can take one area of learning and follow children's development of a principle from easier to harder throughout the year. For example, lessons on phonological awareness begin with songs, rhymes, and chants. You'll help your students become more sensitive to the sounds of language by having them match rhyming pictures and listen for the parts in words. Later in the year you will give closer attention to individual sounds in words and help your students develop insights into the structure of words by identifying and manipulating these sounds. Each area of learning offers room for growth throughout the year.

> ▶ You can look down the columns to get a sense of the understanding students are building across the entire continuum. Working across categories, you ensure that students not only develop phonological awareness but also learn to look at print—distinguish letters and learn their names—as well as think about word meanings and become familiar with some high-frequency words that will help accelerate their learning.

Look at the map both ways. Your students might be more advanced in one area than another. It is obvious that planning instruction is not always neat and tidy; however, the concept of easier to harder, in combination with assessment, should allow you to make effective decisions for your students. Your understandings will allow you to

> ▶ make the most of what students know by allowing them to work at the edge of their knowledge;

> ▶ ensure clear, explicit teaching and meaningful practice to deepen conceptual knowledge;

> ▶ ensure that principles do not have to be taught again and again;

> ▶ avoid spending time on teaching what students already know.

If you wish to have a copy of the Nine Areas of Learning Across the Year for reference or recordkeeping, you can find it in Online Resources.

Nine Areas of Learning

4 Letter-Sound Relationships   LSR

Early	Middle	Late
LSR 1 Recognize and Say Consonant Clusters That Blend Two or Three Consonant Sounds (Onsets)	**LSR 10** Recognize and Use Consonant Letters That Represent Two or More Different Sounds at the End of a Word	**LSR 18** Understand How to Use the Computer Keyboard
LSR 2 Recognize and Use Consonant Clusters (Blends) at the End of a Word	**LSR 11** Recognize and Use Consonant Letters That Represent No Sound	**LSR 19** Understand How to Form Cursive Letters Correctly, Efficiently, and Fluently
LSR 3 Recognize and Use *y* as a Vowel Sound	**LSR 12** Recognize and Use Consonant Letters That Represent No Sound	
LSR 4 Recognize and Use Letter Combinations That Represent Long Vowel Sounds	**LSR 13** Understand That Some Consonant Sounds Can Be Represented by Several Different Letters or Letter Clusters	
LSR 5 Recognize and Use Letter Combinations That Represent the /o/ Vowel Sound (as in *saw*) ["o" with dot over it]	**LSR 14** Recognize and Use Vowel Sounds with *r*	
LSR 6 Recognize and Use Letter Combinations That Represent Two Different Vowel Sounds	**LSR 15** Recognize and Use Vowel Sounds in Closed Syllables (CVC)	
LSR 7 Recognize and Use Two Consonant Letters That Usually Represent One Sound at the Beginning of a Word	**LSR 16** Recognize and Use Vowel Sounds in Open Syllables (CVC)	
LSR 8 Recognize and Use Two Consonant Letters That Usually Represent One Sound at the End of a Word	**LSR 17** Understand How to Use Capital Letters Correctly	
LSR 9 Recognize and Use Middle Consonant Sounds Sometimes Represented by Double Consonant Letters		

5 Spelling Patterns   SP

SP 1 Recognize and Use Less Common Phonograms with a VC Pattern	**SP 9** Recognize and Use Phonogram Patterns with the /ü/ Vowel Sound in Single-Syllable Words
SP 2 Recognize and Use Phonogram Patterns with a Short Vowel Sound in Single-Syllable Words	**SP 10** Recognize and Use Phonogram Patterns with the /u/ Vowel Sound in Single-Syllable Words ["u" with dot over it]
SP 3 Recognize and Use Phonograms with a Vowel-Consonant-Silent *e* (VC*e*) Pattern	**SP 11** Recognize and Use Phonogram Patterns with the /o/ Vowel Sound (as in *saw*) in Single-Syllable Words ["o" with dot over it]
SP 4 Recognize and Use Phonograms That End with a Double Consonant (VCC)	**SP 12** Recognize and Use Phonogram Patterns with the /ou/ Vowel Sound in Single-Syllable Words
SP 5 Recognize and Use Phonograms with Ending Consonant Clusters (VCC)	**SP 13** Recognize and Use Phonogram Patterns with the /oi/ Vowel Sound in Single-Syllable Words
SP 6 Recognize and Use Phonograms with a Double Vowel (VVC)	**SP 14** Recognize and Use Phonogram Patterns with Vowels and *r* in Single-Syllable Words
SP 7 Recognize and Use Phonograms with Vowel Combinations (VVC)	**SP 15** Understand That Some Words Have a Double Consonant
SP 8 Recognize and Use Phonogram Patterns with a Long Vowel Sound in Single-Syllable Words	**SP 16** Recognize and Use Frequently Appearing Syllable Patterns in Multisyllable Words
	SP 17 Recognize and Use Frequently Appearing Syllable Patterns in Multisyllable Words

Across the Year

6	**High-Frequency Words** HFW		

Early	Middle	Late
HFW 1 Recognize and Use High-Frequency Words with Three or More Letters	**HFW 4** Recognize and Use Longer High-Frequency Words, Some with More Than One Syllable	**HFW 6** Read and Write Approximately 500 High-Frequency Words
HFW 2 Recognize and Use High-Frequency Words with Three or More Letters	**HFW 5** Acquire a Large Core of High-Frequency Words	
HFW 3 Recognize and Use Longer High-Frequency Words, Some with More Than One Syllable		

7	**Word Meaning/Vocabulary** WMV		

WMV 1 Recognize and Use Concept Words That Can Have Sets and Subsets	**WMV 7** Recognize and Use Synonyms	**WMV 17** Recognize and Use Compound Words with Common Parts
WMV 2 Recognize and Use Concept Words That Can Have Sets and Subsets	**WMV 8** Recognize and Use Synonyms	**WMV 18** Recognize and Use Compound Words with Common Parts
WMV 3 Recognize That Words Can Be Related in Many Ways: Category	**WMV 9** Recognize and Use Antonyms	**WMV 19** Recognize and Use Onomatopoetic Words
WMV 4 Recognize That Words Can Be Related in Many Ways: Category	**WMV 10** Recognize and Use Antonyms	**WMV 20** Recognize That Some Words Have Literal and Figurative Meanings
WMV 5 Recognize and Use Compound Words	**WMV 11** Recognize and Use Homophones	**WMV 21** Recognize That Some Words Have Literal and Figurative Meanings
WMV 6 Recognize and Use Compound Words	**WMV 12** Recognize and Use Homophones	**WMV 22** Understand the Concept of Suffixes and Recognize Their Use in Determining the Meaning of Some English Words
	WMV 13 Recognize and Use Homographs	**WMV 23** Understand the Concept of Prefixes and Recognize Their Use in Determining the Meaning of Some English Words
	WMV 14 Recognize and Use Homographs	
	WMV 15 Recognize and Use Words with Multiple Meanings	
	WMV 16 Recognize and Use Words with Multiple Meanings	

8	**Word Structure** WS		

WS 1 Recognize and Use Compound Words	**WS 4** Recognize and Use Syllables in Words with Double Consonants	**WS 20** Recognize and Use the Suffixes -er, -or, -ar, and -ist to Form a Noun
WS 2 Recognize and Use Compound Words That Have Frequently Used Words	**WS 5** Identify Syllables in Words with Three or More Syllables	**WS 21** Recognize and Use the Prefix re-, Meaning "again"
WS 3 Recognize and Use Contractions with *not*	**WS 6** Recognize and Use Open Syllables	**WS 22** Recognize and Use the Prefixes That Mean "not"
	WS 7 Recognize and Use Closed Syllables	
	WS 8 Recognize and Use *r*-Influenced Syllables	
	WS 9 Recognize and Use Vowel Combination Syllables	
	WS 10 Recognize and Use VC*e* Syllables	

8 Word Structure   WS (Continued)

Early	Middle		Late
	WS 11	Recognize and Use Syllables in Words with the VCCV Pattern	
	WS 12	Understand That the Ending -*ed* Can Represent Several Different Sounds	
	WS 13	Recognize and Use Common Abbreviations	
	WS 14	Recognize and Use Plurals That Add -*es* to Words that End with the Letters *ch, sh, s, x,* or *z*	
	WS 15	Recognize and Use Plurals That Add -*es* to Words That End with a Consonant and *y*	
	WS 16	Recognize and Use Plurals That Add -*es* to Words After Changing the Final *f* or *fe* to *v*	
	WS 17	Recognize and Use Plurals That Add -*s* to Words That End with *o*	
	WS 18	Recognize and Use Plurals That Add -*es* to Words That End with a Consonant and *o*	
	WS 19	Recognize and Use the Suffixes -*er* and -*est* to Show Comparison	

9 Word-Solving Actions   WSA

WSA 1	Recognize and Use Onsets and Rimes to Read Words
WSA 2	Recognize and Use Onsets and Rimes to Read Words
WSA 3	Recognize and Use Onsets and Rimes to Read Words
WSA 4	Use Onsets and Rimes in Known Words to Read and Write Other Words with the Same Parts
WSA 5	Break a Word into Syllables to Decode Manageable Units
WSA 6	Recognize and Use Word Parts to Solve an Unknown Word and Understand Its Meaning
WSA 7	Use Alphabetical Order to Locate Information About Words in a Variety of Reference Tools
WSA 8	Use Alphabetical Order to Locate Information About Words in a Variety of Reference Tools
WSA 9	Use a Dictionary to Solve and Find Information About Words
WSA 10	Use a Study Routine to Spell a Word: Choose, Write, Build, Mix, Fix, Mix (Partner Study 1)
WSA 11	Use a Study Routine to Spell a Word: Look, Say, Cover, Write, Check (Partner Study 2)
WSA 12	Use Known Words to Spell an Unknown Word (Partner Study 3)
WSA 13	Attempt to Spell an Unknown Word (Partner Study 4)

A Suggested Sequence for Word Study Lessons

The Comprehensive Phonics, Spelling, and Word Study Guide is organized into nine areas of learning. The lessons here are presented for six areas. Within each area, lessons are organized from easier to harder, although some lessons are just about equivalent and are learned within the same time period—early, middle, or late in the year. Also, the lessons are designed to build on each other. So you can see the suggested sequence within each area of learning from the beginning of the year to near the end. (Some areas will be under good control by the middle of the year.) But you will want to create a yearlong sequence that works across the nine areas, taking easier principles first and building on them. A tremendous amount of learning goes on in the area of word study and phonics.

To help you plan your year and make good decisions about the students you teach, we have created a suggested sequence for teaching *Word Study Lessons, Grade 3*. The suggested sequence, from 1 to 100, includes

- lesson titles and lesson numbers across the nine areas of learning;
- designation as a generative lesson (see page 31);
- specific suggestions for extending learning of the principle;
- specific suggestions for working with students who find the principle difficult;
- page numbers for each lesson so that you can find them in the lessons book quickly;
- blank space for your notes (you'll want to note whether you used the lesson and in what way).

You'll notice that the lessons are sequenced by typical appropriateness within each of the six areas, so there is variety in the kinds of lessons that fall early in the year, then in the middle, and then late in the year. This sequence will serve simultaneously as a planning document and as a record of teaching. Use it to plan lessons for the coming week and to keep a record and notes of the lessons you have taught. Here are some suggestions for using the sequence effectively. A reproducible list is provided in Online Resources.

- Think about what students already know as you select and plan lessons. You may want to use some simple assessments. The Assessment Guide (in Online Resources) will help you consider students' strengths and needs. You'll also be gathering information as you work with students in lessons and as you observe them in application activities and group share. If a principle is firmly established, skip the lesson.

- Students may have learned a great deal in shared reading and early guided reading lessons so that early literacy behaviors are well established. You might not need to use all of the lessons in this area.

- You may identify a small group of students who need more support in establishing a principle. You can hold a brief small-group meeting to repeat the lesson and help them with the application activity.

- Remember that you can repeat the lesson using other examples if you think your whole class needs more work on the principle.

- Some lessons may need to be repeated or extended over several days because there is a great deal of content to be covered—for example, consonants and related sounds.

- You can make adjustments in the sequence. If you are working on a series of lessons on one topic (for example, phonogram patterns), you may want to stick with it for a few more days to get it firmly into place.

- It's important to remember that you can skip over lessons if children already understand and can apply the principle. Don't teach a lesson just because it is there.

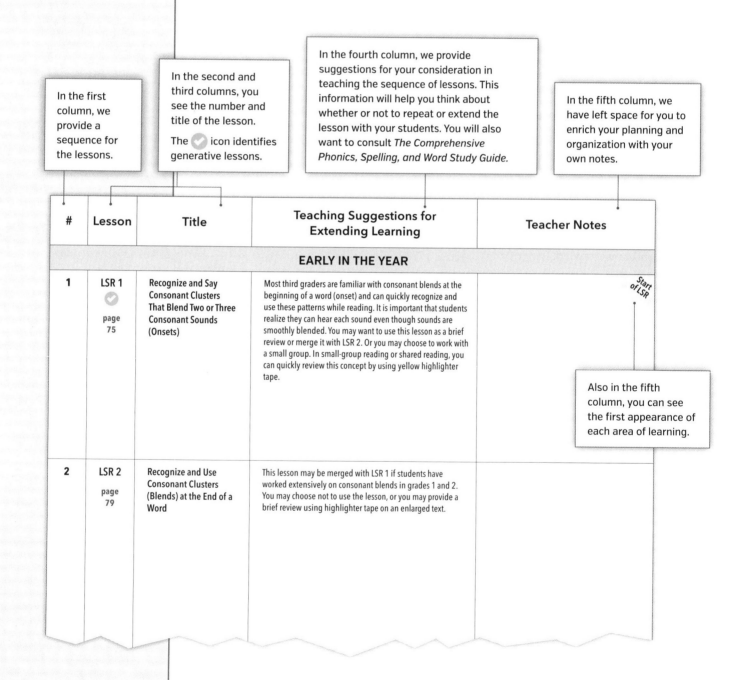

In the first column, we provide a sequence for the lessons.

In the second and third columns, you see the number and title of the lesson.

The ✓ icon identifies generative lessons.

In the fourth column, we provide suggestions for your consideration in teaching the sequence of lessons. This information will help you think about whether or not to repeat or extend the lesson with your students. You will also want to consult *The Comprehensive Phonics, Spelling, and Word Study Guide.*

In the fifth column, we have left space for you to enrich your planning and organization with your own notes.

#	Lesson	Title	Teaching Suggestions for Extending Learning	Teacher Notes
			EARLY IN THE YEAR	
1	LSR 1 ✓ page 75	Recognize and Say Consonant Clusters That Blend Two or Three Consonant Sounds (Onsets)	Most third graders are familiar with consonant blends at the beginning of a word (onset) and can quickly recognize and use these patterns while reading. It is important that students realize they can hear each sound even though sounds are smoothly blended. You may want to use this lesson as a brief review or merge it with LSR 2. Or you may choose to work with a small group. In small-group reading or shared reading, you can quickly review this concept by using yellow highlighter tape.	*Start of LSR*
2	LSR 2 page 79	Recognize and Use Consonant Clusters (Blends) at the End of a Word	This lesson may be merged with LSR 1 if students have worked extensively on consonant blends in grades 1 and 2. You may choose not to use the lesson, or you may provide a brief review using highlighter tape on an enlarged text.	

Also in the fifth column, you can see the first appearance of each area of learning.

MASTER LESSON GUIDE

#	Lesson	Title	Teaching Suggestions for Extending Learning	Teacher Notes
			EARLY IN THE YEAR	
1	LSR 1 ✅ page 75	Recognize and Say Consonant Clusters That Blend Two or Three Consonant Sounds (Onsets)	Most third graders are familiar with consonant blends at the beginning of a word (onset) and can quickly recognize and use these patterns while reading. It is important that students realize they can hear each sound even though sounds are smoothly blended. You may want to use this lesson as a brief review or merge it with LSR 2. Or you may choose to work with a small group. In small-group reading or shared reading, you can quickly review this concept by using yellow highlighter tape.	*Start of LSR*
2	LSR 2 page 79	Recognize and Use Consonant Clusters (Blends) at the End of a Word	This lesson may be merged with LSR 1 if students have worked extensively on consonant blends in grades 1 and 2. You may choose not to use the lesson, or you may provide a brief review using highlighter tape on an enlarged text.	
3	WSA 1 ✅ page 433	Recognize and Use Onsets and Rimes to Read Words	Students will have been working to hear onsets and rimes since kindergarten as they develop the concepts of the first part and the last part of words. This lesson may not be needed. Or you may want to introduce students to the technical words onset and rime and have a discussion of the relationship between rime and rhyme. Noticing word pairs helps students break words apart and make connections between them. Here, magnetic letters are used for emphasis and are easy to incorporate into small-group work for those students who need more support.	*Start of WSA*

MASTER LESSON GUIDE

#	Lesson	Title	Teaching Suggestions for Extending Learning	Teacher Notes
			EARLY *(continued)*	
4	WSA 2 ✓ page 437	Recognize and Use Onsets and Rimes to Read Words	You may want to merge this lesson with WSA 3 as a quick review or skip it entirely if students are automatically using large parts of words as they read and write. If they need practice, the word sort will provide a quick way for them to review the concepts.	
5	WSA 3 ✓ page 441	Recognize and Use Onsets and Rimes to Read Words	Students may need no more than a quick review of the concepts of first part and last part of a word. This concept is important in learning to take words apart to decode them. Students may be able to play Follow the Path with just a few instructions; but if some are confused, work with them in a small group.	
6	WSA 4 ✓ page 445	Use Onsets and Rimes in Known Words to Read and Write Other Words with the Same Parts	Effective readers and writers make connections between the words they know and the new words they try to read or spell. Students will have been working with onsets and rimes for several years (beginning with being able to hear them). But the words in grade three become increasingly complex. Notice that the example words in this lesson contain fewer vowel pairs. You want students to become very flexible with words—noticing the parts and changing them to make new words. In the process, they will build up knowledge of word parts and will learn to take words apart and put them together. Be sure students know the meaning of the words with which they work, and explain that all words they make must be "real."	

Suggested Sequence for Phonics Lessons

#	Lesson	Title	Teaching Suggestions for Extending Learning	Teacher Notes
			EARLY *(continued)*	
7	WSA 5 ✓ page 449	Break a Word into Syllables to Decode Manageable Units	Students need to know that when they encounter a long multisyllable word, they can break it up into manageable parts, or syllables. Help them notice that each syllable has one vowel sound. Students may be taking words apart in reading but not fully aware that they can also spell words in parts. Help them see the connections between what they do in reading and in writing.	
8	WSA 6 ✓ page 453	Recognize and Use Word Parts to Solve an Unknown Word and Understand Its Meaning	Many multisyllable words are long because they have affixes (suffixes and prefixes). Identifying the base word helps in solving the word; and students will soon understand that the affixes add meaning and sometimes change the part of speech. Once students have a repertoire of frequently used prefixes and suffixes, they can greatly expand the number of words they can read and spell. If students are experienced at recognizing and using word parts, you may wish to include some words that have both prefixes and suffixes. The goal of this lesson is to help students become more aware of word parts. They will be studying prefixes and suffixes later in the year.	
9	WSA 7 ✓ page 457	Use Alphabetical Order to Locate Information About Words in a Variety of Reference Tools	Alphabetical order is a frequently used tool that students will find valuable when consulting reference materials, so it is placed early in the sequence. Both hard copy and electronic references tools use the alphabet as the quickest way for people to find information. This lesson is the first on using alphabetical order in a complex way. If students have extensive experience with glossaries, that will help them learn this principle quickly. You may also want to extend the lesson by teaching students to use electronic tools that are searchable.	
10	WSA 8 ✓ page 461	Use Alphabetical Order to Locate Information About Words in a Variety of Reference Tools	WSA 8 builds on WSA 7. Students in third grade are ready to begin more serious research. While they will often be doing an Internet search, you will want them to have the ability to use traditional reference tools such as the dictionary as a check. Many people do not know how to search quickly for what they need.	

#	Lesson	Title	Teaching Suggestions for Extending Learning	Teacher Notes
			EARLY *(continued)*	
11	WSA 9 ✓ page 465	Use a Dictionary to Solve and Find Information About Words	In this lesson, students continue to develop some basic understanding of how dictionaries "work." They need to develop skill and to begin to learn the kind of information that can be gained from using this kind of tool. For example, students can find pronunciation guides and the origins and meanings of word roots and base words as well as affixes. Students can also use searchable dictionaries online to look for the same kind of information. It is time for students to become independent in the development of their own word knowledge.	
12	WSA 10 page 469	Use a Study Routine to Spell a Word: Choose, Write, Build, Mix, Fix, Mix (Partner Study 1)	This lesson and the next three can be used to teach your students some powerful study techniques that will help them attend to (and remember) the details and patterns in words so that they can spell them accurately. Probably all students will need all four Partner Study lessons either as new learning or as a review from the year before. The words they will have each week come partly from those you assign and partly from words they choose themselves. This process gives students power over their own learning and helps them realize their progress. The lesson provides tactile experience in building, breaking apart, and rebuilding words. Using magnetic letters or cards helps them notice the parts and patterns as they look closely at words. Be sure that the words are "high utility" in that students will need to spell them often (for example, more complex high-frequency words) and that they know the meaning of each word. Throughout the year, you may choose to have students study a short list of words each week. Some words can be examples from the lessons.	
13	WSA 11 page 473	Use a Study Routine to Spell a Word: Look, Say, Cover, Write, Check (Partner Study 2)	In this lesson students learn another Partner Study technique– Look, Say, Cover, Write, Check. This study routine helps them to look closely at a word to remember it, test themselves by writing the word without a model, and then checking it letter by letter. This is a "slowed-down" way of considering a word. Soon the process of looking closely at a word will become automatic. Some students may need support in a small group to perform the five steps in order. Demonstrate the steps for the class using an enlarged version of the folder.	

#	Lesson	Title	Teaching Suggestions for Extending Learning	Teacher Notes
			EARLY *(continued)*	
14	WSA 12 page 477	Use Known Words to Spell an Unknown Word (Partner Study 3)	Using the same words they studied yesterday and the day before, students use another study routine for learning how to spell words. This routine will help them develop a network of knowledge about words. They learn to use their current knowledge of words to learn new words. This habit of making word connections will benefit them in both reading and spelling. Partners will enjoy connecting words by parts. If they have difficulty or need to become more sophisticated as they explore longer words, you can repeat or review this lesson several times.	
15	WSA 13 page 481	Attempt to Spell an Unknown Word (Partner Study 4)	This is the last Partner Study routine students will learn. They use the same words over four days; by the time they use this routine, they have a pretty good understanding of their words. Ultimately, spellers must call to mind all of the features of a word and hold it in the mind while writing (or typing). This process is so automatic for known words that we seldom stop to think about it, and that is the way it should be. It is very important that spellers know how to look at a word and tell whether it "looks right." Letter boxes are a tool that provides a scaffold for writing a word left to right in sequence. It is useful for students to write the word in the boxes and then check it. Working with a partner throughout this entire process promotes teamwork, and students often learn more words than their own!	
16	HFW 1 ✓ page 223	Recognize and Use High-Frequency Words with Three or More Letters	This lesson brings students to conscious awareness that they need to continuously acquire words that appear often in reading and writing. Having a large quantity of known words supports problem-solving in reading and writing, because attention is freed for this work. It also supports comprehension and fluency. Children have been adding to a repertoire of known words since kindergarten, and you can use this generative lesson to get third graders started again for the year. They will learn some simple procedures (make, check/mix, write) for studying words that are hard to spell.	*Start of HFW*
17	HFW 2 ✓ page 227	Recognize and Use Longer High-Frequency Words, Some with More Than One Syllable	HFW 3 includes longer words as well as words of more than one syllable. You can teach the routine Word Grid as a way to connecting words. The more students can connect words, the faster they add more words to the repertoire. You may want to check the knowledge base by assessing their knowledge of 200 high-frequency words (see *Ready Resources*). This may provide guidance for some of the words you want students to study weekly.	

#	Lesson	Title	Teaching Suggestions for Extending Learning	Teacher Notes
			EARLY *(continued)*	
18	HFW 3 ✓ page 231	Recognize and Use Longer High-Frequency Words, Some with More Than One Syllable	HFW 3 includes longer words as well as words of more than one syllable. You can teach the routine Word Grid as a way to connecting words. The more students can connect words, the faster they add more words to the repertoire. You may want to check the knowledge base by assessing their knowledge of 200 high-frequency words (see *Ready Resources*). This may provide guidance for some of the words you want students to study weekly.	
19	WS 1 ✓ page 343	Recognize and Use Compound Words	The concept of compound words is easy, and students may have a good grasp of it. You may want to omit this lesson but point out examples occasionally in guided or shared reading. Keep in mind that ease with this concept requires recognition and understanding of the component words.	*Start of WS*
20	WS 2 ✓ page 347	Recognize and Use Compound Words That Have Frequently Used Words	If students have experienced a strong word study program in kindergarten and the first two grades, it is unlikely that you will need to use this lesson. You can review the concepts in WS 3 and ask students to incorporate some compound words into their word study lists. But if the concept is new, use this lesson to help students work quickly and easily with compound words--recognizing the component words and their meanings. You can repeat this lesson with a different variety of compound words.	
21	WS 3 ✓ page 351	Recognize and Use Contractions with *not*	Third graders have been using contractions since acquiring oral language and have been reading them for several years (although they may be a challenge for students new to English). If the concept is well understood, expand this generative lesson to include contractions with *will*, *am*, *are*, and *have*.	

Suggested Sequence for Phonics Lessons

#	Lesson	Title	Teaching Suggestions for Extending Learning	Teacher Notes
			EARLY *(continued)*	
22	LSR 3 page 83	Recognize and Use *y* as a Vowel Sound	Most third graders will have good control of the sounds of long and short vowels and the individual letters that represent them. They also may know a number of words in which y represents the vowel sound of i for words of one syllable and the sound of e for words of two syllables; this lesson helps students notice this difference. Even this concept, though, has some frequently occurring exceptions. You may want to teach this lesson in a small group.	
23	LSR 4 page 87	Recognize and Use Letter Combinations That Represent Long Vowel Sounds	Children are likely to know that letter combinations can represent long vowel sounds in words (*vowel digraphs* or *pairs*). But many students are still adding to the repertoire of examples that they know. You may want to dictate a few words to determine the breadth of understanding. This lesson helps them pair words that have the same vowel combination and then use the game Crazy Eights to develop quick noticing of the patterns.	
24	LSR 5 page 91	Recognize and Use Letter Combinations That Represent the /ò/ Vowel Sound (as in *saw*)	The vowel sound /ò/ (as in *saw*) can be represented by many different letter combinations. Students need to develop the ability to recognize these letter combinations quickly; third graders will know some but usually not all of them. These combinations appear in very complex words and are the source of many spelling errors. Use this lesson when students have full control of long and short vowel sounds, when they understand that vowel sounds can be represented by several letter patterns, and when they have some known words that they can connect to the principle.	
25	LSR 6 page 95	Recognize and Use Letter Combinations That Represent Two Different Vowel Sounds	By the time you teach this lesson, students should be well aware that letters and sounds in English can be related in varying ways. You may want to present this lesson over several days to give students experience in connecting vowel pairs that can represent two different sounds (e.g., *book, moon*). Readers will have many high-frequency words on which to draw as they explore this principle. It will help them to compare and connect letter patterns and to sort them by sound. If students find this concept easy, repeat with other letter combinations that represent two different vowel sounds (e.g., *they, key; snow, cow*).	

#	Lesson	Title	Teaching Suggestions for Extending Learning	Teacher Notes
			EARLY *(continued)*	
26	LSR 7 ✓ page 99	Recognize and Use Two Consonant Letters That Usually Represent One Sound at the Beginning of a Word	This lesson may be a review for most students, and you may want to omit it or to select more complex words including many with more than one syllable. Sorting words quickly will help students recognize these letter clusters as useful word parts. You can also think about combining this lesson with LSR 8.	
27	LSR 8 page 103	Recognize and Use Two Consonant Letters That Usually Represent One Sound at the End of a Word	If students understand the principle of LSR 7, you can omit it and then expand this lesson to look first at ending clusters and then alternate between beginning and ending consonant digraphs. Point out these words in guided reading.	
28	LSR 9 ✓ page 107	Recognize and Use Middle Consonant Sounds Sometimes Represented by Double Consonant Letters	Students will already know many words that have double consonants in the middle and probably will have noticed this pattern. The double consonants make words easy to take apart, because you divide the word between the two like letters. Often, the letter is doubled when you add an inflectional ending to the word (and that sometimes adds a syllable). The group routine Word Grid promotes quick recognition and connection between words that have the same letter pattern. You can repeat this lesson to teach a variety of words with double consonant letters in the middle.	
29	SP 1 page 153	Recognize and Use Less Common Phonograms with a VC Pattern	Students will have worked with words that have a VC pattern for several years (e.g., *it*, *sit*, *at*, *bat*), but in this lesson they encounter less common patterns that often appear in more complex words. Knowing these spelling patterns and recognizing them quickly will make word solving more efficient. Be sure students know the meaning of the words they are making. Stress that when they put words together in the Apply, they must use real words. They can use a glossary or dictionary if needed.	*Start of SP*

Suggested Sequence for Phonics Lessons

#	Lesson	Title	Teaching Suggestions for Extending Learning	Teacher Notes
			EARLY *(continued)*	
30	SP 2 ✓ page 157	Recognize and Use Phonogram Patterns with a Short Vowel Sound in Single-Syllable Words	Students may be able to take words apart using recognition of phonogram patterns with a short vowel sound in single-syllable words; in that case, this lesson may not be necessary. It is important to be sure that students can easily recognize and use these patterns, because they will need to use this knowledge when solving multisyllable words. You can quickly review such words in guided or shared reading.	
31	SP 3 page 161	Recognize and Use Phonograms with a Vowel-Consonant-Silent *e* (VC*e*) Pattern	Students should already be familiar with the VC*e* pattern in single-syllable words; in this lesson, they will expand their understanding to work with multisyllable words. Many of these are compound words. A three-way sort will help them take on and connect these words easily. You can repeat this exercise with more words using other VC*e* phonograms.	
32	SP 4 page 165	Recognize and Use Phonograms That End with a Double Consonant (VCC)	Some students may need more experience with one-syllable words that end with a double consonant (VCC); decide whether to work with the whole class or with a small group on this content. It is important that students recognize phonograms and other regular spelling patterns, because they will be using them in solving multisyllable words. These patterns make word solving efficient.	
33	SP 5 ✓ page 169	Recognize and Use Phonograms with Ending Consonant Clusters (VCC)	As with other patterns that students know and recognize in one-syllable words, students will need a strong foundation in recognizing these patterns so that they can quickly recognize and use them to solve multisyllable words. If some students need more experience and practice in this area, work with them in a small group to perform the four-way sort and to write lists. They can read lists to a partner. Emphasize that the words should be real words. When in doubt, they can use a dictionary to check.	
34	SP 6 ✓ page 173	Recognize and Use Phonograms with a Double Vowel (VVC)	Double vowels appear in many common phonograms; they are easy for students to notice and use in solving both one-syllable and multisyllable words. If some students are not noticing these words, help them in a small group. They are also learning about the variability of sounds in English; double vowel patterns often stand for two different sounds, and it is important for students to understand that there is variety. In this lesson students learn about these patterns, and at the same time they notice the variety in pronunciations. The three-way sort helps them notice both concepts.	

#	Lesson	Title	Teaching Suggestions for Extending Learning	Teacher Notes
EARLY *(continued)*				

#	Lesson	Title	Teaching Suggestions for Extending Learning	Teacher Notes
35	SP 7 ✓ page 177	Recognize and Use Phonograms with Vowel Combinations	Third graders need to expand and solidify their ability to notice and use phonograms with vowel combinations. Many of these letter-sound relationships are regular (with the sound being that of the first vowel in the pair), but sometimes the combination represents other sounds (e.g., *boil*). You may wish to use this lesson with the regular patterns first and then to repeat it to include other sounds.	
36	SP 8 ✓ page 181	Recognize and Use Phonogram Patterns with a Long Vowel Sound in Single-Syllable Words	This lesson provides opportunity for students to work with a variety of phonogram patterns that include a long vowel sound. This may be a challenge, because it requires flexibility in noticing and using these patterns (as opposed to working with one or two). Making and writing twenty words will give students practice in distinguishing the patterns quickly. You may want to dictate six to ten words as a quick check on understanding to see whether you want to repeat the lesson.	
37	WMV 1 ✓ page 249	Recognize and Use Concept Words that Can Have Sets and Subsets	By third grade, students will have acquired many words that represent concepts, and they can see how words are related to each other: e.g., food words. Students may have spontaneously (or as part of a simple lesson) grouped words into categories. This lesson builds on those understandings by presenting clear examples of sets and subsets. Graphic organizers are used to help students understand this basic idea, which will be important in enhancing reading comprehension. Learning to use word webs is a simple way to organize information for greater understanding, and it can be expanded for use in the different content areas.	*Start of WMV*
38	WMV 2 ✓ page 253	Recognize and Use Concept Words That Can Have Sets and Subsets	This lesson expands WMV 1 by helping students understand that some content words stand for larger ideas and some stand for smaller ideas that fit within the larger category. Students will continue to grow in their conceptual ability to distinguish categories and subcategories, skills that are basic to understanding nonfiction. This lesson can be expanded for use in the different content areas.	

Suggested Sequence for Phonics Lessons

#	Lesson	Title	Teaching Suggestions for Extending Learning	Teacher Notes
			EARLY *(continued)*	
39	WMV 3 ✓ page 257	Recognize That Words Can Be Related in Many Ways: Category	Sorting words according to their meanings and placing them into categories will help students form strong ideas of word relationships. It will add to their ability to understand categorization, which is helpful in comprehending nonfiction. The existence of strong connections between words will help students expand vocabulary faster. Use the two-way sort to help them create categories in a constructive way, and repeat the lesson so that students acquire a variety of ways to connect words by meaning.	
40	WMV 4 ✓ page 261	Recognize That Words Can Be Related in Many Ways: Category	As students expand their ability to place words in categories by applying several different criteria, they learn to make finer distinctions within categories. This demanding conceptual work will tell you much about how they think and solve problems. This lesson uses color words for this first category division, but you will want to check to see whether there are children in the class that are color blind in a way that may interfere. In that case, select another group of related words. You can repeat this generative lesson several times to increase power in making these distinctions.	
41	WMV 5 ✓ page 265	Recognize and Use Compound Words	Typically, by this time, students will have had a great deal of experience in using compound words, so you may want to omit this lesson or combine it with WMV 6. If the concept is well understood, you can omit both.	
42	WMV 6 ✓ page 269	Recognize and Use Compound Words	As mentioned in WMV 5, students may well understand the concept of compound words; however, it begins a series of lessons that explore and create a set of learning related to special types of words. Use WMV 6 for a quick review and the game Concentration to help students expand the variety of compound words they know.	

#	Lesson	Title	Teaching Suggestions for Extending Learning	Teacher Notes
			MIDDLE OF THE YEAR	
43	WMV 7 ✓ page 273	Recognize and Use Synonyms	You can use this lesson to provide a review of the concept of synonyms and expand knowledge of examples of pairs (or even triads). You want students to be able to generate synonyms quickly. In reading, connecting synonyms can greatly expand vocabulary and can support reading comprehension. It also can make writing more interesting.	
44	WMV 8 ✓ page 277	Recognize and Use Synonyms	In this lesson students go farther with synonym exploration, and they also examine some of the subtleties of how words are used in English. For example, synonyms are not interchangeable in the context of every sentence, and they are *similar* rather than exact in meaning. The game Go Fish will help students match synonyms quickly.	
45	WMV 9 ✓ page 281	Recognize and Use Antonyms	This first lesson on antonyms may serve as a review of a concept with which students are already familiar. Recognition of antonyms and of synonyms helps students in a similar way. It is important for students to develop the ability to recognize antonyms quickly and to bring prior knowledge of words to understanding the meaning of new ones. Using antonyms will help them expand vocabulary. Observe students in the Concentration routine and identify some who may need small group work to understand the concept.	
46	WMV 10 ✓ page 285	Recognize and Use Antonyms	WMV 10 builds on previous learning by inviting students to locate and connect antonyms within continuous text. If you notice students having difficulty with this concept, use other poems to repeat the lesson with the whole class or with a small group. Have students quickly locate and connect antonyms in guided reading, and show them how to use these understandings to better understand the text.	

Suggested Sequence for Phonics Lessons

#	Lesson	Title	Teaching Suggestions for Extending Learning	Teacher Notes
			MIDDLE *(Continued)*	
47	WMV 11 ✓ page 289	Recognize and Use Homophones	Some word pairs are homophones, and these special words cause many spelling errors in writing. Begin teaching this lesson by using words that students already know, because the concept presented in this lesson can be confusing to many students. Using words in sentences will help a great deal; invite students to describe the homophones.	
48	WMV 12 ✓ page 293	Recognize and Use Homophones	In this lesson, students continue to expand their knowledge of homophones and how they are used in sentences. Even when students understand the concept and know some examples, it may be challenging for them to select the right word for a given context. Work with children in writing conferences and guided writing to help them expand knowledge. Repeat the lesson if needed to expand examples and the way students use them in sentences.	
49	WS 4 ✓ page 355	Recognize and Use Syllables in Words with Double Consonants	WS 4 goes back to the idea of taking words apart by syllables. Students will use their understanding of one-syllable word patterns and of phonogram patterns to help them notice and use these patterns in longer words. Using larger known word parts that are recognized quickly makes word solving efficient and automatic. In this lesson, students work with words that have the CVC pattern in the first syllable and thus have a double consonant. Putting together words to apply the concept will help students learn many examples.	
50	WS 5 ✓ page 359	Identify Syllables in Words with Three or More Syllables	Students will already know how to clap words and identify the number of syllables in words. WS 5 helps students acquire a set of examples of longer words so that they can begin to take them apart by syllables. This will help not only with decoding but also with pronouncing words. Help students pronounce the words, and suggest the breaks so that they begin to get an intuitive feel for the way each syllable sounds. The next lessons will expand students' use of syllables to make their understanding more precise.	
51	WS 6 ✓ page 363	Recognize and Use Open Syllables	Students will have noticed (or you can draw to their attention) the idea that every syllable has a vowel; however, the way the vowel is pronounced is related to the syllable divisions. It makes a difference whether the syllable ends with a consonant or a vowel; so students should have a sense of the pronunciation (from oral language) even before they take the word apart. Lessons WS 6 and WS 7 focus on open and closed syllables, beginning with open syllables that end in a vowel. WS 6 presents examples that will help students remember the principle that the vowel sound is long.	

#	Lesson	Title	Teaching Suggestions for Extending Learning	Teacher Notes
			MIDDLE *(continued)*	
52	WS 7 ✓ page 367	Recognize and Use Closed Syllables	WS 7 focuses on closed syllables that end in a consonant sound and in which the vowel sound is short. When students apply this principle to a known word (that they can pronounce) it will be easy for them to distinguish between an open and closed syllable and to divide the word accordingly. Working with magnetic letters will help them physically move the syllables to remember and understand them. If needed, repeat the lesson using both types of syllables. To solve a new word in guided reading, students can try pronouncing the word both ways to connect it with a word in their oral vocabulary.	
53	WS 8 ✓ page 371	Recognize and Use *r*-Influenced Syllables	In a syllable, the letter *r* influences the sound of the vowel, which is usually neither long nor short but unique. Before teaching this lesson, be sure that students have had experience with *r*-influenced vowels in single-syllable words. Students will be working with all five vowels; but if they have difficulty, you can limit the lesson to two or three.	
54	WS 9 ✓ page 375	Recognize and Use Vowel Combination Syllables	Students will have worked with vowel combinations in single-syllable words, but this lesson has them recognizing those word parts in syllables in longer words. You may wish to review the idea that sometimes *y* and *w* represent a vowel sound in such pairs. It will help for students to know that usually the vowel pairs stay together when you take a word apart by syllables.	
55	WS 10 ✓ page 379	Recognize and Use VC*e* Syllables	Students will be familiar with the VC*e* pattern in single-syllable words, and now they transfer these understandings to their work in taking words apart by syllables. They encounter examples in this lesson that give them experience in noticing the silent e pattern within multisyllable words. They apply this understanding in a five-way sort. If some students have difficulty, work with them in a small group to sort the words.	
56	WS 11 ✓ page 383	Recognize and Use Syllables in Words with the VCCV Pattern	Use this lesson after students understand the concept of syllables and know to identify vowels, consonants, and consonant digraphs; most third graders will be ready for WS 11 and will also have had experience in noticing double letters and consonant blends in words. This pattern signals that the word will have two syllables and that you divide the word between the two consonants.	

#	Lesson	Title	Teaching Suggestions for Extending Learning	Teacher Notes
			MIDDLE *(continued)*	
57	WS 12 ✅ page 387	Understand That the Ending -ed Can Represent Several Different Sounds	Students will have read many words with the -ed ending and possibly will have studied the three sounds related to -ed in second grade. They may know quite a few high-frequency words that end in -ed as they form the past tense. Recognizing the different sounds for this word ending will help them standardize their pronunciation and correctly spell words in the past tense.	
58	WS 13 ✅ page 391	Recognize and Use Common Abbreviations	By the time you teach this lesson, students will be expected to read and write many common abbreviations, which they may have previously learned in relation to names and proper nouns. You may want to teach it earlier in the year if there is a need. You may have taught this convention as part of writing workshop and so can omit it here.	
59	WS 14 ✅ page 395	Recognize and Use Plurals That Add -es to Words That End with the Letters *ch*, *sh*, *s*, *x*, or *z*	Plurals are the source of many spelling errors, and students will continue to learn about the spelling of plurals over several years. Be sure that they have a good understanding of adding -s to create simple plurals (and consider using some of those examples as contrast in this lesson). Pronunciation will also help students to spell plurals, so model it and have them say the words. You may want to repeat this lesson to be sure students have this concept under control.	
60	WMV 13 ✅ page 297	Recognize and Use Homographs	Homographs are a subset of homonyms, so students need to gradually build the larger category and the distinctions within it. It may also help students to know that word pairs in this category (and each subcategory) are alike in some way (spelling, pronunciation). Homographs are a source of pronunciation error in reading because students must make choices based on the meaning within the larger message. Awareness of syntax, built through hearing and constructing sentences, will help students search for pronunciation that "sounds right and makes sense."	
61	WMV 14 ✅ page 301	Recognize and Use Homographs	Students will enjoy finding these homographs and talking about the differences in meaning of the two pronunciations. This lesson gives them more practice in identifying and pairing the homographs as the words are used in sentences. If students understand the concepts very well and have many examples in mind, you may wish to omit this lesson but to follow up in guided reading or shared writing homographs when they encounter examples.	

#	Lesson	Title	Teaching Suggestions for Extending Learning	Teacher Notes
			MIDDLE *(continued)*	
62	WMV 15 ✓ page 305	Recognize and Use Words with Multiple Meanings	As students begin to acquire a large oral and written vocabulary, they realize that a word may mean two or more different things. A word can be different parts of speech, depending on how it is used in a sentence. This lesson begins with very simple examples and uses the words in sentences. If students understand the concept very well, consider compiling a chart of words with multiple meanings that children have noticed.	
63	WMV 16 ✓ page 306	Recognize and Use Words with Multiple Meanings	In this lesson, help students expand their repertoires of examples of words with multiple meanings. This lesson can help them use the context of a sentence to determine word meaning and to check their understanding. Students will enjoy creating riddles, which increases their power over words.	
64	WS 15 ✓ page 399	Recognize and Use Plurals That Add -es to Words That End with a Consonant and *y*	This lesson returns to the concept of plurals and is the first of a series of lessons that will help students to compare and contrast the various ways of creating plural nouns. There may be a difference in both the spelling and the pronunciation of a noun, depending on the letters in the word. Students have previously learned to add -es to nouns to make plurals, but in this lesson they learn that there is a spelling change for nouns that end in consonant and *y*.	
65	WS 16 ✓ page 403	Recognize and Use Plurals That Add -es to Words After Changing the Final *f* or *fe* to *v*	Since plurals are the source of many spelling errors, it is useful to spend time in WS 15, WS 16, WS 17, and WS 18 to be sure students understand the basic rules that will help them. You may want to extend the learning by teaching a summary lesson.	

Suggested Sequence for Phonics Lessons

#	Lesson	Title	Teaching Suggestions for Extending Learning	Teacher Notes
			MIDDLE *(continued)*	
66	WS 17 ✓ page 407	Recognize and Use Plurals that Add *-es* to Words That End with *o*	After students have encountered, written, and sorted many words with this pattern, they will develop automatic ability to write them. Connecting words will help. They should recognize that there are a few exceptions to this rule (e.g., *zeroes*).	
67	WS 18 ✓ page 411	Recognize and Use Plurals that Add *-es* to Words That End with a Consonant and *o*	Here students have the opportunity to explore the exceptions. Some nouns are made plural with *-s* and some with *-es*. Students will eventually develop automatic understanding of the different noun plurals; however, these examples may be the source of spelling errors for several years.	
68	WS 19 ✓ page 415	Recognize and Use the Suffixes *-er* and *-est* to Show Comparison	Understanding base words and suffixes is basic to efficient word solving. Proficient readers approaching an unfamiliar word with affixes will automatically notice these word parts and will use them both for pronunciation and for understanding of meaning. A basic understanding is that adding a suffix to a noun changes the meaning in some way and often changes the function (part of speech) of the word in the sentence. In this lesson students add suffixes to adjectives. It may help to use pictures to increase understanding. It will help students to write the three versions of the base word. Students will have familiarity with the *-er* and *-est* suffixes. They can study affixes more later in the year.	
69	LSR 10 page 111	Recognize and Use Consonant Letters That Represent Two or More Different Sounds at the End of a Word	Students should have a strong understanding of regular consonant letter-sound relationships and also of the fact that sometimes two or more sounds are connected to a single letter or letter cluster. In this lesson, students systematize their knowledge and develop categories of words. They will extend their understanding of the complex letter-sound relationships in English. This lesson will contribute to students' spelling knowledge and can be used as they proofread their writing.	

#	Lesson	Title	Teaching Suggestions for Extending Learning	Teacher Notes
			MIDDLE *(continued)*	
70	LSR 11 page 115	Recognize and Use Consonant Letters That Represent No Sound	Silent consonants are another source of spelling errors, because students have to think not only about how a word sounds but also about how it *looks*. It's part of developing a visual memory for words that is gained through reading but that also deserves direct study of the words in this category. You may wish to use sound and letter boxes as well to emphasize visual memory. The game Follow the Path will help students recognize these words quickly and build visual memory as well.	
71	LSR 12 page 119	Recognize and Use Consonant Letters That Represent No Sound	In this lesson students use a study method (make-say-check-mix-write-read) to develop visual memory of words with silent consonants. If students have difficulty with this activity, work with a small group to study the words. You can repeat this lesson with more examples, and students may add them to their spelling lists.	
72	LSR 13 page 123	Understand That Some Consonant Sounds Can Be Represented by Several Different Letters or Letter Clusters	There are some very complex letter-sound relationships in English. Third-grade students will encounter these complex relationships in the words they read, and they will be expected to spell them. These consonant sounds are the source of many spelling errors. It will be very helpful to students to have a category of words in their heads, all of which can represent a particular consonant sound. Visual memory of the features of words will be helpful, so they need to work with many examples.	
73	LSR 14 ✓ page 127	Recognize and Use Vowel Sounds with *r*	The consonant *r* appears in many syllables with a vowel letter in a way that modifies the sound of the vowel. This is the source of many spelling errors, because students must learn that the same letter combination may represent more than one vowel sound (e.g., *bear, dear*). At the same time, several different letter combinations (e.g., *-er, -ir,* and *-ur*) may represent the same vowel sound. Many third graders will be unsure about the spellings of these words. They need opportunities to work with many examples so that they have a repertoire of common patterns. You may want to return to this lesson to examine more examples. You may wish to use sound and letter boxes as well to emphasize visual memory of these patterns.	

#	Lesson	Title	Teaching Suggestions for Extending Learning	Teacher Notes
			MIDDLE *(continued)*	
74	LSR 15 page 131	Recognize and Use Vowel Sounds in Closed Syllables (CVC)	In this lesson, students return to the idea of open and closed syllables. Dividing words into syllables is basic to pronunciation and to rapid and efficient decoding. When students approach an unfamiliar word that has a single consonant in the middle of the first syllable, they should try alternative ways to say the word–*short vowel sound* and *long vowel sound*. It helps if the word is in the oral vocabulary. If needed, pronounce it for them and make sure they know the meaning.	
75	LSR 16 page 135	Recognize and Use Vowel Sounds in Open Syllables (CVC)	This lesson continues the study of closed and open syllables in words. Students will enjoy using word parts to make words, and they can add some examples in their word study notebooks or to a class chart. You may want to extend this lesson by giving students words with open and closed syllables in the first syllable. They can sort the words and say them.	
76	LSR 17 page 139	Understand How to Use Capital Letters Correctly	You may have taught a lesson on the use of capital letters during writing workshop, so this lesson will not be needed. But if not, it is time to help students systematize the understandings they have already developed implicitly. The game Lotto will give them experience to help in acquiring a repertoire of known proper nouns that they can use as examples. You can also draw attention to capital letters in shared writing and during writing conferences.	
77	HFW 4 page 235	Recognize and Use Longer High-Frequency Words, Some with More Than One Syllable	In HFW 4 and HFW 5, third graders become highly conscious of their own acquisition of known words that appear often in written language. They should understand that they can use this core of known high-frequency words as an anchor to monitor and check their reading and spelling. These words acquaint students with a large number of spelling patterns and word parts that they can use to decode more complex words. Having a large core of words supports fluent reading and writing. Use this lesson to help students notice parts of words that they need to remember in order to spell them accurately.	
78	HFW 5 page 239	Acquire a Large Core of High-Frequency Words	Each student should have an individualized high-frequency word list (see Online Resources) from which they can select new words to learn. (You may also assign some words you think will benefit the class.) In the process of acquiring high-frequency words, students should be noticing visual patterns; the process should get easier because they are developing a sophisticated *system for learning new words*.	

#	Lesson	Title	Teaching Suggestions for Extending Learning	Teacher Notes
			LATE IN THE YEAR	
79	SP 9 ✓ page 185	Recognize and Use Phonogram Patterns with the /u/ Vowel Sound in Single-Syllable Words	SP 9 returns to the study of phonogram patterns by focusing on the long *u* vowel sound, which is varied both in pronunciation and spelling (*tune, suit, mule*). In fact, this sound can be represented by twenty-nine different letter patterns. Students need to learn to look for visual patterns. You can choose to focus on three or four patterns. Or, if students are very strong in this area, use all of them. Students will be fascinated by the complexity of these letter-sound relationships. The more they can connect these words, the easier they will find it to learn, pronounce, and spell them.	
80	SP 10 ✓ page 189	Recognize and Use Phonogram Patterns with the /ủ/ Vowel Sound in Single-Syllable Words	This lesson focuses on phonogram patterns with the /ủ/ sound as in *book, moon, you, should, push*. Here, even single-syllable words can be complex. It will help students to pair examples, and the game Follow the Path will help them notice and practice more of these words. They can make lists of the words and write memorable examples in their word study notebooks.	
81	SP 11 ✓ page 193	Recognize and Use Phonogram Patterns with the /ò/ Vowel Sound (as in *saw*) in Single-Syllable Words	SP 11 continues the study of phonogram patterns with the sound of /o/ that are phonetically regular and those that are represented by other visual patterns (e.g., *wall, paw, taught, cost, long*). Learning will be enhanced if students understand a limited number of ways to represent the pattern and also learn to look at words so they can remember something important about them.	
82	SP 12 ✓ page 197	Recognize and Use Phonogram Patterns with the /ou/ Vowel Sound in Single-Syllable Words	Words that have phonogram patterns with the /ou/ vowel sound also may be represented by a variety of spelling patterns (e.g., *ou, ow*). Probably students have many known words to use as examples. In this lesson they systematize their knowledge by creating categories of words with each kind of spelling.	

Suggested Sequence for Phonics Lessons

#	Lesson	Title	Teaching Suggestions for Extending Learning	Teacher Notes
LATE (continued)				
83	SP 13 ✓ page 201	Recognize and Use Phonogram Patterns with the /oi/ Vowel Sound in Single-Syllable Words	The /oi/ vowel sound is associated with seven phonogram patterns and can be the source of many spelling errors. This lesson focuses on words with *oy* or *oi* in phonograms. Readers and writers who know to choose one of these two representations and who use knowledge of consonant sounds and CVC*e* phonograms can quickly build up experience with these useful parts of words. The game Concentration will help them connect words quickly.	
84	SP 14 ✓ page 205	Recognize and Use Phonogram Patterns with Vowels and *r* in Single-Syllable Words	As students work on spelling throughout the year, *r*-influenced vowels will continue to be a challenge. Once students understand that certain vowels appear with r in words and once they know to look for specific patterns, they can apply this information with increased efficiency. Phonograms that include *at*, *er*, *ir*, *or*, and *ur* will be familiar to students, but patterns like ear are less predictable. The game Follow the Path will give practice in reading and pronouncing these words and will build visual memory of patterns.	
85	SP 15 ✓ page 209	Understand that Some Words Have a Double Consonant	Students will be familiar with words that end in double consonants and also will have noticed double consonants in the middle of words. In this lesson, they combine their understandings to notice the position of the double consonants within a word. A basic understanding is that the two consonants together stand for a single sound. Working with the different kinds of words increases flexibility.	

#	Lesson	Title	Teaching Suggestions for Extending Learning	Teacher Notes
			LATE *(continued)*	
86	WMV 17 ✓ page 313	Recognize and Use Compound Words with Common Parts	If students are very familiar with compound words and have a large repertoire of words that have common parts, you may want to combine WMV 17 and WMV 18. Used in sequence, they can greatly increase the number of words students connect, and this can lead to a rapid expansion of vocabulary. Quickly recognizing frequently appearing words will help students become automatic in reading and writing a large number of compound words.	
87	WMV 18 ✓ page 317	Recognize and Use Compound Words with Common Parts	Students are likely to understand the concept of compound words and have a repertoire of examples. In this lesson, they expand the repertoire and create some word "families" by looking at words that contain the same component word. Knowing that some smaller words appear frequently in compound words will help students quickly take apart the compound words (of which there are many) that they encounter in reading and construct them in writing. Using a word map will make these connections visible.	
88	SP 16 ✓ page 213	Recognize and Use Frequently Appearing Syllable Patterns in Multisyllable Words	Just as they recognize component parts of compound words, students can recognize frequently appearing syllable patterns in multisyllable words, and this is key to rapid, automatic word solving. Recognizing commonly recurring syllable patterns will help students become more flexible in reading and spelling words. In this lesson, students examine word examples that have *a* as in *among* and *be* as in *before*. Most of these examples will be known words, but students may not have connected them in this way.	
89	SP 17 ✓ page 217	Recognize and Use Frequently appearing Syllable Patterns in Multisyllable Words	This lesson extends SP 16 by helping students to notice frequently occurring syllable patterns at the ends of words and to connect the words as they engage in word solving. The game Concentration will provide practice in noticing these patterns and prompt students to begin to notice other frequently appearing syllable patterns.	

#	Lesson	Title	Teaching Suggestions for Extending Learning	Teacher Notes
			LATE *(continued)*	
90	HFW 6 ✓ page 243	Read and Write Approximately 500 High-Frequency Words	As a result of this lesson, you want to have students take learning of high-frequency words into their own control. They need a clear sense of the words they already know, as well as a goal to learn some words that they don't yet know. Do not move to the list of 500 words until students have almost all of the 200 words under control. This move is tricky because some students will have many more words to learn than others. Emphasize the continuous nature of learning, and, if needed, differentiate to give very high progress students a different word list. Reduce the number of words if needed so word study doesn't take too much time. Students can highlight words they know and identify words they need to know for weekly lists.	
91	WMV 19 ✓ page 321	Recognize and Use Onomatopoetic Words	Students will have encountered onomatopoetic words from the first books they have heard read aloud (although even in grade 3 you would not want to use this long technical word). It will be helpful if students have been exposed to poetry and have created their own persona poetry books. They can identify words for sound in many poems they have read and illustrated. The goal of this lesson is to bring sound words to conscious attention and have students become more aware of how writers have created words to represent sounds.	
92	WMV 20 ✓ page 325	Recognize That Some Words Have Literal and Figurative Meanings	Lesson WMV 20 helps students examine another kind of literary language–comparisons. Writers use words that have not only literal meanings but also figurative meanings, and this presents a special challenge to English language learners. It's important to recognize that in order for students to understand a word's figurative meaning, they must first understand its literal meaning. The figurative meaning of a word is a challenge, but at the same time metaphors and similes give the language of texts appeal and interest. This lesson uses simple examples to illustrate the principle.	
93	WMV 21 ✓ page 329	Recognize That Some Words Have Literal and Figurative Meanings	This lesson helps students expand understanding of multiple meanings of words by further exploration of figurative meaning. Again, simple examples are used, but students should be able to apply this understanding to many more examples as they sort sentence strips. Distinguishing literal and figurative meanings is an important understanding.	

#	Lesson	Title	Teaching Suggestions for Extending Learning	Teacher Notes
			LATE *(continued)*	
94	WS 20 ✓ page 419	Recognize and Use the Suffixes *-er*, *-or*, *-ar*, and *-ist* to Form a Noun	In this example, students move back to word structure to examine base words and suffixes, concepts that they will continue to acquire over the next few years. In this lesson, they explore suffixes that change the part of speech of a word. Not only does a word's spelling (and pronunciation) change when you add the suffixes *-er*, *-or*, *-ar*, and *-ist*, but its function changes from a verb to a noun and its meaning becomes "one who does something." Writing twenty words that name a person who does something will provide a number of examples that will help students read and write other words.	
95	WS 21 ✓ page 423	Recognize and Use the Prefix *re-*, Meaning "again"	Grade 3 students will have noticed prefixes in reading, and they will have used them in their own writing. Students may have had experience with and may fully understand the prefix *re-*, meaning "again," and in that case you can move into more complex words and word histories (for example *memory* and *remember* connected to the root *mem*). Students can learn that words have evolved over time, created by people as they used language. These word parts are meaning bearing, and when students understand this, it contributes not only to knowledge of word structure but also to vocabulary.	
96	WS 22 ✓ page 427	Recognize and Use the Prefixes That Mean "not	WS 22 is another lesson on prefixes, this time focusing on prefixes that mean "not." Once students learn the added meaning of this prefix, they can apply it to many words. Dividing words into base words, roots, and affixes is foundational to both word solving and vocabulary in the upper elementary grades. Many English words are made up of more than one meaning-bearing part. Students need to know that all of these word parts have meaning, and this knowledge will help them not only in accurate reading but also in knowing what words mean.	
97	WMV 22 ✓ page 333	Understand the Concept of Suffixes and Recognize Their Use in Determining the Meaning of Some English Words	Students will have noticed suffixes in reading and used them in their own writing. There is huge variety in suffixes, and they function in different ways, so learning about them will take place over several years. All suffixes add meaning to words, and many change the part of speech or the tense of a word. Students will have had experience using suffixes that change adjectives to nouns, for example, or change verbs from present to past tense. In this lesson students examine suffixes that change a base word or word root, and they focus on common suffixes like *-ful* and *-less*. The game Follow the Path helps them visually locate the word parts quickly.	

#	Lesson	Title	Teaching Suggestions for Extending Learning	Teacher Notes
			LATE *(continued)*	
98	WMV 23 ✓ page 337	**Understand the Concept of Prefixes and Recognize Their Use in Determining the Meaning of Some English Words**	Over the next few years students will be exploring and learning more about base words, root words, and affixes, because these are basic understandings for taking words apart and hypothesizing their meanings. Understanding word parts and their relationships will help students to greatly expand vocabulary and to take words apart with efficiency.	
99	LSR 18 ✓ page 143	**Understand How to Use the Computer Keyboard**	LSR 18 and LSR 19 are placed late in grade 3 because selection of these lessons depends very much on the policies and curriculum in your school. You may choose to use either of these lessons much earlier in the year if no other keyboarding instruction exists and if your observations tell you that students could be more productive with efficient moves on the computer. Practice could be accomplished as an independent activity if students do not have individual computers.	
100	LSR 19 ✓ page 147	**Understand How to Form Cursive Letters Correctly, Efficiently, and Fluently**	LSR 18 and LSR 19 are placed late in grade 3 because selection of these lessons depends very much on the policies and curriculum in your school. You may choose to use either of these lessons much earlier in the year. Handwriting, for example, may be part of writer's workshop minilessons. If you teach students efficient cursive writing, it will be easier to read their responses and they can become more fluent as writers.	

Letter-Sound Relationships

The sounds of oral language are related in both simple and complex ways to the twenty-six letters of the alphabet. Learning the connections between sounds and letters is basic to understanding written language. Students first learn simple relationships that are regular in that one phoneme is connected to one grapheme, or letter. Then they learn that consonant clusters blend two or three consonant sounds and that such clusters can also be consonant digraphs (e.g., *ch, ph, sh, th, wh*), which stand for a sound that is different from either of the individual consonant sounds. Long vowel sounds can be represented by letter combinations (e.g., *ai, ea, igh, oa, ue*) that stand for the sound of the name of the first vowel. (Some exceptions exist, usually in words adopted from other languages.) Students learn to look for and recognize these letter combinations as units, which makes their word solving more efficient. It is important to remember that students will be able to hear and connect the easy-to-identify consonants and vowels early and progress to the harder-to-hear and more difficult letter-sound relationships (e.g., consonant sounds that are represented by several different letters or letter clusters; letter combinations that represent two different vowel sounds; or vowel sounds influenced by *r*). You will want to connect initial and final consonant clusters and digraphs to the two charts provided in *Ready Resources*. It is not necessary to teach every cluster as a separate lesson.

Connect to Assessment

See related (optional) LSR Assessment tasks in Online Resources.

- Assessment A: Identifying and Writing Beginning Consonant Clusters in Words

- Assessment B: Identifying and Writing Ending Consonant Clusters in Words

- Assessment C: Reading Words with Consonant Clusters

- Assessment D: Recognizing and Using Double Consonants in Words

- Assessment E: Reading and Writing Words with Vowel Combinations

- Assessment F: Class Record (Consonant Clusters)

- Assessment G: Individual Record (Consonant Clusters)

- Assessment H: Class Record (Reading Words with Consonant Clusters)

- Assessment I: Individual Record (Vowel Combinations)

- Assessment J: Class Record (Vowel Combinations)

Develop Your Professional Understanding

See *The Fountas & Pinnell Comprehensive Phonics, Spelling, and Word Study Guide*. 2017. Portsmouth, New Hampshire: Heinemann. Related pages: 2-12, 26-31.

See *The Fountas & Pinnell Literacy Continuum: A Tool for Assessment, Planning, and Teaching*. 2017. Portsmouth, New Hampshire: Heinemann. Related pages: 357-397.

See *Word Matters: Teaching Phonics and Spelling in the Reading/Writing Classroom* by G.S. Pinnell and I.C. Fountas. 1998. Portsmouth, New Hampshire: Heinemann. Related pages: 46–48, 71–73, 90–93, 123, 141.

Recognize and Say Consonant Clusters That Blend Two or Three Consonant Sounds (Onsets)

Plan

▶ Consider Your Students

In this lesson, students read a variety of words with *l* clusters, *r* clusters, and *s* clusters, as well as *tw.* The lesson can serve as a useful reminder of the concept of consonant clusters. However, if students have learned a great deal about consonant clusters in first and second grades and can quickly recognize them as a pattern while reading, you may not want to use this lesson. Alternatively, if students have little experience recognizing consonant clusters, you may choose to teach this lesson over several days, focusing on a limited number of clusters at a time. You may also find it helpful to have students use highlighter tape to focus on specific consonant clusters or even individual letters (when teaching that you can hear the sound of each letter in a consonant cluster).

▶ Working with English Language Learners

Once English language learners understand that some consonants often appear in pairs or groups of three, they will more easily notice consonant clusters in words. Knowing these larger parts of words gives students better access to the words they read and spell. Keep in mind that it may be difficult for some students to hear or say the sounds represented by certain letters (e.g., *s* and *r*). In these instances, they may need to give more attention to the visual features of the word–how it looks as well as the sound-to-letter relationships.

UNDERSTAND THE PRINCIPLE

Consonants frequently occur together in words. It is important for students to continue to notice consonant clusters (also called *blends*) and to understand that you can hear the sound connected to each of the letters, although the sounds are blended smoothly when you say the word. Eventually students will recognize these particular letter patterns as a unit, making decoding even more efficient.

YOU WILL NEED

PWS Ready Resources
- ▶ Initial Consonant Clusters and Digraphs Chart

Online Resources
- ▶ LSR 1 Action Tags
- ▶ LSR 1 Word Cards
- ▶ LSR 1 List Sheets

Other Materials
- ▶ chart paper

Generative Lesson

A generative lesson has a simple structure that you can use to present similar content or concepts. Use this lesson structure to teach students to recognize and read a variety of consonant clusters at the beginning of words.

EXPLAIN THE PRINCIPLE

A group of two or three consonant letters is a consonant cluster.

You can usually hear each sound in a consonant cluster.

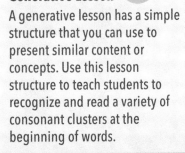

Comprehensive Phonics, Spelling, and Word Study Guide

Refer to: page **27**, row **7**

ACTIVITY: WORD LISTS

INSTRUCTIONAL PROCEDURE

NOTICE PARTS

See page 32 for detailed descriptions of Instructional Procedures.

EXPLAIN THE PRINCIPLE

A group of two or three consonant letters is a consonant cluster.

You can usually hear each sound in a consonant cluster.

Comprehensive Phonics, Spelling, and Word Study Guide

Refer to: page **27**, row **7**

closet   drank   freeze

glance   plenty   stream

Teach

1. On chart paper, write five or six words that begin with two- and three-letter consonant clusters, such as *closet, drank, freeze, glance, plenty,* and *stream.* Read the words with students and use each word in a sentence if students don't know the meaning. *What do you notice about all of these words?* • *Each word begins with two or three consonants.*

2. Explain the principle of consonant clusters to students. *As you've noticed, some words have groups of two or three consonants. These groups of letters are called* consonant clusters. Underline the consonant cluster in each word.

3. *Notice the sounds you hear at the beginning of each word.* • Give students time to notice and conclude that each beginning consonant stands for a sound. *You can hear each sound in a consonant cluster: /k/ /l/ -oset, /d/ /r/ -ank, /s/ /t/ /r/ -eam.*

4. Invite students to name more words beginning with consonant clusters. Students may find it helpful to refer to the Initial Consonant Clusters and Digraphs chart for ideas. Write several more examples on the chart.

5. Have students read each word on the chart again. To reinforce the principle, occasionally ask students to name the sounds they hear in the consonant cluster.

6. Tell students that they will make words by matching beginning consonant clusters with word endings. Use the cards to demonstrate how they can mix and match different beginnings and endings to make a variety of words. Students will then write twenty of the words on a list sheet.

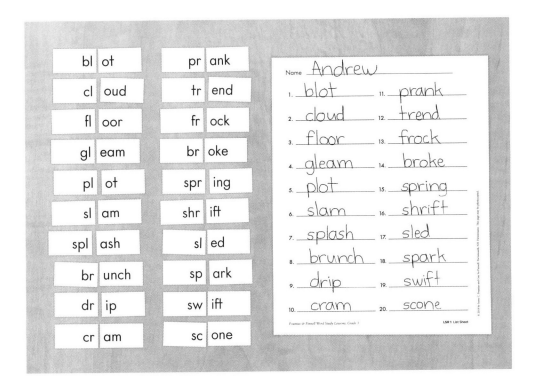

ACTIVITY: WORD BUILDING

INSTRUCTIONAL PROCEDURE

MAKE WORDS

See page 32 for detailed descriptions of Instructional Procedures.

ACTION TAGS

make words

write twenty words

read words

tell sounds

Apply

- Encourage students to experiment with many different combinations of consonant clusters and word endings. Tell them that they may need to read words softly to themselves to decide if a particular combination makes a real word.

- After students write twenty words on a list sheet, have them read each word to a partner and tell the consonant sounds they hear at the beginning.

Share

- Invite students to share some words they made. Add a few new words to the class chart.

- Encourage students to share any discoveries they made about words beginning with consonant clusters.

- Review the principle and remind students to notice beginning consonant clusters when they read and write.

Assess

- Notice whether students are using knowledge of consonant clusters to solve words efficiently while reading.

- Ask students to write ten to twelve words with consonant clusters you have taught. Check to see whether all letters in the consonant clusters are represented.

- You may wish to use Letter-Sound Relationships Assessment A, C, F, G, or H.

Letter-Sound Relationships: Recognize and Say Consonant Clusters That Blend Two or Three Consonant Sounds (Onsets)

Connect Learning Across Contexts

Guided Reading As students are reading texts, prompt them to "look at the first part" when they are trying to solve unknown words beginning with consonant clusters. Some readers may find it helpful to cover the last part of the word in order to focus on the letters and sounds at the beginning.

Independent Reading While students read books independently, instruct them to solve words by using known word parts, e.g., *Look at the first part. Where can you break that word? Do you know a part that can help you?*

Shared Writing When students want to write a word beginning with a consonant cluster, guide them to think about each sound they hear. You may want to add words that are generated in shared writing to the class chart.

Independent Writing During conferences, point out words with consonant clusters that students have spelled correctly. Guide students to review and respell words that begin with consonant clusters they know but that are not spelled conventionally.

Extend Learning

- Repeat the lesson by focusing on specific "families" of consonant clusters: *r* clusters (*br, cr, dr, fr, gr, pr, tr*), *l* clusters (*bl, cl, fl, gl, pl, sl*), two-letter *s* clusters (*sc, sk, sm, sn, sp, st, sw*), and three-letter *s* clusters (*scr, spl, spr, squ, str*). You can use the Initial Consonant Clusters and Digraphs chart as a reference tool. You may not need to teach a lesson for every type of letter cluster, but you may want to summarize each on a chart to which students can refer.

- Print copies of the beginning consonant clusters sheet from Online Resources, and have students say and sort the words.

▶ Connect with Home

Give students sets of beginning consonant cluster cards and word ending cards to mix and match with family members.

Recognize and Use Consonant Clusters (Blends) at the End of a Word

Plan

▶ Consider Your Students

Students should have a great deal of experience with beginning consonant clusters and good control of them before you present this lesson. If students have learned a great deal about consonant clusters in first and second grades and can quickly recognize them at the end of words while reading, you may wish to present even more than seven consonant clusters in this lesson. Alternatively, if students have little experience recognizing consonant clusters, you may choose to teach this lesson over several days, focusing on just two or three consonant clusters at a time. You may also find it helpful to have students use highlighter tape to focus on specific consonant clusters or even individual letters (when teaching that you can hear the sound of each letter in a consonant cluster). The Final Consonant Clusters and Digraphs chart (found in *Ready Resources*) will be a useful tool for summarizing the principle.

▶ Working with English Language Learners

Pronounce each word with students, helping them notice the consonant cluster at the end. When appropriate, help them make connections to the same consonant cluster at the beginning of words that they know well. Sometimes ending sounds of words are especially difficult for English language learners to hear and produce. Give them many opportunities to say the words and to generate word pairs with support.

UNDERSTAND THE PRINCIPLE

Consonants frequently occur together in words. It is important for students to continue to notice consonant clusters (also called *blends*) and to understand that you can hear the sound connected to each of the letters, although the sounds are blended smoothly when you say the word. Eventually students will recognize these particular letter patterns as a unit, making decoding even more efficient.

YOU WILL NEED

PWS Ready Resources
- ▶ Final Consonant Clusters and Digraphs Chart

Online Resources
- ▶ **LSR 2** Action Tags
- ▶ **LSR 2** Word Cards
- ▶ **LSR 2** Word Pairs Sheets

Other Materials
- ▶ blank chart paper

EXPLAIN THE PRINCIPLE

Some words end with a consonant cluster.

You can hear each sound in a consonant cluster at the end of a word.

Comprehensive Phonics, Spelling, and Word Study Guide

Refer to: page **28**, row **15**

ACTIVITY: WORD LISTS

INSTRUCTIONAL PROCEDURE

NOTICE PARTS

See page 32 for detailed descriptions of Instructional Procedures.

EXPLAIN THE PRINCIPLE

Some words end with a consonant cluster.

You can hear each sound in a consonant cluster at the end of a word.

Comprehensive Phonics, Spelling, and Word Study Guide

Refer to:
page **28**, row **15**

lif**t**	drift
itsel**f**	wolf
stum**p**	stamp
spe**nd**	round
bli**nk**	wink
eve**nt**	paint
twi**st**	chest

Teach

1. Write the following words on a chart: *lift, itself, stump, spend, blink, event, twist.* Read the words with students and use the word in a sentence if the students may not know the meaning.

2. *Think about the consonant sounds and letters in the words. What do you notice about all of these words?* • *Each word ends with two consonants.* Remind students that the two consonants together are called a consonant cluster. *You can hear each sound in the consonant cluster.*

3. Ask students to read each word again. Underline the consonants at the end of each word, and have students say the sounds the letters stand for. You may wish to refer to the Final Consonant Clusters and Digraphs chart to help students connect the letters and sounds.

4. Invite students to tell more words that end in the consonant clusters -*ft*, -*lf*, -*mp*, - *nd*, -*nk*, -*nt*, and -*st*. Write at least one additional word for each consonant cluster. Students may suggest words in which the consonant *l* is silent, such as *half* and *calf.* Encourage students to discuss what they notice about these exceptions.

5. Have students read the new list of words as you reinforce the principle. *You can hear each sound in a consonant cluster at the end of a word.*

6. Tell students that today they are going to write pairs of words with the same consonant cluster at the end. Explain that they will take a word card and write the word in the first column of a word pairs sheet. Then they think of another word with the same ending consonant cluster. They write the new word in the second column. Ask students to write at least seven different word pairs, one for each consonant cluster in the lesson. They read all of their word pairs to a partner.

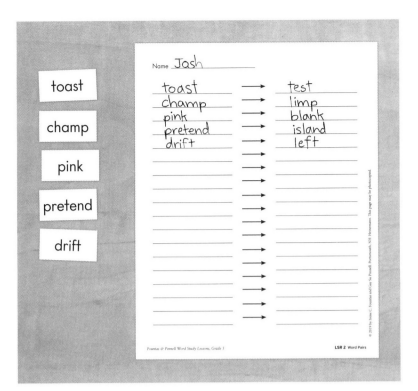

ACTIVITY: WORD PAIRS

INSTRUCTIONAL PROCEDURE

NOTICE PARTS

See page 32 for detailed descriptions of Instructional Procedures.

ACTION TAGS

take card
write word
think of a new word
write word
read words

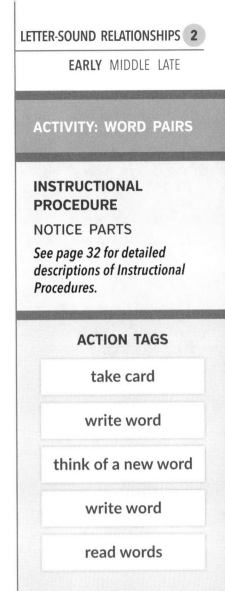

Apply

- You may need to remind students that they are creating word pairs that have the same final consonant cluster. The words do not need to rhyme to count as a word pair. For example, the words *pretend* and *island* create a pair because they both end in the sounds /nd/ and the consonant cluster *-nd.*

- To help students learn to recognize consonant clusters, you may wish to have them highlight the consonant cluster in each word.

- Remind students to read each word pair on their sheet to a partner.

Share

- Have students share more words ending with each consonant cluster. You may wish to add several of the words to the class chart.

- Review the principle and remind students to notice words with consonant clusters at the end of a word clusters when they read and write.

Assess

- Observe students reading words that end with consonant clusters. Notice the patterns they recognize quickly and easily and the patterns with which they need more experience.

- Dictate ten to twelve words that end with consonant clusters. Notice how students represent the ending consonant sounds in writing.

- You may wish to use Letter-Sound Relationships Assessment B, C, F, G, or H.

Letter-Sound Relationships: Recognize and Use Consonant Clusters (Blends) at the End of a Word

Connect Learning Across Contexts

Shared Reading During shared reading, you may wish to use the following title from *Fountas & Pinnell Classroom*™ to locate a few words that end with a consonant cluster.

SR *Wolf Pack* by Annette Bay Pimentel

Guided Reading Select several words in the text that end with consonant clusters. During word work, help students apply their understanding of consonant clusters to solve the words.

Shared Writing As you write words with consonant clusters at the end, guide students to say each word slowly, listening for each sound in the consonant cluster.

Independent Writing As you confer with writers, point out words that have consonant clusters at the end. Prompt them to say each sound at the end and check the letters. Remind them to use the class chart and the Final Consonant Clusters and Digraphs chart as resources.

Extend Learning

- Repeat the lesson using different consonant clusters, such as *ct, ft, ld,* and *sp.*
- Have students take turns choosing a word card and using magnetic letters or letter cards to make another word that ends with the same consonant cluster.

▶ Connect with Home

Send home a set of game cards with students, and encourage them to play Concentration with family members. Explain that words with the same ending consonant cluster count as a match.

Recognize and Use y as a Vowel Sound

Plan

▶ Consider Your Students

To benefit most from this lesson, students need to have good control of long and short vowel sounds. They will likely have noticed that many words end with *y* but may not have noticed the conditions in which it stands for a long vowel sound. If students already understand this letter-sound relationship and can efficiently solve words in which the letter *y* functions as a vowel, you may not need to present the lesson to the whole class.

▶ Working with English Language Learners

Understanding that a letter can represent different sounds depending on its place in a word is an important concept for students who are learning to speak, read, and write English. Some languages are more regular than English in their letter-sound relationships; others do not use an alphabetic system. The words you use to illustrate the sounds represented by *y* should be clear examples that English language learners can understand and perhaps read and write. Establish the concept firmly with these examples. In the beginning, remove any words that students do not understand.

UNDERSTAND THE PRINCIPLE

The letter *y* can function as a consonant or a vowel. When at the end of a word and typically when preceded by a consonant, the letter *y* can stand for either the long *e* sound or the long *i* sound. It most often represents the long *e* sound at the end of words with more than one syllable and the long *i* sound at the end of words with one syllable. There are a number of frequently occurring exceptions, including the words *July, apply, satisfy,* and *reply.*

EXPLAIN THE PRINCIPLE

Y *is a letter that sometimes stands for a vowel sound.*

Y *can stand for a long* e *vowel sound as in words such as* family, funny, happy.

Y *can stand for a long* i *vowel sound as in words such as* by, my, sky.

Comprehensive Phonics, Spelling, and Word Study Guide

Refer to: page **30**, row **26**

ACTIVITY: TWO-WAY SORT

INSTRUCTIONAL PROCEDURE

SAY AND SORT

See page 32 for detailed descriptions of Instructional Procedures.

EXPLAIN THE PRINCIPLE

Y *is a letter that sometimes stands for a vowel sound.*

Y *can stand for a long e vowel sound as in words such as family, funny, happy.*

Y *can stand for a long i vowel sound as in words such as by, my, sky.*

Comprehensive Phonics, Spelling, and Word Study Guide

Refer to:
page **30**, row **26**

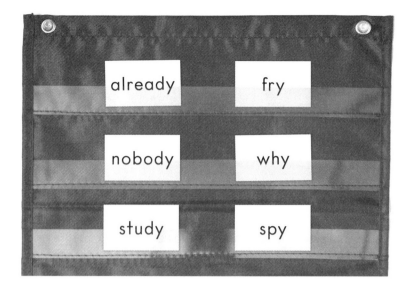

Teach

1. In a pocket chart, display the following words in a random way: *already, fry, nobody, why, study, spy.* Read the words with students and use the word in a sentence if the students may not know the meaning. *What do you notice about all of these words?* • Students will likely notice that the words all end in *y.* As needed, prompt students to continue to think about the words. *Who can say more about the sound you hear at the end of these words?* • Students may observe that the letter *y* stands for two different vowel sounds, that some words are short (have one syllable) and some are longer (have two or more syllables), and that the letter *y* sounds like long *i* in the short words and like long *e* in the longer words.

2. Build on students' observations to explain the principle: *The letter* y *sometimes stands for a vowel sound. As you've noticed,* y *sometimes stands for the long e sound, /ē/. At other times,* y *stands for the long i sound, /ī/.* Depending on students' awareness of syllables, you may wish to explain that *y* usually stands for the long *e* sound at the end of words with more than one syllable. You may also wish to point out that there are a few common exceptions, such as the words *July* and *reply.*

3. Ask students to say the words again and sort the cards in two columns based on the vowel sound of *y.*

4. Tell students that today they are going to practice sorting words. Students will use a two-way sort to sort the words that appear on the word cards. Once the words are sorted, students should then write the words on the sheet.

INSTRUCTIONAL PROCEDURE

NOTICE PARTS

See page 32 for detailed descriptions of Instructional Procedures.

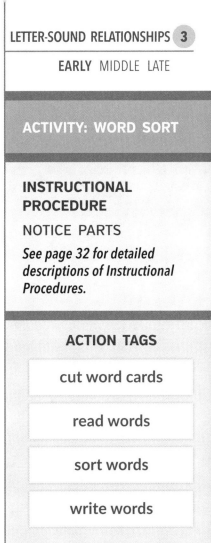

ACTION TAGS

cut word cards

read words

sort words

write words

Apply

Point out the key words *study* and *spy* at the top of the two-way sort. Encourage students to sort the word cards and write the words in the correct column.

Share

■ Have students share a few words with a partner by taking turns reading the words from their two-way sort. You may wish to add new words to the pocket chart using blank pocket-chart word cards found in *Ready Resources*.

■ Review the principle and remind students to notice words in which *y* functions as a vowel when they read and write.

Assess

■ Dictate six to eight words that end with *y* to assess students' control of words in which *y* functions as a vowel.

■ As you observe students reading, notice how efficient they are in recognizing and solving words that have *y* at the end.

Connect Learning Across Contexts

Shared Reading During shared reading, you may wish to use the following title from *Fountas & Pinnell Classroom*™ to locate a few words that use *y* as a vowel.

SR *Tiny but Fierce* by Cheri Colburn

Guided Reading During word work, write a few words ending in *y* on a whiteboard. Call for students to recognize and read the words quickly.

Shared Writing As you construct a piece of writing with students, prompt them to notice the spelling of words in which *y* stands for a vowel sound.

Independent Writing When conferring with writers, point out instances in which they have represented a vowel sound with the letter *y*. As needed, guide students to use conventional spellings.

Extend Learning

- Distribute blank Follow the Path game boards (found in Online Resources), and have students work together to create boards with new sets of words in which *y* stands for a vowel sound.

- Encourage students to write rhyming poems that use words from their two-way sorts.

▶ Connect with Home

Send home the lesson's word cards along with blank word cards from Online Resources. Have students add new words with the *y* vowel sound to the blank word cards and practice sorting.

Recognize and Use Letter Combinations That Represent Long Vowel Sounds

Plan

▶ Consider Your Students

Use this lesson after students have worked with vowels and also understand that letter combinations sometimes stand for single sounds in words. You may wish to have students write and read a few words with long vowel combinations to assess their understanding of the principle and determine which patterns will be most beneficial to teach and include in the game. Once students have learned to play Crazy Eights, you can substitute new words containing long vowel letter combinations to give students additional experience.

▶ Working with English Language Learners

It will be helpful to English language learners to notice vowel patterns in words that they know. Understanding these vowel combinations will help students solve words more efficiently. Use frequently occurring words that are already part of students' speaking, listening, and reading vocabularies. The lesson will help them analyze the words and systematize their knowledge. You may wish to bring together a small group of English language learners to support their understanding of Crazy Eights and how to play it successfully. Quickly review the words on the game cards to be sure they can read and understand them.

UNDERSTAND THE PRINCIPLE

Vowel combinations are also called *vowel digraphs, vowel pairs,* and *vowel teams.* Many long vowel combinations, including *ai, ay,* and *ee,* are highly predictable. They have consistent letter-sound relationships that are valuable for students to notice and remember. Once students understand that vowels often appear together in words and they know to look for specific patterns, they can apply this information to read text and spell words with increased efficiency and accuracy.

YOU WILL NEED

PWS Ready Resources
- ▶ LSR 4 Pocket-Chart Cards
- ▶ Blank Pocket-Chart Cards

Online Resources
- ▶ LSR 4 Action Tags
- ▶ LSR 4 Game Cards
- ▶ LSR 4 Directions for Crazy Eights

Other Materials
- ▶ pocket chart

EXPLAIN THE PRINCIPLE

In some words, two vowels together stand for one sound.

When there are two vowels, they usually stand for the sound of the name of the first vowel.

In some words, one or more vowels together with one or more consonants can stand for one vowel sound.

Comprehensive Phonics, Spelling, and Word Study Guide

Refer to: page **30**, row **27**

ACTIVITY: WORD PAIRS

INSTRUCTIONAL PROCEDURE

NOTICE PARTS

See page 32 for detailed descriptions of Instructional Procedures.

EXPLAIN THE PRINCIPLE

In some words, two vowels together stand for one sound.

When there are two vowels, they usually stand for the sound of the name of the first vowel.

In some words, one or more vowels together with one or more consonants can stand for one vowel sound.

Comprehensive Phonics, Spelling, and Word Study Guide

Refer to: page **30**, row **27**

Teach

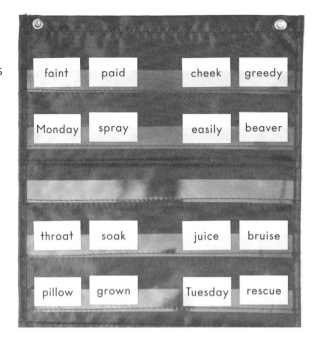

1. In the pocket chart, display the following pairs of words: *faint, paid* and *Monday, spray.* Read the words with students and use the word in a sentence if the students may not know the meaning. *What do you notice about all of the words?* • *Each word has the long a sound, /ā/.* Encourage students to notice and discuss the letters that stand for the long *a* sound. • *In the words* faint *and* paid, *the letters a and i together stand for the sound /ā/. In the words* Monday *and* spray, *the letters a and y together stand for the sound /ā/.*

2. Repeat the procedure with the long *e* word pairs *cheek, greedy* and *easily, beaver;* with the long *o* word pairs *throat, soak* and *pillow, grown;* and with the long *u* word pairs *juice, bruise* and *Tuesday, rescue.* Encourage students to make comparisons among all the words and talk about patterns they are noticing.

3. Ask students to read all of the words again. You may wish to invite them to give one more example for each pattern. Write the new words on blank pocket-chart cards and add them to the chart. If students suggest a word that has a different long vowel pattern, display the word to the side. Use the opportunity to talk about how the pattern is different from the others.

4. Building on students' earlier observations, guide them to compare all of the words and make generalizations. *In some of the words, such as* faint *and* throat, *two vowels together stand for one sound. The two vowels stand for the sound of the name of the first vowel. In some of the words, such as* spray *and* grown, *a vowel together with a consonant stand for one vowel sound.*

5. Tell students that today they are going to play Crazy Eights using a deck of cards with long vowel words. Explain that each player takes eight cards to start. The remaining cards are placed facedown in a deck. One card is turned up beside the deck to create the beginning of the discard pile. On a player's turn, she reads the word on the top of the discard pile, puts down a card with the same long vowel sound, and reads the word. If a player does not have a card that matches, she must either discard a Crazy Eight card or take new cards from the deck until she finds a match to discard. After a Crazy Eight card is played, the next player may choose to discard any card (not necessarily a card matching the previous long vowel sound). The first player to discard all her cards wins the game.

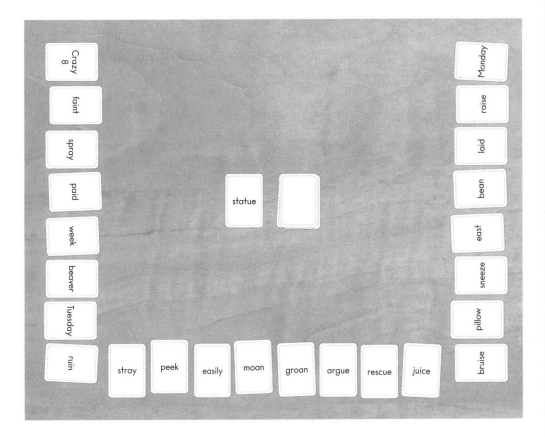

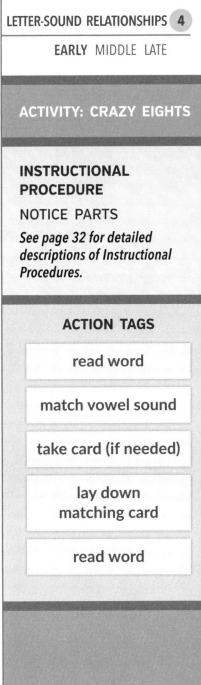

ACTIVITY: CRAZY EIGHTS

INSTRUCTIONAL PROCEDURE

NOTICE PARTS

See page 32 for detailed descriptions of Instructional Procedures.

ACTION TAGS

read word

match vowel sound

take card (if needed)

lay down matching card

read word

Apply

Have students play Crazy Eights in small groups using a deck of game cards. You may need to remind students that they are matching the long vowel sound, not the letter combination. For example, the words *cheek* and *feast* match because they both have the long *e* sound.

Share

- Invite students to name more words with the long vowel letter combinations *ai*, *ay*, *ee*, *ea*, *oa*, *ow*, *ui*, and *ue*. You may wish to add additional words to the chart using blank pocket-chart cards.

- Review the principle and remind students to notice words with long vowel sounds when they read and write.

Assess

- Notice if students are able to read words with vowel digraphs. Take note of any vowel pattern that students have difficulty reading.

- Notice students' use of long vowel patterns in their writing.

- You may wish to use Letter-Sound Relationships Assessment E, I, or J.

Letter-Sound Relationships: Recognize and Use Letter Combinations That Represent Long Vowel Sounds

Connect Learning Across Contexts

Shared Reading During shared reading, you may wish to use the following title from *Fountas & Pinnell Classroom*™ to locate a few words that have vowel combinations.

 *From Beans to Chocolate* by June Schwartz

Guided Reading Select a few words from the text that have long vowel letter combinations. Write the words on a whiteboard. Ask students to read the words and identify the letters that stand for long vowel sounds.

Shared Writing As you construct a piece of writing, ask students to notice words with long vowel letter combinations.

Independent Writing During the editing process, encourage writers to reread their writing and check for the correct spellings of long vowel patterns. Prompt them to think of other words with the same pattern. *Do you know a word like that?*

Extend Learning

- Repeat the lesson with other long vowel combinations, such as *ie, igh, oe,* and *ew.*

- Have students use the game cards to play Concentration. Before the game, decide if matching words contain only the same vowel sound (e.g., *cheek, feast*) or the same vowel sound and the same letter combination (e.g., *cheek, needle*).

▶ Connect with Home

Send home a deck of game cards so that students can play Crazy Eights with family members.

Recognize and Use Letter Combinations That Represent the /ȯ/ Vowel Sound (as in *saw*)

Plan

▶ ### Consider Your Students

For this lesson to be most effective, students should have full control of long and short vowel sounds and considerable experience noticing the various letters and patterns that represent them in words. If students have little knowledge of variant vowels or little experience recognizing the various letter combinations that represent the vowel sound /ȯ/, you may wish to focus on a single letter-sound relationship at a time.

▶ ### Working with English Language Learners

Help English language learners notice the letter combinations by linking them to common words that they know. When appropriate, use pictures and actions to help students make connections to these concepts so that the words are meaningful. Accept approximate pronunciations if the vowel sound is difficult for students to say. Pronounce each sound in a word clearly, and give students many opportunities to repeat words that are challenging. Encourage them to watch how the shape of your mouth changes as you say the sounds in a word.

UNDERSTAND THE PRINCIPLE

In their reading, students will increasingly encounter words with variant vowel sounds that are neither "long" nor "short." One such sound, /ȯ/, is represented in commonly occurring words by a range of letter combinations: *al, au, augh, aw, o,* and *ough.* The ability to quickly recognize the letter combinations related to this vowel sound will make students' reading more efficient and effortless. Understanding this principle also helps students continue to systematize the complex relationships between English vowel sounds and letters.

YOU WILL NEED

Online Resources
- ▶ **LSR 5** Action Tags
- ▶ **LSR 5** Word Cards
- ▶ **LSR 5** List Sheets

Other Materials
- ▶ blank chart paper

EXPLAIN THE PRINCIPLE

Some letters together stand for the vowel sound heard in saw.

Comprehensive Phonics, Spelling, and Word Study Guide

Refer to: page **30**, row **29**

ACTIVITY: WORD LISTS

INSTRUCTIONAL PROCEDURE

NOTICE PARTS

See page 32 for detailed descriptions of Instructional Procedures.

EXPLAIN THE PRINCIPLE

Some letters together stand for the vowel sound heard in saw.

Comprehensive Phonics, Spelling, and Word Study Guide

Refer to:
page **30**, row **29**

t<u>a</u>lk	already
a<u>u</u>tumn	pause
t<u>au</u>ght	daughter
p<u>a</u>w	awful
s<u>o</u>ft	lost
b<u>ou</u>ght	thought

Teach

1. On chart paper, write the following words in a column: *talk, autumn, taught, paw, soft, bought.* Read the words with students and use the word in a sentence if the students may not know the meaning. *What do you notice about all of the words?* • *Each word has the same vowel sound, /ȯ/. The sound is neither "long" nor "short."*

2. *What letters stand for the vowel sound /ȯ/ in the word* talk? • Underline or highlight the letters *al.* Continue to ask students to identify the letter or letters that stand for the vowel sound, and underline or highlight the letters in each word.

3. Have students name additional words with the vowel sound /ȯ/. Write at least one more example of each letter combination.

4. Ask students to read the words again. Then reinforce the principle: *Some letters together stand for the vowel sound /ȯ/.*

5. Tell students that they will be sorting and writing words. Display a set of words cards and explain that students will sort words into six groups, one for each letter combination that stands for the vowel sound /ȯ/. Once the words are sorted, students read the words in each group to a partner and then write three examples from each group on a list sheet, for a total of eighteen words.

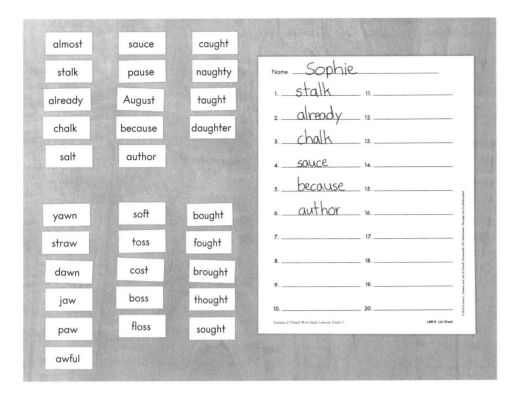

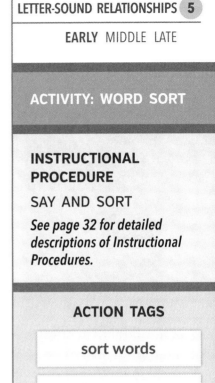

ACTIVITY: WORD SORT

INSTRUCTIONAL PROCEDURE

SAY AND SORT

See page 32 for detailed descriptions of Instructional Procedures.

ACTION TAGS

sort words
read words
write words

Apply

- Remind students to read the words that they have sorted to a partner. Encourage them to talk about other words they know that have each letter combination.

- You may wish to have students highlight the letter combination that stands for the vowel sound in each word on the list sheet.

Share

- Ask students to share some of the words that they wrote on their list sheets. You may wish to add a few new words to the class chart. Encourage students to share any discoveries they made about words with the vowel sound /ȯ/.

- Review the principle and remind students to notice words with the vowel sound /ȯ/ when they read and write.

Assess

- Dictate several words with the vowel sound /ȯ/. Observe students' spelling to determine their ability to apply their knowledge of letter-sound relationships.

- As you observe students' reading, notice how efficient they are in recognizing and solving words with the vowel sound /ȯ/. Take note of any letter combination with which students need more experience.

- You may wish to use Letter-Sound Relationships Assessment E, I, or J.

Letter-Sound Relationships: Recognize and Use Letter Combinations That Represent the /ȯ/ Vowel Sound (as in saw*)*

Connect Learning Across Contexts

Shared Reading During shared reading, you may wish to use the following title from *Fountas & Pinnell Classroom*™ to locate a few words that have the /ȯ/ vowel sound.

SR *Trapped in Tar* by Hannah Cales

Guided Reading After reading a text, have students locate and read words with the vowel sound /ȯ/. Make connections to the letter combinations represented on the class chart.

Shared Writing As you construct a piece of writing, involve students in thinking about the spelling of words with the vowel sound /ȯ/.

Independent Writing As you confer with writers, guide them to think about the spelling of words with the vowel sound /ȯ/. Prompt them to refer to the class chart and other resources to determine conventional spellings.

Extend Learning

- Encourage students to record in their word study notebooks other words with the vowel sound /ȯ/ that they encounter in their reading. Invite students to share their discoveries during group shares.

- Using the words on their list sheets, as well as other examples that they know, students can create and cut out game cards with words that have the vowel sound /ȯ/. A printable game card template is available in Online Resources. Partners and small groups may then use the game cards to play Concentration. Words containing the same letter combinations count as a match, e.g., *because* and *sauce*.

▶ Connect with Home

Send home sets of word cards for students to read and sort with family members.

Recognize and Use Letter Combinations That Represent Two Different Vowel Sounds

Plan

▶ Consider Your Students

Before you present this lesson, students will need to have good control of long and short vowel sounds and an awareness that letters and sounds can be related in varying ways. Depending on their experience, you may wish to present this lesson over several days (e.g., teaching only the two sounds for *oo* on the first day). Some students may also need several encounters with the letter combinations in a whole-group setting before they can successfully identify matches in the game. If students have a great deal of experience with these letter combinations and know many examples, you may wish to identify letter-sound relationships with which students need more experience and tailor the lesson accordingly.

▶ Working with English Language Learners

Be sure that English language learners have encountered and read (or written) common words with the letter combinations *oo*, *ie*, and *ea* many times prior to the lesson. Take time to demonstrate each vowel sound. You may wish to work with a small group to help students notice and contrast the different sounds. Observe them as they match and read words while sorting to be sure they are saying the correct vowel sounds.

UNDERSTAND THE PRINCIPLE

Some letter combinations represent more than one vowel sound. The vowel pair *oo* represents a longer sound, as in *moon,* and a shorter sound, as in *book.* The vowel pair *ie* represents the long *e* sound in words such as *chief, relief,* and *believe* and the long *i* sound in words such as *lie, spied,* and *science.* The vowel pair *ea* represents the long *e* sound in many words, such as *team, beach,* and *feast.* In a few words, the vowel pair *ea* represents the long *a* sound, as in *break.* This lesson will help students be more alert to patterns within words and search for the complex ways in which letters and sounds are related in English.

YOU WILL NEED

PWS Ready Resources
- ▶ LSR 6 Pocket-Chart Cards

Online Resources
- ▶ LSR 6 Action Tags
- ▶ LSR 6 Word Cards
- ▶ LSR 6 Two-Way Sorts

Other Materials
- ▶ pocket chart

Generative Lesson

A generative lesson has a simple structure that you can use to present similar content or concepts. Use this lesson structure to teach students to recognize and use letter combinations that represent two different vowel sounds.

EXPLAIN THE PRINCIPLE

Two letters together can stand for different vowel sounds in different words.

Comprehensive Phonics, Spelling, and Word Study Guide

Refer to: page **30**, row **30**

ACTIVITY: WORD SORT

INSTRUCTIONAL PROCEDURE

SAY AND SORT

See page 32 for detailed descriptions of Instructional Procedures.

EXPLAIN THE PRINCIPLE

Two letters together can stand for different vowel sounds in different words.

Comprehensive Phonics, Spelling, and Word Study Guide

Refer to: page **30**, row **30**

Teach

1. In the pocket chart, display the following words in a random order: *hoop, spoon, tool, loose, brook, wood, cook, hook.* Read the words with students and use the word in a sentence if the students may not know the meaning.

2. *What do you notice about all of the words?* • Students will notice that each word has the letters *oo.* If needed, prompt them to think about the sounds that the letters oo stand for. *Think about the vowel sounds. What do you notice?* • *The letters* oo *together stand for different sounds in different words.*

3. Move the word *hoop* to the top of the chart. *What vowel sound do the letters* oo *stand for in the word* hoop? • *In some words, such as* hoop, *the letters* oo *stand for the sound /ü/.* Then move the word *brook* to the top of the chart. *What vowel sound do the letters* oo *stand for in the word* brook? • *In some words, such as* brook, *the letters* oo *stand for the sound /u̇/.*

4. Have students sort the remaining words below the word *hoop* or the word *brook* according to vowel sound. After all of the words are sorted, have students read each column of words again.

5. Remove the words from the pocket chart, and repeat the process with words in which the letters *ie* together stand for the long *e* sound or the long *i* sound. Use the words *chief* and *lie* as column heads for the sort.

6. Remove the words from the pocket chart, and repeat the process a third time with words in which the letters *ea* together stand for the long *e* sound or the long *a* sound. Use the words *team* and *break* as column heads for the sort. You may wish to point out that there are very few words in which the letters *ea* stand for the long *a* sound.

7. Summarize the principle, building on students' previous observations. *Two letters together can stand for different vowel sounds in different words.* You may wish to display the pairs of key words in the pocket chart as a reference for students.

8. Tell students that they are going to practice sorting words using word cards and two-way sorts. They will sort the word cards while thinking about letter combinations *oo, ie,* and *ea,* and then write the words in the appropriate columns.

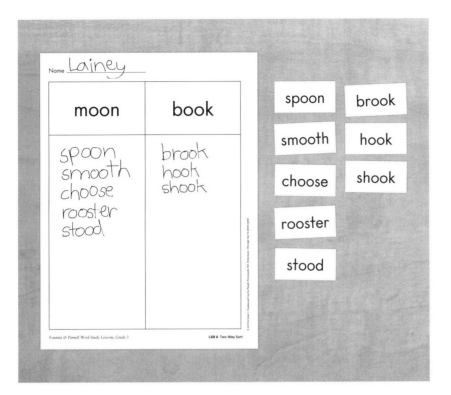

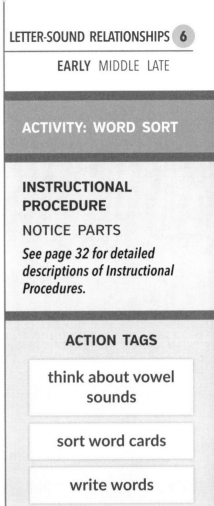

ACTIVITY: WORD SORT

INSTRUCTIONAL PROCEDURE

NOTICE PARTS

See page 32 for detailed descriptions of Instructional Procedures.

ACTION TAGS

think about vowel sounds

sort word cards

write words

Apply

- Have students sort words using the lesson's word cards and two-way sorts while thinking about letter combinations and vowel sounds. After sorting, students should write their findings on the sorts. You may need to remind students that they are matching the vowel sound and the letter combination. For example, the words *steak* and *great* match because they both have the letter combination *ea* and the long *a* sound.

- After working with the words from the word cards, invite students to think of some more words with a partner to add to their sorts.

Share

- Invite students to share a word they added to their sorts with the class. Ask them to specify which letter combination the word has.

- Review the principle and remind students to notice words with letter combinations that represent two different vowel sounds when they read and write.

Assess

- Observe students' use of *oo, ie,* and *ea* to represent vowel sounds in the words they write.

- As students read aloud, take note of any letter-sound relationships for *oo, ie,* or *ea* with which students need more experience.

- You may wish to use Letter-Sound Relationships Assessment E, I, or J.

Letter-Sound Relationships: Recognize and Use Letter Combinations That Represent Two Different Vowel Sounds

Connect Learning Across Contexts

Shared Reading During shared reading, you may wish to use the following title from *Fountas & Pinnell Classroom*™ to locate a few words that represent letter combinations *ei, ea,* or *ie.*

SR *A Meerkat Day* by Geerhardt Heever

Guided Reading During word work, have students identify words with the letter combinations *oo, ie,* or *ea.* Guide them to discuss the vowel sounds that are represented by the letters.

Shared Writing As you construct pieces of writing, point out the letter combinations *oo, ie,* and *ea* in words. Encourage students to make connections to the key words in the pocket chart.

Independent Writing As you confer with the students, help them notice words that are like the key words in the pocket chart. Encourage them to compare the letter combinations that stand for the vowel sounds.

Extend Learning

- Repeat the lesson with other letter combinations that represent two different vowel sounds, such as *ey* [*they, key*] and *ow* [*snow, cow*].
- Have students use the word cards to play Concentration. Remind students that words must have the same vowel sound and the same letter combination [e.g., *hoop, spoon*] to count as a match.

▶ Connect with Home

Send home sets of word cards, and encourage students to practice sorting the words with family members for additional practice. You may wish to add more words to make the task more challenging.

Recognize and Use Two Consonant Letters That Usually Represent One Sound at the Beginning of a Word

Plan

▶ Consider Your Students

This lesson draws students' attention to consonant digraphs at the beginning of words. Students may notice that the digraph *wh* is unique. *Wear* and *where* are close, but slightly different in pronunciation (depending on local dialects). *Wh* has another associated sound, as in *who*. Students may also observe that the digraph *th* can represent two sounds: the (voiced) sound in *these* and the (unvoiced) sound in *thought*. You can decide whether it is appropriate to use the technical term *digraph* with your students.

▶ Working with English Language Learners

Be sure that students are familiar with the meanings of the words used during the lesson and in the application activity. Keep in mind that some sounds may be difficult for English language learners to pronounce because they vary so much from the sounds in their own languages. Accept approximations and provide many opportunities for them to say the words and to make their own connections to letters based on what they hear.

UNDERSTAND THE PRINCIPLE

Consonants frequently occur together in words. Some combinations, known as *consonant digraphs,* stand for a single sound that is different from either sound represented by the individual letters. Quick, automatic recognition of these letter patterns and the associated sound at the end of words makes decoding more efficient.

EXPLAIN THE PRINCIPLE

Some clusters of consonant letters stand for one sound that is usually different from either of the individual consonant sounds. They are consonant digraphs.

You can hear the sound of a consonant digraph at the beginning of a word.

Comprehensive Phonics, Spelling, and Word Study Guide

Refer to: page **27**, row **8**

*Letter-Sound Relationships: Recognize and Use Two Consonant Letters
That Usually Represent One Sound at the Beginning of a Word*

99

EARLY MIDDLE LATE

ACTIVITY: WORD SORT

INSTRUCTIONAL PROCEDURE

SAY AND SORT

See page 32 for detailed descriptions of Instructional Procedures.

EXPLAIN THE PRINCIPLE

Some clusters of consonant letters stand for one sound that is usually different from either of the individual consonant sounds. They are consonant digraphs.

You can hear the sound of a consonant digraph at the end of a word.

Comprehensive Phonics, Spelling, and Word Study Guide

Refer to:
page **27**, row **9**

ch	th	wh	sh
chimney	thin	white	shampoo
choose	there	wheel	ship
choice	thoughtful	what	shore
chapter	thankful	whisper	shimmer

Teach

1. On chart paper, write the words *chimney, thin, white,* and *shampoo,* leaving space above each word for a heading. Read the words with students and use the word in a sentence if the students may not know the meaning.

2. *What do you notice about all of the words?* ● Students may initially notice that each word has the letter *h* or that many of them have the letter *i.* Guide them to think more about the beginning letters and sounds. *Who can say more about the beginning of the words?* ● Build on students' observations to explain the principle. *Each word begins with two consonants. The two consonants together stand for one sound. The sound is different from either of the individual consonant sounds.*

3. Write the consonant digraphs *ch-, th-, wh-,* and *sh-* at the top of the columns. Reinforce the letter-sound relationships. *The letters* ch *stand for the sound /ch/ as in* chimney. *The letters* th *can stand for the sound /th/ as in* thin *or /th/ as in* there. *The letters* wh *stand for the sound /w/ as in* white *or the /h/ sound as in* who. *The letters* sh *stand for the /sh/ sound in* shampoo.

4. Tell students you are going to say a word beginning in one of the sounds. Ask them to tell you the column in which the word belongs. *The word is* choose. *Where should I write this word?* ● Continue to say additional words beginning in *ch, th, wh,* and *sh,* and have students sort them based on the beginning consonant sound.

5. Have students read each column of words again.

6. Explain to students that they will now sort words on their own. Give each student a four-way sort and the lesson's word cards. Students should sort the word cards before writing their answers in the sort. After sorting and writing the words, instruct students to try and think of a few more words that fit into the sort.

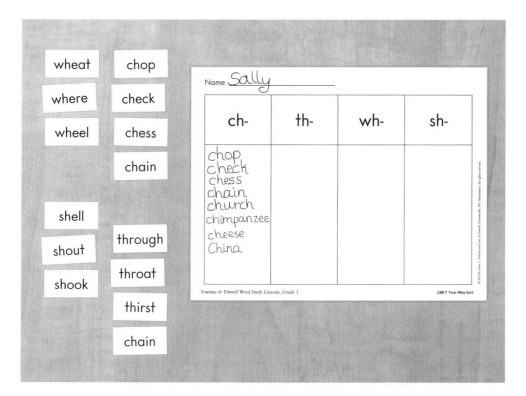

ACTIVITY: FOUR-WAY SORT

INSTRUCTIONAL PROCEDURE

SAY AND SORT

See page 32 for detailed descriptions of Instructional Procedures.

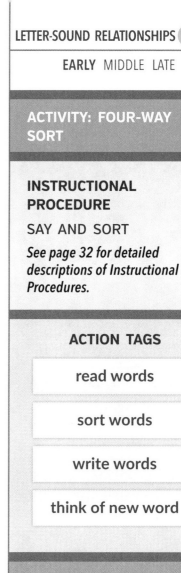

ACTION TAGS

read words

sort words

write words

think of new word

Apply

Have students sort the word cards independently. After sorting, students should use the four-way sorts to write their findings. You may need to remind students that they are matching the beginning consonant digraph only. Once students have completed the task, instruct them to work independently or with a partner to think of a few more words that have one or more of the beginning consonant digraphs and write the word(s) on the four-way sort.

Share

- Invite students to share the words they added to their sorts. You may wish to add any new words to the beginning consonant digraphs class chart.

- Review the principle and remind students to notice words with consonant digraphs at the beginning when they read and write.

Assess

- Dictate four to six words with beginning consonant digraphs for students to write and read. Notice if students are correctly pronouncing and representing the digraphs at the beginnings of words.

- You may wish to use Letter-Sound Relationships Assessment A, C, F, G, or H.

Letter-Sound Relationships: Recognize and Use Two Consonant Letters That Usually Represent One Sound at the Beginning of a Word

Shared Reading During shared reading, you may wish to use the following title from *Fountas & Pinnell Classroom*™ to locate a few words with consonant digraphs.

SR *From Buds to Bananas* by Betty Riggs

Guided Reading As students are reading new words with consonant digraphs, prompt them to read the first or last part of the word and notice the digraph.

Shared Writing Model checking the spelling of a word with a beginning consonant digraph.

Independent Writing During conferences, point out words with beginning consonant digraphs that students have spelled correctly. Guide students to review and respell words that begin with consonant digraphs they know but that are not spelled conventionally.

Extend Learning

Repeat the apply activity with a new set of words beginning in *ch, sh, th,* and *wh*. If students need additional experience with a particular consonant digraph, include more words with that ending.

▶ Connect with Home

Send home the lesson's word cards for students to play Go Fish with a family member to practice matching beginning consonant digraphs.

Plan

▶ Consider Your Students

This lesson draws students' attention to consonant digraphs at the ends of words. If students have very little familiarity with consonant digraphs, you may want to focus on only a few digraphs and gradually teach the others in later lessons. On the other hand, if students have considerable experience with digraphs, one lesson that reinforces all of the letter-sound relationships may be sufficient. Students may notice that the digraph *th* can represent two sounds: the (voiced) sound in *with* and the (unvoiced) sound in *path.* You can decide whether it is appropriate to use the technical term *digraph* with your students.

▶ Working with English Language Learners

Be sure that students are familiar with the meanings of the words used during the lesson and in the application activity. Keep in mind that some sounds may be difficult for English language learners to pronounce because they vary so much from the sounds in their own languages. Accept approximations and provide many opportunities for them to say the words and to make their own connections to letters based on what they hear. Playing Lotto should be a familiar routine for them. If not, play the game with students the first time to be sure they know the routine and the words used.

UNDERSTAND THE PRINCIPLE

Consonants frequently occur together in words. Some combinations, known as *consonant digraphs,* stand for a single sound that is different from either sound represented by the individual letters. Quick, automatic recognition of these letter patterns and the associated sound at the end of words makes decoding more efficient.

YOU WILL NEED

Online Resources
- ▶ **LSR 8** Action Tags
- ▶ **LSR 8** Lotto Game Boards
- ▶ **LSR 8** Word Cards
- ▶ **LSR 8** Directions for Lotto

Other Materials
- ▶ blank chart paper
- ▶ game markers

EXPLAIN THE PRINCIPLE

Some clusters of consonant letters stand for one sound that is usually different from either of the individual consonant sounds. They are consonant digraphs.

You can hear the sound of a consonant digraph at the end of a word.

Comprehensive Phonics, Spelling, and Word Study Guide

Refer to: page **27**, row **9**

Letter-Sound Relationships: Recognize and Use Two Consonant Letters That Usually Represent One Sound at the End of a Word

103

EARLY MIDDLE LATE

ACTIVITY: WORD LIST

INSTRUCTIONAL PROCEDURE

NOTICE PARTS

See page 32 for detailed descriptions of Instructional Procedures.

EXPLAIN THE PRINCIPLE

Some clusters of consonant letters stand for one sound that is usually different from either of the individual consonant sounds. They are consonant digraphs.

You can hear the sound of a consonant digraph at the end of a word.

Comprehensive Phonics, Spelling, and Word Study Guide

Refer to: page **27**, row **9**

---

brush	cloth	much
mash	mouth	sandwich
trash	north	beach

song	kick	tough
king	stack	laugh
young	knock	rough

Teach

1. Write *brush, cloth, much, song, kick,* and *tough* on chart paper, leaving room for a few words under each. Read the words with students and use the word in a sentence if the students may not know the meaning.

2. *What do you notice about all of the words?* • Students may initially notice that each word ends with the letter *h.* Guide them to think more about the ending letters and sounds. *Who can say more about the endings of the words?* • Build on students' observations to explain the principle. *Each word ends with two consonants. The two consonants together stand for one sound. The sound is different from either of the individual consonant sounds.*

3. Invite students to provide a second example for each pattern. Underline the digraph as you write them on the chart. Remind students that they will have to attend to both the way words sound and the way they look.

4. Have students read each column of words again.

5. Tell students that they will play Lotto with words having consonant digraph ending patterns. Demonstrate the game with one or two students if the routine is new. Each player has a Lotto game board. Players take turns drawing word cards, reading the words, and searching for a word on their card that has the same ending consonant digraph. If they find a match, they cover the space with a game marker. The first player to cover the entire card wins the game.

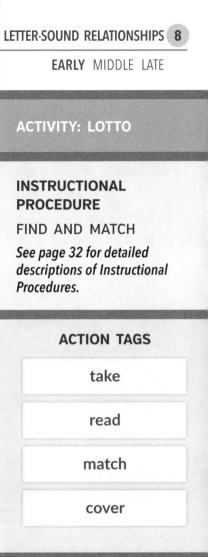

ACTIVITY: LOTTO

INSTRUCTIONAL PROCEDURE

FIND AND MATCH

See page 32 for detailed descriptions of Instructional Procedures.

ACTION TAGS

take

read

match

cover

Apply

- Have students play Lotto in groups of two to four.
- After playing, they write three words on an index card and highlight the ending digraph.
- Have students bring their cards to share and contribute to the group's learning.

Share

- Ask students to suggest one more word for each pattern on the chart and review the lesson principle.
- Listen for comments like: "A digraph can be at the end of a word" or "The two letters in a digraph stand for only one sound."
- Review the principle and remind students to notice words with two consonant letters that usually represent one sound at the end of a word when they read and write.

Assess

- Dictate four to six words with ending consonant digraphs for students to write and read. Notice if students are correctly pronouncing and representing the digraphs at the ends of words.
- Observe students' ability to write words with ending consonant clusters.
- Have students read a typed list of words and then highlight consonant clusters.
- You may wish to use Letter-Sound Relationships Assessment B, C, F, G, or H.

Letter-Sound Relationships: Recognize and Use Two Consonant Letters
That Usually Represent One Sound at the End of a Word

Connect Learning Across Contexts

Shared Reading During shared reading, you may wish to use the following title from *Fountas & Pinnell Classroom*™ to locate a few words with consonant digraphs.

SR *From Buds to Bananas* by Betty Riggs

Guided Reading When students come to an unknown word with a consonant digraph, prompt them by asking, "Do you know another word that ends like that?"

Shared Writing Model checking the spelling of a word with an ending consonant digraph.

Independent Writing During conferences, point out words with ending consonant digraphs that students have spelled correctly. Guide students to review and respell words that end with consonant digraphs they know but that are not spelled conventionally.

Extend Learning

Create Lotto cards that include beginning and ending consonant clusters (including digraphs) for a comprehensive review.

▶ Connect with Home

Have students take home the Lotto game boards and word cards to play the game with a family member. As an alternative, students can make their own game boards to share with their families.

Recognize and Use Middle Consonant Sounds Sometimes Represented by Double Consonant Letters

Plan

▶ Consider Your Students

In this lesson, students work with two-syllable words that have a double consonant pattern in the middle. They should know consonants and short vowel sounds well and have worked with two-syllable words. If students have plenty of experience with this pattern, you may wish to include words in which the double consonant is followed by an inflected ending. Examples include words such as *setting* and *zipped.*

▶ Working with English Language Learners

Observe students carefully to determine their knowledge of consonants and their ability to identify them at the beginning and end of words. While it may be easy for students to spot the double consonants in the middle of words, they should also understand the meaning of these words. It will help them to notice some of the word endings that are common to words that have double consonants, such as *–er.*

YOU WILL NEED

Online Resources
- ▶ **LSR 9** Action Tags
- ▶ **LSR 9** Word Grid Game Boards
- ▶ **LSR 9** Game Cards

Other Materials
- ▶ blank chart paper

Generative Lesson ✓
A generative lesson has a simple structure that you can use to present similar content or concepts. Use this lesson structure to teach a variety of words with double consonant letters in the middle.

UNDERSTAND THE PRINCIPLE

Noticing letter patterns in words makes reading more efficient. Some two-syllable words contain double consonants in the middle, such as the consonants *pp* in the word *slipper.* The first syllable is usually stressed and has a short vowel sound. Students must learn that the double consonants stand for a single sound (although the consonant sound may be pronounced twice when breaking the word into two syllables).

EXPLAIN THE PRINCIPLE

Sometimes double consonant letters stand for one consonant sound in the middle of a word.

Comprehensive Phonics, Spelling, and Word Study Guide

Refer to: page **28**, row **11**

*Letter-Sound Relationships: Recognize and Use Middle Consonant
Sounds Sometimes Represented by Double Consonant Letters*

107

ACTIVITY: WORD LIST

INSTRUCTIONAL PROCEDURE

NOTICE PARTS

See page 32 for detailed descriptions of Instructional Procedures.

EXPLAIN THE PRINCIPLE

Sometimes double consonant letters stand for one consonant sound in the middle of a word.

Comprehensive Phonics, Spelling, and Word Study Guide

Refer to: page **28**, row **11**

---

slipper
mitten
lesson
ladder
follow

Teach

1. Across the top of a piece of chart paper, write four or five words with double consonants in the middle, such as *slipper, mitten, lesson, ladder,* and *follow.* Read the words with students and use the word in a sentence if the students may not know the meaning.

2. *What do you notice about all of these words?* • Students will likely notice that the words have double consonants in the middle. They may also observe that each word has two syllables and that the first vowel sound in each word is stressed.

3. As needed, guide students to think about the principle by drawing their attention to the sounds associated with the double consonants. *What do you notice about the consonant sounds in the middle of the words?* • *The two consonant letters stand for just one consonant sound. For example, the double* p *in the middle of the word* slipper *stands for the sound /p/.*

4. Invite students to think of other words with double consonants in the middle and add the words to the chart.

5. Tell students that today they are going to play Word Grid. The first player takes a card, reads the letters aloud, looks for a word on his grid that contains the same double consonant, then reads the word on his grid and crosses it out. He turns the card over and the next person takes a turn. The goal is to cross out all of the words on the grid.

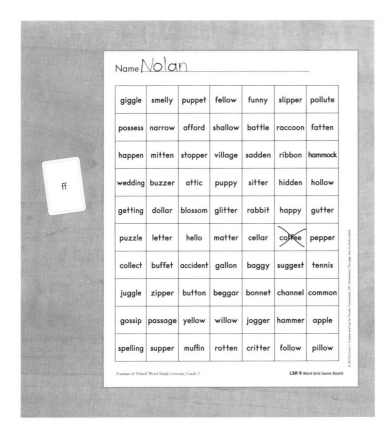

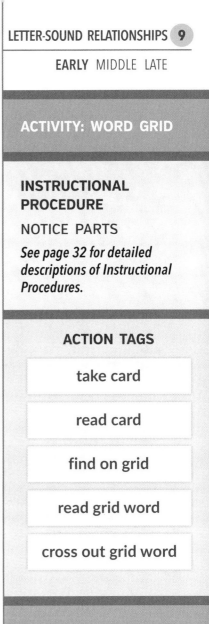

INSTRUCTIONAL PROCEDURE

NOTICE PARTS

See page 32 for detailed descriptions of Instructional Procedures.

ACTION TAGS

take card

read card

find on grid

read grid word

cross out grid word

Apply

Have students play Word Grid in pairs or groups of three using a game board and game cards.

Share

- Invite students to tell a few more words with the double consonant pattern to add to the class chart.
- Review the principle and remind students to notice words with double consonants when they read and write.

Assess

- Dictate four or five words, such as *little, saddle, hollow, sniffing,* and *wobble,* with double consonants in the middle. Notice how students represent the medial consonant sound in writing.
- Observe students solving words with medial double consonants while they are reading aloud. Notice if they smoothly represent the double consonants as a single sound.
- You may wish to use Letter-Sound Relationships Assessment D or G.

Letter-Sound Relationships: Recognize and Use Middle Consonant Sounds Sometimes Represented by Double Consonant Letters

Connect Learning Across Contexts

Shared Reading During shared reading, you may wish to use the following title from *Fountas & Pinnell Classroom*™ to locate a few words with double consonant letters.

> **SR** *Saving Cranes* by Brenda Iasevoli

Guided Reading When students come to an unknown word with double consonants, prompt them by asking, "Do you know another word with two consonants in the middle like this one?"

Interactive or Shared Writing As you and the students construct words with double consonants in the middle, point out the pattern and remind students of the principle.

Independent Writing As you confer with writers, point out words that have double consonants in the middle.

Extend Learning

- Distribute blank Word Grid game boards (found in Online Resources), and have students work together to create boards with new sets of words with double consonants. Make the additional boards available for students to choose when playing the game.

- Keep the lesson chart posted in your classroom, and have students add words with double consonants that they find in books they read.

▶ Connect with Home

Send Word Grid game boards home so that students can play the game with family members.

Plan

▶ Consider Your Students

This lesson extends students' knowledge of the sounds represented by consonants. Use this lesson after your students have developed a strong understanding of regular consonant letter-sound relationships and also understand that sometimes two or more sounds are connected to a single letter or letter cluster. Students should have already worked with consonant letters that represent two or more different sounds at the beginnings of words. This lesson focuses on the consonants *c* and *g* and the digraphs *ch* and *th*.

▶ Working with English Language Learners

Some students may just be beginning to make simple connections between letters and sounds, and they may need help realizing that these relationships are complex. Their own languages may not have as much variation in letter-sound relationships as English does. This lesson will help these students look at the words in a more systematic and formal way so that they can develop categories for the way sounds and letters work in words.

UNDERSTAND THE PRINCIPLE

To become flexible readers and writers, students need to learn that letters and sounds do not necessarily have a one-to-one relationship. Some sounds are represented by several different letters, and some letters can stand for more than one sound. Knowing this principle will help students develop a broader understanding of letter-sound relationships and how they can be used to solve words. For example, students will be less likely to substitute *s* for *c* or *j* for *g* when writing.

EXPLAIN THE PRINCIPLE

Some consonants or consonant clusters stand for two or more sounds at the end of a word.

Comprehensive Phonics, Spelling, and Word Study Guide

Refer to: page **28**, row **13**

Letter-Sound Relationships: Recognize and Use Consonant Letters That Represent Two or More Different Sounds at the End of a Word

111

ACTIVITY: WORD LISTS

INSTRUCTIONAL PROCEDURE

NOTICE PARTS

See page 32 for detailed descriptions of Instructional Procedures.

EXPLAIN THE PRINCIPLE

Some consonants or consonant clusters stand for two or more sounds at the end of a word.

Comprehensive Phonics, Spelling, and Word Study Guide

Refer to:
page **28**, row **13**

picnic	voice
clinic	peace
bag	wage
sag	stage
which	stomach
catch	ache
booth	smooth
moth	bathe

Teach

1. Write the following words on a whiteboard: *picnic, voice, clinic, and peace.* Read the words with students and use the word in a sentence if the students may not know the meaning. *What do you notice about all of these words? • They all have a* c *at the end, but the letter stands for two different sounds. In the word* picnic, *the letter* c *stands for the sound /k/. In the word* voice, *the letter* c *stands for the sound /s/.*

2. Say the words *clinic* and *peace. Which word ends like* picnic? • *Which word ends like* voice? *Erase the two words from the board and write* clinic *beneath* picnic *and* peace *beneath* voice.

3. Repeat the process using the words *bag* and *wage* to discuss the sounds of *g;* the words *which* and *stomach* to discuss the sounds of *ch;* and the words *booth* and *smooth* to discuss the sounds of /th/.

4. Encourage students to tell more words that end in each consonant or consonant digraph.

5. Tell students that they are going to sort, make, and write words that have different sounds at the ends of words. The students should sort the word cards by the sound they hear and the letters they see at the end of a word, make the word with magnetic letters, and then write the word on a list sheet.

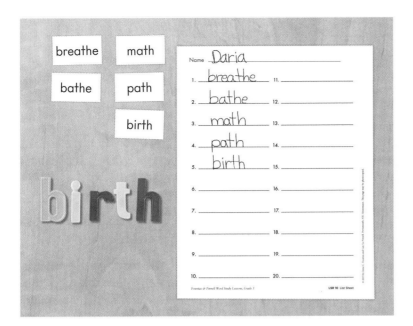

ACTIVITY: MAGNETIC LETTERS

INSTRUCTIONAL PROCEDURE

NOTICE PARTS

See page 32 for detailed descriptions of Instructional Procedures.

ACTION TAGS

sort words
make word
write word

Apply

- Using word cards, magnetic letters, and a list sheet, students will sort, make, and write the words. You may need to remind students that they are sorting the words by the final sound and letters only; the words do not need to rhyme to be sorted together. For example, the words *bath* and *north* match because they both end in the voiceless sound of *th*.

- If students need more of a challenge, have them write a few new words that they come up with on an index card.

Share

- Invite students to talk about any patterns they noticed as they completed the word sorts. Listen for comments such as these:

    "When the letter *c* is followed by *e*, the *c* sounds like *s*."

    "When the letter *g* is followed by *e*, the *g* sounds like *j*."

    "There are a lot more words that have the *ch* sound like at the end of *lunch*."

    The observations students make may not hold in every case. The important thing is for them to observe words closely and search for patterns.

- Have each student share the words they wrote on their index cards and describe what sound and letters the word has at the end.

- Review the principle and remind students to notice words with consonant letters that represent two or more different sounds at the end when they read and write.

Assess

- Notice whether students are spelling words with *c*, *g*, *ch*, and *th* conventionally in their writing.

- As students read aloud, take note of any letter-sound relationships for *c*, *g*, *th*, and *ch* with which students need more experience.

Letter-Sound Relationships: Recognize and Use Consonant Letters That Represent Two or More Different Sounds at the End of a Word

Connect Learning Across Contexts

Shared Reading During shared reading, you may wish to use the following title from *Fountas & Pinnell Classroom™* to locate a few words (when rereading) with consonant letters that represent two or more different sounds at the end of a word.

SR *Above Earth: A Day on the Space Station* by Jane Simon

Guided Reading When students come to an unknown word with consonant letters that represent two or more different sounds at the end of a word, prompt them by asking, "Do you know another word that ends like that?"

Shared Writing Model and check the spelling of a word with consonant letters that represent two or more different sounds at the end of a word.

Independent Writing As you confer with writers, remind them that some consonants, such as *c, g, th* and *ch*, stand for more than one sound at the ends of words. As they write, encourage students to say words slowly, think about the final sound or sounds, and recall spelling patterns that they have learned or observed.

Extend Learning

- Have students sort the game cards by ending sound.
- Challenge students to come up with other words that end in these consonants, and add them to the word wall. Read the words as a class.

▶ Connect with Home

Send home a deck of game cards so that students can play Go Fish with family members.

Recognize and Use Consonant Letters That Represent No Sound

Plan

▶ Consider Your Students

Students have already encountered silent letters as parts of word patterns (e.g., *walk*) and probably automatically read many words with silent letters. However, they may not have formally made the connection that sometimes letters are silent in a word. Take an informal inventory of students' knowledge of silent letters by noticing how often they represent them in their writing. Once students are aware of silent letters, this lesson will expand their knowledge.

▶ Working with English Language Learners

Letters that are not connected with sounds may be confusing to English language learners, especially if they have been taught to expect a direct sound-to-letter relationship. Use this lesson to help them realize that there can be silent letters in words. Help them attend to the larger patterns in words and to see silent letters as part of word parts connected to sounds.

YOU WILL NEED

Online Resources
- ▶ **LSR 11** Action Tags
- ▶ **LSR 11** Follow the Path Game Board
- ▶ **LSR 11** Directions for Follow the Path

Other Materials
- ▶ blank chart paper
- ▶ game markers
- ▶ dice

UNDERSTAND THE PRINCIPLE

Most consonants in the alphabet are occasionally silent. In some words, consonants are silent because the pronunciation has changed over time and the letters are no longer reflected in speech. Other words with silent letters have come into English from other languages. As students become familiar with common silent-letter patterns, they will become more efficient at decoding and spell with greater accuracy.

EXPLAIN THE PRINCIPLE

Some words have consonant letters that are silent.

Comprehensive Phonics, Spelling, and Word Study Guide

Refer to: page **28**, row **17**

ACTIVITY: WORD LISTS

INSTRUCTIONAL PROCEDURE

NOTICE PARTS

See page 32 for detailed descriptions of Instructional Procedures.

EXPLAIN THE PRINCIPLE

Some words have consonant letters that are silent.

Comprehensive Phonics, Spelling, and Word Study Guide

Refer to:
page **28**, row **17**

Words with Silent Consonants

silent b	silent k
lamb	knot
crumb	know
thumb	knife
	knee

silent l	silent t
walk	whistle
calf	

Teach

1. On chart paper, write the words *lamb, crumb,* and *thumb* in a column. Read the words with students and use the word in a sentence if the students may not know the meaning. *What do you notice about all of these words?* • *They each have a* b *at the end, and you do not hear the* b *sound when you say the word.*

2. Write *silent b* at the top of the column.

3. Write the words *knot, know, knife,* and *knee* in a column. Read the words with students. *What do you notice about these words?* • *They all start with* k, *but the* k *is silent.* Write *silent k* at the top of the column.

4. Based on the examples above, guide students to understand the principle: *What can you tell about some letters in words?* • *Some words have a consonant letter or letters that we do not say. These letters are silent.*

5. Repeat the process with words with silent *l* and silent *t*. Write the silent consonant at the top of each column and title the chart Words with Silent Consonants.

6. Have students read each word on the chart with you. To reinforce the principle, occasionally ask students to name the letter they do not hear in each word.

7. Preview the application activity by telling students that they are going to play Follow the Path. They will each have a marker and will share a board with a partner. Taking turns, they will throw a die, move the correct number of spaces, read the word on the space, and identify the silent letter in the word.

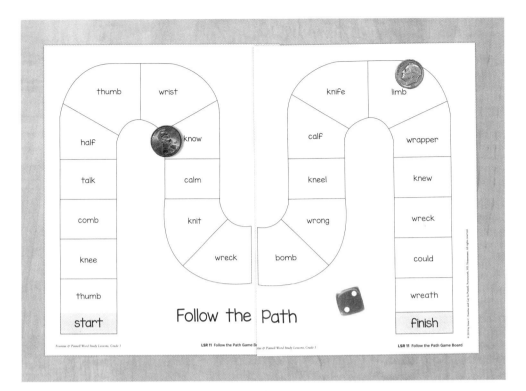

ACTIVITY: FOLLOW THE PATH

INSTRUCTIONAL PROCEDURE

SEE AND SAY

See page 32 for detailed descriptions of Instructional Procedures.

ACTION TAGS

roll die
move
read
tell

Apply

Distribute markers and Follow the Path game boards to partners. Each space has a word containing a silent letter. Students take turns throwing the die, moving the marker, reading the word, and telling the silent letter.

Share

- Ask students to read a few examples of words on the game board and tell the silent letter.
- Review the principle and remind students to notice words with silent consonants when they read and write.

Assess

- Point to words on the class chart, and have students read them. Check their pronunciation.
- Dictate three to five words with silent letters. Notice whether students represent the silent letter in their writing.

Letter-Sound Relationships: Recognize and Use Consonant Letters That Represent No Sound

Connect Learning Across Contexts

Shared Reading During shared reading, you may wish to use the following title from *Fountas & Pinnell Classroom*™ to locate a few words with silent consonants after reading.

> SR *Saving Cranes* by Brenda Iasevoli

Guided Reading When students come to an unknown word with a silent consonant, prompt them by asking, "Do you know another word that looks like that?"

Shared Writing Model and check the spelling of a word with a silent consonant.

Independent Writing Help students think about word patterns with silent letters when they write new words.

Extend Learning

Repeat the lesson with other patterns that include silent letters: *ghost, ghoul, gnat, bought, would, should, scent, scene, scissors, rhyme, rhino, khaki, calf, talk, calm, faster, listen, whistle, write, wrap, wrist.*

▶ ## Connect with Home

Give students a copy of the Follow the Path game board so that they can play the game at home with a family member.

Recognize and Use Consonant Letters That Represent No Sound

Plan

▶ Consider Your Students

Students need strong control of letter-sound relationships prior to this lesson. Many different letters can be silent in words, so attention to the visual pattern is critical. Some silent letters are more common than others. While Lesson LSR 11 helps students begin to notice silent letters, this lesson will help them create categories to organize their knowledge. They will also work with more challenging letter patterns.

▶ Working with English Language Learners

Silent letters in words can be especially challenging to students who are learning to speak, read, and write English. Once students grasp the idea, they are more likely to notice words with silent consonants when they read. You can build their knowledge of words in this category by keeping a group chart or individual lists that they can refer to as part of the word work component of guided reading. For accurate word solving, students should think about how a word *looks* as much as they do about the sounds of its letters. Learning about silent letters is a good way to help students make this shift.

YOU WILL NEED

PWS Ready Resources
▶ Lowercase Letter Cards

Online Resources
▶ **LSR 12** Action Tags
▶ **LSR 12** Make-Say-Check-Mix Sheets

Other Materials
▶ blank chart paper
▶ magnetic letters

UNDERSTAND THE PRINCIPLE

Most consonants in our alphabet are occasionally silent. In some words, consonants are silent because the pronunciation has changed over time and the letters are no longer reflected in speech. Other words with silent letters have come into English from other languages. As students become familiar with common silent letter patterns, they will become more efficient at decoding and spell with greater accuracy.

EXPLAIN THE PRINCIPLE

Some words have consonant letters that are silent.

Comprehensive Phonics, Spelling, and Word Study Guide

Refer to: page **28**, row **17**

ACTIVITY: WORD LISTS

INSTRUCTIONAL PROCEDURE

NOTICE PARTS

See page 32 for detailed descriptions of Instructional Procedures.

EXPLAIN THE PRINCIPLE

Some words have consonant letters that are silent.

Comprehensive Phonics, Spelling, and Word Study Guide

Refer to: page **28**, row **17**

<u>g</u>   <u>t</u>
gnat   castle
gnaw   whistle
                             listen

knife
write
rhyme
sign

Teach

1. On chart paper, write the words *gnat* and *gnaw* in a column. Read the words with students and use the word in a sentence if the students may not know the meaning. *What do you notice about all of these words?* • *They each have a* g *at the beginning, and you do not hear the* g *sound when you say the word.*

2. Write *g* at the top of the column.

3. Write the words *castle, whistle,* and *listen* in a column. Read the words with students. *What do you notice about these words?* • *They all have a* t, *but the* t *is silent.* Write *t* at the top of the column.

4. Guide students to understand the principle: *Some words have a consonant letter or letters that you do not hear. The letters are silent. What do you notice about the position of silent letters in a word?* • *Silent letters can be at the beginning, middle, or end of a word.*

5. Invite students to name other words with silent letters. They may add words to the columns you created today, or they may suggest words with silent letter patterns they learned in LSR 11.

6. Have students read each word on the chart with you. To reinforce the principle, occasionally ask students to name the letter they do not hear in each word.

7. Tell students that they will use a make-say-check-mix sheet to make and read words that have silent letters. Using letter cards or magnetic letters, demonstrate making a word on a sheet, saying the word, checking the word, and placing a check mark in the first box. Explain that students will mix up the letters and repeat the process two more times, checking the second and third boxes. Then they write the word.

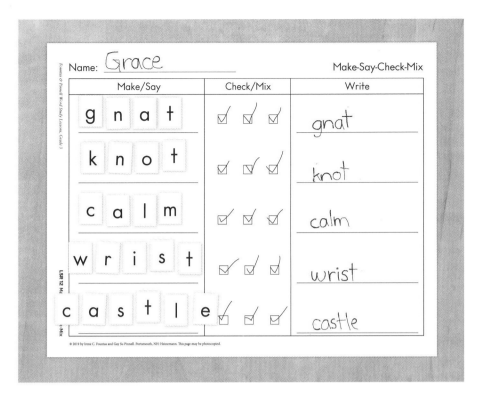

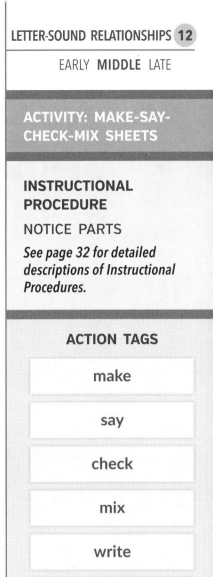

ACTIVITY: MAKE-SAY-CHECK-MIX SHEETS

INSTRUCTIONAL PROCEDURE

NOTICE PARTS

See page 32 for detailed descriptions of Instructional Procedures.

ACTION TAGS

make
say
check
mix
write
read

Apply

- Distribute make-say-check-mix sheets and letter cards or magnetic letters.
- Remind students that they can use the class chart as a resource for checking their words. Encourage them to include other silent words that they know.
- In preparation for the group share, ask students to read their words to a partner.

Share

- In groups of four, have students take turns reading all the words on their make-say-check-mix sheets. Add new words to the class chart as you reinforce the principle.
- Review the principle and remind students to notice words with consonant letters that are silent when they read and write.

Assess

- Check to see if individual students can read words with silent letters on the class chart.
- Dictate three to five words with silent letters. Notice how students represent the letters in writing.

Letter-Sound Relationships: Recognize and Use Consonant Letters That Represent No Sound

Connect Learning Across Contexts

Shared Reading During shared reading, you may wish to use the following title from *Fountas & Pinnell Classroom*™ to locate a few words with silent consonants after reading.

    ▪ *Saving Cranes* by Brenda Iasevoli

Guided Reading When students come to an unknown word with a consonant letter that represents no sound, prompt them by asking, "Do you know another word that looks like that?"

Shared Writing Model and check the spelling of a word with a consonant letter that represents no sound.

Independent Writing Help students think about word patterns with silent letters when they write new words.

Extend Learning

Use a different variety of words with silent letters for playing Word Grid.

▶ ## Connect with Home

Invite students to have family members help them find five words with silent letters on signs, in the newspaper, or in magazines. Students share their lists of words with the class.

Understand That Some Consonant Sounds Can Be Represented by Several Different Letters or Letter Clusters

Plan

▶ Consider Your Students

Students should have strong control of basic letter sound relationships prior to this lesson. In this lesson, students will review familiar letters associated with the /k/ sound–*c, k,* and *ck.* They will also be exposed to some less common spelling patterns for this sound, including *ch* and *que.* If students easily gain control of the principle, you may wish to incorporate additional examples for the /f/ sound, including *f, ff, gh,* and *ph.*

▶ Working with English Language Learners

If possible, collect a few words in students' first languages that have the sound of *k* (for example, *Enrique, quiero,* or *que* in Spanish). Have students notice the different letters that are used to represent the /k/ sound. For examples, select words that are in students' listening and speaking vocabularies. Building words with magnetic letters helps them make connections between sounds and letter patterns.

YOU WILL NEED

Online Resources
- ▶ **LSR 13** Action Tags
- ▶ **LSR 13** Word Cards
- ▶ **LSR 13** List Sheets

Other Materials
- ▶ blank chart paper

UNDERSTAND THE PRINCIPLE

In their reading and writing, students will notice that some consonant sounds can be represented by several different letters or letter clusters. For example, the sound of /k/ can be represented by *c, k, ck, ch,* or *que.* Learning to recognize and use different letter patterns for the same sound will help make students' reading more efficient and their spelling more effective.

EXPLAIN THE PRINCIPLE

Some consonant sounds are represented by several letters or letter clusters.

Comprehensive Phonics, Spelling, and Word Study Guide

Refer to: page **28**, row **18**

Letter-Sound Relationships: Understand That Some Consonant Sounds Can Be Represented by Several Different Letters or Letter Clusters

123

ACTIVITY: WORD LISTS

INSTRUCTIONAL PROCEDURE

NOTICE PARTS

See page 32 for detailed descriptions of Instructional Procedures.

EXPLAIN THE PRINCIPLE

Some consonant sounds are represented by several letters or letter clusters.

Comprehensive Phonics, Spelling, and Word Study Guide

Refer to: page **28**, row **18**

attic   unique   sick

picnic   antique   pack

stomach   bank

chorus   pink

Teach

1. On chart paper, write the words *attic, unique, sick, stomach,* and *bank*. Read the words with students and use the word in a sentence if the students may not know the meaning. *What do you notice in all of these words?* • *They all have the /k/ sound.* • *What do you notice about the letters that stand for the /k/ sound in each word?* • *They are all different. Sometimes two letters stand for the /k/ sound.*

2. Invite volunteers to come to the board and underline the letter or letters that stand for /k/ in each word.

3. Have students suggest additional words for each spelling. Students may bring up words like *rocket* that have the pattern in the middle of the word. If so, write them and highlight the pattern. They may also mention words like *park,* in which *r* and *k* are blended, or *act* in which *c* and *t* are blended. Make sure they can hear and identify both sounds in the blend.

4. If students need additional practice with the principle, repeat the procedure using the words *panic, plaque, talk, ache,* and *duck*.

5. Reinforce the principle as you conclude the lesson. *You can see that some consonant sounds are represented by several different letters or letter clusters that stand for the /k/ sound. As we read each word today, you were able to identify the different letters that can stand for the /k/ sound.*

6. Tell students that they will select four words with each of the four patterns, make them with magnetic letters, then write them on a list sheet, and read their lists to a partner.

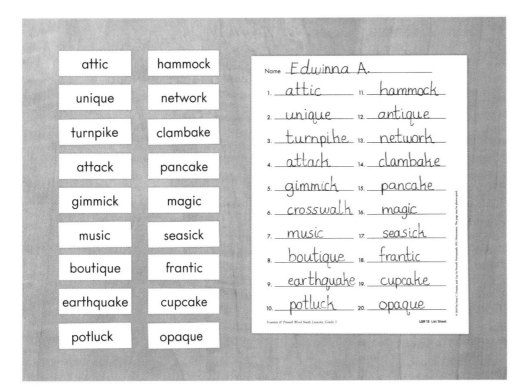

INSTRUCTIONAL PROCEDURE

MAKE WORDS

See page 32 for detailed descriptions of Instructional Procedures.

ACTION TAGS

take

make

write

read

Apply

■ Distribute word cards, magnetic letters, and list sheets. Have students select, make, and write a total of twenty words with different representations of the /k/ sound.

■ Some students may think of and write words that are not on the cards.

■ Have students read their completed list to a partner.

Share

■ Invite students to add one more word to each category on the class chart. They may think of words that were not included in the word card set.

■ Review the principle and remind students to notice words with consonant sounds that can be represented by several different letters or letter clusters when they read and write.

Assess

■ Dictate five or six words with the /k/ sound to assess students' control of the letter patterns. You may wish to use the words *attic, stack, king, antique, picnic,* and *kiss.*

Letter-Sound Relationships: Understand That Some Consonant Sounds Can Be Represented by Several Different Letters or Letter Clusters

125

Connect Learning Across Contexts

Shared Reading During shared reading, you may wish to use the following title from *Fountas & Pinnell Classroom*™ to locate a few words with varying letters or letter clusters that represent the /k/ sound after reading.

SR *From Flower to Honey* by June Schwartz

Guided Reading When students come to an unknown word with a consonant sound that can be represented by several different letters or letter clusters, prompt them by asking, "Do you know another word that looks like that?"

Shared Writing Model and check the spelling of a word with a consonant sound that can be represented by several different letters or letter clusters.

Independent Writing Guide students to think about the different letter patterns for /k/ when they write new words.

Extend Learning

Help students notice other sounds that can be represented different ways in words (e.g., *stiff, cough*).

▶ **Connect with Home**

Invite students to have family members help them find five words with different spellings of the /k/ sound on signs, in the newspaper, or in magazines. Students share their list of words with the class.

Recognize and Use Vowel Sounds with *r*

Plan

▶ Consider Your Students

This lesson will be most effective if students are familiar with a number of common words that have *r*-influenced vowels, such as *her*, *first*, *learn*, *corn*, and *farm*. In this lesson, students consider the different spellings for the same *r*-controlled sound. If students are more experienced with *r*-controlled vowels, you may wish to include several more vowel sounds or multisyllabic words. You may also wish to analyze how students represent *r*-influenced vowels in their writing. You can adapt the lesson to focus on letter-sound relationships with which students need more experience in order to understand and control.

▶ Working with English Language Learners

Depending on their first languages, English language learners may find it difficult to pronounce words with *r*-influenced vowels. Accept approximate pronunciations. Draw students' attention to the visual features of words. Then help them form categories of words for the different vowel sounds.

UNDERSTAND THE PRINCIPLE

When the consonant sound /r/ follows a vowel sound in a syllable, the sounds blend in a way that modifies the vowel sound. These modified sounds are known as *r*-influenced, or *r*-controlled, vowels. The letter-sound relationships among *r*-influenced vowels are complex. The same letter combination may represent more than one vowel sound, e.g., -*ear* in the words *bear*, *dear*, and *learn*. Conversely, several different letter combinations may represent the same vowel sound, e.g., -*er*, -*ear*, -*ir*, and -*ur* in the words *her*, *learn*, *bird*, and *hurt*. To solve increasingly complex words efficiently, students need many opportunities to explore these relationships and learn common patterns.

YOU WILL NEED

Online Resources
- ▶ LSR 14 Action Tags
- ▶ LSR 14 Word Cards
- ▶ LSR 14 Two-Way Sorts

Other Materials
- ▶ chart paper

Generative Lesson ✓

A generative lesson has a simple structure that you can use to present similar content or concepts. Use this lesson structure to teach students a variety of vowel sounds influenced by the letter *r*.

EXPLAIN THE PRINCIPLE

When the letter r *follows a vowel or vowel combination, blend the vowel sound with* r.

Comprehensive Phonics, Spelling, and Word Study Guide

Refer to: page **30**, row **31**

14 LETTER-SOUND RELATIONSHIPS

EARLY **MIDDLE** LATE

ACTIVITY: WORD LISTS

INSTRUCTIONAL PROCEDURE

NOTICE PARTS

See page 32 for detailed descriptions of Instructional Procedures.

EXPLAIN THE PRINCIPLE

When the letter r follows a vowel or vowel combination, blend the vowel sound with r.

Comprehensive Phonics, Spelling, and Word Study Guide

Refer to:
page **30**, row **31**

---

he
her
first   purr   worm   fern

do
door
soar   fork   four

Teach

1. On chart paper, write the word *he*, and read the word with students. *What vowel sound do you hear in this word?* • *The word* he *has the long* e *sound, /ē/.*

2. Write the word *her* beneath *he.* Read the word with students. *What do you notice about both of these words? What is different?* • *The last letter is different. Is there anything else different about the words?* • *The letter* r *changes the vowel sound to /er/.*

3. Write the words *first, purr, worm,* and *fern* on chart paper. *What do you notice about all of these words?* • *They all have the vowel sound /er/. What do you notice about the spelling of all of these words?* • *The sound is spelled differently in each word.* Have volunteers underline the letters that stand for the /er/ sound in each word.

4. Draw attention to the word *worm. Sometimes* or *can stand for the /or/ sound, and sometimes it can stand for the /er/ sound. If you're not sure which sound to use, try saying the word both ways to see which pronunciation sounds like a word you know.*

5. If students have good control over the /er/ words, repeat the procedure for the /or/ sound using the words *do* and *door* to emphasize the change in the vowel sound caused by adding *r.* Then add the words *soar, fork,* and *four.*

6. Read both lists of words again with students. Invite them to talk about what they notice. Some comments students might have are:

   "The letter *r* changes long vowel sounds to /er/ or /or/."

   "If the letter *r* were another letter, the vowel sound would be regular."

   "There are different vowel combinations that can stand for the /or/ sound."

   Build on students' comments as you guide students to understand the principle: *When the letter* r *follows a vowel or vowel combination, the vowel sound changes to /er/ or /or/.*

7. Tell students that they are going to practice sorting words by thinking about the two vowel sounds /er/ and /or/. If the sound in the word sounds like the vowel sound in *store,* they will write the word under the column for *store.* If the sound in the word sounds like the vowel sound in *earn,* they will write the word under the column for *earn.*

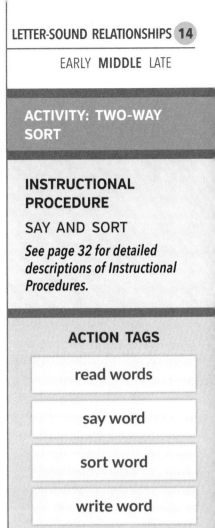

ACTIVITY: TWO-WAY SORT

INSTRUCTIONAL PROCEDURE

SAY AND SORT

See page 32 for detailed descriptions of Instructional Procedures.

ACTION TAGS

read words

say word

sort word

write word

Apply

Have students sort words with /er/ and /or/ vowel sounds using a two-way sort and word cards. They should first sort the word cards on their desks, and then write the words in the sort.

Share

- Have students share a word that they found difficult to sort with a classmate. The students can help each other as needed. You may wish to add new words to the pocket chart using blank pocket-chart cards.

- Review the principle and remind students to notice vowel sounds with *r* when they read and write.

Assess

- During shared reading and guided reading, notice whether students can quickly locate and read words with vowels followed by the letter *r.*

- Examine students' writing for evidence that they are beginning to represent *r*-influenced vowels accurately.

- You may wish to use Letter-Sound Relationships Assessment E, I, or J.

Letter-Sound Relationships: Recognize and Use Vowel Sounds with r

Connect Learning Across Contexts

Shared Reading During shared reading, you may wish to use the following title from *Fountas & Pinnell Classroom*™ to locate a few words that blend the vowel sound with *r* after reading.

SR *Exploring Underground* by Louis Petrone

Guided Reading When students come to an unknown word with vowel sounds with *r*, prompt them by asking, "Do you know another word that looks like that?"

Shared Writing Model and check the spelling of a word with a vowel sound with *r*.

Independent Writing When students are attempting to write a longer word with an *r*-influenced vowel, remind them that there are usually a few possible spellings for the sound. Encourage them to try a letter pattern, see if it looks correct, and then confirm or revise their spelling.

Extend Learning

- Repeat the lesson with two-syllable examples of words containing *r*-influenced vowels, such as *barber, carpet, alarm, garbage, market, partner, sparkle, prepare, careful, repair, dairy, merry, alert, perfect, gerbil, learner, nearby, yearly, cheerful, sincere, dirty, birthday, admire, coral, florist, ignore, curtain, turkey, surely, person, squirrel, normal, important, purple, urgent,* and *surprise.*

- Distribute blank Follow the Path game boards (found in Online Resources), and have students work together to create boards with new sets of words with *r*-influenced vowels. Students can then play Follow the Path in groups.

▶ **Connect with Home**

Send word cards home so that students can practice sorting with family members.

Recognize and Use Vowel Sounds in Closed Syllables (CVC)

Plan

▶ Consider Your Students

In order to read longer words, it is helpful for students to be able to divide words into syllables. While some students will have a natural sense of syllabication, most will need direct instruction in dividing words into syllables. In this lesson, students will focus on the vowel sounds in closed syllables. This lesson can precede or follow the lesson on *open* syllables.

▶ Working with English Language Learners

Closed syllables will be more challenging for many learners because in languages such as Spanish and Chinese, syllables typically end with a vowel rather than a consonant. Have students work with magnetic letters to divide words into syllables. Pronounce each syllable, emphasizing the short vowel sound in the first syllable. Have students repeat after you.

UNDERSTAND THE PRINCIPLE

A syllable is a unit of pronunciation within a word. Every syllable has one vowel sound. The vowel can be a single letter, or it can have other vowels or consonants with it. Some syllables end in consonants (*hel*-met or *muf*-fin) and are called *closed* syllables. Others end in vowels (*ba*-by or *fro*-zen) and are called *open* syllables. When students approach an unfamiliar word that has a single consonant in the middle, they should try alternatives: pronounce the word (1) with the first vowel *short,* as a closed syllable, or (2) with the first vowel *long,* as an open syllable. They can then see which pronunciation sounds like a word they know or have heard before.

YOU WILL NEED

Online Resources
- ▶ **LSR 15** Action Tags
- ▶ **LSR 15** Syllable Cards
- ▶ **LSR 15** List Sheets

Other Materials
- ▶ magnetic letters
- ▶ magnetic whiteboard

EXPLAIN THE PRINCIPLE

Some syllables end with a consonant, and the vowel sound is usually short.

Comprehensive Phonics, Spelling, and Word Study Guide

Refer to:
page **30**, row **32**

EARLY **MIDDLE** LATE

ACTIVITY: CLOSED SYLLABLES

INSTRUCTIONAL PROCEDURE

NOTICE PARTS

See page 32 for detailed descriptions of Instructional Procedures.

EXPLAIN THE PRINCIPLE

Some syllables end with a consonant, and the vowel sound is usually short.

Comprehensive Phonics, Spelling, and Word Study Guide

Refer to: page **30**, row **32**

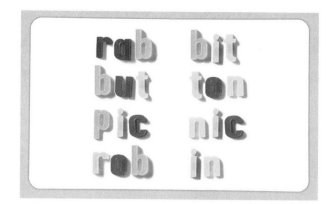

Teach

1. Make the words *rabbit, button,* and *picnic* with magnetic letters. *Read these words. Where would you break each word?*

2. Separate the magnetic letters to break all of the words into syllables—*rab-bit, but-ton, pic-nic. What do you notice about the first syllable?* • *It ends with a consonant, and the vowel sound is short.*

3. *Do you notice anything else about all of these words?* • *The first syllable always ends with a consonant letter. Each word has a short vowel sound in the beginning of the word.*

4. Guide students to understand the principle during the discussion: *Some syllables end with a consonant, and the vowel sound is usually short. You usually divide the word after the short vowel sound.*

5. Point out that the mouth is closed when they finish saying the first syllable, which is a closed syllable (CVC). Write the principle at the top of the whiteboard: *When a syllable ends with a vowel and at least one consonant, the vowel sound is usually short.*

6. *Let's look at another word.* Make the word *robin. What do you notice about the syllables in the word* robin? • *There are two syllables in* robin. Break the word apart on the whiteboard. *The word* robin *is divided after the consonant letter,* b, *that follows the vowel, the letter* o. *What do you notice about the vowel sounds in the word* robin? • Robin *has a short vowel sound in the first closed syllable.*

7. *Can you think of other words (like* robin *or* rabbit*) that have a closed first syllable with a short vowel sound?* • Make the words the students come up with on the whiteboard. Ask them to identify the vowel sound in the closed syllable for each word on the list.

8. Tell students they will be combining syllable cards to make twenty words with closed first syllables and short vowel sounds. They will write the words they make on a list sheet and then read their lists to a partner.

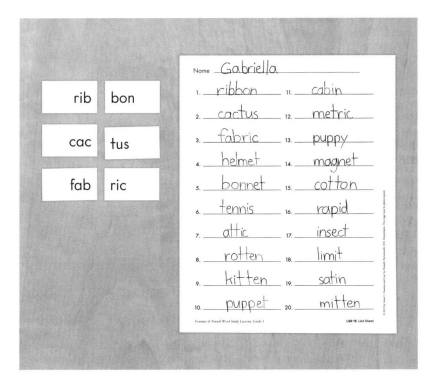

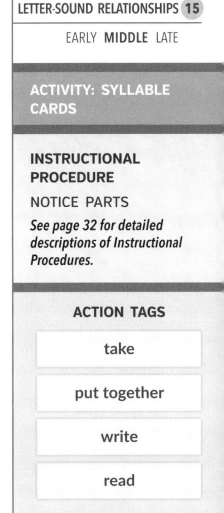

ACTIVITY: SYLLABLE CARDS

INSTRUCTIONAL PROCEDURE

NOTICE PARTS

See page 32 for detailed descriptions of Instructional Procedures.

ACTION TAGS

| take |
| put together |
| write |
| read |

Apply

Distribute syllable cards and list sheets. Tell students that they may use a syllable more than once.

Share

- Have students share a few words that they made. You may wish to add new words to the class chart.
- Review the principle and remind students to notice words with vowel sounds in closed syllables (CVC) when they read and write.

Assess

During shared reading and guided reading, notice whether students can quickly locate and read words with closed syllables.

Connect Learning Across Contexts

Shared Reading During shared reading, you may wish to use the following title from *Fountas & Pinnell Classroom*™ to locate a few words with a short vowel sound within a closed syllable.

SR *Trapped in Tar* by Hannah Cales

Guided Reading When students come to an unknown word with a vowel sound in a closed syllable (CVC), prompt them by asking, "Do you know another word that looks like that?"

Shared Writing Model and check the spelling of a word with a vowel sound in a closed syllable (CVC).

Independent Writing Prompt students to say words and write consecutive sounds. Point out words in their writing that have closed syllables.

Extend Learning

Repeat the lesson with a new set of words with closed syllables. Include a mix of words that have two consonants in the middle, such as *batter,* and words that have one consonant in the middle, such as *rapid.*

▶ Connect with Home

Send syllable cards home with students so that they can make and read words with family members.

Recognize and Use Vowel Sounds in Open Syllables (CVC)

Plan

▶ Consider Your Students

In order to read longer words, it is helpful for students to be able to divide words into syllables. While some students will have a natural sense of syllabication, most will need direct instruction in dividing words into syllables. In this lesson, students will focus on the vowel sounds in open syllables. This lesson can precede or follow the lesson on *closed* syllables.

▶ Working with English Language Learners

Varying pronunciation of English words may be a barrier to students' understanding the principle of the lesson. Model pronunciation and give students a chance to repeat the words. They will be able to hear your pronunciation and connect it to each word, even if they cannot pronounce it exactly as you do. Clapping the words while saying them may be helpful. Use magnetic letters to build the words, and then pull the letters apart to show the two syllables.

UNDERSTAND THE PRINCIPLE

A syllable is a unit of pronunciation within a word. Every syllable has one vowel sound. The vowel can be a single letter, or it can have other vowels or consonants with it. Some syllables end in consonants (*hel*-met or *muf*-fin) and are called *closed* syllables. Others end in vowels (*ba*-by or *fro*-zen) and are called *open* syllables. When students approach an unfamiliar word that has a single consonant in the middle, they should try alternatives: pronounce the word (1) with the first vowel *short,* as a closed syllable, or (2) with the first vowel *long,* as an open syllable. They can then see which pronunciation sounds like a word they know or have heard before.

YOU WILL NEED

PWS Ready Resources
- ▶ Lowercase Letter Cards

Online Resources
- ▶ **LSR 16** Action Tags
- ▶ **LSR 16** Word Cards
- ▶ **LSR 16** List Sheets

Other Materials
- ▶ chart paper
- ▶ magnetic letters

EXPLAIN THE PRINCIPLE

Some syllables end with a vowel, and the vowel sound is usually long.

Comprehensive Phonics, Spelling, and Word Study Guide

Refer to: page **30**, row **33**

ACTIVITY: OPEN SYLLABLES

INSTRUCTIONAL PROCEDURE

NOTICE PARTS

See page 32 for detailed descriptions of Instructional Procedures.

EXPLAIN THE PRINCIPLE

Some syllables end with a vowel, and the vowel sound is usually long.

Comprehensive Phonics, Spelling, and Word Study Guide

Refer to: page **30**, row **33**

Teach

1. Write the words *cozy, major, donut,* and *minor* on chart paper. *What do you notice about these four words?* • *What do you notice about the syllables in these words?* • *Each word has two syllables.*

2. *Think about the parts or syllables in the word* cozy. *Where would you break the word* cozy? • *Rewrite* cozy with a dash in between the letters *o* and *z* to represent the break in the word. Repeat the process for the words *major, donut,* and *minor.*

3. *What do you notice about the first part of all of the words?* • *The beginning part of each word has a long vowel sound. The vowel sound says its name. Do you notice anything else about these words?* • Some student responses might be:

   "All of the words have two syllables."

   "Break each word after the first two letters."

   "Divide the word after the long vowel sound."

   During the discussion, guide students to understand the principle.

4. *When the first syllable ends with a vowel, it usually has a long vowel sound and is called an open syllable.* Guide students to notice that the mouth is open when they finish saying the first syllable. Write the principle at the top of the chart paper: *Some syllables end with a vowel, and the vowel sound is usually long.*

5. *When you want to read a new or longer word, you can start by dividing the word into syllables.* Write the word *silent* on the chart paper. *What do you notice about the word* silent? • Silent *has two syllables and in the first syllable, the vowel sound is long.* Underline the *i* in silent. *When you see a word, like* silent, *with a single consonant in the middle, you can try dividing the word into syllables after the first vowel. Then say the word with a long vowel sound to see if it sounds like a word you know. Si-lent sounds correct. This word is pronounced with the long sound of* i *in the first syllable.* If students are ready, point out that if the word doesn't sound like a real word, they should try dividing it after the consonant and pronouncing the vowel with the short sound, as in *cab-in.*

6. Tell students that they are going to practice dividing words into syllables and reading them. Explain that they will take a word card, read it, make each syllable with magnetic letters, push the syllables together, and then write the word on a list sheet or in their word study notebook.

cozy

co-zy

major

ma-jor

donut

do-nut

minor

mi-nor

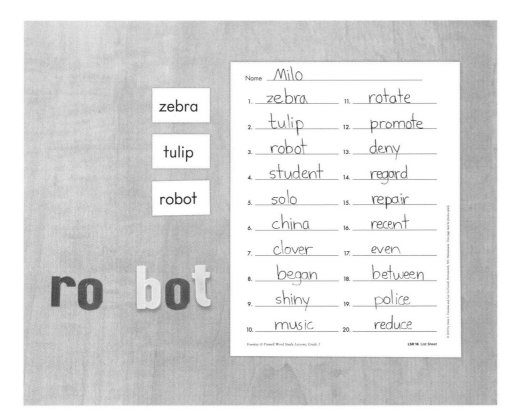

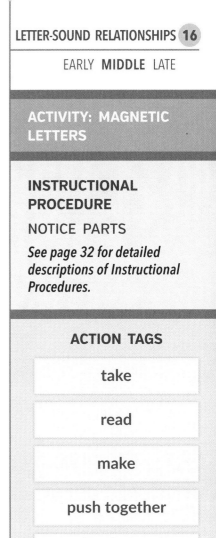

INSTRUCTIONAL PROCEDURE

NOTICE PARTS

See page 32 for detailed descriptions of Instructional Procedures.

ACTION TAGS

take
read
make
push together
write

Apply

Distribute word cards, magnetic letters, and list sheets. Tell students to make at least twenty words.

Share

- Have students share a few words that they made. Add five words, one representing each long vowel sound, to the class chart.
- Review the principle and remind students to notice words with vowel sounds in open syllables (CVC) when they read and write.

Assess

- During shared reading and guided reading, notice whether students can quickly locate and read words with open syllables.
- During shared reading and guided reading, notice whether students can use their knowledge of open and closed syllables to decode longer or unfamiliar words.

Letter-Sound Relationships: Recognize and Use Vowel Sounds in Open Syllables (CVC)

Connect Learning Across Contexts

Shared Reading During shared reading, you may wish to use the following title from *Fountas & Pinnell Classroom*™ to locate a few words (after reading) with a long vowel sound within an open syllable.

SR *A Meerkat Day* by Geerhardt Heever

Guided Reading When students come to an unknown word with a vowel sound in an open syllable (CVC), prompt them by asking, "Do you know another word that looks like that?"

Shared Writing Model and check the spelling of a word with a vowel sound in an open syllable (CVC).

Independent Writing Prompt students to say words and write consecutive sounds. Point out words in their writing that have open syllables.

Extend Learning

Repeat the lesson with a new set of words with open syllables. If students are very proficient with syllables, provide a mix of words with open and closed syllables.

▶ Connect with Home

Send magnetic letters and word cards home with students so that they can make and read words with family members.

Understand How to Use Capital Letters Correctly

Plan

▶ Consider Your Students

Students learn the differences between uppercase (capital) letters and lowercase (small) letters early, but it takes many years to learn their relevance for different kinds of nouns as well as how they function in sentences. Even competent adult writers sometimes misuse these conventions. Use this lesson with students who have had exposure to capitalization and discussed it during shared writing and in writer's workshop. Students may have done some editing of their writing and know that all kinds of names are capitalized. Select familiar people, places, things, or sentences to write in the squares of the Lotto Game Board to make the game enjoyable. The game is played like Lotto, using a die.

▶ Working with English Language Learners

Although English language learners will probably be familiar with capital letters from their experience with their own first language, the rules for English capitalization are likely to be somewhat different and, therefore, challenging. For example, the English pronoun *I* is always capitalized, but many languages do not capitalize the equivalent pronoun. Similarly, in many languages, the names of days and months are also not capitalized. Students may require extra practice to begin to gain automaticity with the standard rules for English capitalization. For the Apply exercise, use texts that are within their control–proper nouns will be simpler and sentences will be shorter and easier to work with.

UNDERSTAND THE PRINCIPLE

Capital letters contribute to readers' fluency and comprehension. They alert readers that a new sentence is beginning, signify proper names and important words in titles, and set apart the pronoun *I*. Paying attention to these signals helps students read smoothly and with greater comprehension. Capital letters also help others understand our writing. By this point, students have had a great deal of exposure to capital letters in their reading and writing, so they are ready to focus in on their specific functions.

YOU WILL NEED

Online Resources
- ▶ **LSR 17** Action Tags
- ▶ **LSR 17** Lotto Board
- ▶ **LSR 17** Game Die
- ▶ **LSR 17** Directions for Lotto

Other Materials
- ▶ chart paper
- ▶ game markers

Generative Lesson ✓

A generative lesson has a simple structure that you can use to present similar content or concepts. Use this lesson structure to present a variety of rules for capitalization.

EXPLAIN THE PRINCIPLE

A capital letter at the beginning of the first word shows the beginning of a sentence.

Capital letters at the beginning of some words show the names of specific people, places, and events.

Use a capital letter for the pronoun I.

Comprehensive Phonics, Spelling, and Word Study Guide

Refer to: page **31**, row **35**

ACTIVITY: CAPITAL LETTERS

INSTRUCTIONAL PROCEDURE

NOTICE PARTS

See page 32 for detailed descriptions of Instructional Procedures.

EXPLAIN THE PRINCIPLE

A capital letter at the beginning of the first word shows the beginning of a sentence.

Capital letters at the beginning of some words show the names of specific people, places, and events.

Use a capital letter for the pronoun I.

Comprehensive Phonics, Spelling, and Word Study Guide

Refer to: page **31**, row **35**

1. On chart paper, write the following sentence: *Today, Samantha will go to ballet class. What do you notice about the capital letters you see?* • Students will observe that the *T* in *Today* and the *S* in *Samantha* are capitalized.

   > Today, Samantha will go to ballet class.

2. *Why do you think the* T *in* Today *is capitalized?* • *The* T *is capitalized because it is the first word in the sentence.* • *What about the* S? • *The* S *is capitalized because it is the first letter in the name of a specific person.* Guide students to notice that they probably already use these capitalization rules automatically when they start a sentence or write their name.

   > Todd and I play on the same soccer team.

3. Now write this sentence: *Todd and I play on the same soccer team.* • *The person's name is capitalized. What other words do you notice that are capitalized?* Students will identify the pronoun *I*. *I is a pronoun that takes the place of your name. It is always capitalized, even when it appears in the middle of the sentence.* Help students make this connection: *Since you capitalize your own name, you should also capitalize I because it takes the place of your name.*

   > I like to play at the park.

   > My favorite is Ward Park.

4. Write on the chart paper these sentences: *I like to play at the park. My favorite is Ward Park. How has the word* park *changed from the first sentence to the second sentence?* • *It is capitalized.* • *Why do you think it has a capital letter in the second sentence?* • *It is the name of a specific park, so both words in the name of the park are capitalized.*

   > On New Year's Day, we have a parade.

5. Now write this sentence. *On New Year's Day, we have a parade. What do you notice about the words "New Year's Day"?* • *Each word has a capital letter.* • *Why do you think we capitalize* New Year's Day? • *It names a specific event or holiday. You capitalize the names of specific events or holidays, like New Year's Day or Labor Day.*

6. Tell students that they will play Lotto. Each player has a card that has squares randomly marked with familiar names of a person, place, thing, pronoun, or the beginning of sentence. Players take turns rolling the game die and finding matching examples on their board. Each player reads the label on the die and the example on his card and tells how they are the same and why they are capitalized. If the other players agree, then he covers the square with a marker or slip of paper. If a player is incorrect or cannot find an example that matches the die, then he passes. The first player to cover all the squares on his card wins the game.

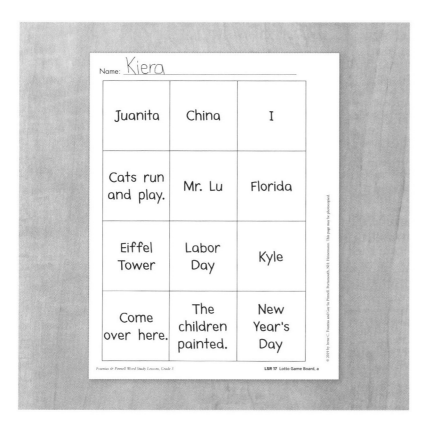

INSTRUCTIONAL PROCEDURE

FIND AND MATCH

See page 32 for detailed descriptions of Instructional Procedures.

ACTION TAGS

read

explain

cover

Apply

Distribute game die, markers, and game boards. Have students play Lotto in small groups.

Share

■ Students come to group share with one example of a capitalized word to share with the group.

■ Ask students to summarize what they have learned about capitalizing words. You may want them to check their own writing for more examples.

■ Review the principle and remind students to notice words with capital letters when they read and write.

Assess

■ Observe students' writing to determine whether they apply what they know about capitalization to their own writing.

■ Dictate two or three sentences that include a few words that require capitals. Analyze the results to learn the types of capitals for which you need to plan more lessons.

Connect Learning Across Contexts

Shared Reading During shared reading, you may wish to use the following title from *Fountas & Pinnell Classroom*™ to locate a few words using capitalization, such as *La Brea Tar Pits, Mexico,* and *Canada* after reading.

　　SR *Trapped in Tar* by Hannah Cales

Guided Reading When students come to an unknown word with a capital letter, prompt them by asking, "Do you know another word that begins like that?"

Shared Writing Model and check the spelling of a word with a capital letter.

Independent Writing: Have students proofread their writing for correct capitalization each time they write.

Extend Learning

- Repeat this lesson and focus on other capitalization principles, such as words in a title, first word in dialogue, and so forth.
- Repeat this lesson with other examples of people, places, and things.

▶ Connect with Home

Send home game boards and dice so that students can play Lotto with family members.

Understand How to Use the Computer Keyboard

Plan

▶ Consider Your Students

If students have had opportunities to use computers, then they already have considerable experience in the general operations of them. More than likely, they know how to turn a computer on and off, use simple programs, navigate with a mouse, and so on. However, they are not likely to be able to keyboard efficiently. You may wish to begin with a brief demonstration and explanation to the whole class, and then work with a small group as they learn to use the computer keyboard. If available, students can use small portable keyboards for a large group lesson.

▶ Working with English Language Learners

If English language learners know the names of the letters, then they can easily learn efficient keyboarding. Computer skills are advantageous when students are expanding their control of English. When typing simple words, phrases, and sentences, they are practicing writing English words and gaining fluency with keyboarding. If their native language uses the same alphabet, they can type words in that language as well. Provide concrete demonstrations that students can easily see, and let them practice the operation immediately afterward.

UNDERSTAND THE PRINCIPLE

Effective use of the computer keyboard is an asset to students in becoming fluent, efficient users of technology. It may seem awkward to them at first, and they will be tempted to use the "hunt and peck" method. However, if they learn keyboarding early, then it becomes automatic, allowing more attention to composing messages, stories, and reports. Fluent keyboarding allows a writer to put thoughts down quickly and leads to greater productivity in writing as well as in Internet research.

YOU WILL NEED

Online Resources
- ▶ **LSR 18** Action Tags
- ▶ **LSR 18** A Sequence for Learning Effective Keyboarding
- ▶ **LSR 18** Keyboard

Other Materials
- ▶ portable keyboards
- ▶ computers (optional)

Generative Lesson

A generative lesson has a simple structure that you can use to present similar content or concepts. Use this lesson structure to present a variety of keyboarding lessons and skills.

EXPLAIN THE PRINCIPLE

Use efficient finger movements to type words on a computer keyboard.

Comprehensive Phonics, Spelling, and Word Study Guide

Refer to: page **31**, row **34**

ACTIVITY: KEYBOARDING TECHNIQUES

INSTRUCTIONAL PROCEDURE

MAKE WORDS

See page 32 for detailed descriptions of Instructional Procedures.

EXPLAIN THE PRINCIPLE

Use efficient finger movements to type words on a computer keyboard.

Comprehensive Phonics, Spelling, and Word Study Guide

Refer to: page **31**, row **34**

Teach

1. Tell students that they will learn a skill that will help them write more efficiently.

2. *You already know how to use a computer. Today you will begin practicing the finger movements that will help you type faster.*

3. Students each have a portable keyboard or keyboard facsimile for this first practice session. *I'm going to show you the finger movements now. We will practice them for about 10 minutes every day this week.*

4. Highlight the "home row" on the enlargement or transparency. *It is important to remember that your eight fingers rest on the home row most of the time. Your thumbs are on the space bar. Let's identify each finger. On your right hand, hold up your index finger, then your middle finger, then your ring finger, and then your little finger. These names will help you follow directions. Now put them on the home row of keys–index finger on J, middle finger on K, ring finger on L, little finger on the semicolon/colon. Just touch the keys lightly. Your thumb barely touches the space bar. Now put your left hand on the home row–index finger on F, middle finger on D, ring finger on S, little finger on A. Your thumb is in the air, ready to touch the space bar when needed."*

5. Have students type: *jkl* [space] *jkl* [space] *jkl* [space] *jkl* [space]. Then repeat with the left hand: *asdf* [space] *asdf* [space] *asdf* [space] *asdf* [space]. Have students practice using the home row to practice random combinations of the letters. You can give them an exercise to follow, but also encourage them to use the correct finger when striking each key in the home row.

6. *You will use those same four fingers to strike the other keys. Sometimes you will reach up or out with the index finger. Look at your keys. Which letters do you think the index finger can easily reach?* Students will respond by suggesting *RTGV* for the left hand and *UYHNM* for the right hand. Explain that each finger will always strike the nearest keys and that each finger always returns to its place in the home row.

7. Introduce the finger movements as indicated in A Sequence of Effective Keyboard Learning [see Online Resources], and have students practice daily to gain fluency.

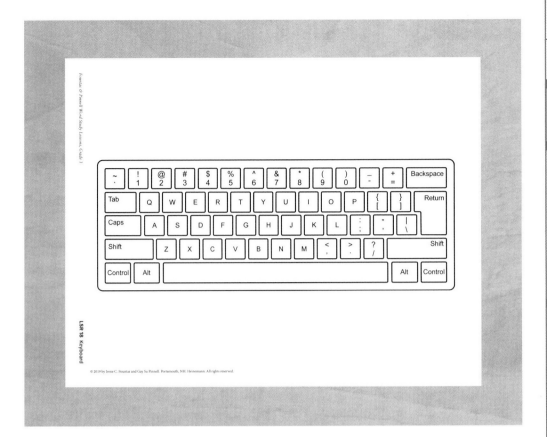

LSR 18 Keyboard

ACTIVITY: KEYBOARDING PRACTICE

INSTRUCTIONAL PROCEDURE

MAKE WORDS

See page 32 for detailed descriptions of Instructional Procedures.

ACTION TAGS

place fingers

type

Apply

Students practice keyboarding on portable computer keyboards or take turns at a computer. There will be some drill when learning this skill because you want them to become very familiar with the home row. Students may tire of the repetition, so if they seem comfortable, go on to introduce new keys, each time having them practice until they are comfortable.

Share

Have students demonstrate how quickly their fingers can find the home row. Discuss the idea that while they are learning, they should work for accuracy, smoothness, and comfort rather than speed. The more they practice using accurate finger movements, the faster they will be able to type on the computer.

Assess

- Collect students' practice documents to assess their accuracy.
- Observe students to determine the degree to which they are using efficient keyboarding. Some may have become quick with the "hunt and peck" method and have established habits that are hard to overcome.
- You may decide that finger movements can be the child's choice rather than a requirement. Remember that efficient keyboarding benefits students.

Connect Learning Across Contexts

Shared Reading When reading poetry, point out different keyboarding options that make the poem more interesting; for example, white space is created deliberately by pressing *Enter*.

Guided Reading When reading informational text, point out specialized uses of the computer to create interesting layouts.

Shared Writing As you compose together, model proper keyboarding techniques.

Independent Writing As soon as students develop some keyboard fluency, encourage them to type their writing pieces or to compose directly on the keyboard. If students develop the skill of composing while typing, they will have a faster way of producing text. Some writers prefer cursive or manuscript writing for some pieces and use the computer for others.

Extend Learning

■ Continue offering minilessons and practice time for the eight steps outlined on A Sequence of Finger Movements for Effective Computer Keyboarding (see Online Resources). Monitor students' progress, and work with those who find the process more difficult.

■ Give students the choice of typing poems to include in their poetry anthology.

■ Establish email capability among the members of your class. Remind students to keyboard correctly when writing their messages.

▶ **Connect with Home**

■ If students have access to a computer at home, encourage them to practice for at least five minutes each day.

■ Let students take home a keyboard facsimile to show family members the finger movements.

Understand How to Form Cursive Letters Correctly, Efficiently, and Fluently

Plan

▶ Consider Your Students

In this lesson, students learn how to form cursive letters. Teach several letters in a lesson, and if that is too much, then introduce only one or two letters at a time. As soon as you have introduced enough letters, work the letters into words to practice. As soon as possible, give students a simple sentence or two to write. Help students understand that letters should slant slightly to the right. You will need to decide the timing of this lesson as it relates to your school's curriculum. You may want to have students use lined paper to gain control of proportions. (Remember that some left-handed students may slant to the left, and that is fine if writing is legible.)

▶ Working with English Language Learners

Many English language learners already know how to write the letters of an alphabetic language system in manuscript, and some may have cursive skills. With English words, however, they will use letters in a different order than they are accustomed. If students have just begun writing English words, begin with manuscript print and then move to cursive. Assess writing skills and, if necessary, form small groups for daily writing practice. If students learn efficient movements, they will become fluent more quickly. Demonstrate as you use language that describes the movements.

UNDERSTAND THE PRINCIPLE

Students learn to write more efficiently when they move from manuscript to cursive form. For right-handed students, cursive letters are formed with a more continuous movement that *slants to the right* as it flows; some left-handed students may slant letters to the left, and that is fine if the writing is legible. Practice in larger form makes it easier to form letters in a smaller size. Even though handwriting develops as an individual style, it is important to establish the habit of efficient movements.

YOU WILL NEED

Online Resources
- ▶ **LSR 19** Action Tags
- ▶ **LSR 19** A Suggested Order for Cursive Letter Formation
- ▶ **LSR 19** Verbal Path for Cursive Formation
- ▶ **LSR 19** Cursive Letter Models
- ▶ **LSR 19** Lined Sheets

Other Materials
- ▶ chart paper
- ▶ lined paper

Generative Lesson

A generative lesson has a simple structure that you can use to present similar content or concepts. Use this lesson structure to present a variety of cursive letters and strokes.

EXPLAIN THE PRINCIPLE

Write letters smoothly and efficiently in cursive form.

Comprehensive Phonics, Spelling, and Word Study Guide

Refer to: page **31**, row **36**

EARLY MIDDLE **LATE**

ACTIVITY: CURSIVE LETTERS

INSTRUCTIONAL PROCEDURE

MAKE WORDS

See page 32 for detailed descriptions of Instructional Procedures.

EXPLAIN THE PRINCIPLE

Write letters smoothly and efficiently in cursive form.

Comprehensive Phonics, Spelling, and Word Study Guide

Refer to: page **31**, row **36**

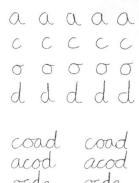

Teach

1. Tell students that they are going to learn another way to write letters.

2. On a large surface such as a large whiteboard or chalkboard, form the letter *a*. As you form it, use simple words (a verbal path) that will guide the learning (*pull back, around, up, down, and swing up*). *How is this letter similar to a regular* a? *How is it different?* Students may observe that it has the same basic shape but that it is slanted to the right and "curvier."

3. Make a few large cursive *a*s, then erase them and start again. Explain that the movement should be smooth and continuous and that writing in cursive should help them write more easily and faster. Also show them how the letters slant to the right so it flows.

4. Have students move the finger in the air to mirror your movement. An alternative is to have them use small notebooks or paper on a clipboard to practice the formation.

5. Repeat the process with *c, o,* and *d,* giving students a few minutes to practice a line of the letters on their lined paper.

6. Next show the students how to join the letters by "going up and over" each time. *How are these letters different from the way we write printed words?* ● *They are connected.* ● *Why do you think some people connect their letters like this when they write?* ● *You can write faster if you don't take your pen or pencil off the paper.*

7. Have them make a line of *coad, acod, ocda, doac* so they can practice smooth, continuous writing. Ask them to circle their best group of letters.

8. Explain that today they will practice one line of each letter (*a, o, c, d*) and one line of each group (*coad, acod, ocda, doac*) in their handwriting notebook.

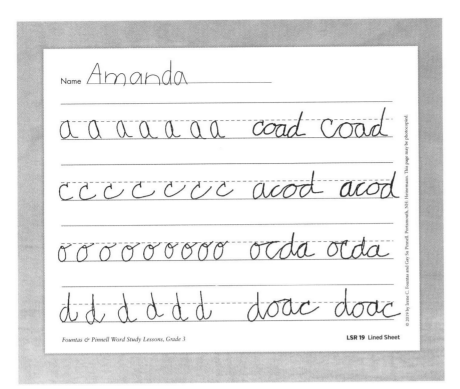

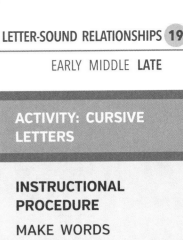

Fountas & Pinnell Word Study Lessons, Grade 3

LSR 19 Lined Sheet

ACTIVITY: CURSIVE LETTERS

INSTRUCTIONAL PROCEDURE

MAKE WORDS

See page 32 for detailed descriptions of Instructional Procedures.

ACTION TAGS

write

slant

circle

Apply

Have students practice one line of each letter and each group of letters on lined paper or in their handwriting notebook. Reinforce the importance of a slant to the right. Ask them to circle the best formation in each line.

Share

Invite each child to make a letter or group of letters on a chalkboard or whiteboard while the other students make the formation in the air or on paper on their clipboards.

Assess

Assign students to write in cursive form for particular tasks. Observe how fluently, efficiently, and proportionally the letters are formed.

Connect Learning Across Contexts

Shared Reading During shared reading, you may wish to read a text that features cursive writing.

Guided Reading When introducing books that have some parts written in cursive (e.g., *Amber Brown*), point out the cursive writing and read those parts with children.

Shared Writing As you write together, model proper cursive handwriting. Invite children to come to the board to write some words in cursive.

Independent Writing: Work with students in small groups when they need guided support forming cursive letters.

Extend Learning

- Repeat the lesson to review *a, c, o,* and *d* and add *g* and *q.*
- Teach the lesson with four other letters that begin the same way (*e, i, t, j*).
- Continue the lessons with (*p, s, u, w*), (*b, f, l, h, k*) (*m, n, v, x, y, a*) and *r.*

▶ Connect with Home

Send home the cursive letter models sheet for students to use as a reference when they practice writing at home (see Online Resources). The Verbal Path information may also be helpful to family members.

Spelling Patterns

Phonograms are spelling patterns that represent the sounds of rimes. In a one-syllable word, the *rime* is the ending part containing the letters that represent the vowel sound and the letters that follow. The part before the vowel is called the *onset*. Phonograms are sometimes called *word families*. You will not need to teach students the technical word *phonogram*, although you may want to use *pattern* or *word part*. We have included a large list of common phonograms in *Ready Resources* that will be useful to students in reading or writing, but you will not need to teach every phonogram separately. Once students understand that there are patterns and learn how to look for them, they will quickly discover more for themselves.

Another way to look at phonograms is to examine the way simple words and syllables are put together. Here we include the consonant-vowel-consonant (CVC) pattern in which the vowel often has a short, or *terse*, sound; and the consonant-vowel-consonant-silent *e* (CVC*e*) pattern in which the vowel usually has a long, or *lax*, sound; the VCC pattern in which words end with double consonants or with consonant clusters; the pattern involving vowel combinations (VVC) that sound like the name of the first vowel or that stand for other sounds; as well as patterns with other vowel sounds including those influenced by the letter *r*. Knowing spelling patterns helps students notice and use larger parts of words, thus making word solving faster and more efficient. Patterns are also helpful to students in writing words because they will quickly write down the patterns rather than laboriously work with individual sounds and letters. The fourteen most common phonograms are marked with an asterisk in rows 8 and 9 of the Spelling Patterns section of *The Fountas & Pinnell Comprehensive Phonics, Spelling, and Word Study Guide* (page 35).

Connect to Assessment

See related (optional) SP Assessment tasks in Online Resources.

- Assessment A: Reading Words with Phonogram Patterns
- Assessment B: Writing Words with Phonogram Patterns
- Assessment C: Individual Record (Reading Words with Phonogram Patterns)
- Assessment D: Individual Record (Writing Words with Phonogram Patterns)

roof
rude
tool
gloom
room
chew
suit
hoot
mood
soon
snoop
coop
clue
true
due

Develop Your Professional Understanding

See *The Fountas & Pinnell Comprehensive Phonics, Spelling, and Word Study Guide*. 2017. Portsmouth, New Hampshire: Heinemann. Related pages: 2-12, 34-38.

See *The Fountas & Pinnell Literacy Continuum: A Tool for Assessment, Planning, and Teaching*. 2017. Portsmouth, New Hampshire: Heinemann. Related pages: 357-397.

See *Word Matters: Teaching Phonics and Spelling in the Reading/Writing Classroom* by G.S. Pinnell and I.C. Fountas. 1998. Portsmouth, New Hampshire: Heinemann. Related pages: 65, 82, 95, 236.

Recognize and Use Less Common Phonograms with a VC Pattern

Plan

▶ **Consider Your Students**

This lesson will be appropriate for students who have good control of the CVC pattern but have little experience noticing words with less common VC patterns, such as *-em, -ib,* and *-ud.* You can tailor this lesson to focus on phonograms with which students need more experience. You will not need to teach all phonograms in formal lessons. Once students understand that there are patterns and learn how to look for patterns, they will quickly discover more for themselves.

▶ **Working with English Language Learners**

Making words is very helpful to English language learners as it provides an opportunity for them to notice and think extensively about word parts. Explicitly demonstrate making words. You may have students who have minimal English vocabularies. At first, limit this activity to words they know well and help them to make these words. Gradually increase the number of patterns with which they are working.

UNDERSTAND THE PRINCIPLE

As students encounter increasingly complex words, they will notice visual patterns and larger parts of words, which is an important step in understanding how words work. Sorting and connecting words according to a variety of features will heighten students' awareness of word parts and patterns and increase their flexibility in working with words.

EXPLAIN THE PRINCIPLE

Look at the spelling pattern to read a word.

Use the spelling pattern to write a word.

Make new words by putting a letter or a letter cluster before the pattern.

Comprehensive Phonics, Spelling, and Word Study Guide

Refer to: page **34**, row **4**

ACTIVITY: WORD CHART

INSTRUCTIONAL PROCEDURE

NOTICE PARTS

See page 32 for detailed descriptions of Instructional Procedures.

EXPLAIN THE PRINCIPLE

Look at the spelling pattern to read a word.

Use the spelling pattern to write a word.

Make new words by putting a letter or a letter cluster before the pattern.

Comprehensive Phonics, Spelling, and Word Study Guide

Refer to: page **34**, row **4**

-ib	-em	-ud	-us
rib	stem	mud	bus
bib	gem	bud	plus
crib	problem	thud	circus
fib	them	cud	focus
	anthem		cactus
			bonus
			minus

Teach

1. Tell students they are going to talk about what they know about words.

2. On chart paper, create a summary chart of several spelling patterns that you would like students to review, compare, and think about. Begin by writing two or three words ending in the first pattern you would like to review, such as *rib, bib, crib.* Use any words students may not understand in a sentence. Have students read the words with you. *What do you notice about the words?* • Allow time for students to observe that the words rhyme and that all three words end in the same two letters. Write *-ib* above the words.

3. Invite students to say other words they know that end with the spelling pattern *-ib,* and write the words on the chart. Students may be unable to name additional words with certain phonograms because either there aren't any or they're so rare that students haven't encountered them.

4. Encourage students to make observations about the words. Build on their observations to help them generalize the principle. *The letters -ib are a pattern that can help you read and write more words.*

5. Continue the process to add more patterns and examples to the chart. Encourage students to discuss patterns they notice in longer words, e.g., CVC + CVC in words such as *cactus.*

6. Have students take turns choosing a pattern and reading the words in that column. Then summarize the principle. *Look for spelling patterns as you read, and use spelling patterns as you write. You can make new words by putting a letter or letter cluster before each pattern.*

7. Explain to students that they will make words using the spelling patterns. Demonstrate the process of making words using word cards. (The word cards in Online Resources are based on the four spelling patterns above. You can create different word cards using blank word cards in Online Resources.) Encourage students to make at least a couple of words for each spelling pattern. They then write the words on a list sheet, and read the words to a partner.

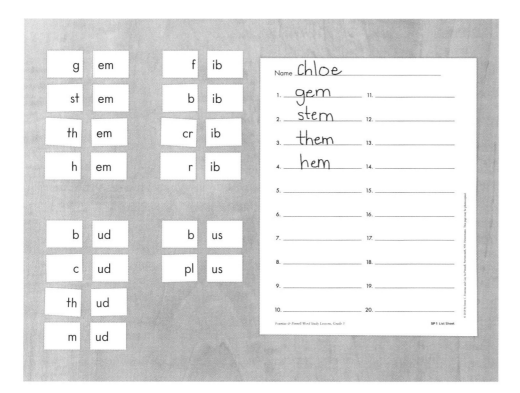

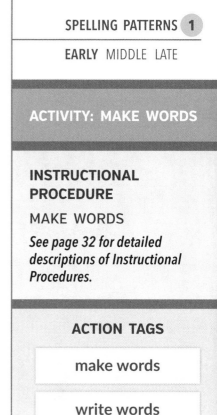

ACTIVITY: MAKE WORDS

INSTRUCTIONAL PROCEDURE

MAKE WORDS

See page 32 for detailed descriptions of Instructional Procedures.

ACTION TAGS

make words

write words

read words

Apply

Remind students that they will make words by matching the beginning consonant word cards with ending spelling pattern word cards. Encourage students to check that each word is real by using it in a sentence.

Share

- Have students share a few words from their lists. You may wish to add one or two more words to each list on the summary chart.

- Review the principle and remind students to notice and use less common phonograms with a VC pattern when they read and write.

Assess

- Point to words on the summary chart in random order, and have students read them. Notice if students are able to read the words quickly and effortlessly or if certain patterns need more review.

- Dictate words representing each pattern, and have students write them. Mix in a few high-frequency words for an added challenge.

- You may wish to use Spelling Patterns Assessment A, B, C, or D.

Spelling Patterns: Recognize and Use Less Common Phonograms with a VC Pattern

Connect Learning Across Contexts

Shared Reading You may wish to use the following Shared Reading title from *Fountas & Pinnell Classroom*™ to point out less common phonograms with a VC pattern.

SR *Trapped in Tar* by Hannah Cales

Guided Reading During word work, have students locate any words containing VC spelling patterns.

Shared Writing As you compose a piece of writing, point out words that contain a VC spelling pattern. You may wish to revisit completed pieces to search for words containing specific patterns that you are reviewing.

Guided/Independent Writing When students become pattern seekers, they are able to edit their spelling more effectively. Prompt students to use patterns they know to check the spelling of words.

Extend Learning

- Repeat the lesson to add more VC spelling patterns to the summary chart.
- Have students play Concentration using game cards with words that have the VC spelling pattern. Blank game cards are available in Online Resources.

▶ Connect with Home

Reproduce the summary chart (or parts of it) for each student to take home and read to family members.

Recognize and Use Phonogram Patterns with a Short Vowel Sound in Single-Syllable Words

Plan

▶ Consider Your Students

The goal of this lesson is to help students recognize common phonograms with short vowel sounds. Use this lesson if students need more experience with words having one syllable and a short vowel sound. You may wish to tailor the lesson to focus on a single short vowel at a time, e.g., you may wish to teach five short *a* phonograms rather than various phonograms for each of the five vowels.

▶ Working with English Language Learners

As students work with spelling patterns, they internalize both the phonology and the letter-sound relationships in English words. A key goal is making connections among words, which will accelerate students' learning of English as well as their literacy development. Work with students to be sure they understand and can pronounce the words you are using as examples. Keep in mind that short vowels may be challenging for some English language learners because the sounds can vary in pronunciation and are sometimes difficult to distinguish.

UNDERSTAND THE PRINCIPLE

Recognizing phonograms and other regular spelling patterns that appear in many words with short vowel sounds will help students understand that they can apply what they know about word structure to figure out new words. Students will also understand that searching for and recognizing patterns are valuable to them as readers and writers. When readers have strong control of phonograms in single-syllable words, they can more easily solve multisyllable words with the same patterns.

YOU WILL NEED

 **Ready Resources**
- ▶ Lowercase Letter Cards

Online Resources
- ▶ SP 2 Action Tags
- ▶ SP 2 Five-Way Sorts

Other Materials
- ▶ blank chart paper
- ▶ magnetic letters

Generative Lesson
A generative lesson has a simple structure that you can use to present similar content or concepts. Use this lesson structure to teach students a variety of phonograms with a short vowel sound.

EXPLAIN THE PRINCIPLE

Some words have a short vowel pattern. You can hear the short vowel sound [e.g., cap, best, pick, not, rust].

 Comprehensive Phonics, Spelling, and Word Study Guide

Refer to: page **36**, row **11**

ACTIVITY: WORD LISTS

chat	fell	trim	stock	dunk
damp	chest	clip	pot	stump
flap	rent	mill	mob	rust
rack	less	kid	bog	shut

INSTRUCTIONAL PROCEDURE

NOTICE PARTS

See page 32 for detailed descriptions of Instructional Procedures.

EXPLAIN THE PRINCIPLE

Some words have a short vowel pattern. You can hear the short vowel sound [e.g., cap, best, pick, not, rust].

Comprehensive Phonics, Spelling, and Word Study Guide

Refer to: page **36**, row **11**

Teach

1. Tell students that they are going to think more about words.

2. On chart paper, write the words *chat, damp, flap,* and *rack.* Have students read the words with you. Use any words students may not understand in sentences.

3. *What do you notice about the words?* • *Each word has the vowel* a *followed by one or more consonants.* If needed, prompt students to think about the vowel sound. *What vowel sound do you hear in these words?* • *Each word has the short* a *sound, /a/.*

4. Repeat the process with words that have other short vowel patterns. You may wish to create a column of words for each vowel.

5. Encourage students to contribute examples, compare the spelling patterns, and share their thinking throughout the process. Listen for comments that provide evidence that students are recognizing and using the phonograms in their analysis of the words, for example:

   "Every word has just one vowel. The sound is always short."

   "Some of the endings have one consonant, but some have two consonants."

   "I've seen this pattern in a lot of longer words, too."

   "You can make lots of different words by changing the letters at the beginning."

6. Have students read each column of words. Help them generalize the principle based on their earlier observations. *Some words have a short vowel pattern. You can hear the short vowel sound.*

7. Tell students that they will make, write, and read words with short vowel patterns. Using magnetic letters, demonstrate making a word and checking the spelling against the class chart. Explain that students will make two words for each pattern. They will then write examples of each pattern on a five-way sort.

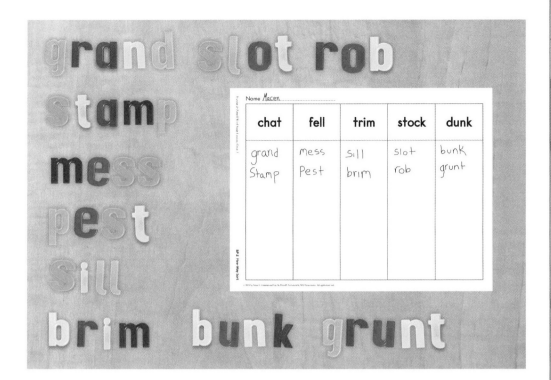

ACTIVITY: MAKE WORDS

INSTRUCTIONAL PROCEDURE

MAKE WORDS

See page 32 for detailed descriptions of Instructional Procedures.

ACTION TAGS

make words

write words

read words

Apply

- Distribute five-way sorts and magnetic letters. (You may also use letter cards from *Ready Resources.*)

- Remind students that they can use the class chart as a resource, but encourage them to make additional words with short vowel patterns.

- In preparation for the group share, ask students to read the words on their sorts to a partner.

Share

- Have students, in turn, read one word for each pattern. Add a few words to the class chart.

- Review the principle and remind students to recognize and use phonogram patterns with a short vowel sound in single-syllable words when they read and write.

Assess

- Ask individual students to use letter cards to make words with specific short vowel patterns.

- Observe students as they read to determine whether they are noticing and using short vowel patterns to solve single-syllable words.

- You may wish to use Spelling Patterns Assessment A, B, C, or D.

Spelling Patterns: Recognize and Use Phonogram Patterns with a Short Vowel Sound in Single-Syllable Words

Connect Learning Across Contexts

Shared Reading You may wish to use the following Shared Reading title from *Fountas & Pinnell Classroom*™ to point out words with short vowel patterns.

SR *Wolf Pack* by Annette Bay Pimentel

Guided Reading After the discussion of the book, identify two or three single-syllable words in the text that have a short vowel pattern. Quickly write the words one at a time on a whiteboard, and have students read the words to develop quick recognition.

Shared Writing When students suggest a new word with a short vowel pattern, ask them to think of a word they know that is like it.

Guided/Independent Writing Prompt students to use patterns they know to check the spelling of words. *This word sounds the same as* stack *at the end. What pattern do you know in the word* stack? *Can you use that pattern here?*

Extend Learning

- Repeat the lesson to add more words with short vowel patterns to the class chart.

- Have students play Concentration using game cards with words that have short vowel patterns. Blank game cards are available in Online Resources.

▶ Connect with Home

Send home a set of letter cards. Ask students to work with family members to make and record words with short vowel patterns.

Recognize and Use Phonograms with a Vowel-Consonant-Silent *e* (VCe) Pattern

Plan

▶ Consider Your Students

Students should already be familiar with the VCe pattern. In this lesson, you will be teaching them to recognize and use this phonogram when solving words with more than one syllable. The VCe pattern may appear in the first or last syllable of the word. Students should have strong control of basic long and short vowel phonograms so they can take apart and solve two-syllable words.

▶ Working with English Language Learners

Quickly review the basic VCe pattern in one-syllable words as you begin this lesson. It is important that English language learners have good control of the basic principle and be able to recognize examples of it. To support pronunciation, say each multisyllable word aloud and have students look at it and repeat it aloud. Observe students as they sort words to be sure they understand the task.

UNDERSTAND THE PRINCIPLE

A helpful generalization that students learn early is that when a word ends in a consonant plus the letter *e*, the *e* usually does not stand for any sound, but it often signals that the vowel preceding the consonant stands for a long vowel sound. This spelling pattern (VCe) is common with the vowels *a, i, o,* and *u*. When the pattern is part of a multisyllable word, it becomes more challenging for readers to notice. Both syllables contain a vowel sound, with one part containing the vowel-consonant-silent *e* pattern. Often, words with VCe in the first syllable are compound words.

EXPLAIN THE PRINCIPLE

Some words have a vowel, a consonant, and silent e. *The vowel sound is usually the name of the first vowel [the* a *in* place, i *in* ripe, o *in* rode, u *in* tube].*

Comprehensive Phonics, Spelling, and Word Study Guide

Refer to: page **35**, row **5**

ACTIVITY: WORD SORT

INSTRUCTIONAL PROCEDURE

SAY AND SORT

See page 32 for detailed descriptions of Instructional Procedures.

EXPLAIN THE PRINCIPLE

Some words have a vowel, a consonant, and silent e. The vowel sound is usually the name of the first vowel [the a in place, i in ripe, o in rode, u in tube].

Comprehensive Phonics, Spelling, and Word Study Guide

Refer to: page **35**, row **5**

Teach

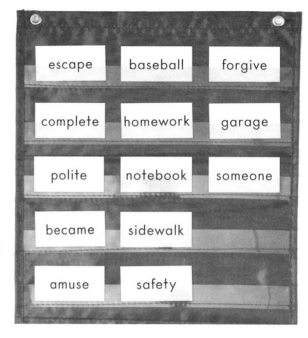

1. In a pocket chart, display the words *escape, complete,* and *polite* in a column. Read the words with students, using any words students may not understand in a sentence.

2. *What do you notice about all of the words?* • Give students the opportunity to make some or all of the following observations: all of the words have two syllables, all end with the letter *e,* and all have a long vowel sound in the second syllable.

3. As needed, draw students' attention to the VCe pattern and to share what they know. *Talk about the pattern of letters at the end of each word.* • *The second syllable of each word has a vowel, then a consonant, and finally a silent* e. *The vowel sound in the second syllable is the name of the first vowel, /ā/ in* escape, */ē/ in* complete, *and /ī/ in* polite.

4. Display the words *baseball, homework,* and *notebook* in a second column. Read the words with students.

5. *What do you notice about all of these words?* • *In these words, the first syllable has a vowel, then a consonant, and finally a silent* e. *The vowel sound in the first syllable is the name of the first vowel, /ā/ in* baseball *and /ō/ in* homework *and* notebook. Students may also observe that the words in the second column are compound words. Explain that words with the VCe pattern in the first syllable are often compound words.

6. Place the remaining words at random along the bottom of the pocket chart. *Today you are going to be sorting words. Let's sort these words according to the syllable in which the vowel-consonant-silent* e *pattern appears.* One at a time, say a word and then sort it into the correct column with students' help. Students will discover that a few words do not fit the pattern. Invite students to talk about how the words are different. • *The vowel sound in the syllable with the VCe pattern is not long.* Use the opportunity to remind students that there will always be exceptions to any generalization. Sort the exceptions into a third column.

7. Explain that students will use a three-way sort to sort word cards below the key words *escape, baseball,* and *forgive* [*forgive* being the column for exceptions]. After they have completed the sort, students write the words on a three-column sort and read their lists to a partner.

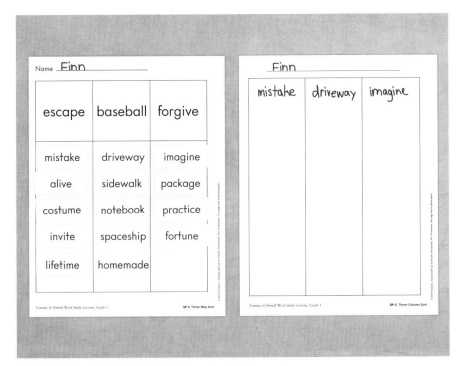

INSTRUCTIONAL PROCEDURE

SAY AND SORT

See page 32 for detailed descriptions of Instructional Procedures.

ACTION TAGS

say words

sort words

write words

read words

Apply

- Have students sort the words according to the syllable in which the vowel-consonant-silent *e* pattern appears. Remind students that it is important to say the words because some are exceptions: in these exceptions, the vowel sound in the syllable with the VC*e* pattern is not long. The exceptions should be sorted under the key word *forgive*.

- Remind students to read to a partner the lists of words that they write on the three-column sort.

- You may wish to have students circle or highlight the VC*e* pattern in each word in the first two columns.

Share

- Ask students to talk about what they learned from sorting and writing the words. Listen for comments such as these, which indicate flexibility and awareness of the VC*e* pattern:

    "*Lifetime* and *homemade* can be sorted two ways!"

    "It's easier to read a word with more than one syllable when you can find a pattern."

- Review the principle and remind students to recognize and use phonograms with a vowel-consonant-silent *e* (VC*e*) pattern when they read and write.

Assess

- Notice whether students can sort two-syllable words by the VC*e* spelling pattern.

- As students read texts, observe how efficiently they solve two-syllable words with the VC*e* pattern.

- You may wish to use Spelling Patterns Assessment A, B, C, or D.

Spelling Patterns: Recognize and Use Phonograms with a Vowel-Consonant-Silent e *(VCe) Pattern*

Connect Learning Across Contexts

Shared Reading You may wish to use the following Shared Reading title from *Fountas & Pinnell Classroom™* to point out phonograms with a vowel-consonant-silent *e* (VC*e*) pattern.

SR *Saving Cranes* by Brenda Iasevoli

Guided Reading During word work, write a few two-syllable words with the VC*e* pattern for students to take apart quickly.

Shared Writing As you construct a text, help students make a connection to words they know containing the same pattern.

Guided/Independent Writing Encourage students to think about the beginning and ending parts of two-syllable VC*e* words as a way to help them spell the words conventionally.

Extend Learning

- Repeat the lesson with other VC*e* phonograms. A blank word card template is available in Online Resources.
- Have students play Follow the Path with two-syllable VC*e* words. A blank game board template is available in Online Resources.

▶ Connect with Home

Have students take the word cards home to sort and read with family members.

Recognize and Use Phonograms That End with a Double Consonant (VCC)

Plan

▶ Consider Your Students

Use this lesson only if students need more experience with one-syllable words that end with a double consonant. If students are ready to apply their knowledge of double consonants to multisyllable words, use lesson SP 15.

▶ Working with English Language Learners

The more English language learners become familiar with the patterns of written language, the easier it will be for them to learn new words. Once they develop the concept of looking for patterns, they will actively try to connect words. You may need to show them how to do this active searching by demonstrating it and taking special care to point out patterns such as double letters in guided reading, shared reading, and shared writing. Be sure that students are noticing patterns in words that are already familiar to them. In the lesson, use words that English language learners have in their speaking or listening vocabularies and also have examined in written form.

YOU WILL NEED

PWS Ready Resources
- ▶ Lowercase Letter Cards

Online Resources
- ▶ SP 4 Action Tags
- ▶ SP 4 List Sheets

Other Materials
- ▶ magnetic letters
- ▶ blank chart paper

UNDERSTAND THE PRINCIPLE

Recognizing phonograms and other regular spelling patterns that appear in many words will help students understand that they can apply what they know about word structure to figure out new words. Students will also begin to understand that searching for and recognizing patterns are valuable to them as readers and writers. In this lesson, students learn to recognize that a double consonant can appear at the end of a word. While the sound of the vowel that precedes the double consonant is usually short, the sounds of the vowels *a, o,* and *u* are sometimes influenced by the consonant *l* (e.g., *small, toll, full*). Other variations include words such as *loss* and *off.*

EXPLAIN THE PRINCIPLE

Some words have a double consonant at the end. The sound of the vowel is usually short [the a *in* class, *the* e *in* bell, *the* i *in* hill, *the* u *in* puff].

Comprehensive Phonics, Spelling, and Word Study Guide

Refer to: page **35**, row **6**

ACTIVITY: WORD SORT

INSTRUCTIONAL PROCEDURE

NOTICE PARTS

See page 32 for detailed descriptions of Instructional Procedures.

EXPLAIN THE PRINCIPLE

Some words have a double consonant at the end. The sound of the vowel is usually short [the a in class, *the e in* bell, *the i in* hill, *the u in* puff].

Comprehensive Phonics, Spelling, and Word Study Guide

Refer to: page **35**, row **6**

gr<u>a</u>ss	sm<u>e</u>ll	ch<u>i</u>ll	str<u>o</u>ll	st<u>u</u>ff
small	dress	hiss	toss	pull
class	shell	spill	roll	fluff
add	mess	inn	floss	fuss
		miss	off	
			odd	

Teach

1. Across the top of a sheet of chart paper, write the words *grass, smell, chill, stroll,* and *stuff.* Have students read the words with you. Use any words students may not understand in a sentence.

2. *What do you notice about all of these words?* • *Each word ends with a double consonant.* If needed, draw students' attention to the vowel sounds. *Think about the vowel sounds. What do you notice?* • *The words* grass, smell, chill, *and* stuff *have a short vowel sound. The word* stroll *has a long vowel sound.* You may wish to underline the vowels *a, e, i, o,* and *u* in the words.

3. Invite students to say more words that end with double consonants. Have students sort the words based on the vowel. Write the words on the chart in the correct column.

4. Students will likely suggest some words with variant or long vowel sounds, such as *ball, roll,* and *full.* If such words are not represented, you may wish to add some examples to the chart.

5. Have students read each column of words. Help them generalize the principle based on their observations. *Some words have a double consonant at the end. The sound of the vowel is usually short, but not always.* • Highlight the words as students identify them. *What do you notice?* • *Words that have the vowels* a, o, *and* u *sometimes have other vowel sounds.*

6. Tell students that they will make, write, and read words that end with double consonants. Using letter cards or magnetic letters, demonstrate making a word and checking the spelling against the class chart. Explain that students will make a couple of words with each vowel. They will then write two words for each vowel on a list sheet, for a total of ten words.

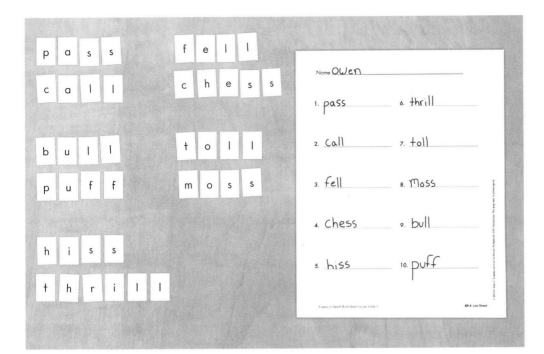

ACTIVITY: MAKE WORDS

INSTRUCTIONAL PROCEDURE

SAY AND SORT

See page 32 for detailed descriptions of Instructional Procedures.

ACTION TAGS

make words

write ten words

read words

Apply

- Distribute list sheets and magnetic letters. (You may also use letter cards from *Ready Resources*.)
- Remind students that they can use the class chart as a resource, but encourage them to make additional words that end with double consonants.
- In preparation for the group share, ask students to read the words on their list sheet to a partner.

Share

- In groups of four, have students take turns reading all the words on their list sheets. Add new words to the appropriate columns on the class chart as you reinforce the principle.
- Review the principle and remind students to notice phonograms that end with a double consonant (VCC) when they read and write.

Assess

- Ask individual students to use letter cards to make words with specific double consonant phonograms.
- Observe students as they read to determine whether they are noticing and using knowledge of double consonants to solve new words.
- You may wish to use Spelling Patterns Assessment A, B, C, or D.

Connect Learning Across Contexts

Shared Reading Read aloud poems that have words with double consonants. Have students locate and circle the words on their own copies of the poem. You may wish to use the following Shared Reading title from *Fountas & Pinnell Classroom*™ to locate one or two words with double consonant letters.

SR *From Buds to Bananas* by Betty Riggs

Guided Reading During word work, use magnetic letters or letter cards to make a few words containing double consonants. Talk with students about the vowel sounds they hear in the words.

Shared Writing Revisit completed pieces to identify and highlight words that have a double consonant at the end.

Guided/Independent Writing When conferring with students, help them spell words by using their knowledge of patterns, including words that end with double consonants.

Extend Learning

Give students additional list sheets, and ask them to "write around the room." They will record on the list sheet any words with double consonants (either at the end or in the middle of the word) that they find on the walls, charts, or books in the classroom.

▶ Connect with Home

Send home word cards with the double consonant pattern for students to sort and read to family members. A blank word card template is available in Online Resources.

Recognize and Use Phonograms with Ending Consonant Clusters (VCC)

Plan

▶ Consider Your Students

This lesson gives students the opportunity to act on and systematize their knowledge of word patterns by comparing the patterns with one another. Students should have familiarity with the VCC pattern and extensive experience sorting words. This lesson will be most effective if it follows lessons about other phonograms. The VCC patterns in this lesson include both consonant clusters and consonant digraphs. You can tailor the lesson to focus on phonograms with which students need more experience noticing and comparing.

▶ Working with English Language Learners

Working with the four phonograms *-and, -ent, -ink,* and *-ush* will allow you to select words that English language learners already have in their speaking or listening vocabularies. Be sure to take advantage of any names of class members that fit these patterns by including them as examples. Repeat the words many times, and work with English language learners in a small group the first time they say and sort words by pattern.

UNDERSTAND THE PRINCIPLE

Noticing parts of words (beginning letter or letters and the ending phonogram, or spelling pattern) makes it easier for students to break words apart in order to analyze them. It is important for students to notice that some phonograms include consonant clusters (in which each letter stands for a separate sound) and some phonograms include consonant digraphs (in which two letters together stand for a single sound that is different from either sound represented by the individual letters).

YOU WILL NEED

PWS Ready Resources
- ▶ SP 5 Pocket-Chart Cards

Online Resources
- ▶ SP 5 Action Tags
- ▶ SP 5 Word Cards
- ▶ SP 5 Four-Way Sorts
- ▶ SP 5 List Sheets

Other Materials
- ▶ pocket chart

Generative Lesson

A generative lesson has a simple structure that you can use to present similar content or concepts. Use this lesson structure to teach students a variety of phonograms with ending consonant clusters.

EXPLAIN THE PRINCIPLE

Some words have consonant clusters at the end. Sometimes the sounds of the two consonant letters are blended together [e.g., ma<u>sk</u>, lu<u>mp</u>]; other times the two consonant letters stand for one sound (digraph) [e.g., pa<u>th</u>, si<u>ng</u>].

Comprehensive Phonics, Spelling, and Word Study Guide

Refer to: page **35**, row **8**

ACTIVITY: WORD SORT

INSTRUCTIONAL PROCEDURE

SAY AND SORT

See page 32 for detailed descriptions of Instructional Procedures.

EXPLAIN THE PRINCIPLE

Some words have consonant clusters at the end. Sometimes the sounds of the two consonant letters are blended together [e.g., ma__sk__, lu__mp__]; other times the two consonant letters stand for one sound (digraph) [e.g., pa__th__, sin__g__].

Comprehensive Phonics, Spelling, and Word Study Guide

Refer to: page **35**, row **8**

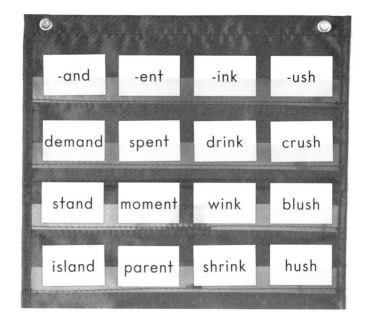

Teach

1. At the top of a pocket chart, display the patterns *-and, -ent, -ink,* and *-ush* as column heads. Explain that each pattern is a word part, and read the patterns to the students. Tell students that these are four spelling patterns at the end of words. Say the four patterns with students.

2. Place the word cards along the bottom of the pocket chart. Invite students to come to the chart one at a time, take a card, read the word to the class, and place it in the appropriate column.

3. After the words are sorted, have students read the lists of words. *What do you notice about these words and patterns?* • Listen for comments that provide evidence that students are recognizing, comparing, and using the phonograms in their analysis of the words, for example:

   "Each ending part has three letters, one vowel and two consonants."

   "Some of the consonants make two sounds, but some of the consonants just stand for one sound."

   "I can hear the *n* sound in *-ent,* but the letter *n* in *-ink* sounds different."

   "The letters *sh* stand for the /sh/ sound."

   "You can make a lot of different words by changing the letter at the beginning."

   "*Island* sounds slightly different from *-and.*"

4. Build on students' observations to summarize the principle. *Some words have patterns with consonant clusters at the end. Sometimes the sounds of the two consonant letters are blended together, as in* -and *and* -ent. *Other times the two consonant letters stand for one sound, as in* -ink *and* -ush.

5. Tell students that today they are going to say, sort, read, and write words with the patterns *-and, -ent, -ink,* and *-ush.* They will say the word on each card and place the card in the correct column on the four-way sort. After sorting all of the words, students read the words in each column to a partner and write examples on a list sheet.

INSTRUCTIONAL PROCEDURE

SAY AND SORT

See page 32 for detailed descriptions of Instructional Procedures.

ACTION TAGS

say words
sort words
read words
write words

Apply

Have students say the words, sort the word cards on the four-way sort, and then read the lists of words to a partner. Partners can help each other make adjustments if they discover that a word is in the wrong column. Students then write examples from their sort on a list sheet.

Share

- Invite students to read several words that they wrote on their list sheets.
- Review the principle and remind students to notice phonograms with ending consonants clusters (VCC) when they read and write.

Assess

- Dictate eight words, two with each phonogram, to determine which patterns students control in their writing and which patterns they need to work with more.
- Notice whether students use the phonograms to solve words when they are reading.
- You may wish to use Spelling Patterns Assessment A, B, C, or D.

Spelling Patterns: Recognize and Use Phonograms with Ending Consonant Clusters (VCC)

Connect Learning Across Contexts

Shared Reading Display a poem that includes words with final consonant clusters and digraphs. Cover the phonograms on the first reading of the text, and ask students to predict the patterns. Then show the words. You may wish to use the following Shared Reading title from *Fountas & Pinnell Classroom*™ to highlight one or two ending consonant clusters or digraphs after reading.

SR *From Beans to Chocolate* by June Schwartz

Guided Reading On a whiteboard, write a variety of words containing the VCC pattern. Ask students to read the words quickly to develop quick recognition of the patterns.

Shared Writing As you write a new word containing a VCC pattern, have students think of another word like it. You may want to show the relationship between the words quickly on chart paper or a whiteboard.

Guided/Independent Writing Teach students how to use phonograms they know to check the spelling of words they have written.

Extend Learning

- Repeat the lesson with other phonograms that end with the VCC pattern. A list of common phonograms, word card templates, and blank sorts and list sheets are available in Online Resources.

- Have students sort the word cards by new criteria that they establish. For example, students might choose to sort words by vowel or by initial letter. Encourage students to read each group of words to a partner and then have the partner guess the criteria upon which the words were sorted.

▶ Connect with Home

Send home sets of word cards for students to sort and read with family members.

Recognize and Use Phonograms with a Double Vowel (VVC)

Plan

▶ Consider Your Students

In this lesson, students learn to notice *ee* and *oo* as a double vowel that is often followed by a consonant in a large number of words. They learn that sometimes a double vowel sounds like the name of the vowel, for example the *ee* in *feed,* and sometimes the double vowel represents other sounds, for example the *oo* in *good* or *room*. This lesson best follows lessons on common phonograms that have consistent letter-sound relationships. It helps students attend to the sequence of letters in words and quickly recognize them.

▶ Working with English Language Learners

English language learners need a large core of known words as well as systems for learning words. If they try to remember each word separately, they will not develop efficient word-solving systems. It is important for them to develop their ability to search for and find patterns. They may need many explicit demonstrations of noticing patterns in words. While they may see the patterns, the words may not be meaningful and/or they may not know how to pronounce the words. Say the words clearly and have students repeat them as many times as needed while you also write them on a small whiteboard. Be sure that students understand the meaning of the words you select as examples.

UNDERSTAND THE PRINCIPLE

Some vowel combinations have double letters, such as *ee* and *oo*. The double vowels appear in a number of common phonograms, making them valuable for students to notice and remember. Once children understand that certain vowels often appear together in words and they know to look for specific patterns, they can apply this information to read text and spell words with increased efficiency and accuracy.

YOU WILL NEED

PWS Ready Resources
- ▶ **SP 6** Pocket-Chart Cards

Online Resources
- ▶ **SP 6** Action Tags
- ▶ **SP 6** Word Cards
- ▶ **SP 6** Two-Way Sorts

Other Materials
- ▶ pocket chart

Generative Lesson ✓
A generative lesson has a simple structure that you can use to present similar content or concepts. Use this lesson structure to teach students a variety of phonograms with a double vowel.

EXPLAIN THE PRINCIPLE

Some words have a double vowel followed by a consonant.

Sometimes a double vowel sounds like the name of the vowel (long sound) [e.g., ee in feed, ee in seem].

Sometimes a double vowel stands for other vowel sounds [e.g., oo in good, oo in room].

Comprehensive Phonics, Spelling, and Word Study Guide

Refer to:
Page **35**, row **7**

ACTIVITY: POCKET CHART

INSTRUCTIONAL PROCEDURE

SAY AND SORT

See page 32 for detailed descriptions of Instructional Procedures.

EXPLAIN THE PRINCIPLE

Some words have a double vowel followed by a consonant.

Sometimes a double vowel sounds like the name of the vowel (long sound) [e.g., ee in feed, ee in seem].

Sometimes a double vowel stands for other vowel sounds [e.g., oo in good, oo in room].

Comprehensive Phonics, Spelling, and Word Study Guide

Refer to: page **35**, row **7**

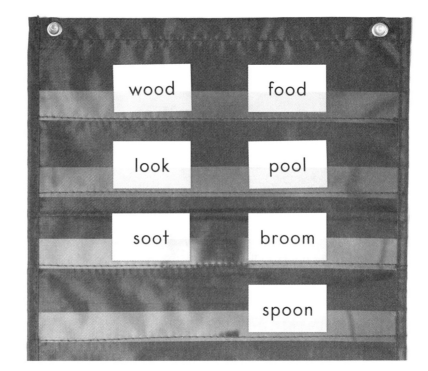

Teach

1. Place *feed, heel, screen, sweep, steer, meet* in the pocket chart. Have students read the words with you. Use any words students may not understand in a sentence.

2. *What do you notice about all of the words?* ● Students will likely notice that they all have a double *e* followed by a consonant. *What do you notice about the vowel sound?* ● *All the words have the long* e *vowel sound.*

3. Remove these word cards and insert *wood, food, look, pool, broom, spoon,* and *soot* in random order in the chart. Read the words with students.

4. *What do you notice about all of the words?* ● Students will likely notice that the words all have the double vowel *oo* followed by a consonant. As needed, prompt students to continue to think about the words. *What are some ways that we can sort the words?* ● Allow time for children to notice that the words can be sorted into two groups by vowel sound. Place the words *wood* and *food* at the top of the chart as column heads. You may wish to underline or highlight the double vowel *oo* in each word to emphasize that students are sorting by the sounds that these letters stand for. Have students sort the remaining words.

5. Have students read each column of words. Build on their earlier observations to explain the principle. *As you noticed, some words have a double vowel followed by a consonant. Sometimes the double vowel sounds like the name of the vowel, such as the letters* ee *in seek. Sometimes the double vowel stands for vowel sounds that are different from the long or short sound of the letter, such as the letters* oo *in wood and the letters* oo *in food.*

6. Tell children that today they are going to sort and write words based on their vowel sound. Once the words are sorted, students read the words in each group to a partner and then write examples from each group on a two-way sort.

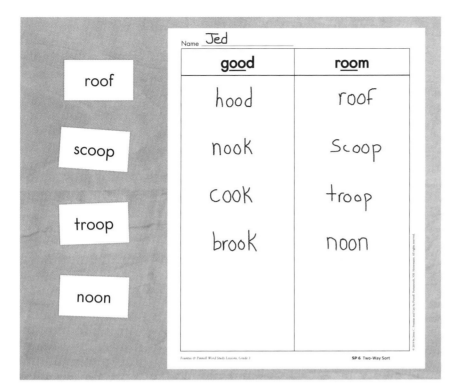

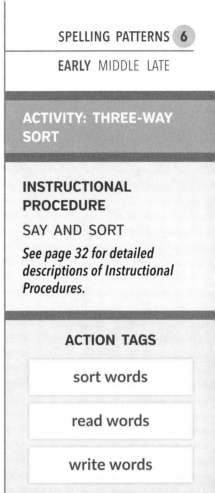

INSTRUCTIONAL PROCEDURE

SAY AND SORT

See page 32 for detailed descriptions of Instructional Procedures.

ACTION TAGS

sort words

read words

write words

Apply

Remind students to read the words they have sorted to a partner. Encourage them to talk about words they know that would fit in each category.

Share

- Have students read their three columns of words to a different partner.
- Invite students to suggest two or three more words to add to each column of the chart.

Assess

- As students read texts, observe how quickly they read phonograms with double vowel patterns.
- Notice how well students' written work reflects their control of double vowel phonogram patterns.
- Notice their use of patterns in two-syllable words, such as *succeed* or *cartoon*.
- You may wish to use Spelling Patterns Assessment A, B, C, or D.

Spelling Patterns: Recognize and Use Phonograms with a Double Vowel (VVC)

Connect Learning Across Contexts

Shared Reading Read a variety of poems with double vowel phonograms. After enjoying the text, write a few words with double vowels on the whiteboard and have students highlight the pattern with a marker. You may wish to use the following nonfiction Shared Reading title from *Fountas & Pinnell Classroom*™ to complete this task.

　　SR *Far Above Earth: A Day on the Space Station* by Jane Simon

Guided Reading As students try to solve unknown words, prompt them to notice and use spelling patterns. Ask, "Do you know another word like that?" or "Do you see a part that can help you?"

Shared Writing Prompt students to think of a word with the *ee*-consonant or *oo*-consonant patterns to write new words with the same pattern.

Guided/Independent Writing During the editing process, encourage students to check words that fit double vowel patterns they know.

Extend Learning

- Create a Follow the Path game with words with the *ee* or *oo* vowel pattern. Blank game boards are available in Online Resources.

- Repeat the lesson with words that have more than one syllable, e.g., *seesaw, beetle, birdseed, weekend, afternoon, classroom, moonlight, raccoon, bookshelf, footsteps, cookies, lookout.*

▶ Connect with Home

Send home a set of word cards for students to read and sort with family members.

Recognize and Use Phonograms with Vowel Combinations

Plan

▶ Consider Your Students

In this lesson, students work with a variety of vowel patterns. They learn that sometimes a vowel combination sounds like the name of the first vowel, for example *oa* in *soak,* and sometimes the vowel combination represents other sounds, for example the *oi* in *boil*. There are many vowel combinations, such as *ai, ea, oa, ie, oi,* and *ou.* You may wish to tailor this lesson by focusing on vowel combinations with which your students need additional experience.

▶ Working with English Language Learners

English language learners need a large core of known words as well as systems for learning words. If they try to remember each word separately, they will not develop efficient word-solving systems. It is important for them to develop their ability to search for and find patterns. This lesson focuses on some of the more complex vowel combinations that may pose spelling and pronunciation challenges. Say the words clearly and have students repeat them as many times as needed while you also write them on a small whiteboard. Be sure that students understand the meaning of the words you select as examples.

UNDERSTAND THE PRINCIPLE

Vowel combinations are also called vowel digraphs, vowel pairs, and vowel teams. Most vowel combinations have consistent letter-sound relationships and appear in a number of common phonograms, making them valuable for students to notice and remember. Once students understand that certain vowels often appear together in words and they know how to look for specific patterns, they can apply this information to read text and spell words with increased efficiency and accuracy.

YOU WILL NEED

Online Resources
- ▶ SP 7 Action Tags
- ▶ SP 7 Word Ladders
- ▶ SP 7 Word Cards

Other Materials
- ▶ magnetic whiteboard
- ▶ magnetic letters

Generative Lesson ✓
A generative lesson has a simple structure that you can use to present similar content or concepts. Use this lesson structure to teach students a variety of phonograms with vowel combinations.

EXPLAIN THE PRINCIPLE

Some words have two vowels together (vowel combination).

Sometimes a vowel combination sounds like the name of the first vowel [e.g., stream, road].

Sometimes a vowel combination stands for other sounds [e.g., soil, hour].

Comprehensive Phonics, Spelling, and Word Study Guide

Refer to:
Page **35**, row **9**

Spelling Patterns: Recognize and Use Phonograms with Vowel Combinations (VVC)

ACTIVITY: MAKE AND SORT WORDS

INSTRUCTIONAL PROCEDURE

SAY AND SORT

See page 32 for detailed descriptions of Instructional Procedures.

EXPLAIN THE PRINCIPLE

Some words have two vowels together (vowel combination).

Sometimes a vowel combination sounds like the name of the first vowel [e.g., stream, road].

Sometimes a vowel combination stands for other sounds [e.g., soil, hour].

Comprehensive Phonics, Spelling, and Word Study Guide

Refer to: page **35**, row **9**

Teach

1. On a magnetic whiteboard, make the words *sneak, peak,* and *weak* with magnetic letters. Use any words students may not understand in a sentence.

2. *What do you notice about all of the words?* • Students will likely notice that they all end with *-eak. What do you notice about the vowel sound?* • All the words have the long e vowel sound. The vowel sound is the name of the first vowel, /ē/, the long e sound.

3. Ask students to continue changing the beginning letter or letters to make more words with the *-eak* spelling pattern. Write the words in the column.

4. Repeat the process with additional phonograms, such as *-oak, -oat, -ail,* and *-ied*.

5. Then build the words *oil, foil,* and *soil. What do you notice about the words?* • Students will likely notice that they all end with *-oil. What do you notice about the vowel sound?* • The vowel combination stands for a different vowel sound than the long or short sound of either vowel.

6. Repeat for words with *-out,* such as *spout, scout,* and *trout*.

7. Build on students' observations to summarize the principle. *As you noticed, some words have two vowels together. They're called a vowel combination. Sometimes the combination sounds like the name of the first vowel. Sometimes it stands for a different sound.*

8. Tell students that they will choose four words and make word ladders by changing the beginning letter or letters. Demonstrate how to make word ladders. Write one word and change the beginning to write another word. The letters added or changed must be consecutive in the words: e.g., *ouch, couch, grouch, slouch, pouch, vouch.*

Name Dean

soil	shout
spoil	out
broil	scout
boil	sprout
coil	snout
toil	pout
foil	

bean	main
mean	pain
clean	chain
lean	rain
dean	stain
	plain
	brain

Fountas & Pinnell Word Study Lessons, Grade 3   SP 7 Word Ladders

ACTIVITY: WORD LADDERS

INSTRUCTIONAL PROCEDURE

NOTICE PARTS

See page 32 for detailed descriptions of Instructional Procedures.

ACTION TAGS

write word

change letters

write new word

underline vowel combination

Apply

Have students make word ladders. Remind them that all the words on a ladder should have the same vowel combination pattern. Only the beginning letter or letters will change.

Share

■ Have students read their word ladders to a partner.

■ Invite students to share a few words from their word ladders. Add them to the class chart.

Assess

■ As students read texts, observe how quickly they read phonograms with vowel combination patterns.

■ Notice how well students' written work reflects their control of vowel combination patterns.

■ Dictate five or six words with vowel combination patterns, and have students write them.

■ You may wish to use Spelling Patterns Assessment A, B, C, or D.

Spelling Patterns: Recognize and Use Phonograms with Vowel Combinations (VVC)

Connect Learning Across Contexts

Shared Reading After rereading books, quickly write down a few words with vowel combination patterns on a whiteboard. Have students underline the vowel combinations and read the words. You may wish to use the following Shared Reading title from *Fountas & Pinnell Classroom*™.

> SR *Far Above Earth: A Day on the Space Station* by Jane Simon

Guided Reading Help students use their knowledge of word patterns. Ask, "Do you know another word like that?" or "Do you know the last part?" or "Do you see a part that you know?"

Shared Writing Prompt students to think of a familiar word with a vowel combination pattern to write new words with the same pattern: e.g., *You know the word* sound. *Can you write the word* pound?

Guided/Independent Writing Draw students' attention to VVC words that they have spelled accurately. Encourage students to talk about what they knew and what they did that helped them write the word.

Extend Learning

- Repeat the lesson, focusing on different vowel combinations.
- Repeat the lesson with words that have more than one syllable, e.g., *rainbow, season, oily, oatmeal.*

▶ Connect with Home

Send home word cards and a word ladder sheet (see Online Resources), and have students make word ladders with family members. Encourage them to choose different words than the ones they used in the Apply activity.

Recognize and Use Phonogram Patterns with a Long Vowel Sound in Single-Syllable Words

Plan

▶ Consider Your Students

This lesson will be appropriate for students who have experience noticing and working with beginning letters and ending spelling patterns. You can use this lesson several times, focusing on words with long vowel sounds with which students need more experience. You will not need to teach all phonograms in formal lessons. By third grade, students likely will have discovered many patterns for themselves. Be sure that students are not overly dependent on spelling patterns. Noticing and recognizing phonograms should be only one part of a flexible repertoire of word-solving actions.

▶ Working with English Language Learners

English learners may need many more encounters with words in order to learn them, because they may not have yet developed efficient decoding systems. Explicitly demonstrate making words. If you have students who have minimal English vocabularies, limit this activity to words they know well, and help them to make these words. More experienced English language learners should already be accustomed to looking for patterns in words. For these students, review the concept of phonograms, and gradually increase the number of patterns with which they are working.

YOU WILL NEED

 **Ready Resources**
- ▶ SP 8 Pocket-Chart Cards

Online Resources
- ▶ SP 8 Action Tags
- ▶ SP 8 Word Cards
- ▶ SP 8 List Sheets

Other Materials
- ▶ pocket chart

Generative Lesson

A generative lesson has a simple structure that you can use to present similar content or concepts. Use this lesson structure to teach students a variety of phonograms that have long vowel sounds.

UNDERSTAND THE PRINCIPLE

Many long vowel patterns are highly predictable. They have consistent letter-sound relationships that are valuable for students to notice and remember. Once students know to look for specific patterns, they can apply this information to read text and spell words with increased efficiency and accuracy. Making and comparing words according to a variety of features, including long vowel patterns, will heighten students' awareness of word parts and patterns and increase their flexibility in working with words.

EXPLAIN THE PRINCIPLE

Some words have a long vowel pattern. You can hear the long vowel sound [e.g., make, green, pie, coat, cute].

 Comprehensive Phonics, Spelling, and Word Study Guide

Refer to:
Page **36**, row **12**

ACTIVITY: POCKET CHART

INSTRUCTIONAL PROCEDURE

NOTICE PARTS

See page 32 for detailed descriptions of Instructional Procedures.

EXPLAIN THE PRINCIPLE

Some words have a long vowel pattern. You can hear the long vowel sound [e.g., make, green, pie, coat, cute].

Comprehensive Phonics, Spelling, and Word Study Guide

Refer to: page **36**, row **12**

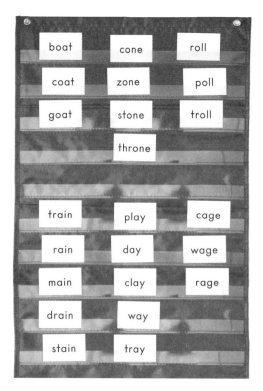

Teach

1. Place the words *boat, coat,* and *goat* in in a pocket chart. Have students read the words with you. *What do you notice about all of these words?* Students may notice that the words rhyme and that all three words end in the same letters.

2. Repeat this process for words with the *-one* and *-oll* pattern. Discuss what students notice about the vowel sound in all of these words. *All of these words have the /ō/ sound.*

3. Clear the chart and repeat the process with words having *-ain, -ay,* and *-age.* Encourage students to compare the spelling patterns and share their thinking.

4. Have students take turns choosing a column and reading the words in it. Then build on students' observations to review the principle: *Some words have a long vowel pattern. You can hear the long vowel sound.*

5. Explain to students that they will make words with long vowel patterns. Demonstrate the process of making words using beginning consonant and ending spelling pattern word cards. Tell students that they will make twenty words with long vowel patterns and write the words on a list sheet. Encourage them to make several words for each spelling pattern. Then they will read their list to a partner.

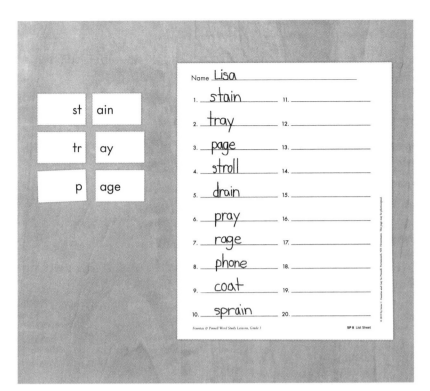

ACTIVITY: MAKE WORDS

INSTRUCTIONAL PROCEDURE
NOTICE PARTS
See page 32 for detailed descriptions of Instructional Procedures.

ACTION TAGS

make words
write twenty words
read words

Apply

Have students make words. Remind them to double-check that each word that they make is a real word. They may use a children's dictionary or check with a partner if they are unsure.

Share

- Have students read a few words from their lists. You may wish to add a few examples to a class word wall or spelling pattern chart.
- Review the principle and remind students to notice phonogram patterns with a long vowel sound in single-syllable words when they read and write.

Assess

- As you read students' writing, make note of the long vowel patterns that are challenging so that you can use them in lessons.
- Dictate six to ten words with long vowel patterns as a quick assessment. Notice how quickly students write the vowel patterns.
- You may wish to use Spelling Patterns Assessment A, B, C, or D.

Spelling Patterns: Recognize and Use Phonogram Patterns with a Long Vowel Sound in Single-Syllable Words

Connect Learning Across Contexts

Shared Reading You may wish to use the following Shared Reading title from *Fountas & Pinnell Classroom*™ to point out phonogram patterns with a long vowel sound in single-syllable words.

　SR *Exploring Underground* by Louis Petrone

Guided Reading When students come to unknown words, prompt them to use the pattern by thinking of other words they know: e.g., "Do you know another word that ends like that?"

Shared Writing Guide students to use spelling patterns they know to help them write an unknown word. Revisit completed pieces to search for words containing specific patterns that you are reviewing.

Guided/Independent Writing Prompt students to use patterns they know to check the spelling of words.

This word sounds the same as stain *at the end. What pattern do you know in* stain? *Can you use that pattern here?*

Extend Learning

- Have students do a blind sort with the words they made for the Apply activity. Check that they have sorted the words by the long vowel spelling pattern.

- Have students play Follow the Path with words that have patterns that you wish to review. Blank game boards are available in Online Resources.

▶ Connect with Home

Have students read their word lists to a family member. Challenge them to think of one or two additional words for each spelling pattern.

Recognize and Use Phonogram Patterns with the /ü/ Vowel Sound in Single-Syllable Words

Plan

▶ Consider Your Students

Some students may think that the /ü/ sound is regular (as in *cute*). In fact, representations of /ü/ are highly varied. There are twenty-nine different spelling patterns that represent the /ü/ sound. You can choose to focus on three or four patterns or all of them, depending on students' strengths and needs. You may wish to work with the patterns that have a vowel, consonant and *e* together as a group.

▶ Working with English Language Learners

The complex range of spellings in this lesson may be difficult for English language learners. Be sure that they can read and understand the words that you use as examples. Have students review examples of words with the /ü/ sound. They may be surprised to find so many different spellings related to this sound and also that there is a slight variation in pronunciation (*moon, cute*). Consider having them begin with words having the vowel-consonant-silent *e* pattern. During word work, create a chart that students can read together and reference as they encounter new words in texts.

YOU WILL NEED

PWS **Ready Resources**
▶ SP 9 Pocket-Chart Cards

Online Resources
▶ SP 9 Action Tags
▶ SP 9 Word Cards
▶ SP 9 Word Pairs Sheet

Other Materials
▶ pocket chart

Generative Lesson

A generative lesson has a simple structure that you can use to present similar content or concepts. Use this lesson structure to teach students a variety of phonograms that have the /ü/ vowel sound.

UNDERSTAND THE PRINCIPLE

Many long vowel patterns are highly predictable. However, the long sound of *u* is varied, both in pronunciation and spelling. The pronunciation can be /ü/, as in *tune* or *suit,* or /yü/, as in *mule.* It can be represented by twenty-nine different letter patterns. Many of the patterns are constructed with a vowel, consonant, and *e* (*fuse, cure*). However, words can also end with *o* (*to, who*) or two *o*'s (*too*) and represent the same sound. Once students know to look for specific patterns, they can apply this information to read text and spell words with increased efficiency and accuracy.

EXPLAIN THE PRINCIPLE

Some words have the /ü/ vowel sound as in moon. *Several patterns of letters can stand for the /ü/ sound [e.g.,* flew, do, zoo, soup*].*

Comprehensive Phonics, Spelling, and Word Study Guide

Refer to:
Page **36**, row **13**

EARLY MIDDLE **LATE**

INSTRUCTIONAL PROCEDURE

NOTICE PARTS

See page 32 for detailed descriptions of Instructional Procedures.

EXPLAIN THE PRINCIPLE

Some words have the /ü/ vowel sound as in moon. *Several patterns of letters can stand for the /ü/ sound [e.g.,* flew, do, zoo, soup].

Comprehensive Phonics, Spelling, and Word Study Guide

Refer to: page **36**, row **13**

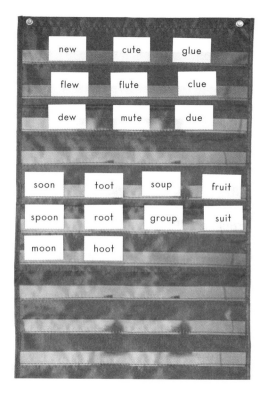

Teach

1. Place the words *new, flew, dew; glue, clue, due;* and *soup, group* randomly in the pocket chart. Have students read the words with you. *What do you notice about all of these words?* • Some example responses might be:

    "Some of the words rhyme."

    "Some of the words have the same ending letters."

    "All of the words have the /ü/ sound."

    "Even though the words have different letters, the vowel sound is the same."

2. Invite a couple of students up to the pocket chart to organize the words by the ending letters: *-ew, -ue, -oup.*

3. Continue the process by adding more patterns and examples to the chart using the reusable blank pocket-chart cards from *Ready Resources.* You may wish to use patterns such as *-ood, -oof, -ool, -oom, -oon,* or *-oot.* Encourage students to compare the spelling patterns and share their thinking.

4. Guide students to understand the principle: *Some words have the /ü/ vowel sound as in* moon. *Several patterns of letters can stand for the /ü/ sound.*

5. Explain to students that they will make words using /ü/ spelling patterns. Demonstrate the process of making words using beginning consonant and ending spelling pattern word cards. Students will use the word parts to make fifteen different words and then write them on the left column of a word pairs sheet. In the right column, they write another word with the same pattern and then underline the /ü/ pattern in each.

ACTIVITY: MAKE WORDS

INSTRUCTIONAL PROCEDURE

NOTICE PARTS

See page 32 for detailed descriptions of Instructional Procedures.

ACTION TAGS

make word
write word
write another word
underline
read

Name **Reneé**

proof	→	roof
crude	→	rude
school	→	tool
groom	→	gloom
bloom	→	room
screw	→	chew
fruit	→	suit
scoot	→	hoot
brood	→	mood
noon	→	soon
hoop	→	snoop
scoop	→	coop
cue	→	clue
glue	→	true
blue	→	due

Fountas & Pinnell Word Study Lessons, Grade 3

SP 9 Word Pairs Sheet

© 2019 by Irene C. Fountas and Gay Su Pinnell. Portsmouth, NH: Heinemann. This page may be photocopied.

Apply

Have students make words. Remind them to double-check that each word that they make is a real word. They may use a children's dictionary or check with a partner if they are unsure.

Share

- Invite each student to read a word pair from his list as you write the words on a chart and underline the pattern that represents the /ü/ sound.
- Have students say words slowly to hear the very small differences in the pronunciation of the vowel sound in words like *suit, cute,* and *cure.* Invite them to discuss the similarity in pronunciation as well as the differences.

Assess

- Dictate six to ten words with /ü/ spelling patterns as a quick assessment. Notice how quickly students write the vowel patterns.
- Give students a list of about twenty words that includes (mixed with others) a variety of six to ten words with /ü/ patterns. They read the words and circle those that have the /ü/ sound.
- You may wish to use Spelling Patterns Assessment A, B, C, or D.

Spelling Patterns: Recognize and Use Phonogram Patterns with the /ü/ Vowel Sound in Single-Syllable Words

Connect Learning Across Contexts

Shared Reading You may wish to use the following Shared Reading title from *Fountas & Pinnell Classroom™* to point out phonogram patterns with the /ü/ vowel sound in single-syllable words.

> *From Buds to Bananas* by Betty Riggs

Guided Reading During word work, have students use magnetic letters to make four or five words with /ü/. Then have them write the words.

Shared Writing Guide students to use spelling patterns they know to help them write an unknown word. Revisit completed pieces to search for words containing /ü/ patterns that you are reviewing.

Guided/Independent Writing Prompt students to use patterns they know to check the spelling of words. *This word sounds the same as* new *at the end. What pattern do you know in* new? *Can you use that pattern here?*

Extend Learning

- Repeat this lesson with a different selection of spelling patterns.
- Give children three key words to write on the top of a three-way sort. Have them write as many words as they can with the same pattern as each key word.

▶ Connect with Home

Have students read their word lists to a family member. Have them read the words aloud several times to family members to increase their speed in recognition. Challenge them to think of one or two additional words for each spelling pattern.

Recognize and Use Phonogram Patterns with the /ù/ Vowel Sound in Single-Syllable Words

Plan

▶ Consider Your Students

This lesson will be most effective if students understand that the sounds connected to vowels can vary. The letters and letter patterns that students will encounter in this lesson, *oo, ou,* and *u,* can stand for other vowel sounds, but this lesson will focus on words in which they stand for the /ù/ sound.

▶ Working with English Language Learners

Depending on their first languages, English language learners may find it difficult to pronounce the /ù/ sound. Accept approximate pronunciations, pointing out that English has more vowel sounds than most languages so it takes time to learn them all. Begin with words that will be familiar to most English language learners. Be sure to review all of the words on the game board before they play the game.

YOU WILL NEED

Online Resources
- ▶ **SP 10** Action Tags
- ▶ **SP 10** Follow the Path Game Boards
- ▶ **SP 10** List Sheets
- ▶ **SP 10** Directions for Follow the Path

Other Materials
- ▶ blank chart paper
- ▶ game die
- ▶ game markers

Generative Lesson

A generative lesson has a simple structure that you can use to present similar content or concepts. Use this lesson structure to teach students a variety of phonograms that have the /ù/ vowel sound.

UNDERSTAND THE PRINCIPLE

Some letter combinations represent more than one vowel sound. For example, the vowel pair *oo* represents a longer sound, as in *moon,* and a shorter sound, as in *book.* The /ù/ sound can also be represented by *ou,* as in *should,* and *u,* as in *push.* Because spelling patterns can often stand for more than one sound, make sure students are not becoming overly dependent them. Noticing and recognizing phonograms should be only one part of a flexible repertoire of word-solving actions.

EXPLAIN THE PRINCIPLE

Some words have the /ù/ vowel sound as in book.

Several patterns of letters can stand for the /ù/ vowel sound [e.g., good, pull*].*

Comprehensive Phonics, Spelling, and Word Study Guide

Refer to: Page **36**, row **14**

ACTIVITY: WORD LISTS

INSTRUCTIONAL PROCEDURE

NOTICE PARTS

See page 32 for detailed descriptions of Instructional Procedures.

EXPLAIN THE PRINCIPLE

Some words have the /ù/ vowel sound as in book.

Several patterns of letters can stand for the /ù/ vowel sound [e.g., good, pull].

Comprehensive Phonics, Spelling, and Word Study Guide

Refer to:
page **36**, row **13**

good
hood
wood

look
book

could
should

bull
pull

Teach

1. Tell students that they are going to learn more about spelling patterns.

2. Place the following words, at random, in a pocket chart: *good, hood, wood; look, book; could, should;* and *bull, pull.* Read the words aloud with students.

3. *What do you notice about all of these words?* • Some example responses might be:

   "Some of the words rhyme."

   "Some of the words have the same ending letters."

   "All of the words have the /ù/ sound."

4. Invite a couple of students up to the pocket chart to organize the words by the ending letters: *-ood, -ook, -ould,* and *-ull.*

5. Encourage students to think of more examples that fit the patterns, and add the words to the appropriate columns.

6. *What is the same in all of these words?* • *They all have vowel sound /ù/. What is different?* • *The vowel sound is spelled differently in each column. Several patterns of letters can stand for the /ù/ vowel sound.*

7. Tell students that today they are going to play Follow the Path. Taking turns, they will toss a die, move that number of spaces, read aloud the word in the new space, and use the word in a sentence. They go back to the space they were on if they can't read the word correctly and use it in a sentence. The first player to reach "finish" wins the game. Students will then write examples of each pattern on a list sheet.

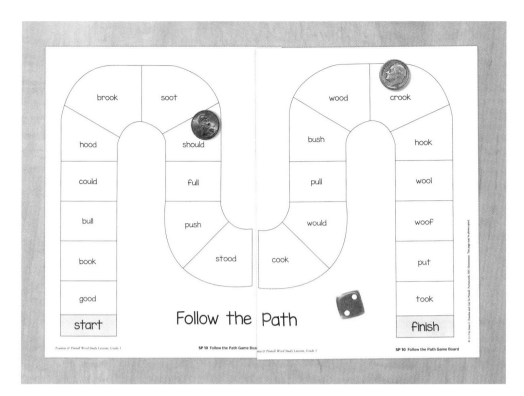

ACTIVITY: FOLLOW THE PATH

INSTRUCTIONAL PROCEDURE

NOTICE PARTS

See page 32 for detailed descriptions of Instructional Procedures.

ACTION TAGS

toss die

move

read word

use in a sentence

write on list sheet

Apply

- Have students play Follow the Path in pairs or groups of three using a game board, a game die, and game pieces to mark their places on the board.

- Then have students write words that represent each pattern on a list sheet.

Share

- Invite students to suggest more words with each pattern to add to the class chart.

- Review the principle and remind students to notice phonogram patterns with the /ù/ vowel sound in single-syllable words when they read and write.

Assess

- Dictate six to ten words with /ù/ spelling patterns while they are reading aloud. Notice their control and use of the spelling pattern to solve words.

- Observe students solving words with /ù/ spelling patterns.

- You may wish to use Spelling Patterns Assessment A, B, C, or D.

Spelling Patterns: Recognize and Use Phonogram Patterns with the /ù/ Vowel Sound in Single-Syllable Words

Connect Learning Across Contexts

Shared Reading You may wish to use the following Shared Reading title from *Fountas & Pinnell Classroom*™ to point out phonogram patterns with the /ù/ vowel sound in single-syllable words.

 *From Buds to Bananas* by Betty Riggs

Guided Reading When students come to difficult words, encourage them to use patterns they know. Ask, "Do you know another word like that?"

Shared Writing Guide students to use spelling patterns they know to help them write an unknown word. Revisit completed pieces to search for words containing /ù/ patterns that you are reviewing.

Guided/Independent Writing Prompt students to use patterns they know to check the spelling of words. *This word sounds the same as* foot *at the end. What pattern do you know in* foot? *Can you use that pattern here?*

Extend Learning

■ Distribute blank Follow the Path game boards (found in Online Resources), and have students work together to create boards with new sets of words with spelling patterns for the /ù/ vowel sound. Make the additional boards available for students to choose when playing the game.

■ Repeat the lesson with words that have two syllables: *cookbook, rosebush, wooden,* and *bookworm.*

▶ ## Connect with Home

Send Follow the Path game boards home so that students can play the game with family members.

Recognize and Use Phonogram Patterns with the /ȯ/ Vowel Sound (as in *saw*) in Single-Syllable Words

Plan

▶ Consider Your Students

In this lesson, students work with a variety of phonogram patterns, some of which are phonetically irregular and more complex. If students have good control over regular phonogram patterns, such as *-ong* and *-oss,* you may wish to focus on irregular phonogram patterns, such as *-aught.* The pronunciation of /ȯ/ is often similar to the pronunciation of /ŏ/. Have students focus on connecting their own pronunciation with the spelling, not on differentiating between the sounds.

▶ Working with English Language Learners

By the time you use this lesson, English language learners should be familiar with the concept of patterns in words and should have plenty of experience noticing and identifying them. If they are still having trouble connecting words by patterns, focus only on the regular patterns. Help make the meanings of example words clear, and discard any examples they find difficult to understand.

YOU WILL NEED

PWS Ready Resources
▸ **SP 11** Pocket-Chart Cards

Online Resources
▸ **SP 11** Action Tags
▸ **SP 11** Game Cards
▸ **SP 11** Directions for Concentration

Other Materials
▸ pocket chart

Generative Lesson

A generative lesson has a simple structure that you can use to present similar content or concepts. Use this lesson structure to teach students a variety of phonograms that have the /ȯ/ vowel sound.

UNDERSTAND THE PRINCIPLE

Phonogram patterns are very useful to readers and writers. Once students know to look for specific patterns, they can apply this information to read text and spell words with increased efficiency and accuracy. All of the spelling patterns in this lesson include the /ȯ/ sound, though the pattern may be phonetically regular (*ost, ong*) or may have a more complex letter sound relationship (*all, aw, alk, aught, ought*). Learning to work with both regular and irregular patterns will increase students' flexibility in working with words.

EXPLAIN THE PRINCIPLE

Some words have the /ȯ/ vowel sound as in saw.

*Several patterns of letters can stand for the /ȯ/ vowel sound [e.g., w*all*, p*aw*, c*ost].*

Comprehensive Phonics, Spelling, and Word Study Guide

Refer to: Page **36**, row **15**

Spelling Patterns: Recognize and Use Phonogram Patterns with the /ȯ/ Vowel Sound (as in saw*) in Single-Syllable Words*

193

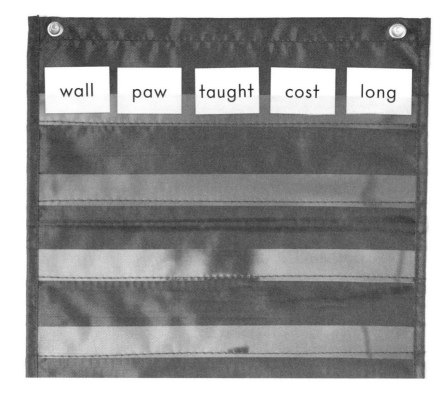

ACTIVITY: POCKET CHART

INSTRUCTIONAL PROCEDURE

NOTICE PARTS

See page 32 for detailed descriptions of Instructional Procedures.

EXPLAIN THE PRINCIPLE

Some words have the /ȯ/ vowel sound as in saw.

Several patterns of letters can stand for the /ȯ/ vowel sound [e.g., wall, paw, cost].

Comprehensive Phonics, Spelling, and Word Study Guide

Refer to: page **36**, row **14**

Teach

1. Place *wall, paw, taught, cost, long* in the first row of a pocket chart. Have students read the words with you.

2. *What do you notice about all of these words?* • Allow time for students to notice that they all have the /ȯ/ sound. If needed, provide this prompt: *What vowel sound do you hear in these words?* • Each word has the /ȯ/ sound.

3. Invite students to think of other one-syllable words with the /ȯ/ sound in the pattern. Write each word on a blank card from *Ready Resources,* place it in the correct column, and underline the pattern. If they suggest words that have other patterns with the /ȯ/ sound, create a new column. Continue the process with a variety of words so they can see the various patterns that represent the /ȯ/ sound.

4. Have students read each column of words. Help them generalize the principle based on their earlier observations: *Some words have the /ȯ/ vowel sound as in saw. Several patterns of letters can stand for the /ȯ/ vowel sound.*

5. Tell students that today they are going to play Concentration. They will take turns turning over a card, reading the word, and identifying the /ȯ/ spelling pattern. They then turn over a second card and repeat the procedure. If the two words have the same spelling pattern, the player keeps the pair of cards. Otherwise the player turns the cards back over, and play passes to the left. The player with the most pairs wins the game.

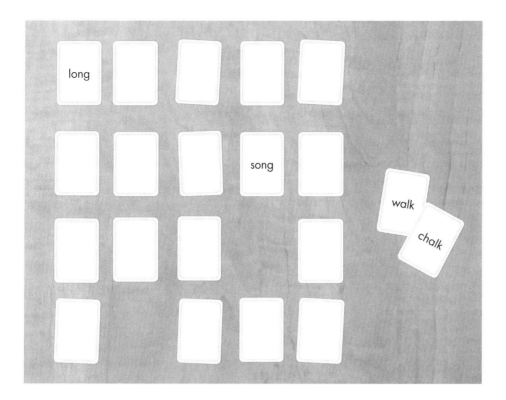

ACTIVITY:
CONCENTRATION

INSTRUCTIONAL
PROCEDURE

FIND AND MATCH

See page 32 for detailed
descriptions of Instructional
Procedures.

ACTION TAGS

turn over card

read word

identify spelling pattern

match pairs

Apply

- Students may play Concentration in pairs or groups of four.
- As students begin to play, remind them that they are matching words that have the same spelling pattern for /ȯ/.

Share

- Have students share a few matches that they made. You may wish to add any new words to the class chart.
- Review the principle and remind students to notice phonogram patterns with the /ȯ/ vowel sound (as in *saw*) in single-syllable words when they read and write.

Assess

- Dictate six to ten words with /ȯ/ spelling patterns while students are reading aloud. Notice their control and use of the spelling pattern to solve words.
- Observe whether students are spelling words with /ȯ/ spelling patterns conventionally in their writing.
- You may wish to use Spelling Patterns Assessment A, B, C, or D.

Spelling Patterns: Recognize and Use Phonogram Patterns with
the /ȯ/ Vowel Sound (as in saw*) in Single-Syllable Words*

195

Connect Learning Across Contexts

Shared Reading You may wish to use the following Shared Reading title from *Fountas & Pinnell Classroom™* to point out phonogram patterns with the /ȯ/ vowel sound (as in *saw*) in single-syllable words.

 *Wolf Pack* by Annette Bay Pimentel

Guided Reading When students come to difficult words, encourage them to use patterns they know. Ask, "Do you know another word like that?"

Shared Writing Guide students to use spelling patterns they know to help them write an unknown word. Revisit completed pieces to search for words containing /ȯ/ patterns that you are reviewing.

Guided/Independent Writing Prompt students to use patterns they know to check the spelling of words. *This word sounds the same as* caught *at the end. What pattern do you know in* caught? *Can you use that pattern here?*

Extend Learning

- Continue to add words to the chart as students encounter interesting words in their reading and writing.

- If students need more experience with the sounds of a particular letter combination, replace most of the cards with words containing the letters, and have them play Concentration again.

- Have students play Go Fish using the game cards. Directions for Go Fish are available in Online Resources.

▶ **Connect with Home**

Send home a deck of Concentration cards for students to play with family members.

Recognize and Use Phonogram Patterns with the /ou/ Vowel Sound in Single-Syllable Words

Plan

▶ Consider Your Students

This lesson will be most effective if students have good control of basic common phonogram patterns. Fourteen different spelling patterns represent the /ou/ sound in single-syllable words. You can use all the patterns or select particular ones to work with.

▶ Working with English Language Learners

This group of phonograms challenges English language learners but helps them realize that larger visual patterns in words relate to sounds. Once they know about this category (/ou/ as in *cow*), they can add spellings that fit within it. Developing these understandings will probably be an ongoing process for several years. Start with simple examples that students understand and gradually expand their repertoire. During word work, reinforce their understanding by having students write or build words.

UNDERSTAND THE PRINCIPLE

Phonogram patterns are very useful to readers and writers. Once students know to look for specific patterns, they can apply this information to read text and spell words with increased efficiency and accuracy. The letters *ow* and *ou* are followed by various consonants to represent several different spelling patterns. The *ow* can represent the entire phonogram or spelling pattern (as in *cow* or *how*) or it can be part of the pattern (*howl, clown*). It is helpful for students to learn the complete pattern.

YOU WILL NEED

Online Resources
- ▶ SP 12 Action Tags
- ▶ SP 12 Word Cards
- ▶ SP 12 Word Pairs Sheets

Other Materials
- ▶ chart paper

Generative Lesson
A generative lesson has a simple structure that you can use to present similar content or concepts. Use this lesson structure to teach students a variety of phonograms that have the /ou/ vowel sound.

EXPLAIN THE PRINCIPLE

Some words have the /ou/ vowel sound as in cow.

Several patterns of letters can stand for the /ou/ vowel sound [e.g., proud, clown*].*

Comprehensive Phonics, Spelling, and Word Study Guide

Refer to:
Page 37, row **17**

EARLY MIDDLE **LATE**

ACTIVITY: WORD LISTS

INSTRUCTIONAL PROCEDURE

NOTICE PARTS

See page 32 for detailed descriptions of Instructional Procedures.

EXPLAIN THE PRINCIPLE

Some words have the /ou/ vowel sound as in cow.

Several patterns of letters can stand for the /ou/ vowel sound [e.g., proud, clown].

Comprehensive Phonics, Spelling, and Word Study Guide

Refer to: page **37**, row **17**

---

cow	growl	clown
plow	howl	frown

loud	mouth	sound
proud	south	pound

Teach

1. On chart paper, write the following pairs of word in three columns: *cow, plow; growl, howl; clown, frown.*

2. *What do you notice about all of the words?* • Students are likely to observe that all of the words have the letters *ow.* As needed, prompt students to think about the spellings at the end of the words. • *The words in the first column end with -ow. The words in the other columns have a consonant after -ow.* Write *-ow, -owl,* and *-own* at the top of the columns.

3. Encourage students to think of more examples that fit the patterns, and add the words to the appropriate columns. Underline the phonogram in each word.

4. Repeat the procedure with the word pairs *loud, proud; mouth, south;* and *sound, pound.* If you wish, you may also include words with *-out, -our, -oul, -ouch,* and *-ouse.*

5. Read each column of words. *What do you notice about the vowel sound in all of these words? If you hear the /ou/ vowel sound at the end of a word, which spelling do you think you would use?*

6. Use students' observations to summarize the principle: *Some words have the /ou/ vowel sound as in* cow. *Several patterns of letters can stand for the /ou/ vowel sound.*

7. Explain to students that they will make words using /ou/ spelling patterns. Demonstrate the process of making words using beginning consonant and ending spelling pattern word cards. Students will use the word parts to make fourteen different words and then write them on the left column of a word pairs sheet. In the right column, they write another word with the same pattern and then circle the /ou/ pattern in each.

INSTRUCTIONAL PROCEDURE

NOTICE PARTS

See page 32 for detailed descriptions of Instructional Procedures.

ACTION TAGS

make word
write word
write another word
circle
read

Apply

Have students make words. Remind them to double-check to be sure that each word that they make is a real word. They may use a children's dictionary or check with a partner if they are unsure.

Share

■ Invite each student to read a word pair from his list as you write the words on a chart and underline the pattern that represents the /ou/ sound.

■ Review the principle and remind students to notice phonogram patterns with the /ou/ vowel sounds in single-syllable words when they read and write.

Assess

■ Observe students solving words with /ou/ patterns while they are reading aloud. Notice their control and use of the phonograms to solve words.

■ Dictate eight to ten words with the /ou/ pattern. Notice if students use the patterns conventionally in their writing.

■ You may wish to use Spelling Patterns Assessment A, B, C, or D.

Spelling Patterns: Recognize and Use Phonogram Patterns with the /ou/ Vowel Sound in Single-Syllable Words

Connect Learning Across Contexts

Shared Reading You may wish to use the following Shared Reading title from *Fountas & Pinnell Classroom*™ to point out phonogram patterns with the /ou/ vowel sound in single-syllable words.

> SR *Far Above Earth: A Day on the Space Station* by Jane Simon

Guided Reading After reading a text, ask students to turn to a particular page and locate two or three words with /ou/ patterns.

Shared Writing Guide students to use spelling patterns they know to help them write an unknown word. Revisit completed pieces to search for words containing /ou/ patterns that you are reviewing.

Guided/Independent Writing In students' writing, point out words with /ou/ spelling patterns. Help students notice when a word they want to write has a pattern like another word they know.

Extend Learning

- Have students create word ladders with /ou/ by changing the beginning or ending consonants.
- Distribute blank Follow the Path game boards (found in Online Resources), and have students work together to create boards with words that have the /ou/ sound. Allow students to play the game during independent learning times.

▶ Connect with Home

Have students share their word pairs with a family member. Challenge them to add additional examples to their list.

Recognize and Use Phonogram Patterns with the /oi/ Vowel Sound in Single-Syllable Words

Plan

▶ Consider Your Students

Before teaching this lesson, be sure that students have worked with many phonograms and word patterns. In this lesson, students learn to notice seven phonogram patterns with the /oi/ sound. If you wish to challenge students, you may wish to also include a mix of /ou/ cards to build their automaticity in distinguishing between similar vowel sounds and spellings.

▶ Working with English Language Learners

As English language learners continue to explore vowel sounds that are represented by many different spellings, they will make deeper connections between spelling and sound. This activity helps them decode and write words. The more they work with patterns like *oin* and *oice,* the more readily they will recognize them as they read and the more alternatives they will consider as they write. During word work, write examples on a whiteboard and have students suggest other words that have the sound of *oy,* as in *boy.*

UNDERSTAND THE PRINCIPLE

Phonogram patterns are very useful to readers and writers. Once students know to look for specific patterns, they can apply this information to read text and spell words with increased efficiency and accuracy. In this lesson, students learn the seven different letter patterns that represent the /oi/ sound. Help students read and write the patterns as a unit, noticing that the /oi/ sound is often followed by a consonant.

YOU WILL NEED

PWS Ready Resources
- ▶ SP 13 Pocket-Chart Cards

Online Resources
- ▶ SP 13 Action Tags
- ▶ SP 13 Game Cards
- ▶ SP 13 Directions for Concentration

Other Materials
- ▶ pocket chart

✓ Generative Lesson

A generative lesson has a simple structure that you can use to present similar content or concepts. Use this lesson structure to teach students a variety of phonograms that have the /oi/ vowel sound.

EXPLAIN THE PRINCIPLE

Some words have the /oi/ vowel sound as in boy.

Several patterns of letters can stand for the /oi/ sound [e.g., coin, joy*].*

Comprehensive Phonics, Spelling, and Word Study Guide

Refer to: Page **37**, row **18**

ACTIVITY: WORD LISTS

INSTRUCTIONAL PROCEDURE

NOTICE PARTS

See page 32 for detailed descriptions of Instructional Procedures.

EXPLAIN THE PRINCIPLE

Some words have the /oi/ vowel sound as in boy.

Several patterns of letters can stand for the /oi/ sound [e.g., coin, joy].

Comprehensive Phonics, Spelling, and Word Study Guide

Refer to: page **37**, row **18**

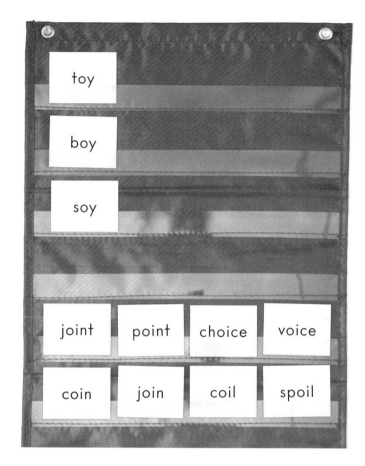

Teach

1. In a pocket chart, randomly place the following word cards: *toy, boy, soy; joint, point; choice, voice; coin, join; coil, spoil.* Have students read the words with you. *What do you notice about all of these words?* • Some example responses might be:

   "Some of the middle and ending letters look the same."

   "All of the words have the /oi/ sound."

   "All of the words have the same vowel sound even though they are spelled differently."

2. Invite a couple of students up to the pocket chart to organize words by the ending letters: *-oy, -oint, -oice, -oin,* and *-oil.*

3. Encourage students to think of more examples that fit the pattern, and add the words to the column. Underline the vowel sound in each word.

4. Read each column of words again with students. Use students' observations to summarize the principle: *Some words have the /oi/ vowel sound as in* boy. *Several patterns of letters can stand for the /oi/ vowel sound.*

5. Tell students that they are going to play Concentration. They will take turns turning over a card, reading the word, and identifying the /oi/ spelling pattern. They then turn over a second card and repeat the procedure. If the two words have the same spelling pattern, the player keeps the pair of cards. Otherwise the player turns the cards back over, and play passes to the left. The player with the most pairs wins the game.

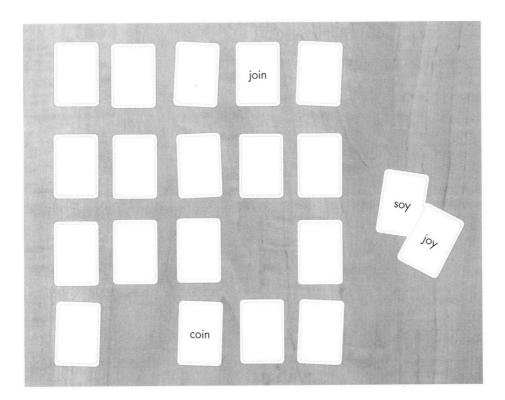

ACTIVITY: CONCENTRATION

INSTRUCTIONAL PROCEDURE

FIND AND MATCH

See page 32 for detailed descriptions of Instructional Procedures.

ACTION TAGS

turn over card
read word
identify spelling pattern
match pairs

Apply

- Students may play Concentration in pairs or groups.
- As students begin to play, remind them that they are matching words that have the same spelling pattern for /oi/.

Share

- Have students share a few matches that they made. You may wish to add any new words to the class chart.
- Review the principle and remind students to notice phonogram patters with the /oi/ vowel sound in single-syllable words when they read and write.

Assess

- Dictate six to ten words with /oi/ spelling patterns while students are reading aloud. Notice their control and use of the spelling pattern to solve words.
- Observe whether students are spelling words with /oi/ spelling patterns conventionally in their writing.
- You may wish to use Spelling Patterns Assessment A, B, C, or D.

Connect Learning Across Contexts

Shared Reading You may wish to use the following Shared Reading title from *Fountas & Pinnell Classroom*™ to point out spelling patterns with the /oi/ vowel sound in single-syllable words.

  SR *Trapped in Tar* by Hanna Cales

Guided Reading After reading a text, ask students to turn to a particular page and locate two or three words with /oi/ patterns.

Shared Writing Guide students to use spelling patterns they know to help them write an unknown word. Revisit completed pieces to search for words containing /oi/ patterns that you are reviewing.

Guided/Independent Writing In students' writing, point out words with /oi/ spelling patterns. Help students notice when a word they want to write has a pattern like another word they know.

Extend Learning

- Include a larger variety of phonogram patterns in the Concentration game card deck.

- Have students use magnetic letters to make twenty words with the /oi/ pattern. Then have them write them on a list sheet.

▶ Connect with Home

Send home a deck of Concentration cards for students to play with family members.

Recognize and Use Phonogram Patterns with Vowels and *r* in Single-Syllable Words

Plan

▶ Consider Your Students

This lesson will be most effective if students are familiar with a number of common words that have *r*-influenced vowels, such as *start, turn, bird, herd,* and *form.* In this lesson, students will work with a variety of words that have phonograms influenced by the letter *r.* Phonograms that include *ar, er, ir, or,* and *ur* will be easier for students than ones with less predictable sounds, such as those that include the letters *-ear.* Tailor the lesson by selecting words that provide an appropriate challenge for your students.

▶ Working with English Language Learners

Depending on their first languages, English language learners may find it difficult to pronounce words with *r*-influenced vowels. Accept approximate pronunciations. It will be helpful to teach only one *r*-influenced vowel sound at a time before introducing other sounds and phonograms. Begin with words that your English language learners know. Be sure to review all of the words on the game board with them before they play the game.

UNDERSTAND THE PRINCIPLE

When the consonant sound /r/ follows a vowel sound in a syllable, the sounds blend in a way that modifies the vowel sound. These modified sounds are known as *r*-influenced, or *r*-controlled, vowels. Many common words contain phonograms with *r*-influenced vowels, making them valuable for students to notice and remember. Once students understand that certain vowels appear with *r* in words and they know to look for specific patterns, they can apply this information to read text and spell words with increased efficiency and accuracy.

YOU WILL NEED

Online Resources
- ▶ **SP 14** Action Tags
- ▶ **SP 14** Follow the Path Game Board
- ▶ **SP 14** List Sheets
- ▶ **SP 14** Directions for Follow the Path

Other Materials
- ▶ blank chart paper
- ▶ game die
- ▶ game pieces or other markers

Generative Lesson

A generative lesson has a simple structure that you can use to present similar content or concepts. Use this lesson structure to teach students a variety of phonograms with vowels followed by the letter *r.*

EXPLAIN THE PRINCIPLE

Some words have a vowel pattern with one or two vowels and r.

When vowels are with r *in words, usually you blend the sound of the vowels with* r *[e.g., third].*

Comprehensive Phonics, Spelling, and Word Study Guide

Refer to:
Page **36**, row **16**

ACTIVITY: WORD LISTS

INSTRUCTIONAL PROCEDURE

NOTICE PARTS

See page 32 for detailed descriptions of Instructional Procedures.

EXPLAIN THE PRINCIPLE

Some words have a vowel pattern with one or two vowels and r.

When vowels are with r in words, usually you blend the sound of the vowels with r [e.g., third].

Comprehensive Phonics, Spelling, and Word Study Guide

Refer to: page **36**, row **16**

girl	born	farm
twirl	corn	charm
whirl	horn	harm

burn	fern
churn	stern
turn	

Teach

1. On chart paper, write the following words in a column: *girl, twirl, whirl.* Use any words that students may not know in a sentence.

2. *What do you notice about all of the words?* • Students are likely to observe that all of the words have the letters *ir* or *irl.* As needed, prompt students to think about the spellings at the end of the words. • *These words end in* -irl.

3. Encourage students to think of more examples that fit the pattern, and add the words to the column. Underline the phonogram in each word.

4. Have students read the column of words. *What do you notice about the vowel sound?* •*The letter* i *doesn't stand for the long sound, /ī/, or the short sound, /ĭ/. The vowel sound is different because it is blended with the sound of* r.

5. Repeat the procedure with the words *born, corn,* and *horn; farm, charm,* and *harm; burn, churn,* and *turn;* and *fern* and *stern.* Guide students to notice how the *r* influences the vowel sound. If students easily grasp the simpler *r*-controlled patterns, you may wish to replace some of these words with word pairs such as *heart, heard* and *dear, bear.*

6. Tell students that today they are going to play Follow the Path. Taking turns, they will toss a die, move that number of spaces, read aloud the word in the new space, and use the word in a sentence. They go back to the space they were on if they can't read the word correctly and use it in a sentence. The first player to reach "finish" wins the game. Students will then write examples of each pattern on a list sheet.

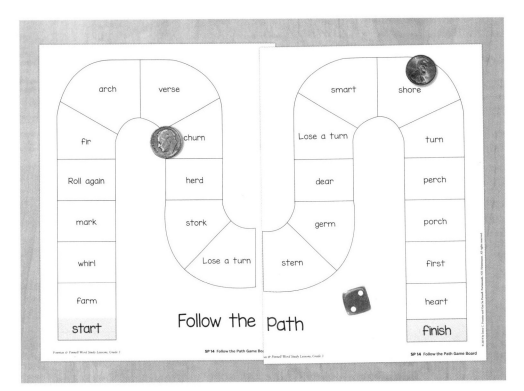

ACTIVITY: FOLLOW THE PATH

INSTRUCTIONAL PROCEDURE

NOTICE PARTS

See page 32 for detailed descriptions of Instructional Procedures.

ACTION TAGS

> toss die

> move

> read word

> use in a sentence

> write on list sheet

Apply

- Have students play Follow the Path in pairs or groups of three using a game board, a game die, and game pieces to mark their places on the board.
- Then have students write words that represent each pattern seen on the chart on a list sheet.

Share

- Invite students to suggest more words with *r*-controlled vowels to add to the chart.
- Review the principle and remind students to notice phonogram patterns with vowels and *r* in single-syllable words when they read and write.

Assess

- Observe students solving words with *r*-controlled vowel patterns while they are reading aloud. Notice their control and use of the phonograms to solve words.
- Dictate eight to ten words with *r*-controlled vowel patterns. Notice if students use spelling patterns conventionally in their writing.
- You may wish to use Spelling Patterns Assessment A, B, C, or D.

Connect Learning Across Contexts

Shared Reading You may wish to use the following Shared Reading title from *Fountas & Pinnell Classroom*™ to point out phonogram patterns with vowel and *r* sounds in single-syllable words.

SR *Trapped in Tar* by Hannah Cales

Guided Reading During word work, write several words with *r*-influenced vowel sounds on a whiteboard to help students develop quick recognition and flexibility with the patterns.

Shared Writing Guide students to use spelling patterns they know to help them write an unknown word. Revisit completed pieces to search for words containing *r*-controlled vowel patterns that you are reviewing.

Guided/Independent Writing In students' writing, point out words with *r*-controlled vowel spelling patterns. Help students notice when a word they want to write has a pattern like another word they know.

Extend Learning

■ Distribute blank Follow the Path game boards (found in Online Resources), and have students work together to create boards with new sets of words with patterns that have one or two vowels followed by the letter *r*. Make the additional boards available for students to choose when playing the game.

■ Keep the lesson chart posted in the classroom. Have students add new words that fit the patterns that they find in books they read.

▶ Connect with Home

Send Follow the Path game boards home so that students can play the game with family members.

Understand That Some Words Have a Double Consonant

Plan

▶ Consider Your Students

This lesson focuses on the concept that double consonants can be found in the middle and at the end of multisyllabic words. The lesson will be most helpful if students are attempting to solve various multisyllabic words as they read and more accurately representing multisyllable words as they write. This lesson will help readers and writers increase their flexibility in analyzing, breaking apart, and spelling longer words.

▶ Working with English Language Learners

The more English language learners become familiar with the patterns of written language, the easier it will be for them to learn new words. Once they develop the concept of looking for patterns, they will actively try to connect words. You may need to show them how to do this active searching by demonstrating it and taking special care to point out patterns such as double consonants in guided reading, shared reading, and the interactive writing that you do with small groups. Be sure that students have the opportunity to notice double consonants in words that are already familiar to them.

UNDERSTAND THE PRINCIPLE

Double consonants appear in the middle and at the end of a number of common multisyllable words. The two consonants together stand for a single sound. Recognizing this recurring spelling pattern will help students become more flexible in breaking apart and solving words with more than one syllable.

YOU WILL NEED

PWS Ready Resources
- ▶ SP 15 Pocket-Chart Cards

Online Resources
- ▶ SP 15 Action Tags
- ▶ SP 15 Word Cards
- ▶ SP 15 Two-Way Sorts

Other Materials
- ▶ pocket chart

Generative Lesson
A generative lesson has a simple structure that you can use to present similar content or concepts. Use this lesson structure to teach students a variety of patterns with double consonants.

EXPLAIN THE PRINCIPLE

Some multisyllable words have a double consonant.

Sometimes a double consonant stands for a consonant sound in the middle of a multisyllable word.

Sometimes a double consonant stands for a consonant sound at the end of a multisyllable word.

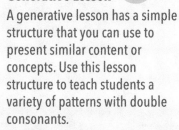

Comprehensive Phonics, Spelling, and Word Study Guide

Refer to: Page **37**, row **19**

ACTIVITY: WORD SORT

INSTRUCTIONAL PROCEDURE

NOTICE PARTS

See page 32 for detailed descriptions of Instructional Procedures.

EXPLAIN THE PRINCIPLE

Some multisyllable words have a double consonant.

Sometimes a double consonant stands for a consonant sound in the middle of a multisyllable word.

Sometimes a double consonant stands for a consonant sound at the end of a multisyllable word.

Comprehensive Phonics, Spelling, and Word Study Guide

Refer to: page **37**, row **19**

Teach

1. On a pocket chart, display the following words in a mixed-up order: *hammer, blizzard, traffic, princess, uphill,* and *recess.* Read the words with students. Use any words students may not know in a sentence.

2. *What do you notice about these words?* • Students will likely notice that all of the words have a double consonant. As needed, prompt them to continue to think about the words. *What are some ways that we can sort these words?* • Allow time for students to notice that the words can be sorted into two groups by the location of the double consonant: in the middle or at the end. Place the words *hammer* and *princess* at the top of the chart as column heads. You may wish to underline or highlight the double consonant(s) in each word. Have students sort the remaining words.

3. Display additional word cards. Students should notice that *mattress* can be sorted into both columns.

4. Have students read each column of words. Summarize the principle. *As you've noticed, some multisyllable words have a double consonant. Sometimes a double consonant stands for a consonant sound in the middle of a multisyllable word, and sometimes a double consonant stands for a consonant sound at the end of a multisyllable word.* Point out that some words, such as *mattress,* have double consonants in the middle and at the end.

5. Tell students that they are going to say and sort and write words with double consonants. Display a set of word cards, and explain that students will sort the words into two groups: words with a double consonant in the middle and words with a double consonant at the end. Once the words are sorted, students read the words in each group to a partner and then write examples from each group on a list sheet.

INSTRUCTIONAL PROCEDURE

SAY AND SORT

See page 32 for detailed descriptions of Instructional Procedures.

ACTION TAGS

sort words

read words

write words

Apply

- Remind students to read the words they have sorted to a partner. Encourage them to talk about other words they know that have double consonants in the middle or at the end.

- Point out the key words *hammer* and *princess* at the top of the sort. Remind students to write the words they sort in the correct column.

Share

- Have students read their two columns of words to a different partner.

- Invite students to suggest two or three more words to add to each column of the chart.

Assess

- Notice whether students use what they know about the sounds associated with the double consonant pattern to solve words when they are reading.

- Dictate a few words with the double consonant pattern for students to write.

- You may wish to use Spelling Patterns Assessment A, B, C, or D.

Spelling Patterns: Understand That Some Words Have a Double Consonant

Connect Learning Across Contexts

Shared Reading You may wish to use the following Shared Reading title from *Fountas & Pinnell Classroom™* to point out words that have a double consonant.

SR *Exploring Underground* by Louis Petrone

Guided Reading During word work, write several words with double consonants and have students read them aloud. If a word has double consonants in the middle, model dividing the word into syllables between the consonants and then blending the parts to read the word.

Shared Writing As you write a piece together, highlight any words that have double consonants in the middle or at the end.

Guided/Independent Writing When students want to write a new word with a double consonant, have them quickly write a similar word they know off to the side. Point out the pattern, and tell them that the same pattern is found in the word they want to write.

Extend Learning

- Have students read and sort a different set of words with double consonants.
- Create a Follow the Path game with multisyllable words that have double consonants. Blank game boards are available in Online Resources.

▶ Connect with Home

Send home a set of word cards for students to sort and read with family members. Encourage them to look for examples of words with double consonants around their homes and neighborhoods.

Recognize and Use Frequently Appearing Syllable Patterns in Multisyllable Words

Plan

▶ Consider Your Students

This lesson focuses on common syllable patterns that often appear at the beginnings of words. The lesson will be most helpful if students can easily separate words into syllables. They should be attempting to solve various multisyllabic words as they read and more accurately representing multisyllable words as they write. This lesson will help readers and writers increase their flexibility in analyzing, breaking apart, and spelling longer words.

▶ Working with English Language Learners

The more English language learners become familiar with the patterns of written language, the easier it will be for them to learn new words. Once they develop the concept of looking for patterns, they will actively try to connect words. You may need to show them how to do this active searching by demonstrating it and taking special care to point out common syllable patterns in guided reading, shared reading, and the interactive writing that you do with small groups. Be sure that students have the opportunity to notice common syllable patterns in words that are already familiar to them.

UNDERSTAND THE PRINCIPLE

Many common syllable patterns appear frequently at the beginning or end of multisyllable words. Recognizing these recurring syllable patterns will help students become more flexible in reading and spelling words with more than one syllable. This lesson focuses on the common syllables *a* as in *among* and *be* as in *before*. You may wish to use a similar format to teach common prefixes that are also the first syllables of words, such as *un-* and *re-*.

YOU WILL NEED

Online Resources
▸ **SP 16** Action Tags
▸ **SP 16** Word Cards
▸ **SP 16** Word and Sentence Sheets

Other Materials
▸ chart paper

Generative Lesson
A generative lesson has a simple structure that you can use to present similar content or concepts. Use this lesson structure to teach students a variety of syllable patterns that appear in multisyllable words.

EXPLAIN THE PRINCIPLE

Some syllable patterns appear often in multisyllable words.

Look for the familiar pattern to read a multisyllable word.

Think about the familiar pattern to spell a multisyllable word.

Comprehensive Phonics, Spelling, and Word Study Guide

Refer to: Page **37**, row **21**

Spelling Patterns: Recognize and Use Frequently Appearing Syllable Patterns in Multisyllable Words

ACTIVITY: WORD LIST

INSTRUCTIONAL PROCEDURE

NOTICE PARTS

See page 32 for detailed descriptions of Instructional Procedures.

EXPLAIN THE PRINCIPLE

Some syllable patterns appear often in multisyllable words.

Look for the familiar pattern to read a multisyllable word.

Think about the familiar pattern to spell a multisyllable word.

Comprehensive Phonics, Spelling, and Word Study Guide

Refer to: page **37**, row **21**

alone become
away behave
again before

Teach

1. Tell students that they are going to learn more about syllable patterns.

2. Write the following words on a piece of chart paper: *alone, away, again.* Read the words with students.

3. *What do you notice about all of these words?* • Students will likely first notice that all of the words start with *a.* As needed, read the words again with students, this time clapping the syllables. Guide them to notice that the *a* has the /ə/ sound in each word and that it forms the first syllable of each word.

4. *Many words have* a *as the first syllable. What are some others that you can think of?* Add students' suggestions to the chart.

5. Repeat the procedure with words such as *become, behave,* and *before.* As students suggest words, be sure to talk about the meanings of any new words.

6. Tell students that they will make five words that start with the syllable *a* and five words that start with the syllable *be.* Then they will write each word in a sentence.

Fountas & Pinnell Word Study Lessons, Grade 3

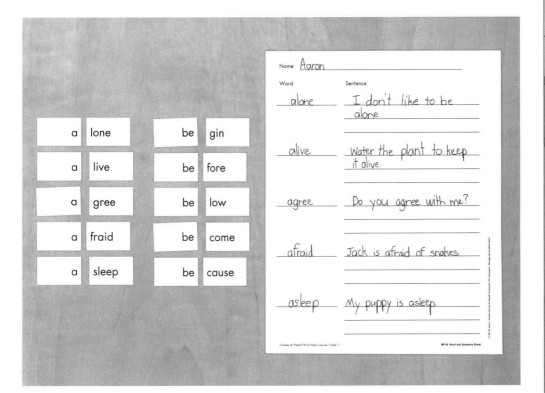

INSTRUCTIONAL PROCEDURE

MAKE WORDS

See page 32 for detailed descriptions of Instructional Procedures.

ACTION TAGS

make words

read words

write words

use in a sentence

Apply

Have students use the word cards to make the words. Tell students to make sure that the words they make are real words. Then have them record their words on a word and sentence sheet and write a sentence for each.

Share

■ Have students choose one sentence to share with a partner and then with the class.

■ Invite students to discuss the meaning of words; for example, *asleep* is connected to *sleep* by meaning, as is *because* to *cause.*

Assess

■ Notice whether students use what they know about common syllable patterns to solve words when they are reading or spelling.

■ Dictate a few words with the *a* or *be* syllable pattern for students to write.

Spelling Patterns: Recognize and Use Frequently Appearing Syllable Patterns in Multisyllable Words

Connect Learning Across Contexts

Shared Reading You may wish to use the following Shared Reading title from *Fountas & Pinnell Classroom*™ to point out frequently appearing syllable patterns in multisyllable words.

SR *Tiny but Fierce* by Cheri Colburn

Guided Reading During word work, write several words that have the *a* or *be* syllable pattern at the beginning. Have students read the words, clap the syllables, divide the words into syllables, and then read the words again.

Shared Writing As you write a piece together, highlight any words that begin with the *a* or *be* syllable pattern.

Guided/Independent Writing When students want to write a new word with an *a* or *be* syllable pattern, remind them that they can use words they know that start the same way to write new words.

Extend Learning

- Have students use the word cards to create more words and use them in sentences.
- Repeat this lesson with a different set of common syllable patterns, such as *en*, *in*, *im*, *un*, or *re*.

▶ Connect with Home

Send home the word cards and have students form new words with family members. Have them read the words aloud and use them in sentences.

Recognize and Use Frequently Appearing Syllable Patterns in Multisyllable Words

Plan

▶ Consider Your Students

This lesson focuses on common syllable patterns that often appear at the ends of words. The lesson will be most helpful if students can easily separate words into syllables and recognize basic word parts. They should be attempting to solve various multisyllabic words as they read and more accurately representing multisyllable words as they write. This lesson will help readers and writers increase their flexibility in analyzing, breaking apart, and spelling longer words.

▶ Working with English Language Learners

The more English language learners become familiar with the patterns of written language, the easier it will be for them to learn new words. Once they develop the concept of looking for patterns, they will actively try to connect words. Some students may benefit from focusing on just one syllable pattern at a time, while others may be ready to work with more. Be sure to use examples that are in students' oral vocabularies.

YOU WILL NEED

Online Resources
- ▸ **SP 17** Action Tags
- ▸ **SP 17** Game Cards
- ▸ **SP 17** Directions for Concentration

Other Materials
- ▸ chart paper

Generative Lesson
A generative lesson has a simple structure that you can use to present similar content or concepts. Use this lesson structure to teach students a variety of syllable patterns that frequently appear in multisyllable words.

UNDERSTAND THE PRINCIPLE

Many common syllable patterns appear frequently at the beginning or end of multisyllable words. Recognizing these recurring syllable patterns will help students become more flexible in reading and spelling words with more than one syllable. This lesson focuses on common syllables at the ends of words.

EXPLAIN THE PRINCIPLE

Some syllable patterns appear often in multisyllable words.

Look for the familiar pattern to read a multisyllable word.

Think about the familiar pattern to spell a multisyllable word.

Comprehensive Phonics, Spelling, and Word Study Guide

Refer to: Page **37**, row **21**

ACTIVITY: WORD LIST

INSTRUCTIONAL PROCEDURE

NOTICE PARTS

See page 32 for detailed descriptions of Instructional Procedures.

EXPLAIN THE PRINCIPLE

Some syllable patterns appear often in multisyllable words.

Look for the familiar pattern to read a multisyllable word.

Think about the familiar pattern to spell a multisyllable word.

Comprehensive Phonics, Spelling, and Word Study Guide

Refer to: page **37**, row **21**

purple   other
trouble   brother
cycle   weather

ready
easy
lucky

Teach

1. Write the following words on a piece of chart paper: *purple, trouble, cycle.* Read the words with students.

2. *What do you notice about all of these words?* • Students will likely notice that all the words end with *le.* As needed, read the words again with students, this time clapping the syllables and underlining the consonant -*le* ending. Help them notice that when you break the word the -*le* is a syllable with the previous consonant. Guide them to notice that this syllable is pronounced by blending the first consonant with the *l.* The *e* is silent.

3. *Many words have the consonant -*le *syllable pattern. What are some others that you can think of?* Add students' suggestions to the chart.

4. Repeat the procedure with words such as *other, brother, weather* and *ready, easy, lucky.* As students suggest words, be sure to talk about the meanings of any new words.

5. Explain to the students that they are going to play Concentration. *You are going to play the game Concentration with syllable patterns. You will pick up a card and read the word. Then you will pick up another card and see if the two words end with the same syllable pattern. If the two words have the same final syllable pattern, you have made a match. The player with the most matches wins the game.*

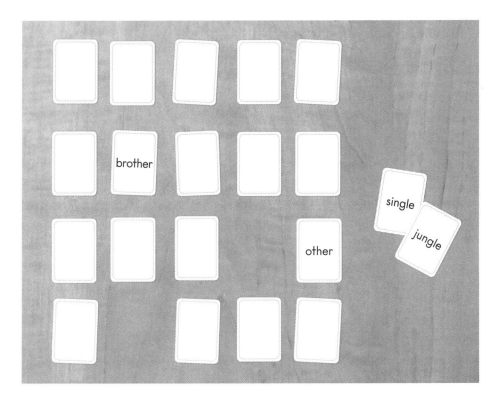

INSTRUCTIONAL PROCEDURE

FIND AND MATCH

See page 32 for detailed descriptions of Instructional Procedures.

ACTION TAGS

turn card

turn another card

match pair

Apply

- Have students play Concentration in groups of two to four players.
- Remind students that they are trying to match the ending syllable pattern. If two words end with the same syllable pattern, they are a match.
- Tell students to list three words with different final syllable patterns to share with the group.

Share

Have the students read their word lists to the group. Add any new words to the class chart.

Assess

- Notice whether students use what they know about common syllable patterns to solve words when they are reading or spelling.
- Dictate a few words with the *y, er,* or *consonant -le* syllable pattern for students to write.

Connect Learning Across Contexts

Shared Reading You may wish to use the following Shared Reading title from *Fountas & Pinnell Classroom*™ to point out frequently appearing syllable patterns in multisyllable words.

A Meerkat Day by Geerhardt Heever

Guided Reading During word work, write several words that have the *y, er,* or *consonant -le* syllable pattern at the end. Have students read the words, clap the syllables, divide the words into syllables, and then read the words again.

Shared Writing As you write a piece together, highlight any words that end with the *y, er,* or *consonant -le* syllable pattern.

Guided/Independent Writing When students want to write a new word, remind them that they can use words they know that have the same syllable pattern to write new words.

Extend Learning

- Repeat this lesson with a different set of common final syllable patterns.
- Have students sort the game cards by final syllable pattern and read the words in each pile.

▶ Connect with Home

Have students play Concentration with someone at home.

High-Frequency Words

A core of known high-frequency words is a valuable resource as students build their reading and writing processes. Students notice words that appear frequently in the texts they read; eventually, their recognition of these words becomes automatic. In this way, their reading becomes more efficient, enabling them to decode new words using phonics as well as to attend to comprehension.

Readers are more able to engage in problem-solving when they do it against a backdrop of accurate reading. They have more information available to them (i.e., language structure, meaning). Also, they can use connections between words in problem solving. Known high-frequency words are powerful examples that help them grasp that a word is always written the same way. They can use known high-frequency words to check on the accuracy of their reading and as resources for solving other words (for example, *thread* starts like *things*). In general, students learn the simpler words earlier and in the process develop efficient systems for learning words. They continuously add to the core of high-frequency words they know. Lessons on high-frequency words help them look more carefully at words and develop more efficient systems for word recognition.

Connect to Assessment

See related (optional) HFW Assessment tasks in Online Resources.

- Assessment A: Reading High-Frequency Words
- Assessment B: Recognizing and Writing High-Frequency Words
- Assessment C: Individual Record (Reading and Writing)

Develop Your Professional Understanding

See *The Fountas & Pinnell Comprehensive Phonics, Spelling, and Word Study Guide.* 2017. Portsmouth, New Hampshire: Heinemann. Related pages: 2-12, 40-41.

See *The Fountas & Pinnell Literacy Continuum: A Tool for Assessment, Planning, and Teaching.* 2017. Portsmouth, New Hampshire: Heinemann. Related pages: 357-397.

See *Word Matters: Teaching Phonics and Spelling in the Reading/Writing Classroom* by G.S. Pinnell and I.C. Fountas. 1998. Portsmouth, New Hampshire: Heinemann. Related pages: 35–41, 44–46, 71–72, 88–90, 237–238.

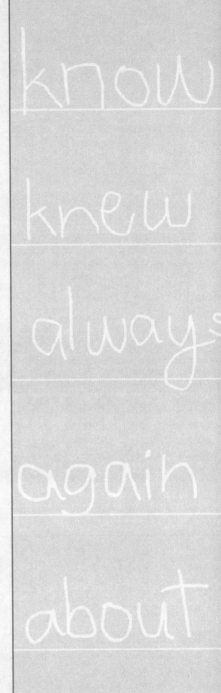

know

knew

always

again

about

Recognize and Use High-Frequency Words with Three or More Letters

Plan

▶ Consider Your Students

In this lesson, you will want to include both known words and unknown words. Using a few well-known words will help students have a base for learning the more difficult words taught in the lesson. In order to choose words for the class, take an inventory of the words students write correctly so you can focus on those they need to learn. (You may wish to use the lists of 200 and 500 high-frequency words found in *Ready Resources*.) During the Apply activity, if the lesson's word cards are not an appropriate selection of words for your class, use blank word cards to write more suitable high-frequency words.

▶ Working with English Language Learners

Use context-rich examples that are easy for English language learners to understand and use in oral language. Remember that high-frequency words such as articles (*an, the*) are abstract rather than concrete. A child's native language syntax may be quite different from English; in fact, counterpart words may not exist in some cases. Give students opportunities to hear and say the high-frequency words in meaningful sentences.

YOU WILL NEED

Online Resources
- ▶ **HFW 1** Action Tags
- ▶ **HFW 1** Make-Say-Check-Mix Sheets
- ▶ **HFW 1** Word Cards

Other Materials
- ▶ magnetic letters
- ▶ chart paper
- ▶ index cards

Generative Lesson
A generative lesson has a simple structure that you can use to present similar content or concepts. Use this lesson structure to teach a variety of high-frequency words.

UNDERSTAND THE PRINCIPLE

Students use a core of known high-frequency words as anchors to monitor and check their reading. Students can connect spelling patterns and word parts in words they know with those in more complex words. Having a large repertoire of high-frequency words supports fluent, meaningful reading and writing.

EXPLAIN THE PRINCIPLE

You see some words many times when you read.

You need to learn words that you see many times because they help you read and write.

Comprehensive Phonics, Spelling, and Word Study Guide

Refer to: page **40**, row **4**

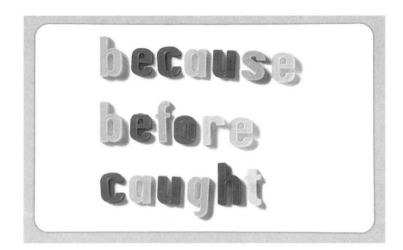

ACTIVITY: MAGNETIC LETTERS

INSTRUCTIONAL PROCEDURE

WORDS TO KNOW

See page 32 for detailed descriptions of Instructional Procedures.

EXPLAIN THE PRINCIPLE

You see some words many times when you read.

You need to learn words that you see many times because they help you read and write.

Comprehensive Phonics, Spelling, and Word Study Guide

Refer to: page **40**, row **4**

Teach

1. Make the word *because* on the whiteboard using magnetic letters. *What is this word?* • *The word is* because. *What do you notice about the spelling of the word* because? • Some example responses might be:

   "The word *because* has two syllables."

   "The word *because* begins with *be* like the words *before* and *become*."

   "The word *because* has the word *cause* in it."

   "*Because* has a silent *e* at the end."

   The word because *means "for the reason of." You could use* because *in a sentence such as, "I like ice cream because it tastes so delicious." When you see the word* because, *a reason is coming next.*

2. *What do you notice about* because *that will help you remember how to read and write the word?* • The students might notice that the *be* and *au* together sounds like a short *o*, the *s* sounds like a *z*, and that a silent *e* is at the end of the word.

3. Mix up the letters and make *because* again, emphasizing meaningful parts that help students learn the word. Then write *because* on chart paper and use a highlighter to draw attention to a word part students might find difficult and therefore want to remember.

4. Repeat the process with several other words, using words most students need to learn such as *continue, reason, enough,* and *difference.* Remind students of how each word will be like other words (e.g., be*cause,* be*fore, caught*). Be sure to use words in meaningful sentences so students can understand them.

5. Guide students to understand the principle. *Why do you think you need to learn words like* because, before, *and* caught? • *These are words that you see many times when you read. You need to learn words that you see many times because they help you read and write.*

6. Explain that students will work with high-frequency words. Using a make-say-check-mix sheet, students write a word, say it, and make and mix it three times with magnetic letters, each time placing a check mark on their sheet. Students then write the word again and highlight a difficult part they want to remember.

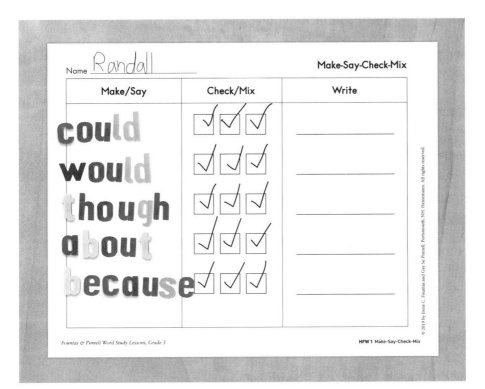

ACTIVITY: MAKE-SAY-CHECK-MIX

INSTRUCTIONAL PROCEDURE

WORDS TO KNOW

See page 32 for detailed descriptions of Instructional Procedures.

ACTION TAGS

write word

say word

make word

mix letters (3x)

check word

write word

highlight word parts

Apply

- Have students use make-say-check-mix sheets, word cards, and magnetic letters to practice fifteen different words from the 200 or 500 high-frequency words list.

- Ask the class to write one word on an index card (or a piece of paper), highlight a part they want to remember, and bring the card (or paper) to group share.

Share

Have each child in the group hold up his card, say the word, and talk about the highlighted word part he wants to remember. Point out other words that have similar parts.

Assess

- Review the students' work and notice the high-frequency words they do not know. Then, use these words to repeat the lesson.

- Notice how quickly students recognize words as they read.

- You may wish to use High-Frequency Words Assessment A, B, or C.

High-Frequency Words: Recognize and Use High-Frequency Words with Three or More Letters

Connect Learning Across Contexts

Shared Reading You may wish to use the following title from *Fountas & Pinnell Classroom*™ to locate a few high-frequency words after the shared reading of the text.

> SR *Far Above Earth: A Day on the Space Station* by Jane Simon

Guided Reading When children come across more difficult high-frequency words, remind them of other words that have the same or some of the same features. Show them how they can use parts of high-frequency words they know to solve new words.

Shared Writing During shared writing, have students approach the chart paper to write the high-frequency words they've been learning.

Independent Writing Hold students accountable for spelling the words they know correctly. Remind them to use words and word parts they know to write new words.

Extend Learning

- Have students select another fifteen words with which to work on a make-say-check-mix sheet.
- Give students a deck of game cards (see Online Resources) with high-frequency words. Have partners take turns turning a card and reading the word as quickly as they can.

▶ Connect with Home

Encourage students to take home their make-say-check-mix sheet and make each word again with magnetic letters or letter cards.

Recognize and Use High-Frequency Words with Three or More Letters

Plan

▶ Consider Your Students

This lesson will show students how to solve new words using known high-frequency words. For example, if a student knows *the*, it helps her to learn *there, they, their;* if she knows *could*, it helps her to learn *would, should*. Students will need to use their knowledge of how sounds stand for different letters and how some words do not always sound the way they look. Keep an ongoing inventory of high-frequency words that are known, almost known, and not known so you can focus on those words that require more attention. (See the Assessment Guide in Online Resources.) Make a list of the words that you will focus on in this lesson so that you can repeat the lesson with other high-frequency words at a later date.

▶ Working with English Language Learners

Help English language learners become very familiar with a core of easy high-frequency words before taking on more difficult ones. Be sure that the base of known words is solid before expanding the word list. Observe students to be sure that they are not simply producing the words mechanically without thinking about them or noticing visual features. Also, it is important for students to understand the meanings of words and to know that word meaning is challenging with abstract terms like *there.* Use such words in sentences that students can understand. If necessary, work with a small group of children to provide the practice that will help them rapidly and automatically recognize words.

UNDERSTAND THE PRINCIPLE

Students use a core of known high-frequency words as anchors to monitor and check their reading. Students can connect spelling patterns and word parts in words they know with those in more complex words. Having a large repertoire of high-frequency words supports fluent, meaningful reading and writing.

YOU WILL NEED

Online Resources
- ▶ HFW 2 Action Tags
- ▶ HFW 2 Word Cards
- ▶ HFW 2 Game Cards
- ▶ HFW 2 Directions for Concentration

Other Materials
- ▶ chart paper
- ▶ word study notebooks

Generative Lesson
A generative lesson has a simple structure that you can use to present similar content or concepts. Use this lesson structure to teach a variety of high-frequency words.

EXPLAIN THE PRINCIPLE

You see some words many times when you read.

You need to learn words that you see many times because they help you read and write.

Comprehensive Phonics, Spelling, and Word Study Guide

Refer to: page **40**, row **4**

ACTIVITY: WORDS WITH SIMILAR PATTERNS

INSTRUCTIONAL PROCEDURE

WORDS TO KNOW

See page 32 for detailed descriptions of Instructional Procedures.

EXPLAIN THE PRINCIPLE

You see some words many times when you read.

You need to learn words that you see many times because they help you read and write.

Comprehensive Phonics, Spelling, and Word Study Guide

Refer to: page **40**, row **4**

---

where   brought
when   bring
which   broke
while

became
began
behind

Teach

1. Write *where, when, which,* and *while* in a list on chart paper. *What do you notice about these four words?* • *All of the words begin with the letters* wh. Underline the letters *wh* in each of the four words.

2. *If you don't know one of these words, you can use words that you do know to try and solve it. You might know the word* when, *but you might not know the word* while. *How could you use the word* when *to learn to spell the word* while? • *Sounding out the word* while *will show you that the beginning sounds like the beginning of the word* when. *This is how you know that both words begin with the letters* wh.

3. *Let's look at some more words.* Write the words *brought, bring,* and *broke* in a separate list on the chart paper. *What do you notice about this group of words?* • *Each word begins with the letters* br. Underline the letters *br* in each of the words.

4. Continue the process with other word groups, such as *became, began, behind; every, even, everything; inside, instead; could, would, should; couldn't, wouldn't, shouldn't; might, right, fight.* Guide students to understand that you can use high-frequency words to learn other words.

5. Reinforce the principle: *You need to learn words that you see many times because they help you read and write.*

6. Tell students they will work with words that are alike in some way. Using word cards, students will find five pairs of words that have parts that are alike and write them in their word study notebooks.

7. Students then play Concentration in groups of three or four. Players take turns turning over two cards and reading the words aloud. If the words match, a player takes the pair of cards. If the words do not match, the player turns the cards facedown again. To make a match, students should look for words that have similar parts at the beginning, middle, or end of the word, e.g., *night* and *fight; bring* and *broke.* The player with the most matches wins the game.

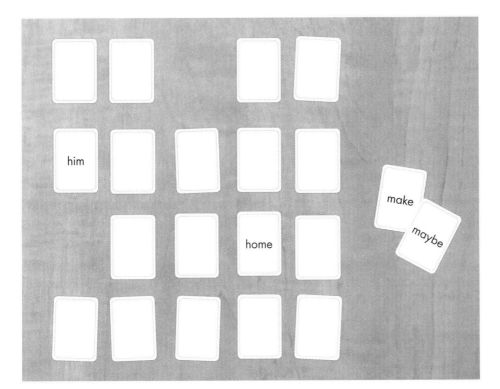

INSTRUCTIONAL PROCEDURE

WORDS TO KNOW

See page 32 for detailed descriptions of Instructional Procedures.

ACTION TAGS

find
match
write
turn
say
match

Apply

■ Have students match five sets of words with similar beginning, ending, or middle parts (such as *ma-* in *make* and *ma-* in *maybe*) using word cards. After matching, students will write the pairs in their word study notebooks.

■ Have students play Concentration using high-frequency words.

Share

■ Have students read three high-frequency words from their word study notebooks to a partner, telling the partner what they want to remember about the word.

■ Make a group chart of the words students find the most difficult to remember, highlighting the difficult part of each word with a marker.

Assess

■ Notice how fluently students read high-frequency words in text.

■ Observe how quickly and accurately they write high-frequency words.

■ For a more systematic assessment, dictate a list of high-frequency words.

■ You may wish to use High-Frequency Words Assessment A, B, or C.

High-Frequency Words: Recognize and Use High-Frequency Words with Three or More Letters

Connect Learning Across Contexts

Shared Reading You may wish to use the following title from *Fountas & Pinnell Classroom*™ to locate a few high-frequency words after the shared reading of the text.

> 🔲 *Trapped in Tar* by Hannah Cales

Guided Reading Remind students that there are many words they know and can read quickly. Guide students to try and solve words that they don't know by thinking about similar words that they do know.

Shared Writing During shared writing exercises, have students write more difficult high-frequency words. Remind students to think of words they do know in order to spell more challenging words.

Independent Writing Remind students to write words they know how to spell correctly each time they use them. During conferences, underline a few words you know a child can spell so she can self-correct.

Extend Learning

- To challenge students further, have them play Concentration with high-frequency words that have five or more letters. Use the 500 High-Frequency Words list from *Ready Resources* for more challenging words.

- Reteach the lesson with words students did not write correctly during the high-frequency word assessment (see Online Resources).

▶ Connect with Home

Send home a deck of blank game cards and the directions for Concentration (see Online Resources). Invite the students to make a deck of high-frequency cards with words they have not yet mastered. They can play Concentration with family members to develop their knowledge.

Recognize and Use Longer High-Frequency Words, Some with More Than One Syllable

Plan

▶ Consider Your Children

In order to better determine the words students know, have students keep a high-frequency words list (see *Ready Resources*) in their word study notebooks. Children can highlight the words they spell correctly as an ongoing record of accomplishment. Before teaching this lesson, determine which words are (to most students) known, almost known, and not known. If you would like to create your own Word Grid with words that are specifically tailored to the class, be sure to create a Word Grid that includes mostly words that are in the "almost known" or "not known" categories, along with a few known words.

▶ Working with English Language Learners

Searching word grids provides valuable practice for English language learners to search for words while noticing visual features. Searching for and creating word matches will aid English language learners in recognizing new words and making connections to words they already know. It may be beneficial to work with small groups. Check to be sure students understand the meaning of high-frequency words, especially abstract words like *through*. Use the words in sentences students understand.

UNDERSTAND THE PRINCIPLE

While learning new, longer words, it is beneficial for students to use a core of known high-frequency words as anchors to monitor and check their reading and spelling. Students can connect spelling patterns and word parts in words they know with those in more complex words. Having a large repertoire of high-frequency words supports fluent, meaningful reading and writing.

YOU WILL NEED

Online Resources
- ▶ HFW 3 Action Tags
- ▶ HFW 3 Word Grids
- ▶ HFW 3 Word Cards
- ▶ HFW 3 Directions for Word Grids

Other Materials
- ▶ chart paper

Generative Lesson ✓

A generative lesson has a simple structure that you can use to present similar content or concepts. Use this lesson structure to teach a variety of high-frequency words.

EXPLAIN THE PRINCIPLE

Some words have more than one syllable.

You need to learn words that you see many times because they help you read and write.

 Comprehensive Phonics, Spelling, and Word Study Guide

Refer to: page **40**, row **6**

ACTIVITY: WORDS WITH SIMILAR PATTERNS

INSTRUCTIONAL PROCEDURE

WORDS TO KNOW

See page 32 for detailed descriptions of Instructional Procedures.

EXPLAIN THE PRINCIPLE

Some words have more than one syllable.

You need to learn words that you see many times because they help you read and write.

Comprehensive Phonics, Spelling, and Word Study Guide

Refer to: page **40**, row **6**

friend
almost
everything
through
hard
finally
favorite
somebody

Teach

1. On chart paper, write the word *friend. What do you notice about the spelling of this word?* • *The word* friend *ends with a word you know how to spell,* end. *Do you notice anything else about the way the word sounds?* • Friend *begins with the letters* fr *like the word* from. Friend *and* from *both also have one syllable.*

2. Write the words *almost, everything, through, hard, finally, favorite,* and *somebody* one at a time, on chart paper. Each time, ask the class what they notice about the word, guiding students to understand that the spelling of the word is similar to another word they know. Remind them to think about the number of syllables, the sounds they hear, and the patterns they notice. Use words in sentences that students can understand.

3. Guide students to generalize the principle: *Some words have more than one syllable. You need to learn words that you see many times because they help you read and write.*

4. Show an enlarged high-frequency Word Grid to the class. Demonstrate how to search for words by reading across and down the grid.

5. *Now you will practice reading the words on your Word Grids out loud to a partner. After you practice reading the words, you will play Word Grid in groups of four.*

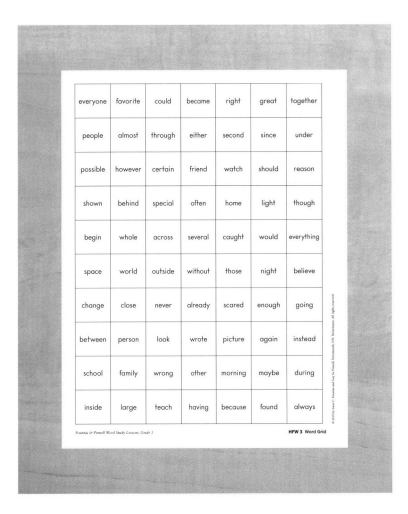

everyone	favorite	could	became	right	great	together
people	almost	through	either	second	since	under
possible	however	certain	friend	watch	should	reason
shown	behind	special	often	home	light	though
begin	whole	across	several	caught	would	everything
space	world	outside	without	those	night	believe
change	close	never	already	scared	enough	going
between	person	look	wrote	picture	again	instead
school	family	wrong	other	morning	maybe	during
inside	large	teach	having	because	found	always

Fountas & Pinnell Word Study Lessons, Grade 3

HFW 3 Word Grid

INSTRUCTIONAL PROCEDURE

WORDS TO KNOW

See page 32 for detailed descriptions of Instructional Procedures.

ACTION TAGS

read to partner

take card

say word

cross out

Apply

- Partners read their word grids to one another.
- In groups of four, students play Word Grid. One player takes a word card and says the word aloud. The player then searches for a word with a similar beginning, ending, or medial word part to make a match, e.g., *-son* in *reason* and *-son* in *person.* If a match can be created, the player crosses out the word on her Word Grid. The other players take their turns in sequence. The first player to cross out all of the words on her grid wins the game.

Share

- Invite children to talk about the words that are the most difficult for them and tell how they will remember these words.
- Children read their Word Grids to a different partner to further develop fluency.

Assess

- Notice how quickly students read high-frequency words with five or more letters.
- Dictate six to ten words used in the lesson to assess children's understanding.
- You may wish to use High-Frequency Words Assessment A, B, or C.

High-Frequency Words: Recognize and Use Longer High-Frequency Words, Some with More Than One Syllable

Connect Learning Across Contexts

Guided Reading As children solve new words, encourage them to use parts of high-frequency words they know (e.g., *begin, behind; everyone, everything*). *Find a part you know.* • *Do you know a word like that?*

Independent Reading While students read books independently, encourage them to use known words to solve high-frequency words that are partially known or not known.

Shared Writing During shared writing, ask students to write the multisyllable high-frequency words they are learning.

Independent Writing As students construct words, help them use known parts of high-frequency words to solve and write new words.

Extend Learning

Have students play Word Grid with a different selection of words. Alternatively, create a variety of grids that are tailored to individual children depending upon the words they know, are beginning to know, and do not know.

▶ **Connect with Home**

Send home a blank grid and have children write the words they know they want to learn. They can then play Word Grid with a family member.

Recognize and Use Longer High-Frequency Words, Some with More Than One Syllable

Plan

▶ Consider Your Students

Continue to monitor students as they learn to spell high-frequency words. If you choose to select words for this lesson, use your knowledge of the high-frequency words students need to learn. Keep in mind that words with five or more letters can be challenging, so students will need repeated practice. Giving each student a notebook used specifically for word study will help you monitor students' progress and also help students regulate their own progress. If the words you choose differ from the words provided, you can use a blank Lotto game board from Online Resources to customize the game.

▶ Working with English Language Learners

You may want to prepare Lotto game boards mostly with words that students know or almost know. You can limit the new words by repeating a word twice or even three times on a particular game board. Students may cover a word only once at any turn. Remember that students need many experiences with a word before they can read or write it quickly and without conscious thought. It is important that words be meaningful to students. Use them in sentences that they can understand.

YOU WILL NEED

Online Resources
- ▶ **HFW 4** Action Tags
- ▶ **HFW 4** Lotto Game Boards
- ▶ **HFW 4** Word Cards
- ▶ **HFW 4** Directions for Lotto

Other Materials
- ▶ chart paper or whiteboard
- ▶ game markers

Generative Lesson ✓

A generative lesson has a simple structure that you can use to present similar content or concepts. Use this lesson structure to teach a variety of high-frequency words.

UNDERSTAND THE PRINCIPLE

As students are learning new, longer words, it is beneficial for them to use a core of known high-frequency words as anchors to monitor and check their reading and spelling. Students can connect spelling patterns and word parts in words they know with those in more complex words. Having a large repertoire of high-frequency words supports fluent, meaningful reading and writing.

EXPLAIN THE PRINCIPLE

You need to learn words that you see many times because they help you read and write.

Comprehensive Phonics, Spelling, and Word Study Guide

Refer to: page **40**, row **6**

ACTIVITY: WORD STUDY NOTEBOOKS

INSTRUCTIONAL PROCEDURE

WORDS TO KNOW

See page 32 for detailed descriptions of Instructional Procedures.

EXPLAIN THE PRINCIPLE

You need to learn words that you see many times because they help you read and write.

Comprehensive Phonics, Spelling, and Word Study Guide

Refer to:
page **40**, row **6**

although
heard

although

Teach

1. Tell the students that they will be learning more high-frequency words.

2. On a whiteboard (or on chart paper) quickly write the word *although*. *What do you notice about the word* although? ● *Are there any parts of this word that you find challenging and that you want to remember?* ● Underline the more difficult parts that the class identifies, erase the word, and write it again quickly. Continue this process with several words, such as *heard, found, between,* and *themselves.*

3. Have students write each of the words in their word study notebooks, one at a time. *Write the word* although. *Take your time writing* although *from left to right without stopping.* Proceed word by word, writing the word on the whiteboard for them to check upon completion. If a student writes a word incorrectly, the student should cross out and fix the word, underlining the part that is incorrect or especially challenging.

4. Guide students to generalize the principle. *Why are these words important?* ● *You need to learn words that you see many times because they help you read and write.*

5. Tell the class they will practice reading high-frequency words by playing Lotto. The first player to cover all of the words on his Lotto game board wins the game.

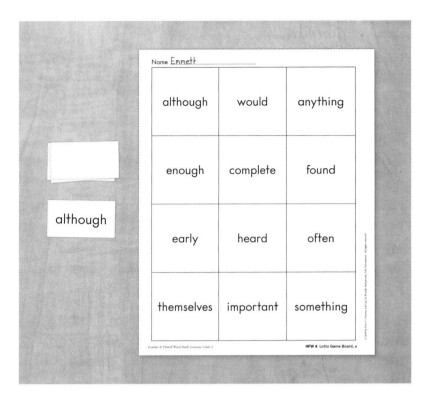

ACTIVITY: LOTTO

INSTRUCTIONAL PROCEDURE

WORDS TO KNOW

See page 32 for detailed descriptions of Instructional Procedures.

ACTION TAGS

take card

say word

cover word

Apply

Have students play Lotto with high-frequency words in groups of two to four. In turn, each player takes a word card, reads it aloud, and checks for a match on her Lotto game board. Students can use pennies or buttons for markers. The first player to fill his Lotto game board wins.

Share

Have students write the words they learned to read fluently, and then read them to a partner.

Assess

- Notice student errors and accurate reading of high-frequency words when taking reading records.

- Dictate six to ten words to students so you can assess their control of particular high-frequency words having five or more letters.

- On a regular basis, review student's highlighted individual high-frequency word lists located in their word study notebooks (see Online Resources or *Ready Resources* for high-frequency word lists). These lists provide a way for students to keep track of their own learning. Over several days, you may wish to test students on these words. They highlight words they know and choose others with which to work during Partner Study.

- You may wish to use High-Frequency Words Assessment A, B, or C.

High-Frequency Words: Recognize and Use Longer High-Frequency Words, Some with More Than One Syllable

Connect Learning Across Contexts

Shared Reading You may wish to use the following title from *Fountas & Pinnell Classroom*™ to locate additional high-frequency words after the shared reading of the text.

 *Tiny but Fierce* by Cheri Colburn

Guided Reading During word work, have students make and mix three or four high-frequency words they have been seeing while reading. Then have them write the words. (For long words, have them write and then check with a model.)

Shared Writing During shared writing, ask students to write the multisyllable high-frequency words they are learning.

Independent Writing During writing conferences, discuss any misspelled high-frequency words and have them underline difficult parts (or parts they want to remember).

Extend Learning

- Have students play Lotto with game cards that have a different variety of high-frequency words.

- Alternatively, have students select words they need to learn to place on the Lotto game boards.

▶ Connect with Home

Photocopy each student's highlighted high-frequency word lists and send it home periodically so that the students can share their increasing knowledge.

Acquire a Large Core of High-Frequency Words

Plan

▶ Consider Your Students

Use this lesson once students have worked with high-frequency words in many different ways. Each student should have an individual high-frequency word list (see Online Resources) from which to learn new words. In this lesson, students take an inventory of words that they know as well as those with which they need more practice. You can use this lesson to help determine which high-frequency words require focus in your classroom. After the lesson, highlight the words that students spell correctly, and return these highlighted lists to students. These lists can also be used for words to learn in the Partner Study System (see Word-Solving Actions lessons 10–13).

▶ Working with English Language Learners

Self-assessing and taking charge of student's own learning is beneficial to all students, including English language learners, but this requires a complex series of tasks. Work with students in a small group to be sure they understand how to keep a record of the words they know and the ones they don't know. Also, help them understand the purpose of keeping a record of known and unknown words.

YOU WILL NEED

PWS Ready Resources
- ▶ 200 High-Frequency Word List
- ▶ 500 High-Frequency Word List

Online Resources
- ▶ HFW 5 Action Tags
- ▶ HFW 5 Make-Say-Check Mix Sheets

Other Materials
- ▶ whiteboard
- ▶ index cards or paper
- ▶ magnetic letters
- ▶ word study notebooks

Generative Lesson

A generative lesson has a simple structure that you can use to present similar content or concepts. Use this lesson structure to teach a variety of high-frequency words.

UNDERSTAND THE PRINCIPLE

It is important for students to be able to write a large number of words quickly and accurately. Fluency in writing high-frequency words is acquired when children have worked with them in many different ways. Keeping a vocabulary list of known words allows learners to see their progress as well as visualize the words they still need to learn. Routinely referring to this list provides each student with a personal goal as well as freedom to choose the words they want to learn next independently. Having a large repertoire of high-frequency words supports fluent, meaningful reading and writing.

EXPLAIN THE PRINCIPLE

Add to the number of high-frequency words you can read and write.

Read and write high-frequency words quickly.

Check to see how many high-frequency words you know.

Comprehensive Phonics, Spelling, and Word Study Guide

Refer to: page **41**, row **8**

ACTIVITY: SPELLING STRATEGIES

INSTRUCTIONAL PROCEDURE

WORDS TO KNOW

See page 32 for detailed descriptions of Instructional Procedures.

EXPLAIN THE PRINCIPLE

Add to the number of high-frequency words you can read and write.

Read and write high-frequency words quickly.

Check to see how many high-frequency words you know.

Comprehensive Phonics, Spelling, and Word Study Guide

Refer to: page **41**, row **8**

---

200 High-Frequency Words

a	by	get
able	came	girl
above	can	give
across	can't	go
after	children	goes
again	city	going
all	close	gone
almost	come	good
always	could	got
am	dad	great
an	dark	grow
and	day	had
any	did	happy
anything	do	has
are	does	have
as	don't	he
ask	down	help
at	each	her
away	end	here
back	enough	hide
bad	even	him
be	every	his
because	fast	how
become	father	I
been	feel	I'm
before	find	if
begin	first	in
behind	five	inside
between	for	into
big	four	is
both	friend	it
boy	from	just
brother	fun	knew
but	game	know

Teach

1. Explain to the students that you will help them think about words they know how to write as well as words they don't know how to write or do not yet know.

2. Show an example of a list of high-frequency words with several words highlighted. *The highlighted words are words this student has already learned. The words that are not highlighted are words the student has not yet learned. This student is using a list of high-frequency words to keep track of the words he can write accurately.*

3. *Look at the list of 200 High-Frequency Words you have. There are probably many words on this list that you know how to read already. Some of these words you may know how to write already. Do you see any words that you do not know at all?* • You might suggest that students draw a small star next to a few words that are absolutely unfamiliar to them.

4. *Do you see any words that you think you know how to read and write, but you're not sure?* • You might suggest that students draw a small dot next to a few words that may be known or somewhat known.

5. Select twenty or twenty-five words of varying difficulty, dictate them to students, and have students attempt to write them correctly on a numbered list. Then review the correct spelling of these words so students can check their knowledge and annotate their list of 200 High-Frequency Words accordingly. *Any word that I said and that you wrote accurately can be highlighted on your own list, because you know that word.*

6. Encourage students to choose from the list ten or fifteen unfamiliar words that they wish to learn. Tell students that they will work with these words, practicing making and writing them using a make-say-check-mix sheet.

ACTIVITY: MAKE-SAY-CHECK-MIX

INSTRUCTIONAL PROCEDURE

WORDS TO KNOW

See page 32 for detailed descriptions of Instructional Procedures.

ACTION TAGS

select words
write words
make word
check
mix (x3)
write word
highlight a difficult part

The worksheet image:

Name: Molly — Make-Say-Check-Mix

Make/Say	Check/Mix	Write
know	✓ ✓ ✓	know
knew	✓ ✓ ✓	knew
always	✓ ✓ ✓	always
again	✓ ✓ ✓	again
about	✓ ✓ ✓	about

Fountas & Pinnell Word Study Lessons, Grade 3

HFW 5 Make-Say-Check-Mix

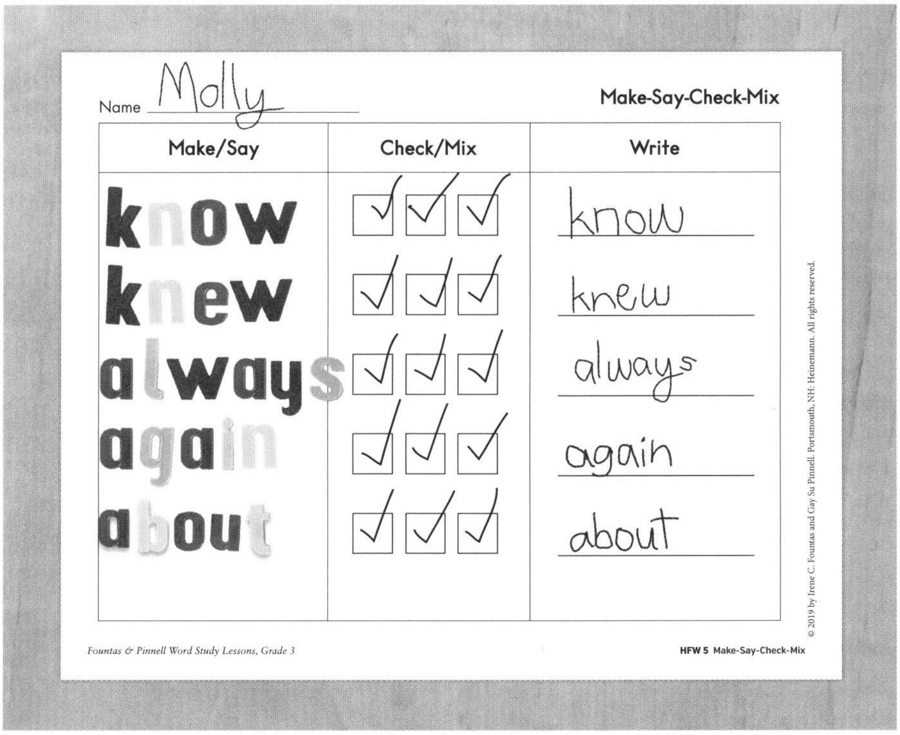

Apply

- Students select ten or fifteen unknown words from their individualized lists of high-frequency words (see Online Resources). Then students write the words on an index card or a piece of paper.

- Using a make-say-check-mix sheet, each student makes a word with magnetic letters, mixes it, and remakes it until she has made the word three times. The student places a check in the box each time she makes it, then writes the word and highlights any difficult part she wants to remember.

Share

Have students (in groups of three) tell two words that they worked on and what they want to remember about how to write them.

Assess

- Observe how students write high-frequency words in their daily writing so you can help them keep an accurate inventory on their lists of high-frequency words.

- You may wish to use High-Frequency Words Assessment A, B, or C.

Connect Learning Across Contexts

Shared Reading You may wish to use the following title from *Fountas & Pinnell Classroom*™ to locate a few high-frequency words after the shared reading of the text.

SR *From Beans to Chocolate* by June Schwartz

Guided Reading During word work, think aloud as you write some high-frequency words that students need to learn. Have them quickly write several of the words. Words that are nearly known can be located quickly within the context of print.

Shared Writing During shared writing, ask students to write the multisyllable high-frequency words they are learning.

Independent Writing Ask students to mark the words that might be incorrect and then use their word lists to check them.

Extend Learning

- Have students create their own high-frequency Word Grids for reading practice (see Online Resources for directions for Word Grids). Each student's grid will contain the particular words he needs to learn.

- Have the children create game cards (see Online Resources) with high-frequency words they need to learn. Then they find a partner and play Concentration with the deck of cards.

▶ **Connect with Home**

- Photocopy each student's high-frequency word inventory to send home or to share during family conferences.

- Have students take home their Word Grids (or Concentration game cards) and practice reading them to (or playing the game with) family members.

Read and Write Approximately 500 High-Frequency Words

Plan

▶ Consider Your Students

In third grade, students are expanding and increasing their vocabulary. In order to do so effectively, it is helpful for students to have a clear sense of the words they already know, as well as a goal to learn some words that they don't yet know. Use this lesson when students are comfortable with most words on the list of 200 High-Frequency Words and appear ready to move onward to 500 High-Frequency Words. If the words provided for this lesson are not words suitable for the class as a whole, think about what words would be most beneficial for the students to learn during this lesson, Use the students' individualized lists of high-frequency words to choose words successfully. Students can add the words they learn during this lesson to those lists.

▶ Working with English Language Learners

It is important for students to learn how to spell words in ways that will help them remember the spellings. Performing multiple actions with a single word is much more beneficial to students than writing the word on paper only. Using a make-say-check-mix sheet while spelling longer, more difficult high-frequency words will help students remember the spelling of words. Be sure that the students are comfortable with list of 200 High-Frequency Words before moving onto the list of 500 High-Frequency Words. Remember that they also need to understand word meaning. Use words in sentences they can understand.

YOU WILL NEED

PWS Ready Resources
- ▶ 500 High-Frequency Words

Online Resources
- ▶ HFW 6 Action Tags
- ▶ HFW 6 Make-Say-Check-Mix Sheets
- ▶ HFW 6 Word Cards

Other Materials
- ▶ whiteboard
- ▶ magnetic letters
- ▶ word study notebooks

Generative Lesson

A generative lesson has a simple structure that you can use to present similar content or concepts. Use this lesson structure to teach a variety of high-frequency words.

UNDERSTAND THE PRINCIPLE

Knowing high-frequency words gives students the foundation needed to write, spell, and read other more challenging words. Recognizing high-frequency words automatically while reading supports fluency and allows students to concentrate on solving words they don't know. The ability to read and write many high-frequency words quickly makes it easier for students to pay attention to the message they are reading or composing.

EXPLAIN THE PRINCIPLE

Read and write high-frequency words.

Comprehensive Phonics, Spelling, and Word Study Guide

Refer to: page **41**, row **9**

EARLY MIDDLE **LATE**

ACTIVITY: HEAR, SAY, AND WRITE: LETTER BOXES

INSTRUCTIONAL PROCEDURE

WORDS TO KNOW

See page 32 for detailed descriptions of Instructional Procedures.

EXPLAIN THE PRINCIPLE

Read and write high-frequency words.

Comprehensive Phonics, Spelling, and Word Study Guide

Refer to: page **41**, row **9**

Teach

1. *Today you are going to learn more about reading and writing some words.* Select words that many students find challenging, such as *brought*. Write *brought* on the whiteboard for the class to see. *What do you notice about the word* brought? • Students may make comments like "*brought* starts like *bring*"; "*brought* is like *bought*"; "*brought* begins with the letters *br* like *break*."

2. Erase the word and write the word again. Use *brought* in a sentence to convey its meaning to students. Talk about a variety of details about the word, such as its onset and its rime: *Brought begins with* br- *and ends with* -ought.

3. Draw seven empty letter boxes on the board. Invite a student to write the word *brought* using one letter per box. Ask the class to help sound out the word to guide spelling as needed.

4. *Let's try another word.* Write *favorite* on the whiteboard for the class to see. *What do you notice about this word?* • Favorite *has a silent* e *at the end of the word.* Erase the word and write *favorite* again before inviting a student to write the word using letter boxes. Use *favorite* in an example sentence.

5. Continue working with the class to make five or six more words (such as *either, might, answer, beautiful,* and *enough*). If students have difficulty using letter boxes, ask the class to identify the first sound, the last sound, and any middle sounds in the word: e.g., *What is the first sound you hear in the word* brought? • *What is the second sound?* • *What letters stand for the sounds* /br/?

6. Guide students to generalize the principle: *It is important to learn to read and write high-frequency words.*

7. Show students the lesson's make-say-check-mix sheet. Explain that they should take a word card, say the word, make the word with magnetic letters, check the word, place a check mark in the box, and mix the letters. Then students make, say, and check the word two more times. Each time, they should check the word they've made letter by letter using the word on the card. Then they write the word quickly in the third column and check it against the card one last time.

brought
favorite
either
might
answer
beautiful
enough

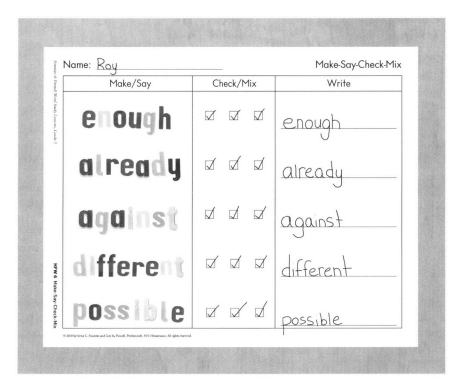

INSTRUCTIONAL PROCEDURE

WORDS TO KNOW

See page 32 for detailed descriptions of Instructional Procedures.

ACTION TAGS

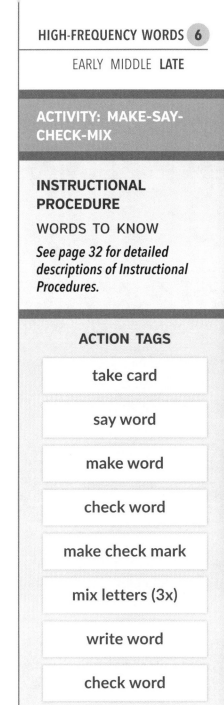

take card

say word

make word

check word

make check mark

mix letters (3x)

write word

check word

Apply

Give the students copies of the make-say-check-mix sheets and the lesson's word cards. Have the students work alone or with a partner. The students can take turns making words and checking each other's work.

Share

Have each student share what he wants to remember about one word that he learned. If time allows, ask students to write the word on the board and underline the word part that the individual student identified.

Assess

- Refer to the students' list of high-frequency words in their word study notebooks. Have students check or highlight words they have learned to write.
- Observe students' high-frequency word accuracy and understanding while reading aloud.
- You may wish to use High-Frequency Words Assessment A, B, or C.

Connect Learning Across Contexts

Shared Reading You may wish to use the following title from *Fountas & Pinnell Classroom*™ to locate a few high-frequency words after the shared reading of the text.

SR *Saving Cranes* by Brenda Iasevoli

Guided Reading During word work, think aloud as you write some high-frequency words that students need to learn. Have them quickly locate a nearly known word.

Shared Writing Invite students to write high-frequency words quickly during shared writing. Point out parts of certain words that are more difficult to remember.

Independent Writing Ask students to mark the words that might be incorrect and then use their word lists to check them.

Extend Learning

Repeat the lesson with other high-frequency words, such as *cause, easily, complete, whole,* and *together.*

▶ Connect with Home

Send home the students' individual word lists and accompanying letter boxes to complete with family members.

Word Meaning/Vocabulary

Students need to know the meaning of the words they are learning to read and write. It is important for them to expand their speaking, reading, writing, and vocabulary constantly as well as to develop a more complex understanding of words they already know. The category of Word Meaning/Vocabulary includes concept words with sets and subsets that are often used in the texts that students read, and they will want to use these words in their own writing. When students learn concept words, they can learn how to form categories that help in retrieving these words when needed. In our complex language, meaning and spelling are intricately connected. Often you must know the meaning of the word you want to spell or read before you can spell it accurately. And vocabulary is certainly a very important element of reading comprehension.

In addition to lists of common concept words that students are often expected to know how to read and spell, we include synonyms and antonyms. Knowing these types of related words will help students build more powerful systems for connecting and categorizing words; it will also help them comprehend texts better and write in a more interesting way. Being able to distinguish homophones from homographs assists in comprehension and helps spellers to avoid mistakes. We also include work with words with multiple meanings as well as words with literal and figurative meanings.

Connect to Assessment

See related (optional) WMV Assessment tasks in Online Resources.

- Assessment A: Recognizing and Reading Concept Words
- Assessment B: Categorizing Words
- Assessment C: Recognizing and Using Compound Words
- Assessment D: Recognizing and Using Synonyms
- Assessment E: Recognizing and Using Antonyms
- Assessment F: Recognizing and Using Homophones
- Assessment G: Recognizing and Using Homographs
- Assessment H: Individual Record

Develop Your Professional Understanding

See *The Fountas & Pinnell Comprehensive Phonics, Spelling, and Word Study Guide*. 2017. Portsmouth, New Hampshire: Heinemann. Related pages: 2-12, 44-49.

See *The Fountas & Pinnell Literacy Continuum: A Tool for Assessment, Planning, and Teaching*. 2017. Portsmouth, New Hampshire: Heinemann. Related pages: 357-397.

See *Word Matters: Teaching Phonics and Spelling in the Reading/Writing Classroom* by G.S. Pinnell and I.C. Fountas. 1998. Portsmouth, New Hampshire: Heinemann. Related pages: 78–81, 88–89, 199–205.

Recognize and Use Concept Words That Can Have Sets and Subsets

Plan

▶ Consider Your Students

Most students will have prior knowledge of a variety of types of concept words, such as colors, number words, days of the week, months of the year, and seasons. They also will likely have some familiarity of grouping words into subsets, such as *animals* and *elephant.* You may want to review the concept with words that represent items or ideas with which they are already familiar, such as food, games, family, clothing, and weather. Then begin integrating content words from areas such as math, science, and social studies.

▶ Working with English Language Learners

English language learners will know the routine of sorting, but make sure they understand that in this lesson they will be arranging words according to the relationship of the words' meanings. It will be helpful for you to demonstrate sorting words by meanings. Categorizing words into sets and subsets will be very helpful to English learners as they expand their speaking, reading, and writing vocabularies. Begin with basic examples, and use pictures if necessary.

UNDERSTAND THE PRINCIPLE

Good word solvers are able to connect words by their meanings. Using meanings to group words into categories creates a useful mental map for readers and writers. Moreover, students can begin to form more sophisticated mental maps by connecting, analyzing, and arranging related words into sets and subsets according to how general or specific the terms are.

YOU WILL NEED

Online Resources
- ▶ WMV 1 Action Tags
- ▶ WMV 1 Word Webs
- ▶ WMV 1 Word Cards

Other Materials
- ▶ chart paper

Generative Lesson ✓
A generative lesson has a simple structure that you can use to present similar content or concepts. Use this lesson to teach a variety of concept words.

EXPLAIN THE PRINCIPLE

Some words stand for big ideas or items.

Find words that stand for smaller ideas or items related to the big ideas.

Comprehensive Phonics, Spelling, and Word Study Guide

Refer to:
page **44**, row **2**

ACTIVITY: WORD WEB

INSTRUCTIONAL PROCEDURE

MAP WORDS

See page 32 for detailed descriptions of Instructional Procedures.

EXPLAIN THE PRINCIPLE

Some words stand for big ideas or items.

Find words that stand for smaller ideas or items related to the big ideas.

Comprehensive Phonics, Spelling, and Word Study Guide

Refer to: page **44**, row **2**

bird

eagle

robin

blue jay

sparrow

Teach

1. Write the words *eagle, robin, blue jay,* and *sparrow* on chart paper. Invite children to read the words with you.

2. *What do you notice about all these words? What is the same about all these words?*

3. Above the list of words, write the word *bird. All the words listed are kinds of birds. The words listed fit into the same group or big idea. The big idea is* bird; *a smaller idea is* robin. *Can you think of other examples where the small ideas fit into one big idea?*

4. Students might offer examples of concept words, such as *airplane* (transportation), *violin* (instruments), *math* (school subjects), and *elephant* (animals).

5. *Sometimes we can start with a big idea and break it down into even smaller groups.* Write the word *plant* in the center of a sheet of chart paper. *What are some words that go with* plant? Invite students to suggest words (*leaves, flowers, grass*), and record them on chart paper in a word web.

6. Tell the students that they are going to sort words into groups. After they sort the words, they will work with a partner to make a word web.

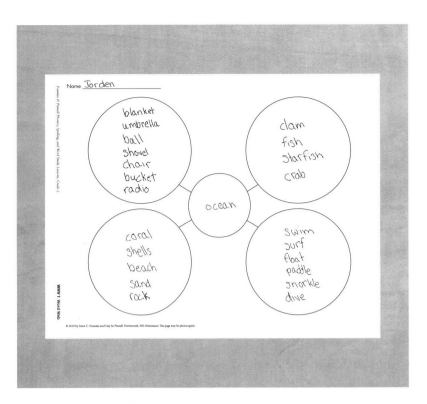

Name Jorden

blanket
umbrella
ball
shovel
chair
bucket
radio

clam
fish
starfish
crab

ocean

coral
shells
beach
sand
rock

swim
surf
float
paddle
snorkle
dive

WMV 1 Word Web

© 2019 by Irene C. Fountas and Gay Su Pinnell. Portsmouth, NH: Heinemann. This page may be photocopied.

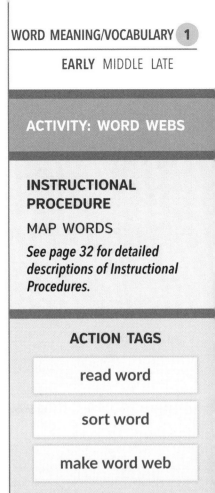

ACTIVITY: WORD WEBS

INSTRUCTIONAL PROCEDURE

MAP WORDS

See page 32 for detailed descriptions of Instructional Procedures.

ACTION TAGS

read word

sort word

make word web

Apply

Have the students work with a partner and sort the ocean word cards into smaller categories. Partners then write *ocean* in the middle of a word web. They write the words in each category to make a final web. Students can draw circles around their categories and/or label them.

Share

■ Partners bring their word webs to share with the group. Students may compare the different webs and the ways students have made their subsets.

■ Review the principle, and remind students to notice words concept words with sets and subsets as they read and write.

Assess

■ Working individually with students, have them identify and say words that stand for smaller ideas or items related to the big idea of a concept word you name.

■ Look at the word webs to see the kind of thinking students have done as they placed words into categories.

■ Have the students do a simple individual word web to see if they understand the concept.

■ You may wish to use Word Meaning/Vocabulary Assessment A or H.

Word Meaning/Vocabulary: Recognize and Use Concept Words That Can Have Sets and Subsets

Connect Learning Across Contexts

Shared Reading You may wish to use the following Shared Reading title from *Fountas & Pinnell Classroom*™ to point out concept words that can have sets and subsets.

> *Exploring Underground* by Louis Petrone

Independent Reading In discussing selections that children have read, point out words that are related to larger concepts or ideas by creating a quick web in the extension part of the lesson.

Shared Writing Write with the class about small idea words related to big ideas such as *jobs, books,* or *sports.*

Independent Writing If you have made some word webs in content areas, prompt students to use them as resources for writing. Prompt the students to use word connecting as a strategy to compose informational writing.

Extend Learning

Create word webs for words in different content areas.

▶ Connect with Home

Give students the assignment of creating a word web for *activities I do at home, things in my house,* or another home-related topic.

Recognize and Use Concept Words That Can Have Sets and Subsets

Plan

▶ Consider Your Students

This lesson is placed early in the year to help students begin forming categories for connecting words. You can choose any category of words for this lesson, so coordinate it with your science or social studies curriculum as a means of developing content vocabulary. The purpose is to help students begin the process of relating words by meaning. Choose a topic with which students have concrete experience, as well as many opportunities to talk about the topic and listen to stories about it.

▶ Working with English Language Learners

Connecting words is a good way to help students expand their English vocabularies. Begin with familiar subject areas and topics, using words that students have encountered in books you read to them and in conversation in the classroom. Provide opportunities for English language learners to use words in meaningful sentences. You may wish to work with them in a small group and to simplify the word web, perhaps using fewer words, to be sure they understand the task. Before beginning the application, test whether students can read the words, and eliminate any that are too difficult.

YOU WILL NEED

Online Resources
- ▶ WMV 2 Action Tags
- ▶ WMV 2 Four-Box Sheets

Other Materials
- ▶ chart paper

Generative Lesson
A generative lesson has a simple structure that you can use to present similar content or concepts. Use this lesson to teach a variety of concept words.

UNDERSTAND THE PRINCIPLE

Good word solvers are able to connect words by their meanings. Using meanings to group words into categories creates a useful mental map for readers and writers. Moreover, students can begin to form more sophisticated mental maps by connecting, analyzing, and arranging related words into sets and subsets according to how general or specific the terms are.

EXPLAIN THE PRINCIPLE

Some words stand for big ideas or items.

Find words that stand for smaller ideas or items related to the big ideas.

Comprehensive Phonics, Spelling, and Word Study Guide

Refer to: page **44**, row **2**

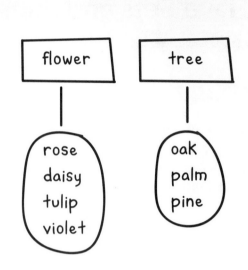

ACTIVITY: WORD MAP: PLANTS

INSTRUCTIONAL PROCEDURE

MAP WORDS

See page 32 for detailed descriptions of Instructional Procedures.

EXPLAIN THE PRINCIPLE

Some words stand for big ideas or items.

Find words that stand for smaller ideas or items related to the big ideas.

Comprehensive Phonics, Spelling, and Word Study Guide

Refer to: page **44**, row **2**

Teach

1. Tell students that they are going to think about how words go together.

2. Write the word *flower* near the top left of a sheet of chart paper. *What is this word? • This word is* flower. Then write the words *rose* and *daisy* below.

3. *What do you notice about these three words when you think about their meanings? •* As necessary, help students recognize that *rose* and *daisy* name types of flowers. Draw a box around the word *flower. What are some other words that go with* rose *and* daisy? Students may offer words such as *tulip* or *violet*. Write these words below, and place a box around these four words.

4. Guide students to generalize the principle: *Some words stand for big ideas or items. You can find words that stand for smaller ideas or items related to a big idea.*

5. Write the word *tree* at the top right, and draw a box around it. *Here is another big idea. What words could go below the word* tree? • Students may mention words such as *oak, palm,* or *pine*. Draw a box around the more specific related words, and invite students to explain the relationship of this group of words and the word *tree*.

6. Continue the lesson with "big idea" words such as *fruit* or *vegetable*.

7. Tell students that they will choose one of these categories: *art, sports,* or *animals*. On a four-box sheet, they will list four groups of words that relate to the category they selected. Then they will trade papers with a partner and see if they can identify the way their partner grouped each set of words.

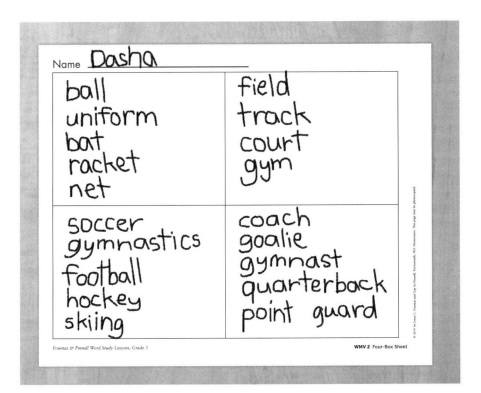

Name **Dasha**

ball uniform bat racket net	field track court gym
soccer gymnastics football hockey skiing	coach goalie gymnast quarterback point guard

Fountas & Pinnell Word Study Lessons, Grade 3   **WMV 2** Four-Box Sheet

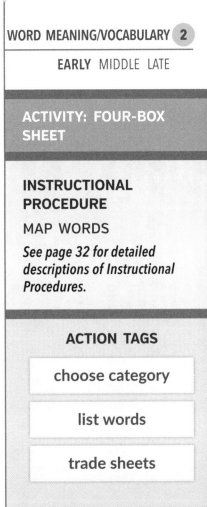

ACTIVITY: FOUR-BOX SHEET

INSTRUCTIONAL PROCEDURE

MAP WORDS

See page 32 for detailed descriptions of Instructional Procedures.

ACTION TAGS

choose category

list words

trade sheets

Apply

Distribute four-box sheets and have students list four groups of words related to each category. Remind them that there is no right or wrong way to group the words, as long as they are grouped in a meaningful way.

Share

- Have students trade lists with a partner. Have partners guess the categories.
- Review the principle, and remind students to notice that words can be related in many ways as they read and write.

Assess

- Work individually with students, and have them identify and say words that stand for smaller ideas or items related to the big idea of a concept word you name.
- Look at the four-box sheets to see the kind of thinking students have done as they wrote words into categories.
- You may wish to use Word Meaning/Vocabulary Assessment A or H.

Word Meaning/Vocabulary: Recognize and Use Concept Words That Can Have Sets and Subsets

Connect Learning Across Contexts

Shared Reading You may wish to use the following Shared Reading title from *Fountas & Pinnell Classroom*™ to point out words that can be related in many ways.

SR *Saving Cranes* by Brenda Iasevoli

Guided Reading In discussing selections that students have read, point out words that are related to larger concepts or ideas by creating a quick web in the extension part of the lesson.

Shared Writing As you work together to write informational texts, prompt students to think about the connections among words.

Independent Writing If you have made some word webs in content areas, prompt students to use them as resources for writing. Encourage them to think about connections among words as a way to organize and elaborate on their writing.

Extend Learning

- As you work in content area, make word webs related to key content ideas.
- Have students make a new word web for one of the categories they did not choose for the Apply activity.
- Have students return to the webs you made together during the Teach activity. Invite students to extend the web "upward" by thinking of a bigger concept (e.g., plants) that relates to *flower*, *tree*, *fruit*, and *vegetable*.

▶ Connect with Home

Have students share their four-box sheets with a family member. Ask them to invite their family member to guess the categories they used to group the words.

Recognize That Words Can Be Related in Many Ways: Category

Plan

▶ Consider Your Students

In this lesson you will teach students a technique for seeing the relationships between and among words. Use very simple words and categories if this is the first time students have sorted words by meaning. Also, limit the number of categories and/or the number of words. If students are experienced sorters, increase the complexity. While the emphasis in this lesson is on sorting words by meaning, you will want to recognize other criteria students use to sort, for example, how words look or sound. Make this first sorting experience easy and obvious; later, you can vary the samples so that there is more than one way to sort the words.

▶ Working with English Language Learners

Word sorting can help English language learners expand their vocabularies. Making connections will help students create richer definitions for English words and better understand how words can be related. Start with only two categories and just a few words in each. Use pictures and words to begin, if necessary, then gradually remove the pictures.

UNDERSTAND THE PRINCIPLE

Connecting words will help students accelerate the development of their vocabularies. Understanding categorization is a foundation for understanding how information is organized and presented.

YOU WILL NEED

PWS Ready Resources
- ▶ WMV 3 Pocket-Chart Cards

Online Resources
- ▶ WMV 3 Action Tags
- ▶ WMV 3 Word Cards
- ▶ WMV 3 Two-Way Sorts

Other Materials
- ▶ pocket chart

Generative Lesson ✓
A generative lesson has a simple structure that you can use to present similar content or concepts. Use this lesson to teach a variety of ways to categorize words.

EXPLAIN THE PRINCIPLE

Some words go together because they are the same in some way [e.g., clothes, family members].

Comprehensive Phonics, Spelling, and Word Study Guide

Refer to: page **45**, row **3**

EARLY MIDDLE LATE

ACTIVITY: FOUR-WAY SORT

INSTRUCTIONAL PROCEDURE

MAP WORDS

See page 32 for detailed descriptions of Instructional Procedures.

EXPLAIN THE PRINCIPLE

Some words go together because they are the same in some way [e.g., **clothes, family members***].*

Comprehensive Phonics, Spelling, and Word Study Guide

Refer to:
page **45**, row **3**

Teach

1. Tell students that they are going to think about how words go together. They have some meaning that shows they can be grouped together.

2. Place some words in random order in a column on the left half of the chart. Leave room on the right side for students to take words from the left column and make categories on the right.

3. *I have some words on the chart today. Some of these words go together. Can you see some words that belong together?* Students will identify the categories as *things you wear, colors, number or position words,* and *ways to move.*

4. Have students take turns suggesting or placing words together into categories. Ask them to label their categories or to talk about why they put certain words together. If students suggest visual aspects of words (such as first letters), recognize that way of connecting words, but remind them to think about the meaning of the words.

5. As students talk about the way they sorted the words, reinforce the principle: *Some words go together because they belong to the same category.*

6. Explain to students that today they will sort more words. If they find any words that they do not know how to group, they can put them aside to sort later. Students select categories, sort the word cards, and then write the words on the two-way sort. Then they write a label for the categories at the top of each column.

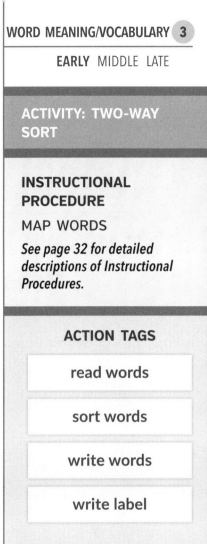

INSTRUCTIONAL PROCEDURE

MAP WORDS

See page 32 for detailed descriptions of Instructional Procedures.

ACTION TAGS

read words

sort words

write words

write label

Apply

Distribute two-way sorts. Have students read and sort the word cards. You may wish to add other words that fit the categories. For each category, students write the words on a two-way sort and then they write a label describing each column.

Share

- Have students share their word sorts with a partner. Ask them to talk about what they have learned about words by sorting them. You may wish to collect and review their word sorts.

- Review the principle, and remind students to notice category words that can be related in many ways when they read and write.

Assess

- Observe students as they sort the words, and talk with them about how they are sorting the words. This will help you understand how they are thinking about words.

- You may wish to use Word Meaning/Vocabulary Assessment B or H.

Connect Learning Across Contexts

Shared Reading You may wish to use the following Shared Reading title from *Fountas & Pinnell Classroom™* to point out category words that can be related in many ways.

SR *Exploring Underground* by Louis Petrone

Guided Reading When students encounter an unfamiliar word, help them connect it by meaning to some words that they already know (e.g., a new way of moving through water as in *gliding*).

Shared Writing As you work together to write texts, point out connections between words. Identify places where you can substitute a different, more specific word that is related by meaning. For example, instead of saying that someone put on a *coat*, you could say that they put on a *parka*.

Independent Writing Suggest that students think of words that are connected to words they usually in order to increase the variety of words they use in their writing.

Extend Learning

Expand the categories of words and make it possible to sort them in several different ways. For example:

- numbers and words relating to numbers: *one, two, three, four, five, fifth, fourth, third, second, first*
- words related to movements: *walk, ride, run, creep, dive, swim, splash, fly*
- names of animals: *turtle, dog, cat, horse, bird, horse, fish, duck*

The same words can be sorted like this:

- words related to living or moving on land: *run, walk, ride, creep, fly, gallop, turtle, dog, cat, horse, bird*
- words related to living or moving in the water: *swim, dive, splash, fish, duck, turtle* (both categories)
- words relating to position: *first, second, third, fourth, fifth*
- number words: *one, two, three, four, five*

▶ Connect with Home

Have students take home words to sort. As they build their collections of words, they can create new categories and sort in different ways.

Recognize That Words Can Be Related in Many Ways: Category

Plan

▶ Consider Your Students

Use this lesson when students have learned the task of sorting words by applying several different criteria. They will work with a variety of related words that can be grouped into sets and subsets. There may be some words in the collection that are new to students, so be sure to explain them before they begin the activity. Eliminate any words that are too difficult. Color words are used in this lesson; you will want to use other categories to expand students' vocabularies. Make note of any students who are color-blind and may have difficulty with the concepts shown here. You can substitute other words (see Extend Learning).

▶ Working with English Language Learners

The words in this lesson may be challenging for English language learners. You may wish to reduce the number of words and be sure that students have a color illustration as a reference. Say each word several times and have students repeat it. Give students time to talk about what the words mean and why they are putting them together.

UNDERSTAND THE PRINCIPLE

Connecting words will help students accelerate the development of their vocabularies. Understanding categorization is a foundation for understanding how information is organized and presented. In this lesson, students are required to notice the more subtle aspects of words and their connections. Colors are used to introduce this kind of thinking.

YOU WILL NEED

Online Resources
- ▶ **WMV 4** Action Tags
- ▶ **WMV 4** Word Cards
- ▶ **WMV 4** Three-Way Sorts

Other Materials
- ▶ blank chart paper

Generative Lesson

A generative lesson has a simple structure that you can use to present similar content or concepts. Use this lesson to teach a variety of ways to categorize words.

EXPLAIN THE PRINCIPLE

Some words go together because they are the same in some way [e.g., clothes, family members].

Comprehensive Phonics, Spelling, and Word Study Guide

Refer to:
page **45**, row **3**

ACTIVITY: TWO-WAY SORT

INSTRUCTIONAL PROCEDURE

MAP WORDS

See page 32 for detailed descriptions of Instructional Procedures.

EXPLAIN THE PRINCIPLE

Some words go together because they are the same in some way [e.g., **clothes, family members***].*

Comprehensive Phonics, Spelling, and Word Study Guide

Refer to: page **45**, row **3**

---

yellow	blue
gold	navy
lemon	indigo
mustard	teal
honey	cobalt

Gold is a darker shade of yellow. These things are all shades of yellow.

All these are things that are blue. They are different shades of blue.

Teach

1. Tell students that they are going to think about how words go together. *You can put them in groups by thinking about what they mean. You know that you can learn new words by making connections. Today you will think about ways that words can go together. Some words you may know, and some may be new to you.*

2. Write *yellow* and *blue* at the top of the chart. *I'm thinking of another color word. I'm thinking of* gold. *Where would I put* gold—*with* yellow *or with* blue?

3. Students will probably respond by saying that *gold* is more like *yellow* than like blue. As needed, find something gold, either in the crayon box or in something students are wearing. *Why did you put* gold *with* yellow? ● Gold *is a shade of* yellow, *so gold* goes under yellow *because it is related to* yellow *by meaning.*

4. Suggest several more color words that fit in either the *yellow* or *blue* category. When you have several in each category, ask students if they can come up with any more color words to place under *yellow* or *blue*. The contrast with blue will help them to make decisions about words like *lemon, mustard,* or *honey.*

5. *What have you noticed about some of these color words?* Students may observe that the colors are lighter, brighter, or darker even though they are all still yellow or blue. Write their statements on the chart, and then use them to restate the principle: *Some words go together because they mean the same or almost the same.*

6. Tell students they will again sort color words for yellow, blue, and a mystery category. Review the words on the word cards, and provide examples if students do not know the color. Have them record the color words on a three-way sort and then record a sentence describing each category on the back of the sort.

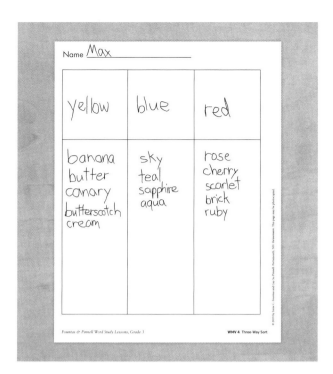

INSTRUCTIONAL PROCEDURE

MAP WORDS

See page 32 for detailed descriptions of Instructional Procedures.

ACTION TAGS

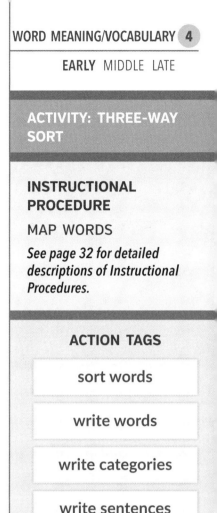

sort words

write words

write categories

write sentences

Apply

Distribute three-way sorts. Have students write *yellow* and *blue* at the top of two columns and leave the third column blank. Then ask them to sort the color word cards and write them in the three columns. Remind them to write a name for the third column and a sentence describing each category on the back of the sheet.

Share

- Have students share their word sorts with a partner and then with the group. Discuss the name that students gave the third category and why. Ask students to talk about what they have learned about words by sorting them. You may wish to collect and review their word sorts.

- Review the principle, and remind students to notice category words that can be related in many ways when they read and write.

Assess

- Observe students as they sort the words, and talk with them about how they are sorting the words. This will help you understand how they are thinking about words.

- Provide another group of related words, and have students determine a category name for the words. Listen for them to choose a meaning-based category.

- You may wish to use Word Meaning/Vocabulary Assessment B or H.

Word Meaning/Vocabulary: Recognize That Words Can Be Related in Many Ways: Category

Connect Learning Across Contexts

Shared Reading You may wish to use the following Shared Reading title from *Fountas & Pinnell Classroom*™ to point out category words that can be related in many ways.

SR *From Flower to Honey* by June Schwartz

Guided Reading Help students notice when writers use interesting words identifying specific shades of colors in descriptions.

Shared Writing As you work together to write texts, point out connections between words. Identify places where you can substitute a different, more specific word that is related by meaning. For example, instead of saying that someone put on a *red* sweater, you could say that he put on a *crimson* sweater.

Independent Writing Suggest to students that they can increase the variety of words they use in their compositions by thinking of words that are connected to the words they usually use.

Extend Learning

Repeat this lesson with other categories that require students to sort words according to related meanings. For example, students may sort words such as *hot, cold, burning, boiling, warm, sizzling, scalding, chilly, icy, freezing, frosty, wintry, frozen, frigid,* and *steamy.*

▶ Connect with Home

Students can take home their lists of color words and ask family members to help them think of new ways to describe colors. Students can work on new lists of words describing colors such as *black* or *orange*.

Recognize and Use Compound Words

Plan

▶ Consider Your Students

Many students find compound words easy to understand, because typically they have had experience with many different examples. If students have not studied compound words formally, introduce the principle by using simple examples such as *sunshine*. Begin with words that are in students' speaking vocabularies, then branch out to include words that they may not have considered but that have meanings that are easily derive.

▶ Working with English Language Learners

Use simple compound words that English language learners can understand. Provide picture support and demonstrations as needed. It may be helpful to work with students in a small group. If you know any compound words in a student's language, add these to the list, and show students how the meanings of the individual words can be combined to determine the meaning of the whole word.

UNDERSTAND THE PRINCIPLE

Compound words are made up of two smaller words. In most compound words (for example, *sidewalk*), each smaller word contributes to the meaning of the whole word. Teaching students to look for smaller words in larger words can be a helpful strategy for figuring out the meaning of longer words.

YOU WILL NEED

Online Resources
- ▶ **WMV 5** Action Tags
- ▶ **WMV 5** Word Cards
- ▶ **WMV 5** List Sheets

Other Materials
- ▶ chart paper

Generative Lesson ✓

A generative lesson has a simple structure that you can use to present similar content or concepts. Use this lesson structure to teach students a variety of compound words.

EXPLAIN THE PRINCIPLE

Some words are made of two smaller words. They are compound words.

Each smaller word helps in thinking about the meaning of the whole word.

Comprehensive Phonics, Spelling, and Word Study Guide

Refer to: page **46**, row **10**

ACTIVITY: COMPOUND WORDS

INSTRUCTIONAL PROCEDURE

NOTICE PARTS

See page 32 for detailed descriptions of Instructional Procedures.

EXPLAIN THE PRINCIPLE

Some words are made of two smaller words. They are compound words.

Each smaller word helps in thinking about the meaning of the whole word.

Comprehensive Phonics, Spelling, and Word Study Guide

Refer to: page **46**, row **10**

sunlight

haircut

anthill

doghouse

footprint

classroom

backpack

Teach

1. Tell students that they are going to learn more about words.

2. Write the words *sunlight, haircut,* and *anthill* on a piece of chart paper. Read the words aloud, and ask: *What do you notice about all of the words on the chart?* Students will likely respond that "there are two words put together." *All of these words are compound words. That means that they are made up of two words that are put together.* Have students identify the two words that make up each compound word.

3. *Let's look at the word* sunlight. *What do you think* sunlight *is? How did you figure out the meaning? • Sometimes we can put together the meanings of the two smaller words in a compound word to figure out the meaning of the larger word.*

4. Repeat this procedure for *haircut* and *anthill.* As students suggest definitions, listen for evidence that they understand the principle.

   "*Haircut* is made up of the words *hair* and *cut.* You get a *haircut* when someone cuts your hair."

   "*Anthill* has the words *ant* and *hill.* It's a little hill of sand that ants make when they build their home."

5. Challenge students to come up with additional examples of compound words, and write them on the chart paper. Discuss the meaning of each word they suggest.

6. Explain to the students that today they are going to make compound words with two word cards. Then they will write the compound word on a list sheet. Finally, they will read their list to a partner and tell what each word means.

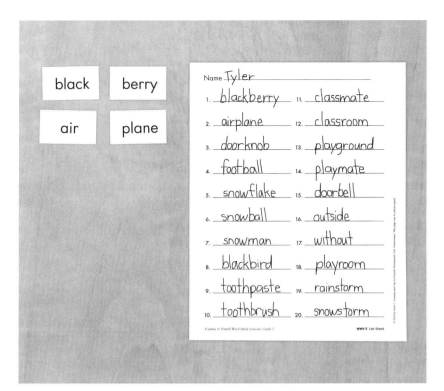

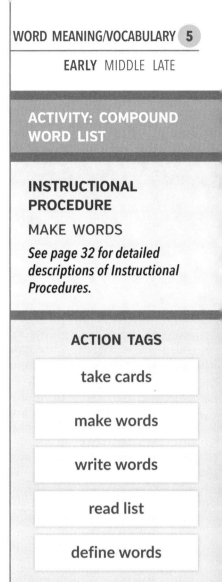

ACTIVITY: COMPOUND WORD LIST

INSTRUCTIONAL PROCEDURE

MAKE WORDS

See page 32 for detailed descriptions of Instructional Procedures.

ACTION TAGS

take cards

make words

write words

read list

define words

Apply

Have students make twenty compound words. Remind them that the words must be real. Be sure that students know that some of the component words can be used more than once. After they write their words, have them read each word and share its definition with a partner.

Share

- Have students read their lists of compound words to a different partner or the group. Be prepared for some creative suggestions. You can always check the dictionary. If children suggest words that are not compound words, validate their thinking by discussing the way that the words in their example go together.

- Review the principle, and remind students to notice compound words they read and write.

Assess

- Make a list of five to ten compound words, and have each child read them. After students have read the compound words, ask them to talk about the meanings of each one. Observe to find evidence of students' ability to think about the meaning of words by noticing their component parts.

- You may wish to use Word Meaning/Vocabulary Assessment C or H.

Connect Learning Across Contexts

Interactive Read-Aloud As you reread books, select one or two compound words to write on a whiteboard, and discuss their meanings. You may wish to use a document camera or projector.

> IRA *The Sunsets of Miss Olivia Wiggins* by Lester M. Laminack

> IRA *Meadowlands: A Wetlands Survival Story* by Thomas F. Yezerski

Guided Reading After students have read a text, write a few compound words on a whiteboard. Have the students talk about the component parts and how they are helpful in thinking about the meaning of the word.

Shared Writing As you work together to write texts, point out compound words. Explain that thinking about how to spell each smaller word can help you spell the compound word.

Independent Writing When conferring with students, point out any compound words that they have used in their own writing.

Extend Learning

Have students brainstorm word families that use compound words, such as *snow*, *snowman*, *snowball*, *snowflake*, *snowshoe*, and *snowplow*.

▶ Connect with Home

Have the students enlist their family members in looking for compound words. They may find some that are commonly used at home: *bathroom, stovetop, raindrop, doghouse, dishtowel, doorbell.*

Recognize and Use Compound Words

Plan

▶ Consider Your Students

Many students find compound words easy to understand, because typically they have had experience with many different examples. If students have not studied compound words formally, introduce the principle by using simple examples such as *sunshine*. Begin with words that are in students' speaking vocabularies, then branch out to include words that they may not have considered but that have meanings that are easily derived.

▶ Working with English Language Learners

Use simple compound words that English language learners can understand. Provide picture support and demonstrations as needed. It may be helpful to work with students in a small group. If you know any compound words in a student's language, add these to the list, and show students how the meanings of the individual words can be combined to determine the meaning of the whole word.

UNDERSTAND THE PRINCIPLE

Compound words are made up of two smaller words. In most compound words (for example, *popcorn*), each smaller word contributes to the meaning of the whole word. Teaching students to look for smaller words in larger words can be a helpful strategy for figuring out the meaning of longer words.

YOU WILL NEED

Online Resources
- ▶ **WMV 6** Action Tags
- ▶ **WMV 6** Game Cards
- ▶ **WMV 6** Directions for Concentration

Other Materials
- ▶ chart paper

Generative Lesson
A generative lesson has a simple structure that you can use to present similar content or concepts. Use this lesson structure to teach students a variety of compound words.

EXPLAIN THE PRINCIPLE

Some words are made of two smaller words. They are compound words.

Each smaller word helps in thinking about the meaning of the whole word.

Comprehensive Phonics, Spelling, and Word Study Guide

Refer to: page **46**, row **10**

ACTIVITY: COMPOUND WORDS

INSTRUCTIONAL PROCEDURE

NOTICE PARTS

See page 32 for detailed descriptions of Instructional Procedures.

EXPLAIN THE PRINCIPLE

Some words are made of two smaller words. They are compound words.

Each smaller word helps in thinking about the meaning of the whole word.

Comprehensive Phonics, Spelling, and Word Study Guide

Refer to: page **46**, row **10**

footprint
blueberry
backyard

inside
    sidewalk
        walkway

sunlight
    lighthouse
        houseboat

Teach

1. Tell students that they are going to learn more about words.

2. Write the words *footprint, blueberry,* and *backyard* on a piece of chart paper. Read the words aloud, and ask: *What do you notice about all of these words?* Students will likely respond that "there are two words put together." Review that these words are called compound words, and have students identify the two smaller words that make up each compound word.

3. *Look at the word* footprint. *How can knowing the meaning of* foot *and the meaning of* print *help you figure out the meaning of this longer word?* ● *A* footprint *is a print, or mark, made by your foot. The meaning of each word,* foot *and* print, *helps you think about the meaning of the longer word.*

4. Repeat this procedure for *blueberry* and *backyard.*

5. Then make compound word ladders with students. Start with one word (*inside,* for example). Invite students to add a compound word that starts with the second word: *inside, sidewalk, walkway.*

6. Complete a few more ladders (e.g., *sunlight, lighthouse, houseboat*) so that students will understand the concept. As students build the ladders, discuss how the meaning of each word on the ladder changes and stays the same. Guide students to notice how each individual word within a compound contributes to the meaning of the compound word as a whole.

7. Explain to the students that today they are going to play Concentration. *You are going to play the game Concentration with compound words. You will pick up a card and read the word. Then you will pick up another card and see if the two words can be combined to make a compound word. If the two words make a compound word, you have made a match. The player with the most matches wins the game.*

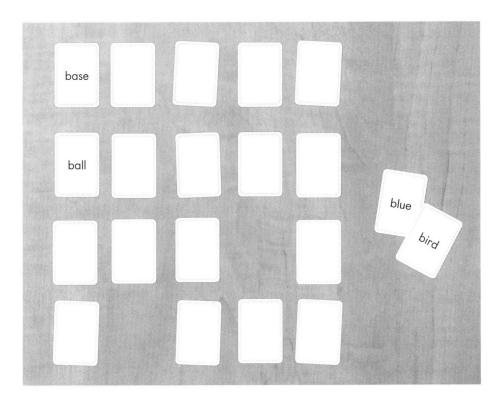

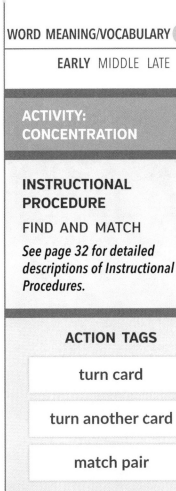

ACTIVITY:
CONCENTRATION

INSTRUCTIONAL PROCEDURE

FIND AND MATCH

See page 32 for detailed descriptions of Instructional Procedures.

ACTION TAGS

turn card

turn another card

match pair

Apply

Have students play Concentration in groups of two to four players. Tell them to list three compound words on an index card to share with the group.

Share

■ Have the students read their lists of compound words to the group, and discuss the meanings. Add any new compound words to the class chart.

■ Review the principle, and remind students to notice compound words when they read and write.

Assess

■ Make a list of five to ten compound words, and have each student read them. After students have read the compound words, ask them to talk about what they mean.

■ Observe to find evidence of students' ability to think about the meaning of words by noticing their component parts.

■ You may wish to use Word Meaning/Vocabulary Assessment C or H.

Connect Learning Across Contexts

Interactive Read-Aloud As you reread books, select one or two compound words to write on a whiteboard, and discuss their meanings.

- [IRA] *The Paperboy* by Dav Pilkey
- [IRA] *Some Birthday!* by Patricia Polacco

Guided Reading After students have read a text, write a few compound words on a whiteboard. Have the students talk about the component parts and how they are helpful in thinking about the meaning of the word.

Shared Writing As you work together to write texts, point out compound words. Explain that thinking about how to spell each shorter word can help you spell the longer word.

Independent Writing When conferring with students, point out any compound words they have used in their own writing.

Extend Learning

- Give students a word card, and have them generate a second word that would form a compound word.
- Repeat the lesson using open compound words, such as *ice cream, French fries,* and *high school.*

▶ Connect with Home

Have students play Concentration using compound words with a family member.

Recognize and Use Synonyms

Plan

▶ Consider Your Students

Use this lesson to provide a review of the concept of synonyms and to increase students' knowledge of good examples. If students have not learned the term *synonym,* this lesson will familiarize them with that term and help them quickly generate pairs of synonyms. You may want to start with limited sets of synonyms that you are sure students know, then increase the number and complexity of the examples over several days.

▶ Working with English Language Learners

Grasping the concept of synonyms helps English language learners expand their knowledge of English; when they truly understand one word, it is easier to learn other words that share similar meanings. At the same time, using words interchangeably increases the complexity of the language for beginners. As needed, work with a small group of students to help them match synonym word cards and repeat the words in sentences.

UNDERSTAND THE PRINCIPLE

When proficient readers encounter unfamiliar words in print, they not only use their decoding skills but also think of alternative words that fit the meaning of the sentence. Knowing that words can mean the same thing helps students begin to connect words by meaning. Knowledge of synonyms allows students to vary the words they use, making their writing more interesting.

YOU WILL NEED

PWS Ready Resources
▶ **WMV 7** Pocket-Chart Cards

Online Resources
▶ **WMV 7** Action Tags
▶ **WMV 7** Word Cards
▶ **WMV 7** Word Pairs Sheets

Other Materials
▶ pocket chart

Generative Lesson

A generative lesson has a simple structure that you can use to present similar content or concepts. Use this lesson to teach a variety of synonyms.

EXPLAIN THE PRINCIPLE

Some words mean the same. They are synonyms.

 Comprehensive Phonics, Spelling, and Word Study Guide

Refer to: page **45**, row **4**

ACTIVITY: POCKET CHART

INSTRUCTIONAL PROCEDURE

MAP WORDS

See page 32 for detailed descriptions of Instructional Procedures.

EXPLAIN THE PRINCIPLE

Some words mean the same. They are synonyms.

Comprehensive Phonics, Spelling, and Word Study Guide

Refer to: page **45**, row **4**

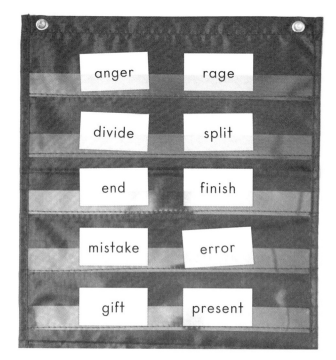

Teach

1. *Today, you are going to think about word meanings.* If students have already learned about synonyms and antonyms, remind them that they already know that some words can mean the same thing and some words can be opposites.

2. Place the words *anger* and *rage* in the pocket chart. Point to *anger. What is this word?* • *This word is* anger. *What about the second word?* • *This word is* rage. *What do you notice about these words?* • Acknowledge responses about the letters and sounds in the words, but guide students to focus on the meanings of the words. Anger *and* rage *are synonyms. Synonyms are words that mean the same, or almost the same.* Students may say that *rage* is a little stronger than *anger.*

3. Place the pocket-chart cards for *divide* and *split* in the pocket chart. Read each word with students. *What do you notice about* divide *and* split? • *The meaning is the same, or similar. Let's look at another pair of words.*

4. Continue placing the word pairs into the pocket chart, each time asking students what they notice about the two words. Do so for a total of about five pairs of words. Use some words in sentences. If students seem very comfortable with synonyms, increase the challenge by placing words and synonyms in two columns and having them match the synonyms instead.

5. Explain to students that they will find synonym matches and choose two pairs to share with a partner. You might wish to provide extra blank cards so that students can add their own synonyms.

Name *Shane*

add	→	total
arrive	→	reach
anger	→	rage
ask	→	question
baby	→	infant
begin	→	start
below	→	under
call	→	yell
close	→	shut
dislike	→	hate
divide	→	split
earth	→	world
end	→	finish
error	→	mistake
fat	→	chubby

Fountas & Pinnell Word Study Lessons, Grade 3   **WMV 7** Word Pairs

ACTIVITY: WORD PAIRS

INSTRUCTIONAL PROCEDURE

MAP WORDS

See page 32 for detailed descriptions of Instructional Procedures.

ACTION TAGS

take card
match words
write words

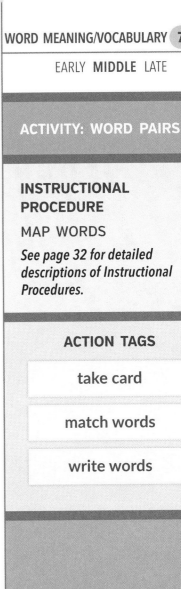

Apply

Distribute word cards and word pairs sheets. Have students work with lesson word cards to make fifteen pairs of synonyms and write them on a sheet. You may also wish to consider doing this activity as a partner activity.

Share

- Have students select and share two synonym pairs with a partner. Students may suggest new synonym pairs, which you can show in a class chart.
- Review the principle, and remind students to notice synonyms when they read and write.

Assess

- Observe students during sharing to notice whether they were able to select synonym pairs.
- Notice the variety and complexity of the pairs they choose.
- Give students a page of words, and ask them to write synonyms for each one.
- You may wish to use Word Meaning/Vocabulary Assessment D or H.

Connect Learning Across Contexts

Interactive Read-Aloud Read aloud books that will help students learn how to think about and/or notice synonyms. You might choose a handful of words and invite students to give two or three synonyms for each one.

> IRA *Confetti: Poems for Children* by Pat Mora

> IRA *Earthquack!* by Margie Palatini

Shared Reading You may wish to use the following Shared Reading title from *Fountas & Pinnell Classroom™* to point out synonyms.

> SR *Saving Cranes* by Brenda Iasevoli

Shared Writing When students are composing a text, encourage them to give synonyms for words that would make the text more interesting. Add to the list of synonyms on the board or chart so that students can use them in their own writing.

Independent Writing As students write independently, highlight a few appropriate words, and ask students to think of synonyms that could be substituted to make the writing more interesting.

Extend Learning

- Repeat the lesson with additional synonyms.
- Set up a synonym board, and invite students to put pairs of similar words on it, along with illustrations.

▶ Connect with Home

Have students take home a sheet of words that they can cut apart and use to make synonym pairs. Alternatively, have students find and write five pairs of synonyms with family members.

Recognize and Use Synonyms

Plan

▶ Consider Your Students

Use this lesson to help students remember the concept of synonyms as well as some examples. The lesson will also help students understand the finer shades of meaning that they find in words related by meaning. Often synonyms do not have exactly the same meaning, and students need to choose between them to express a more precise meaning. Students should work mostly with words that they already know, but they may acquire a few new words as they connect synonyms.

▶ Working with English Language Learners

The concept of synonyms will give English language learners a tool to use in expanding their speaking, reading, and writing vocabularies. Realize that many English language learners will make mistakes as they try to use synonyms interchangeably. Provide opportunities for students to work with easy synonyms that are in their speaking vocabularies. If you can, give students some synonyms in their own language to illustrate the principle.

YOU WILL NEED

Online Resources
- ▶ **WMV 8** Action Tags
- ▶ **WMV 8** Game Cards

Other Materials
- ▶ blank chart paper

Generative Lesson ✓
A generative lesson has a simple structure that you can use to present similar content or concepts. Use this lesson to teach a variety of synonyms.

UNDERSTAND THE PRINCIPLE

When proficient readers encounter unfamiliar words in print, they not only use their decoding skills but also think of alternative words that fit the meaning of the sentence. Knowing that words can mean the same thing helps students begin to connect words by meaning. Knowledge of synonyms allows students to vary the words they use, making their writing more interesting.

EXPLAIN THE PRINCIPLE

Some words mean the same. They are synonyms.

Comprehensive Phonics, Spelling, and Word Study Guide

Refer to: page **45**, row **4**

ACTIVITY: SYNONYMS

INSTRUCTIONAL PROCEDURE

MAP WORDS

See page 32 for detailed descriptions of Instructional Procedures.

EXPLAIN THE PRINCIPLE

Some words mean the same. They are synonyms.

Comprehensive Phonics, Spelling, and Word Study Guide

Refer to: page **45**, row **4**

---

happy	glad
all	every
start	begin
little	small
rich	wealthy
smart	clever

It's time to _____ our work.
Mom tried to_____ the car.

Teach

1. *Today, you are going to think more about word meanings.*

2. Write the word pairs *happy/glad; all/every; start/begin; little/small; rich/wealthy; smart/clever*. Read the pairs aloud with students.

3. *What do you notice about these pairs of words?* • Guide students to recognize that each pair of words has the same or similar meanings. *Each pair means the same thing, or almost the same thing.*

4. *What do you call words that mean the same?* • *Synonyms. One way to remember the word* synonym *is that the word* synonym *and the word* same *have the same sound at the beginning and the same sound at the end.*

5. *Can you think of some more words that are synonyms?* If students have difficulty, suggest some easy words like *big* and *kind,* and have students offer additional synonyms for these words.

6. *Now let's see what happens when we use synonyms in our writing.* Write *It's time to _____ our work.* Have students read the sentence with both *start* and *begin. They mean the same, don't they?*

7. Now try this sentence: Write *Mom tried to _____ the car.* Have students read the sentence with both *start* and *begin.* Help them notice that although *start* fits, the word *begin* does not. *Synonyms can mean almost the same thing, but their meaning also depends on how they are used in sentences.* Generate several more pairs of synonyms, and have students try them in sentences.

8. Tell students that today they are going to play Go Fish using a deck of cards with synonyms. Explain that each child draws five cards to start. Taking turns, one player asks another player for a card with a word that matches the meaning of a card he is holding (e.g., "Do you have a word that means the same thing as *baby*?"). If the other player has a word with a similar meaning, she gives the card to the first player. The first player now has a match and puts the matching words faceup on the table. If the other player does not have a match, she says, "Go fish," and the first player draws a new game card from the deck. The first player to find matches for all of the cards in her hand wins.

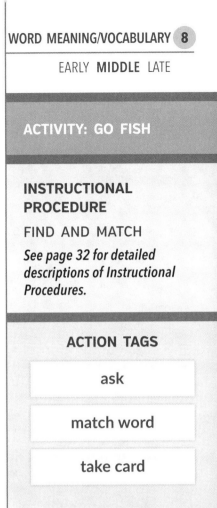

ACTIVITY: GO FISH

INSTRUCTIONAL PROCEDURE

FIND AND MATCH

See page 32 for detailed descriptions of Instructional Procedures.

ACTION TAGS

ask
match word
take card

Apply

Have students play Go Fish in small groups using a deck of game cards. If you include a few more difficult synonyms, with which students have little experience, review those pairs at the end of the lesson. To provide an additional challenge, have players match synonyms and use both words in the same sentence before laying down the synonym pair. If both synonyms do not fit the exact meaning of the sentence, the player should create another sentence.

Share

Have students select and share two synonym pairs with a partner. Students may suggest new synonym pairs, which you can show in a class chart.

Assess

- Observe students as they play Go Fish, and identify those who have difficulty either identifying synonyms or making sentences with them.

- Have students write a list of as many synonym pairs as they can within a five-minute period. Look at the results for the accuracy of matches, the number of pairs produced, and their variety.

- You may wish to use Word Meaning/Vocabulary Assessment D or H.

Connect Learning Across Contexts

Shared Reading Have the students tape a synonym over one or two words in a poem or other text. Then have them reread the text with the new words. They can discuss whether–and how–any of the new words changes the meaning of the text.

SR *Exploring Underground* by Louis Petrone

Guided Reading When the students come to a word and are not sure of the meaning, suggest a synonym, and write the two words. Have students try substituting the synonym in the sentence in place of the new word.

Shared Writing As you compose texts together, invite students to suggest several possible synonyms for a word such as *happy*. Work with them to choose the word that best matches the context of the writing.

Independent Writing When students share their writing, ask if any synonyms could be used to make sentences more interesting. They will have to be thoughtful here, because a substitution may change the meaning too much.

Extend Learning

- Repeat the lesson with additional synonyms.
- Set up a synonym board, and invite students to put pairs of similar words on it, along with illustrations.

▶ Connect with Home

Send home a deck of word cards with pairs of synonyms. Students can play Go Fish with family members.

Recognize and Use Antonyms

Plan

▶ Consider Your Students

Most students are familiar with words that have opposite meanings and may have examined them formally. In this lesson, you will review the concept of antonyms and expand students' repertoires of examples. Be sure to use words that students already have in their speaking, reading, or writing vocabularies. Remember, though, that when working mostly with known words, students can often learn new words.

▶ Working with English Language Learners

English language learners will benefit from connecting words that mean the opposite. Keep this lesson simple by using easy examples and words that students understand and can read (*hot/cold* or *smooth/rough*) until you are sure that they understand the principle. Work with students individually or in a small group to create picture labels, act out meanings of words, or use words in sentences. If you can, give students some antonyms in their own language to illustrate the principle.

UNDERSTAND THE PRINCIPLE

Increasing students' awareness of antonyms helps them understand the meaning of words in sentences and expands their vocabularies. Once students understand the concept of antonyms, they will begin to search for and notice words that have opposite meanings. As students gradually expand their knowledge of opposite terms, their ability to choose more precise words in their independent writing will improve.

YOU WILL NEED

Online Resources
- ▶ **WMV 9** Action Tags
- ▶ **WMV 9** Game Cards
- ▶ **WMV 9** Directions for Concentration

Other Materials
- ▶ blank chart paper

Generative Lesson
A generative lesson has a simple structure that you can use to present similar content or concepts. Use this lesson to teach a variety of antonyms.

EXPLAIN THE PRINCIPLE
Some words have opposite meanings. They are antonyms.

Comprehensive Phonics, Spelling, and Word Study Guide

Refer to: page **45**, row **5**

ACTIVITY: ANTONYMS

INSTRUCTIONAL PROCEDURE

MAP WORDS

See page 32 for detailed descriptions of Instructional Procedures.

EXPLAIN THE PRINCIPLE

Some words have opposite meanings. They are antonyms.

Comprehensive Phonics, Spelling, and Word Study Guide

Refer to:
page **45**, row **5**

fast   slow

good   bad

above   below

dirty   clean

inside   outside

Teach

1. Tell students that they are going to learn more about the meanings of certain words.

2. Write the words *fast* and *slow* on the chart. Read the pair aloud with students. *What does the word* fast *mean?* • *The word* fast *means "moving at a quick speed."* • *What does* slow *mean?* • *The word* slow *means "moving at a low speed."* •

3. *What do you notice about these two words when you think about their meanings?* Students may respond that each pair of words means the opposite and may come up with the word *antonyms*. If not, you can introduce it. *Words that mean the opposite, or almost the opposite, are called* antonyms. Have students say the word *antonym*.

4. Write the words *good* and *bad* on the chart. *What do you notice about these two words?* • *These words have opposite meanings. Can you use the word* good *in a sentence? Can you use the word* bad *in a sentence?*

5. Have students continue to give examples of pairs of antonyms. Continue asking them what they notice about the words, guiding them to understand the principle. Ask them to use each pair of antonyms in sentences that show their opposite meanings.

6. *You are going to play the game Concentration with antonyms. You will pick up a card and read the word. Then you will pick up another card and see if the words are antonyms. If the two words are antonyms, you have a match. The player with the most matches wins the game.*

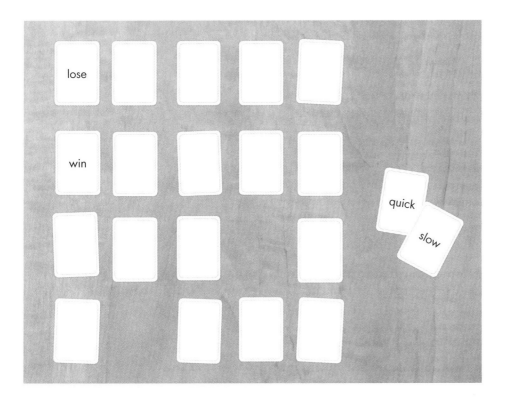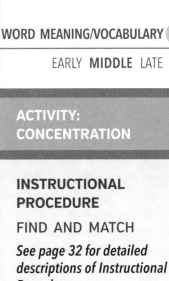

ACTIVITY: CONCENTRATION

INSTRUCTIONAL PROCEDURE

FIND AND MATCH

See page 32 for detailed descriptions of Instructional Procedures.

ACTION TAGS

turn card
turn another card
match pair

Apply

Have students play Concentration in groups of two to four players. Tell them to list three pairs of antonyms on an index card to share with the group.

Share

- Have groups of students share and discuss the pairs of antonyms. Invite students to add a few more examples to the class list.

- Review the principle, and remind students to notice antonyms when they read and write.

Assess

- Observe students as they play Concentration, and identify those who need more work in a small group.

- Give students a list of five to ten words, and have them write an antonym for each one.

- You may wish to use Word Meaning/Vocabulary Assessment E or H.

Connect Learning Across Contexts

Interactive Read-Aloud As you reread books, select one or two antonyms to display on a whiteboard. Help students notice how antonyms are used to create contrasts that help them learn.

IRA *Cat and Rat: The Legend of the Chinese Zodiac* by Ed Young

IRA *Day and Night in the Desert* by Caroline Arnold

Guided Reading Prompt students to notice antonyms after reading a text. Work with a few antonyms on a whiteboard during the word work segment of the lesson.

Shared Writing Help students notice the antonyms they use in shared writing, or have them find an antonym for a word on a class antonym chart.

Independent Writing Help students use antonyms in their own writing to make their writing more colorful and to help improve vocabulary.

Extend Learning

■ Repeat the lesson with other antonyms.

■ Set up an antonym board, and invite students to put pairs of opposite words on it, along with illustrations.

▶ **Connect with Home**

Send home pairs of antonym on game cards for students to match at home or to play Concentration with family members.

Recognize and Use Antonyms

Plan

▶ **Consider Your Students**

Most students are familiar with words that have opposite meanings and may have examined them formally. In this lesson, you will review the concept of antonyms and expand students' repertoires of examples. Remember that working with antonyms often helps students unlock the meaning of related words.

▶ **Working with English Language Learners**

Read the poem in an enjoyable way many times until students are familiar with it and can read along. Talk about the meaning of specific antonym pairs, so that you are sure that students grasp the difference between each word in the pair. Invite students to share their own experiences and connect them to the poem.

YOU WILL NEED

Online Resources
- ▶ **WMV 10** Poem: Old and New
- ▶ **WMV 10** Action Tags
- ▶ **WMV 10** Lotto Game Boards
- ▶ **WMV 10** Word Cards
- ▶ **WMV 10** Directions for Lotto

Other Materials
- ▶ chart paper
- ▶ highlighter

Generative Lesson ✓

A generative lesson has a simple structure that you can use to present similar content or concepts. Use this lesson to teach a variety of antonyms.

UNDERSTAND THE PRINCIPLE

Increasing students' awareness of antonyms helps them understand the meanings of words in sentences and expands their vocabularies. Once students understand the concept of antonyms, they will begin to search for and notice words that have opposite meanings. As students gradually expand their knowledge of opposite terms, their ability to choose more precise words in their independent writing will improve.

EXPLAIN THE PRINCIPLE

Some words have opposite meanings. They are antonyms.

Comprehensive Phonics, Spelling, and Word Study Guide

Refer to:
page **45**, row **5**

EARLY **MIDDLE** LATE

ACTIVITY: OLD AND NEW

INSTRUCTIONAL PROCEDURE

SEE AND SAY

See page 32 for detailed descriptions of Instructional Procedures.

EXPLAIN THE PRINCIPLE

Some words have opposite meanings. They are antonyms.

Comprehensive Phonics, Spelling, and Word Study Guide

Refer to: page **45**, row **5**

Old and New

I have a great new pair of jeans.
They are navy and very cool.
I like to wear my dark blue jeans
Everywhere in school.
I have an old pair of blue jeans.
They're a light and faded blue.
But I wear my old blue jeans
More than I wear the new.
I have a wonderful new pair of shoes.
They're clean and chocolate brown.
I like to wear my great new shoes
Everywhere in town.
I have a pair of running shoes.
They're old with dirty laces.
I wear my old shoes less unless
I want to win the races.

Teach

1. Review the concept of antonyms with students. *Some words have opposite meanings. These words are called* antonyms. *What are some antonyms you can think of?* Students may suggest common antonym pairs, such as *hot/cold, fast/slow,* and *on/off.*

2. On an easel, display the poem "Old and New." Read the poem several times with students.

3. *What do you notice about some of the words in this poem when you think about meanings?* ● *Do you notice any antonyms in this poem?*

4. Invite students to locate pairs of antonyms (e.g., *old* and *new* in the title) and to mark them with a highlighter.

5. Have students continue to give examples of pairs of antonyms. Continue asking them what they notice about the words, guiding them to understand the principle.

6. Tell students that they are going to play Lotto with antonyms. A match is a word that is the opposite of the card drawn. The player who covers all of the words on her card first is the winner.

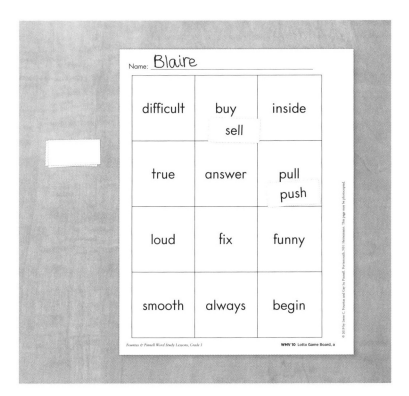

INSTRUCTIONAL PROCEDURE

FIND AND MATCH

See page 32 for detailed descriptions of Instructional Procedures.

ACTION TAGS

take card

say word

match word

cover space

Apply

Have students play Lotto in groups of two to four players. Remind them that they are matching antonyms, or words with opposite meanings.

Share

■ Have students share a pair of antonyms that they matched. Invite them to add a few more examples to the class list.

■ Review the principle, and remind students to notice antonyms when they read and write.

Assess

■ Observe students as they play Lotto in a small group, and identify those who need more work with antonyms.

■ Give students a list of five to ten words, and have them write an antonym for each one.

■ You may wish to use Word Meaning/Vocabulary Assessment E or H.

Word Meaning/Vocabulary: Recognize and Use Antonyms

Connect Learning Across Contexts

Interactive Read-Aloud As you reread books, select one or two interesting words, and quickly write them on a whiteboard. Invite students to think of antonyms for each of the words.

>  *The Contest Between the Sun and the Wind: An Aesop's Fable* by Heather Forest

> *Enemy Pie* by Derek Munson

Guided Reading When the students have read a selection, go back and locate a few words that are antonyms. Write the pairs on a whiteboard.

Shared Writing Help students notice any antonyms they may use in a piece of shared writing.

Independent Writing Help students understand how to use contrasts in their writing and to think of pairs of antonyms that might help make their meaning clear.

Extend Learning

- Repeat the lesson with other antonyms.
- Have students write a poem with antonyms.

▶ Connect with Home

Students can take home word cards to play Lotto with family members.

Recognize and Use Homophones

Plan

▶ Consider Your Students

Use this lesson with students who have not had much formal exposure to homophones. The reading vocabulary that most students have acquired includes many homophones; however, students may not have noticed them. In their writing, students may be prone to homophone substitution (using *to* for *two, to,* or *too,* for example). When first teaching this lesson, use example words that students already know, along with content-rich but simple example sentences, to assist students' learning of the principle.

▶ Working with English Language Learners

Homophones in oral language can be very confusing to English language learners. Noticing the differences in spelling will help students make distinctions among these words that sound the same but have different meanings. Help students compose sentences with homophones during shared writing, but don't attempt too many pairs at once. During the lesson, you may wish to show English language learners a few additional example sentences to convey understanding.

YOU WILL NEED

Online Resources
- ▶ **WMV 11** Action Tags
- ▶ **WMV 11** Word Cards
- ▶ **WMV 11** Sentence Sheets

Other Materials
- ▶ chart paper

Generative Lesson ✓

A generative lesson has a simple structure that you can use to present similar content or concepts. Use this lesson to teach a variety of homophones.

UNDERSTAND THE PRINCIPLE

Students need to understand that words can *sound* the same but have different spellings and meanings. When they encounter a word like this–a homophone–they will know they have to think carefully about the meaning and spelling to understand the message. Once students grasp this important principle, they can begin to develop examples of words that fit into the category of homophones independently. Understanding this concept is necessary to improve spelling and reading comprehension.

EXPLAIN THE PRINCIPLE

Some words sound the same but have different spellings and meanings. They are homophones.

Comprehensive Phonics, Spelling, and Word Study Guide

Refer to: page **45**, row **6**

ACTIVITY: HOMOPHONES

INSTRUCTIONAL PROCEDURE

HEAR AND SAY

See page 32 for detailed descriptions of Instructional Procedures.

EXPLAIN THE PRINCIPLE

Some words sound the same but have different spellings and meanings. They are homophones.

Comprehensive Phonics, Spelling, and Word Study Guide

Refer to: page **45**, row **6**

The moon comes out at <u>night</u>.

The <u>knight</u> went into battle.

Teach

1. Tell students that they are going to learn something interesting about words.

2. Write two sentences on chart paper with *night* and *knight* underlined: *The moon comes out at <u>night</u>. The <u>knight</u> went into battle.* Read each sentence aloud with children.

3. *What do you notice about the two underlined words?* • Guide students to recognize that *night* and *knight* look different but sound the same. *What do you notice about these two words when you think about meaning?* • *These words have different meanings.* Reread the sentences with students, encouraging them to understand that *night* means "the time between evening and morning," whereas a *knight* was a high-ranking officer during the Middle Ages.

4. Repeat the procedure for *aunt/ant* and *hear/here.*

5. Reinforce the principle: *Some words sound the same but have different spellings and meanings. They are homophones.* Homo- *means "same," and* phone *means "sound." Homophones are words that sound the same.*

6. *Now you are going to practice matching homophones and using them to complete sentences. First, you will match homophones on word cards. Then you will use some of the homophones to complete the sentences on a sentence sheet.*

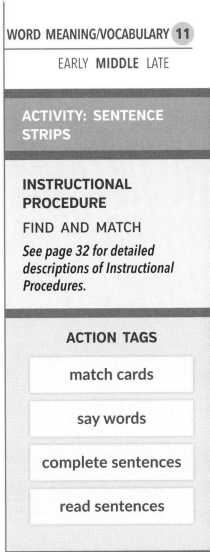

Name Ocean

The red ___rose___ smells sweet.

He knocked at the door. I said, "Come ___in___."

Do you have the ___right___ answer?

The storyteller told a ___tale___ of adventure.

The rabbit had a fluffy ___tail___.

I bought this hat at a good ___Sale___.

Next ___week___ we will have a vacation.

Jan got a ___new___ bike.

___I___ have two brothers.

We ___won___ the game because we played well.

Fountas & Pinnell Word Study Lessons, Grade 1   **WMV 11 Sentence Sheet**

ACTIVITY: SENTENCE STRIPS

INSTRUCTIONAL PROCEDURE

FIND AND MATCH

See page 32 for detailed descriptions of Instructional Procedures.

ACTION TAGS

match cards

say words

complete sentences

read sentences

Apply

Distribute word cards and sentence sheets. Have students match words and complete sentences. Ask them to read each completed sentence aloud.

Share

- Have students share and compare their sentence sheets with a partner. Invite them to name another pair of homophones and to use the words in oral sentences.

- Review the principle, and remind students to notice homophones when they read and write.

Assess

- Notice whether students can accurately use homophones in sentences.

- Observe students' reading and writing to determine whether they are using homophones correctly.

- You may wish to use Word Meaning/Vocabulary Assessment F or H.

Word Meaning/Vocabulary: Recognize and Use Homophones

Connect Learning Across Contexts

Interactive Read-Aloud As you reread books, select one or two homophones to write on a whiteboard, and discuss their spelling and meanings. You may want to use a document camera or projector.

> RA *Odd Boy Out: Young Albert Einstein* by Don Brown

> RA *Button Up!* by Alice Schertle

Guided Reading During word work, write pairs of homophones on the board; discuss them and use them in oral sentences.

Shared Writing As you work with small groups, point out homophones, and ask the students to choose the correct spellings given the context of phrases and sentences.

Independent Writing When you confer with students, help them distinguish between homophones to communicate the correct meaning.

Extend Learning

- Repeat the lesson with other homophones.
- Have students use the pairs of homophones in sentences of their own.

▶ Connect with Home

Have students take home the word cards to match with a family member and to use in sentences.

Recognize and Use Homophones

Plan

▶ Consider Your Students

Use this lesson to help students continue to expand their knowledge of the use of homophones. They should understand the principle that words can sound the same but be spelled differently. They should also know that it is important to consider their intended meaning when they wish to write a sentence using a homophone.

▶ Working with English Language Learners

Use simple, meaningful sentences when working with English language learners. Unless they can read and understand the meaning of the sentences, it will be difficult for students to distinguish between homophones. It will be helpful to act out meanings whenever possible.

YOU WILL NEED

Online Resources
- ▶ **WMV 12** Action Tags
- ▶ **WMV 12** Lotto Game Boards
- ▶ **WMV 12** Word Cards
- ▶ **WMV 12** Sentence Sheets
- ▶ **WMV 12** Directions for Lotto

Other Materials
- ▶ chart paper
- ▶ game markers or chips

Generative Lesson
A generative lesson has a simple structure that you can use to present similar content or concepts. Use this lesson to teach a variety of homophones.

UNDERSTAND THE PRINCIPLE

Students need to understand that words can *sound* the same but have different spellings and meanings. When they encounter a word like this–a homophone–they will know they have to think carefully about the meaning and spelling to decode the message. Once students grasp this important principle, they can begin to develop examples of words that fit into the category of homophones independently. However, even when students understand the concept of homophones and know a range of examples, it might still be challenging for them to select the right word for a given context. Many spelling errors are related to the misuse of homophones, and it is important for spellers to continue to develop knowledge in this area.

EXPLAIN THE PRINCIPLE

Some words sound the same but have different spellings and meanings. They are homophones.

Comprehensive Phonics, Spelling, and Word Study Guide

Refer to: page **45**, row **6**

ACTIVITY: HOMOPHONES

INSTRUCTIONAL PROCEDURE

HEAR AND SAY

See page 32 for detailed descriptions of Instructional Procedures.

EXPLAIN THE PRINCIPLE

Some words sound the same but have different spellings and meanings. They are homophones.

Comprehensive Phonics, Spelling, and Word Study Guide

Refer to: page **45**, row **6**

Teach

1. Write the words *hair* and *hare* on the chart paper, and read them aloud with students.

2. *What do you notice about these two words?* • *They sound the same, but they are spelled differently. What do you notice about the meanings of these two words?* • *They have different meanings.* Help students recognize that *hair* grows on the bodies of some animals, whereas a *hare* is an animal that is somewhat similar to but larger than a rabbit. *These two words are homophones. Sometimes it can be tricky to use homophones correctly.*

3. Have students suggest additional examples of homophones, and write the words on chart paper.

4. Briefly discuss the different meanings of each pair or group of homophones. *What are some ways we can tell homophones apart?* Encourage students to think of some creative ways to distinguish among the words. Students' ideas may be silly or far-fetched–the process of noticing something about the word is what's important. For example:

   "Walking in this *pair* of shoes is like walking on *air*."

   "I *eat* a pear. The pear that you eat has *ea*, just like *eat*."

   "*Four* is the number. The word *four* has four letters in it."

   "I can think about something that would *weigh eight* pounds–the *eigh* is in both."

   "*Oh*, no! I *owe* money!"

5. After discussing the words, have students write words as you read them aloud in a sentence. *I am going to use a word in a sentence. It will be a word that is a homophone. Write the word as quickly as you can, then put down your pencil.* (You may wish to use a few sentences from this lesson's sentences sheet.) Read each sentence; then, after a short pause, have students hold up their predictions of the spelling of the word. Then hold up the right word so students can check themselves. *How did you figure out which word to use?*

6. Tell students that they will play Lotto with homophones. Players will take turns taking a card and reading a sentence with a blank. To mark a square with a game marker, the player must have the word (with the correct spelling) that fits into the sentence. Before marking the square, he must read the sentence with the correct word inserted. The first player to mark all the words wins.

hair/hare
four/for
pear/pair
oh/owe

ACTIVITY: LOTTO

INSTRUCTIONAL PROCEDURE

FIND AND MATCH

See page 32 for detailed descriptions of Instructional Procedures.

ACTION TAGS

take card

read sentence

match word

cover space

Apply

Distribute Lotto game boards, word cards, and game markers. Have students play Lotto in small groups. Remind them to read the sentence with the correct word inserted before covering a square with a marker.

Share

- Have students read aloud one of the sentences they covered. Invite them to name another pair of homophones and use the words in oral sentences.

- Review the principle, and remind students to notice words that are homophones when they read and write.

Assess

- Notice whether students can accurately use homophones in sentences.

- Observe students' reading and writing to determine whether they are using homophones correctly.

- You may wish to use Word Meaning/Vocabulary Assessment F or H.

Word Meaning/Vocabulary: Recognize and Use Homophones

Connect Learning Across Contexts

Interactive Read-Aloud After rereading books, quickly point out one or two homophones, and write them on a whiteboard. Discuss the meanings and spellings of the words.

> IRA *Our Seasons* by Grace Lin and Ranida T. McKneally

> IRA *The Paperboy* by Dav Pilkey

Shared Reading Select poetic texts with a variety of homophones, and have students highlight these words.

> SR *From Flower to Honey* by June Schwartz

Guided Reading During word work, have students practice reading pairs of homophones quickly.

Independent Writing When students want to write a word that is a homophone–especially one that students often confuse, such as *would* and *wood*–ask them to stop and think about the spelling and meaning of each of the words.

Extend Learning

■ Repeat the lesson with other homophones.

■ Have students use homophones in sentences of their own.

▶ Connect with Home

Have students take the game board and sentences home to play Lotto with a family member.

Recognize and Use Homographs

Plan

▶ Consider Your Students

To understand homographs, students should have previous practice solving unknown words during independent and guided reading. Awareness of the syntax of written language, built through hearing and constructing sentences, will help students solve homographs by looking for the pronunciation that "sounds right." The goal of this lesson is for students to understand the principle and notice homographs in sentences. Select words that are appropriate for the class.

▶ Working with English Language Learners

English language learners often find homographs quite difficult to understand and pronounce. They will develop understanding of the various pronunciations over time. It is important that students begin to understand the principle that two words may *look* exactly the same yet be different. Students may find it easier to distinguish the words when listening, especially as you use them in sentences and in stories you read aloud. After the words are established in their speaking and listening vocabularies, you can share the spelling.

UNDERSTAND THE PRINCIPLE

Homographs are a subset of homonyms. It's important for students to understand that these words are spelled the same but can be pronounced differently and have different meanings when used in sentences. When they encounter a homograph, students will learn to think carefully about the meaning and pronunciation to decode the overall message. Once they grasp this important principle, they can begin to develop examples of words that fit into the category of homographs independently. Understanding this concept is important to improve reading comprehension. It will also help them to be more accurate in pronunciation when reading aloud as well as to achieve more accurate spelling when writing independently.

YOU WILL NEED

Online Resources
- ▶ **WMV 13** Action Tags
- ▶ **WMV 13** Word Cards
- ▶ **WMV 13** Four-Box Sheets

Other Materials
- ▶ chart paper

Generative Lesson ✓

A generative lesson has a simple structure that you can use to present similar content or concepts. Use this lesson to teach a variety of homographs.

EXPLAIN THE PRINCIPLE

Some words are spelled the same but have different meanings and origins.

Sometimes they are pronounced differently. They are homographs.

Comprehensive Phonics, Spelling, and Word Study Guide

Refer to: page **45**, row **7**

ACTIVITY: HOMOGRAPHS

INSTRUCTIONAL PROCEDURE

HEAR AND SAY

See page 32 for detailed descriptions of Instructional Procedures.

EXPLAIN THE PRINCIPLE

Some words are spelled the same but have different meanings and origins.

Sometimes they are pronounced differently. They are homographs.

Comprehensive Phonics, Spelling, and Word Study Guide

Refer to: page **45**, row **7**

The actor took a <u>bow</u>.
Lee tied a <u>bow</u> in her hair.

We live <u>close</u> to school.
Please <u>close</u> the door.

The <u>dove</u> flew by.
She <u>dove</u> into the pool.

Teach

1. Tell students that they are going to look at some words in sentences.

2. Demonstrate reading the first pair of sentences. *The first sentence says, "The actor took a bow." The second sentence says, "Lee tied a bow in her hair."* Have students read the sentences after you.

3. Underline or highlight *bow* in both sentences. *What do you notice about both words?* • Students may point out that you say them differently or that they have different meanings but are spelled the same.

4. Discuss the two highlighted words with students, talking about the meaning and pointing out how the words are pronounced differently. Say each sentence with the pronunciation of each word. *Which sounds right?* • *It's important to check and make sure the word "sounds right" in the sentence.* Explain to the class that you have to think about the meaning of the sentence and think about the word meaning to use the right pronunciation.

5. Continue the lesson with homographs *close* and *dove*. With each example, make sure to show students how to check to see which word sounds right, looks right, and makes sense in the sentence.

6. Guide students to generalize the principle: *There are some words that look the same but have different meanings and usually sound different. These words are called homographs.* Invite students to say *homograph*. You may wish to explain that the two parts of this word, *homo* plus *graph*, mean "*same spelling.*"

7. Tell students that they will be writing and illustrating four sentences on a four-box sheet using words that are spelled the same but have different meanings and pronunciations.

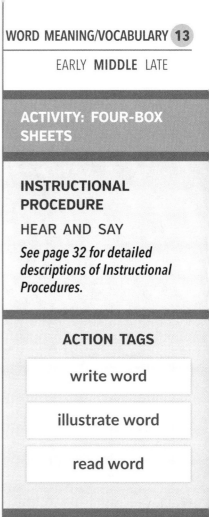

ACTIVITY: FOUR-BOX SHEETS

INSTRUCTIONAL PROCEDURE

HEAR AND SAY

See page 32 for detailed descriptions of Instructional Procedures.

ACTION TAGS

write word

illustrate word

read word

Apply

Hand out the lesson word cards and four-box sheets to the class. Using the word cards, have students choose four homographs to write and illustrate four pairs of sentences. Ask students to read their sentences to a partner.

Share

- Have students read two of their sentences to the class. Add selected sentences to the class chart if you need more examples.

- Review the principle, and remind students to notice homographs when they read and write.

Assess

- When sampling oral reading, notice whether students are accurately pronouncing homographs. Corrections in pronunciation provide evidence that they are using language syntax to monitor their reading and are thinking about meaning.

- Give students several unfamiliar sentences containing homographs, and ask students to read them aloud. Note their pronunciation.

- You may wish to use Word Meaning/Vocabulary Assessment G or H.

Connect Learning Across Contexts

Shared Reading You may wish to use the following Shared Reading title from *Fountas & Pinnell Classroom*™ to point out homographs.

SR *A Meerkat Day* by Geerhardt Heever

Guided Reading During word work, use the whiteboard to write homographs, and ask students to make oral sentences with them.

Shared Writing As you work with small groups, point out homographs, asking students to give pronunciations of both words and to talk about the meanings.

Independent Writing When you confer with students, help clarify the meanings of homographs and provide examples as needed.

Extend Learning

- Repeat the lesson with other homographs.
- Have students collect homographs on a page in their writing workshop folders or in their writer's notebook.

▶ Connect with Home

Have students take home word cards and repeat the activity with family members using different homographs.

Recognize and Use Homographs

Plan

▶ Consider Your Students

To understand homographs, students should have previous practice solving unknown words during independent and guided reading. Awareness of the syntax of written language, built through hearing and constructing sentences, will help students solve homographs by looking for the pronunciation that "sounds right." The goal of this lesson is for students to understand the principle and notice homographs in sentences. Select words that are appropriate for the class.

▶ Working with English Language Learners

English language learners often find homographs quite difficult to understand and pronounce. They will develop understanding of the various pronunciations over time. It is important that students begin to understand the principle that two words may *look* exactly the same yet be different. Students may find it easier to distinguish the words when listening, especially as you use them in sentences and in stories you read aloud. After the words are established in their speaking and listening vocabularies, you can share the spelling.

UNDERSTAND THE PRINCIPLE

Homographs are a subset of homonyms. It's important for students to understand that these words are spelled the same but can be pronounced differently and have different meanings when used in sentences. When they encounter a homograph, students will learn to think carefully about the meaning and pronunciation to decode the overall message. Once they grasp this important principle, they can begin to develop examples of words that fit into the category of homographs independently. Understanding this concept is important to improve reading comprehension. It will also help them to be more accurate in pronunciation when reading aloud as well as to achieve more accurate spelling when writing independently.

YOU WILL NEED

Online Resources
- ▶ **WMV 14** Action Tags
- ▶ **WMV 14** Word Cards
- ▶ **WMV 14** Sentence Sheets

Other Materials
- ▶ chart paper

Generative Lesson ✓
A generative lesson has a simple structure that you can use to present similar content or concepts. Use this lesson to teach a variety of homographs.

EXPLAIN THE PRINCIPLE

Some words are spelled the same but have different meanings and origins.

Sometimes they are pronounced differently. They are homographs.

Comprehensive Phonics, Spelling, and Word Study Guide

Refer to: page **45**, row **7**

ACTIVITY: HOMOGRAPHS

INSTRUCTIONAL PROCEDURE

HEAR AND SAY

See page 32 for detailed descriptions of Instructional Procedures.

EXPLAIN THE PRINCIPLE

Some words are spelled the same but have different meanings and origins.

Sometimes they are pronounced differently. They are homographs.

Comprehensive Phonics, Spelling, and Word Study Guide

Refer to:
page **45**, row **7**

> I had a <u>tear</u> in my eye.
> My shirt had a <u>tear</u> in it.
>
> He always <u>does</u> his homework.
> I saw two <u>does</u> in the woods.
>
> My brother plays the <u>bass</u> drum
> My dad fishes for <u>bass</u>.
>
> A strong <u>wind</u> was blowing.
> Did you <u>wind</u> the clock?

Teach

1. Tell students that they are going to look at the way words are spelled and to notice how they sound.

2. Demonstrate reading the first pair of sentences. *The first sentence says, "I had a tear in my eye." The second sentence says, "My shirt had a tear in it."* Have students read the sentences after you.

3. Underline or highlight *tear* in both sentences. *What do you notice about both words?* • Students may point out that you say them differently or that they have different meanings. *What are the two meanings of* tear *and* tear?

4. Follow the same procedure for the remaining sentences on the chart. *When words are spelled the same but have different pronunciations, how do you know which way to say the words?* • *If you listen carefully, you can think whether one of the words makes sense and whether it sounds right to check your pronunciation.*

5. Review that fact that some words that look the same but have different meanings and often have different pronunciations are called *homographs*. Have students repeat the word *homograph*.

6. Tell students that they will choose five word cards and write two sentences for each homograph. Then they will trade sentence sheets with a partner and read their partner's sentences aloud.

Name Oscar

1. I live in a white house.

2. There will be live music at the parade

3. Don't desert me.

4. I rode a camel through the desert.

5. Did you buy me a present?

6. I am present at school today

7. Does our team have practice today?

8. The does ate the corn.

9. Tom will lead the way.

10. My pencil has no lead

Fountas & Pinnell Word Study Lessons, Grade 3

WMV 14 Sentence Sheet

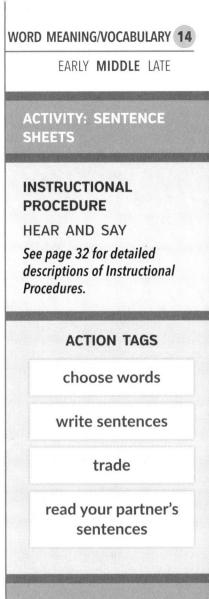

INSTRUCTIONAL PROCEDURE

HEAR AND SAY

See page 32 for detailed descriptions of Instructional Procedures.

ACTION TAGS

choose words

write sentences

trade

read your partner's sentences

Apply

Hand out the sentence sheets to the class. Remind students to listen for their partner's pronunciation of homographs.

Share

- Have students read two of their partner's sentences to the class. Add selected sentences to the class chart if you need more examples.

- Review the principle, and remind students to notice homographs when they read and write.

Assess

- When sampling oral reading, notice whether students are accurately pronouncing homographs. Corrections in pronunciation provide evidence that they are using language syntax to monitor their reading and are thinking about meaning.

- Give students several unfamiliar sentences containing homographs, and ask students to read them aloud. Note their pronunciation.

- You may wish to use Word Meaning/Vocabulary Assessment G or H.

Connect Learning Across Contexts

Shared Reading You may wish to use the following Shared Reading title from *Fountas & Pinnell Classroom*™ to point out words with homographs.

SR *A Meerkat Day* by Geerhardt Heever

Guided Reading During word work, use the whiteboard to write a couple of homographs, and ask students to make oral sentences with them.

Shared Writing As you work with small groups, point out homographs, and ask students to give pronunciations of both words and to talk about the meanings.

Independent Writing When you confer with students, help clarify the meanings of homographs, and provide examples as needed. Ensure that students use the correct spelling of the word meaning in their writing.

Extend Learning

- Repeat the lesson with other homographs.
- Have students collect homographs on a page in their writing workshop folders or in their writer's notebooks.

▶ Connect with Home

Have students take home word cards and repeat the activity with family members using different homographs.

Recognize and Use Words with Multiple Meanings

Plan

▶ Consider Your Students

Before using this lesson, students should be familiar with the idea that words can have different meanings. Students should also have a beginning understanding of the fact that some words can be different parts of speech, depending on how they are used in a sentence. As you choose words for this lesson, select words that have concrete, easy-to-visualize definitions, and use them in context-rich sentences or examples.

▶ Working with English Language Learners

Pay particular attention to whether English language learners know the words you are using in the lesson and have been exposed to both meanings. You may want to limit the lesson to three or four familiar words. Create sentences that students can read and understand, and have them read them orally several times. You may want to work with students in a small group as they make their sentences. Have students read their sentences several times aloud before illustrating.

YOU WILL NEED

Online Resources
- ▶ **WMV 15** Action Tags
- ▶ **WMV 15** Word Cards
- ▶ **WMV 15** Four-Box Sheets

Other Materials
- ▶ chart paper

Generative Lesson ✓

A generative lesson has a simple structure that you can use to present similar content or concepts. Use this lesson to teach a variety of words with multiple meanings.

UNDERSTAND THE PRINCIPLE

Understanding that a word can have more than one meaning is important to better reading comprehension. Encountering a word with multiple meanings, students will begin to think carefully about the meaning and pronunciation to decode the overall message. Students can use context clues to help them figure out which meaning fits according to how the word is used in a sentence. They can also consult a dictionary.

EXPLAIN THE PRINCIPLE

Some words are spelled the same but have more than one meaning.

Comprehensive Phonics, Spelling, and Word Study Guide

Refer to: page **45**, row **8**

ACTIVITY: MULTIPLE-MEANING WORDS

INSTRUCTIONAL PROCEDURE

MAP WORDS

See page 32 for detailed descriptions of Instructional Procedures.

EXPLAIN THE PRINCIPLE

Some words are spelled the same but have more than one meaning.

Comprehensive Phonics, Spelling, and Word Study Guide

Refer to: page **45**, row **8**

Some words are spelled the same but have more than one meaning.

park
The friends play at the <u>park.</u>
Mom will <u>park</u> the car.

spring
My favorite season is <u>spring.</u>
The cat can <u>spring</u> into the air.

roll
I eat my sandwich on a <u>roll.</u>
<u>Roll</u> the ball to me.

fly
Birds can <u>fly.</u>
The <u>fly</u> buzzed in my ear.

Teach

1. Start with a blank chart, writing sentences as you introduce each word noted in the steps below.

2. *You are going to look at some words you already know, and you are going to think about what each word means.* Write the word *park* on the chart. *Can you think of a meaning for the word* park? • As necessary, help students articulate a definition such as "land set apart for the pleasure of the public." *Are there any other meanings for the word* park? • Guide students to recognize that the word *park* can also mean "to leave a vehicle for a time in a certain place."

3. *Now let's think of a sentence for each meaning of* park *we mentioned.* • Have students suggest sentences for multiple meanings of the word. Write the sentences on the chart paper. Be sure that the sentences are easy for students to understand and that different meanings of the word are clear and distinct in each sentence.

4. Repeat the procedure for a few other words, such as *spring, roll,* and *fly.*

5. *What do you notice about the words you've seen today?* • Listen for responses such as:

   "Some words mean more than one thing."

   "You have to think about the sentence to find out the meaning for some words."

   "Some words can be nouns or verbs."

   Write a summary statement on the chart to reflect on the principle: *Some words are spelled the same but have more than one meaning.*

6. Tell students that they are going to create sentences for words that have more than one meaning.

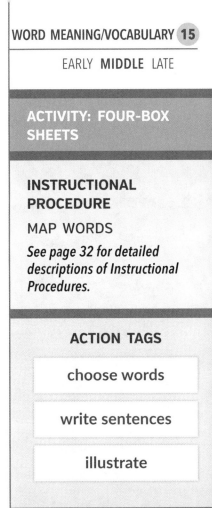

INSTRUCTIONAL PROCEDURE

MAP WORDS

See page 32 for detailed descriptions of Instructional Procedures.

ACTION TAGS

choose words

write sentences

illustrate

Apply

Have students select four word cards. Using two four-box sheets, they will write and illustrate a sentence for each meaning of each word.

Share

- Have students take turns reading some of their sentences aloud to the class. Discuss how the way they used the words in the sentences helped show the words' different meanings.

- Review the principle, and remind students to notice words with multiple meanings when they read and write.

Assess

- Notice whether students can create sentences that reflect different meanings of words.

- Assign students a word with more than one meaning. Ask them to write at least two sentences in which the word is used with a different meaning.

Connect Learning Across Contexts

Shared Reading You may wish to use the following Shared Reading title from *Fountas & Pinnell Classroom™* to point out words with multiple meanings.

SR *Wolf Pack* by Annette Bay Pimentel

Guided Reading As you read sentences that include words with multiple meanings, guide students to use sentence context to determine the intended meaning.

Shared Writing As you work with small groups, point out multiple-meaning words, and ask students to talk about the meanings.

Independent Writing When you confer with students, help them recognize that if they use a word with multiple meanings, they need to make sure the words and phrases around that word help a reader understand the meaning students intend.

Extend Learning

- Repeat the lesson with other multiple-meaning words.
- Compile an ongoing classroom chart of words with multiple meanings.

▶ **Connect with Home**

Have students take home their sentences and illustrations to share with family members.

Recognize and Use Words with Multiple Meanings

Plan

▶ Consider Your Students

Before using this lesson, students should be familiar with the idea that words can have different meanings. Students should also have a beginning understanding of the fact that some words can be different parts of speech, depending on how they are used in a sentence. As you choose words for this lesson, select words that have concrete, easy-to-visualize definitions, and use them in context-rich sentences or examples.

▶ Working with English Language Learners

Pay particular attention to whether English language learners know the words you are using in the lesson and have been exposed to both meanings. You may want to limit the lesson to words that have two distinct meanings that are easy to show through either visuals or demonstrations. Create sentences that students can read and understand, and have them read them orally several times. You may want to work with students in a small group as they write their riddles.

UNDERSTAND THE PRINCIPLE

Understanding that a word can have more than one meaning is important to better reading comprehension. Encountering a word with multiple meanings, students will begin to think carefully about the meaning and pronunciation to decode the overall message. Students can use context clues to help them figure out which meaning fits according to how the word is used in a sentence. They can also consult a dictionary.

YOU WILL NEED

Online Resources
- ▶ **WMV 16** Action Tags
- ▶ **WMV 16** Word Cards
- ▶ **WMV 16** Four-Box Sheets

Other Materials
- ▶ chart paper

Generative Lesson ✓

A generative lesson has a simple structure that you can use to present similar content or concepts. Use this lesson to teach a variety of words with multiple meanings.

EXPLAIN THE PRINCIPLE

Some words are spelled the same but have more than one meaning.

Comprehensive Phonics, Spelling, and Word Study Guide

Refer to: page **45**, row **8**

EARLY **MIDDLE** LATE

ACTIVITY: MULTIPLE-MEANING WORDS

INSTRUCTIONAL PROCEDURE

MAP WORDS

See page 32 for detailed descriptions of Instructional Procedures.

EXPLAIN THE PRINCIPLE

Some words are spelled the same but have more than one meaning.

Comprehensive Phonics, Spelling, and Word Study Guide

Refer to: page **45**, row **8**

---

chest
The boy had a scratch on his <u>chest.</u>
Please get the fancy plates out of
the <u>chest</u> in the kitchen.

change
Do you have <u>change</u> for a dollar?
Dad can <u>change</u> the tire.

break
We took a quick <u>break</u> from working.
Don't <u>break</u> the vase!

Teach

1. Write the following sentences on the board with the word *chest* underlined. *The boy had a scratch on his <u>chest</u>. Please get the fancy plates out of the <u>chest</u> in the kitchen.*

2. *What do you notice about the word* chest *in these sentences?* • Students may observe that the word has a different meaning in each sentence.

3. *How did you figure out the meaning of* chest *in the first sentence?* • Guide students to recognize that knowing the meanings of words like *scratch* and *boy* can help them determine that in this sentence *chest* means "the front part of the body between the neck and the stomach." • *How did you figure out the meaning of* chest *in the second sentence?*

4. If students easily grasp the concept of using context clues, you may also wish to introduce using a dictionary to identify various meanings of a word. You will want to draw students' attention to the numbered definitions and the abbreviations for the parts of speech in dictionary entries.

5. Repeat the procedure for the words *change* and *break*.

6. Conclude by reviewing the principle: *Some words are spelled the same but have more than one meaning.*

7. Tell students that they are going to choose four words with more than one meaning. Then they will write riddles for these words. Remind them that they should not write the solution to their riddles. They will give their riddles to partners to solve. You may wish to provide this example: *What will take you high if you sit on it?* (a swing)

Name Shawn

An elephant's nose or a place to pack your things.	The covering of a tree, or the sound a dog makes.
Something you put on a letter or to pound your feet.	A kind of tree or part of your hand.

Fountas & Pinnell Word Study Lessons, Grade 3   **WMV 16** Four-Box Sheet

ACTIVITY: WORD RIDDLES

INSTRUCTIONAL PROCEDURE

MAP WORDS

See page 32 for detailed descriptions of Instructional Procedures.

ACTION TAGS

choose words

write riddles

trade and solve

Apply

Have students select four word cards. Using a four-box sheet, they will write a riddle for a particular definition of a multiple-meaning word. If students need help focusing a definition for their riddles, suggest they use a dictionary to find or confirm the different meanings. Have students trade riddles with a partner and write solutions to the riddles they receive.

Share

- Have students take turns reading aloud some of the riddles they solved. Discuss how a variety of riddles shows a word's different meanings.
- Review the principle, and remind students to notice words with multiple meanings when they read and write.

Assess

- Notice whether students can create riddles that reflect different meanings of words.
- Assign students a word with more than one meaning. Ask them to write at least two sentences in which the word is used with different meanings.

Connect Learning Across Contexts

Shared Reading You may wish to use the following Shared Reading title from *Fountas & Pinnell Classroom*™ to point out words with multiple meanings.

 *Wolf Pack* by Annette Bay Pimentel

Guided Reading As you read sentences that include words with multiple meanings, guide students to use sentence context to determine the intended meaning.

Shared Writing As you work with small groups, point out multiple-meaning words, and ask students to talk about the meanings they intend.

Independent Writing When you confer with students, discuss word choice, especially any words with multiple meanings that they have included.

Extend Learning

- Repeat the lesson with other multiple-meaning words.
- Compile a classroom book of words with multiple meanings.

▶ Connect with Home

Have students take home the riddles they wrote and share them with a family member. Challenge family members to solve their child's riddles.

Recognize and Use Compound Words with Common Parts

Plan

▶ Consider Your Students

This lesson should follow other lessons, such as WMV 5 and WMV 6, that help students understand the concept of compound words. Students should have a repertoire of compound words that they can recognize and break down into their component parts. In this lesson, students apply principles to more examples and connect words by studying categories of compound words.

▶ Working with English Language Learners

Understanding the concept of compound words helps students understand a word's meaning. Students can look for the two smaller words that make the compound word and can use them as clues to find the meaning of the larger word. Help students understand the words' meanings by talking about the words and using them in sentences. Give students opportunities to repeat the words and make them with magnetic letters. This allows them to break the compound words into smaller words and then put them together again. Use simple examples that clearly illustrate the principle.

YOU WILL NEED

Online Resources
- ▶ **WMV 17** Action Tags
- ▶ **WMV 17** Word Cards
- ▶ **WMV 17** Four-Way Sorts

Other Materials
- ▶ chart paper

Generative Lesson ✓

A generative lesson has a simple structure that you can use to present similar content or concepts. Use this lesson structure to teach students a variety of compound words.

UNDERSTAND THE PRINCIPLE

Word solving is more efficient when students can recognize large units within a word. Compound words are a good way to illustrate this principle. For simple compound words, students will readily recognize the component parts. This lesson helps them group compound words into categories. They will learn that some smaller words appear frequently in compound words; quickly recognizing these words as components of compound words will help students become more automatic in word solving.

EXPLAIN THE PRINCIPLE

Some smaller words appear in many compound words.

Comprehensive Phonics, Spelling, and Word Study Guide

Refer to: page **46**, row **11**

ACTIVITY: COMPOUND WORDS

INSTRUCTIONAL PROCEDURE

NOTICE PARTS

See page 32 for detailed descriptions of Instructional Procedures.

EXPLAIN THE PRINCIPLE

Some smaller words appear in many compound words.

Comprehensive Phonics, Spelling, and Word Study Guide

Refer to:
page **46**, row **11**

air	fire	hair	snow
airmail	fireplace	hairdo	snowball
airtight	fireman	hairbrush	snowman
airport	firefly	haircut	snowflake
airline	fireworks		snowstorm
airplane			

Teach

1. Write the words *airmail, airtight,* and *airport* on a piece of chart paper. Read the words aloud, and ask: *What do you notice about all of the words on the chart?* • *They are all made up of two words that are put together. They all include the word* air. *Can you think of some other words that would fit in this category?* Students may suggest words such as *airline* or *airplane.*

2. *You know that all of these words have* air *in them, so their meanings are related but different. What differences do you notice?* Listen for students to make comments that show how the second word affects the meaning of the compound word. For example,

   "Airmail *is mail that is carried by* airplanes. *An* airport *is a place for* airplanes *to take off and land.*"

3. Repeat this process to have students make and discuss compound words with the words *fire, hair,* and *snow.*

4. Have students read each word on the chart with you. To reinforce the principle, occasionally ask students to name the smaller word that a group of compound words has in common. Guide them to summarize the principle: *Some smaller words appear in many compound words.*

5. Explain to students that they are going to sort compound words. They can look for the smaller words in the compound words and place them into categories on the four-way sort.

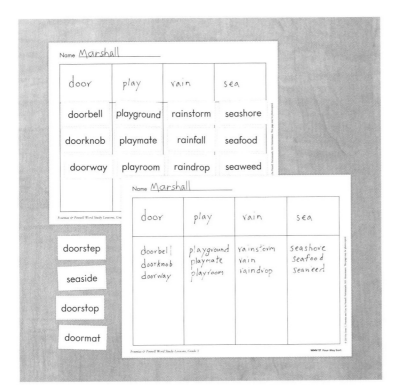

INSTRUCTIONAL PROCEDURE

SAY AND SORT

See page 32 for detailed descriptions of Instructional Procedures.

ACTION TAGS

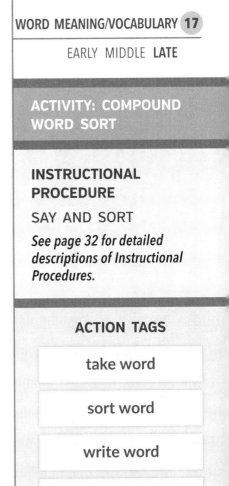

take word
sort word
write word
read word

Apply

Remind students to write their words on the four-way sort, read them to a partner, and explain how they sorted the words.

Share

- Have students share their word lists with the whole group and compare the ways they sorted words. Address any problems students had sorting words, and talk about the smaller word that each group of compound words has in common.

- Review the principle, and remind students to notice words with multiple meanings when they read and write.

Assess

- Give students a word that is common to many compound words, such as *house* or *side*. See if they can come up with at least two or three compound words that include the smaller word.

- You may wish to use Word Meaning/Vocabulary Assessment C or H.

Word Meaning/Vocabulary: Recognize and Use Compound Words with Common Parts

Connect Learning Across Contexts

Shared Reading You may wish to use the following Shared Reading title from *Fountas & Pinnell Classroom*™ to point out compound words with common parts.

SR *Exploring Underground* by Louis Petrone

Guided Reading During word work, write compound words on the board, and invite students to make more words with the parts.

Shared Writing As you work together to write texts, point out compound words. Explain that thinking about how to spell each smaller word can help you spell the larger word.

Independent Writing When conferring with students, point out any compound words they have used in their own writing.

Extend Learning

- Create a wall chart to collect and display compound words. Arrange the words in families.
- Repeat the lesson with more compound words. Some possible sorts are:

  bed: bedroom, bedspread, bedtime

  night: nightfall, nightgown, nightmare, nighttime

  tooth: toothbrush, toothpick, toothpaste

  any: anybody, anyone, anything, anytime, anywhere

  every: everybody, everything, everywhere

▶ Connect with Home

Have students take home a set of word cards to sort with family members. Students can search for compound words in magazines and bring examples to class to share.

Recognize and Use Compound Words with Common Parts

Plan

▶ Consider Your Students

This lesson should follow other lessons, such as WMV 5 and WMV 6, that help students understand the concept of compound words. Students should have a repertoire of compound words that they can recognize and break down into their component parts. In this lesson, students apply the principle to more examples and connect words by creating "word families" of compound words that contain the same word.

▶ Working with English Language Learners

Understanding the concept of compound words helps students understand a word's meaning. Students can look for the two smaller words that make the compound word and can use them as clues to find the meaning of the larger word. To help students understand compound words and their meanings, work with magnetic letters, a whiteboard, or compound words written on strips of paper to help them take apart and put together compound words. You may want to work with English language learners in a small group for the Apply activity.

YOU WILL NEED

Online Resources
- ▸ **WMV 18** Action Tags
- ▸ **WMV 18** Word Cards
- ▸ **WMV 18** Word Maps

Other Materials
- ▸ chart paper

Generative Lesson
A generative lesson has a simple structure that you can use to present similar content or concepts. Use this lesson structure to teach students a variety of compound words.

UNDERSTAND THE PRINCIPLE

Word solving is more efficient when students can recognize large units within a word. Compound words are a good way to illustrate this principle. For simple compound words, students will readily recognize the component parts. This lesson helps them group compound words into categories. They will learn that some smaller words appear frequently in compound words; quickly recognizing these words as components of compound words will help students become more automatic in word solving.

EXPLAIN THE PRINCIPLE

Some smaller words appear in many compound words.

Comprehensive Phonics, Spelling, and Word Study Guide

Refer to: page **46**, row **11**

ACTIVITY: COMPOUND WORDS

INSTRUCTIONAL PROCEDURE

MAP WORDS

See page 32 for detailed descriptions of Instructional Procedures.

EXPLAIN THE PRINCIPLE

Some smaller words appear in many compound words.

Comprehensive Phonics, Spelling, and Word Study Guide

Refer to: page **46**, row **11**

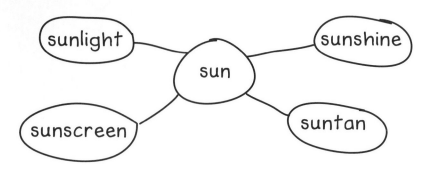

everywhere
everybody
everything

sunlight — sun — sunshine

sunscreen — sun — suntan

Teach

1. Write the words *everywhere, everybody,* and *everything* on a piece of chart paper. Read the words aloud, and ask: *What do you notice about the words on the chart?* • *They are all made up of two words that are put together so they are compound words. They all include the word* every. *Can you think of some other words that would fit in this category?* Students may suggest words such as *everyone* or *every.*

2. *You know that all of these words have* every *in them. How can this help you read them and figure out their meanings?* Listen for students to make comments that show an understanding of the principle, such as:

    "Knowing that *every* is a part of the word helps me pronounce it. If I know how to say *every*, it helps me read the whole word."

    "I know that the compound word has a meaning that relates to the word *every*, which means 'all of them.'"

3. Repeat this process to have students make and discuss compound words with the words *light, house,* and *sun.* To help students visualize the connections, you may want to create word maps for these examples. Put the common word in the center circle, and write the compound words that students suggest in the outer circles.

4. Have students read each word on the chart with you. To reinforce the principle, occasionally ask students to name the smaller word that a group of compound words has in common. Guide them to summarize the principle: *Some smaller words appear in many compound words.*

5. Explain to students that they are going to create a word map of compound words. They will choose a smaller word and write it in the center of the map. Then they will write compound words that include the smaller word in the outer circles.

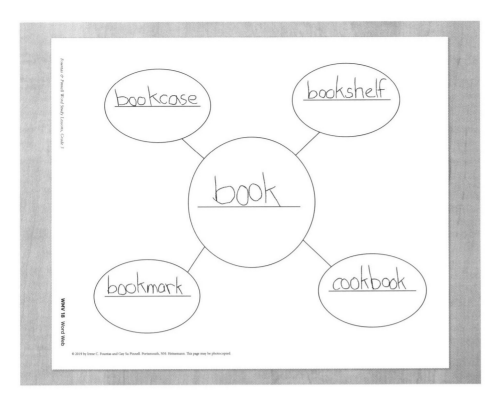

ACTIVITY: COMPOUND WORD MAP

INSTRUCTIONAL PROCEDURE

MAP WORDS

See page 32 for detailed descriptions of Instructional Procedures.

ACTION TAGS

take word

write word in center circle

write compound words in outer circles

read words

Apply

Distribute word cards and blank word maps. Have students write as many compound words as they can. Point out that they can add more circles if they need to.

Share

■ Have students share their word maps with the whole group and compare the words they came up with. Add any new examples to the class chart.

■ Review the principle, and remind students to notice compound words with common parts when they read and write.

Assess

■ Give students a different word that is common to many compound words, such as *book* or *water.* See if they can come up with at least two or three compound words that include the smaller word.

■ You may wish to use Word Meaning/Vocabulary Assessment C or H.

Connect Learning Across Contexts

Shared Reading You may wish to use the following Shared Reading title from *Fountas & Pinnell Classroom*™ to point out compound words with common parts.

SR *Trapped in Tar* by Hannah Cales

Guided Reading During the word work part of the lesson, write compound words on the board, and invite students to make additional words with either of the smaller words.

Shared Writing As you create texts together, draw students' attention to the components of various compound words.

Independent Writing When conferring with students, note compound words they have used in their own writing.

Extend Learning

Create word chains with compound words. Start with a common word. Students will make a compound word from that word. Then they will use one of the words from that compound word in another compound word, and so on: e.g., *eye, eyeball, ballgame, baseball*.

▶ Connect with Home

Have students share their word maps with a family member. Challenge them to come up with additional examples to add to their maps or to make a new map for a different set of compound words.

Recognize and Use Onomatopoetic Words

Plan

▶ Consider Your Students

Use this lesson after students have explored many books of poetry and other literature and have experienced listening to and reading poetry for themselves. Since preschool, they probably have experienced many words that represent or evoke sounds. It will also be helpful if students have collected their own poems in poetry notebooks. This lesson can be especially helpful to students who are searching for techniques to make their own writing more interesting and enjoyable to read.

▶ Working with English Language Learners

English language learners will enjoy saying and working with words that imitate sounds. They also have such words in their home language. Have students offer examples once they understand the principle. Students can compare how different languages represent the same sounds (e.g., the sound a kitten makes). They may notice some important similarities. Be sure that students have experience with the sounds being imitated (e.g., animals they know or sounds they have heard and can identify). Play audio of actual sounds when appropriate, and help students compare the actual sounds with the sounds of the words.

UNDERSTAND THE PRINCIPLE

Onomatopoeia is the representation of sound with words, e.g., the words *buzz* and *hiss*. It is not necessary to teach students to pronounce the terms *onomatopoeia* or *onomatopoetic*. The goal is to help students create a category for and identify examples of onomatopoetic words. Through this process, students become more sensitive to the use of language. This sensitivity is a step toward noticing other literary devices that make language descriptive, vivid, and poetic.

YOU WILL NEED

Online Resources
- ▶ **WMV 19** Action Tags
- ▶ **WMV 19** Poem: Porridge Is Bubbling
- ▶ **WMV 19** Poem: Some One
- ▶ **WMV 19** Poem: A Thunderstorm

Other Materials
- ▶ blank chart paper

Generative Lesson
A generative lesson has a simple structure that you can use to present similar content or concepts. Use this lesson structure to teach students to recognize and use a variety of onomatopoetic words.

EXPLAIN THE PRINCIPLE

Some words imitate the sound of a thing or an action. They are onomatopoetic words.

Comprehensive Phonics, Spelling, and Word Study Guide

Refer to: page **47**, row **16**

EARLY MIDDLE **LATE**

ACTIVITY:
ONOMATOPOETIC WORDS

INSTRUCTIONAL PROCEDURE

HEAR AND SAY

See page 32 for detailed descriptions of Instructional Procedures.

EXPLAIN THE PRINCIPLE

Some words imitate the sound of a thing or an action. They are onomatopoetic words.

Comprehensive Phonics, Spelling, and Word Study Guide

Refer to: page **47**, row **16**

The Rain

Splish, splash,

Splish, splash,

Drip, drop,

Drip, drop,

Will the rain ever stop?

Words That Imitate Sounds

splish

splash

ping

whoosh

hiss

buzz

tick tock

smack

knock

back

quack

Teach

1. Write the poem "The Rain" on chart paper, and read it with students.

2. *Think about the sound of the words. Which words in the poem imitate the sound of rain?* • *The pronunciations of the words* splish *and* splash *sound like water hitting something.*

3. Write the words *splish* and *splash* on another sheet of chart paper. *What other words have you read or used in your writing that imitate the sound of something?* • Create a list of onomatopoetic words with students. Stretch their thinking to include words such as *bark, cluck, quack,* and *knock.* You may also wish to include a heading and simple drawings.

4. Invite students to share what they have noticed about onomatopoetic words. *Why do writers use words like these?* • *Words that imitate sounds can make writing more interesting, vivid, and enjoyable.*

5. Tell students that they will read poems and identify words that imitate sounds. You may wish to provide copies of the poems in Online Resources as well as books of poetry. Students will find a poem that has at least one word that imitates a sound, copy the poem in their personal poetry notebook, and highlight the onomatopoetic words. If students do not have personal poetry notebooks, they can copy the poem on a sheet of paper.

Porridge Is Bubbling

Porridge is Bubbling, bubbling hot.
Stir it 'round and 'round in the pot,
The bubbles plip,
The bubbles plop.
It's ready to eat all bubbling hot.
Wake up, children.
Wake up soon.
We'll eat the porridge with a spoon.

**ACTIVITY:
ONOMATOPOETIC WORDS**

**INSTRUCTIONAL
PROCEDURE**

HEAR AND SAY

*See page 32 for detailed
descriptions of Instructional
Procedures.*

ACTION TAGS

read poems

find words

copy a poem

highlight words

Apply

■ You may need to tell students to copy poems exactly as they are printed, with the same lines and spaces, so they notice and value the line breaks.

■ Remind students to highlight the onomatopoetic words in the poems they copy. You may also wish to have students illustrate their poems.

Share

■ Invite students to share their selected poems. You may wish to add onomatopoetic words to the class chart.

■ Review the principle, and remind students to notice onomatopoetic words when they read and write.

Assess

Ask students to read a short text and identify examples of onomatopoetic words.

Connect Learning Across Contexts

Shared Reading You may wish to use the following Shared Reading title from *Fountas & Pinnell Classroom*™ to point out onomatopoetic words.

SR *Wolf Pack* by Annette Bay Pimentel

Guided Reading As you guide discussion of a text that includes onomatopoetic words, prompt students to notice and think about the writer's use of words that imitate sounds. *Why do you think the writer uses words that imitate sounds in this book?*

Shared Writing When appropriate, include an onomatopoetic word in a piece of writing. Involve students in deciding how and where to incorporate the word to make the piece more enjoyable and interesting.

Independent Writing During conferences, talk with writers about opportunities to use onomatopoetic words. Together, think about places in a piece of writing in which a sound is described or is key to the development of an idea. *Would the use of a word that imitates the sound make your piece more interesting?*

Extend Learning

■ Encourage students to record onomatopoetic words in their writer's notebooks.

■ Have students perform short texts with onomatopoetic words as readers' theater. Guide them to emphasize the sounds of onomatopoetic words in their performance.

▶ **Connect with Home**

Encourage students to share with family members the poems they copied.

Recognize That Some Words Have Literal and Figurative Meanings

Plan

▶ Consider Your Students

The concept of figurative language is challenging. Students may need to consider many examples over several days before they understand the principle sufficiently to apply their learning. It will be helpful to begin with words that have literal meanings that are very familiar to students, such as simple adjectives (e.g., *dry*, *sharp*), common, tactile nouns (e.g., *stream, heart, army*), and vivid action verbs (e.g., *jump, gnaw*). Be sure that students are familiar with the structure and components of dictionary entries, including multiple definitions and illustrative examples.

▶ Working with English Language Learners

English language learners understand that many words have multiple meanings. However, words that are used figuratively are likely to present a special challenge. Be sure that students understand the literal meanings of the words in the lesson. You may find it helpful to use picture cards, photographs, and videos to establish that students thoroughly understand the literal meaning of a word. Describe the figurative meaning of a word in simple terms. You may need to use the word in a variety of sentences over the course of several lessons to build adequate context for the figurative meaning.

UNDERSTAND THE PRINCIPLE

For comprehension and coherence, students need to know the meaning of the words in the texts they read and write. Even as they constantly expand their listening, speaking, reading, and writing vocabularies, it is important for them to develop more complex understandings of words they already know, including the fact that some words have a literal meaning but may also be used figuratively. The *literal* meaning of a word is its usual meaning, without exaggeration or imaginative use. *Figurative* language changes or goes beyond literal meaning.

YOU WILL NEED

Online Resources
- ▶ **WMV 20** Action Tags
- ▶ **WMV 20** Word Cards
- ▶ **WMV 20** Two-Way Sorts

Other Materials
- ▶ blank chart paper

✓ Generative Lesson

A generative lesson has a simple structure that you can use to present similar content or concepts. Use this lesson structure to teach students to recognize a variety of words that have both literal and figurative meanings.

EXPLAIN THE PRINCIPLE

Some words have a literal meaning and a figurative meaning.

Comprehensive Phonics, Spelling, and Word Study Guide

Refer to:
page **47**, row **17**

ACTIVITY: WORD MEANINGS

INSTRUCTIONAL PROCEDURE

MAP WORDS

See page 32 for detailed descriptions of Instructional Procedures.

EXPLAIN THE PRINCIPLE

Some words have a literal meaning and a figurative meaning.

Comprehensive Phonics, Spelling, and Word Study Guide

Refer to: page **47**, row **17**

Teach

1. On chart paper, write the following sets of sentences with the word *bug* underlined:

    I watched a <u>bug</u> crawl onto a stick.

    My brother started to <u>bug</u> me, asking the same question over and over.

2. Read the sentences with students. *What do you notice about the underlined words in these sentences? • What do you notice about the meaning of* bug *in these sentences? • The meanings are different.* Allow time for students to explain the two meanings. *In the first sentence,* bug *means "an insect, usually without wings and with a pointed beak for piercing and sucking." In the second sentence,* bug *means "to annoy."*

3. Repeat the process for the word *sharp*. Write the following sets of sentences on the chart with the word *sharp* underlined.

    Be careful, it's a very <u>sharp</u> knife.

    He's a <u>sharp</u> dresser who likes fancy clothes.

4. Read the sentences with students. *What do you notice about the words in these sentences? •* Encourage students to discuss the two meanings of the word *sharp. In the first sentence,* sharp *means "having a thin cutting edge or a fine point." In the second sentence,* sharp *means "intelligent, clever."*

5. Build on students' observations and ideas to explain the principle. *Some words have a literal meaning and a figurative meaning. The first sentences use the literal meanings of* bug *and* sharp. *The second sentences use figurative meanings of* bug *and* sharp. Invite students to name other words that have literal and figurative meanings. Guide them to use the words in sentences that provide context for the meanings.

6. Tell students that they are going to draw pictures to illustrate the literal and figurative meanings of a word. Display a set of word cards. Explain that each word has a literal meaning and at least one figurative meaning. Students will choose a word and draw two pictures on a two-way sort. The picture in the first column illustrates the literal meaning of the word. The picture in the second column illustrates a figurative meaning of the word. At the top of each column, students write a sentence that uses the word and corresponds to the picture below.

I watched a <u>bug</u> crawl onto a stick.

My brother started to <u>bug</u> me, asking the same question over and over.

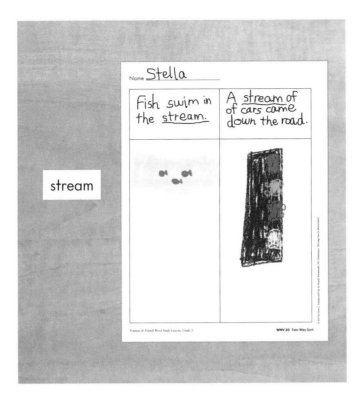

INSTRUCTIONAL PROCEDURE

MAP WORDS

See page 32 for detailed descriptions of Instructional Procedures.

ACTION TAGS

choose word

draw pictures

write sentences

Apply

- Students may need to consult a dictionary to identify or understand the figurative meaning of a word. Most dictionaries also provide example phrases and sentences that students may find helpful.

- Remind students to write a sentence at the top of each column that corresponds to the picture they have drawn. You may wish to have students underline or highlight the key word in each sentence.

Share

- Invite students to share their pictures and sentences. Encourage students to talk about what they have learned and observed about the figurative meanings of words.

- Review the principle, and remind students to notice figurative meanings of words when they read and write.

Assess

- Write new sets of sentences that use the literal meaning and a figurative meaning of a word. Ask students to describe both meanings.

- Have students read a short text and identify words that are used figuratively.

Word Meaning/Vocabulary: Recognize That Some Words Have Literal and Figurative Meanings

Connect Learning Across Contexts

Interactive Read-Aloud Read aloud books that include figurative language.

 *Bedhead* by Margie Palatini

 *My Rotten Redheaded Older Brother* by Patricia Polacco

Guided Reading Prompt students to notice a writer's use of figurative meanings. You may wish to ask students to think about and describe how the figurative meaning of a word differs from the literal meaning of the word.

Shared Writing Take time to identify words with figurative meanings within pieces of writing that you have completed together as a class. Guide students to recognize how the use of words with figurative meanings makes the writing more interesting.

Independent Writing During conferences, talk with writers about opportunities to use figurative meanings of words.

Extend Learning

■ Encourage students to begin a list of words with literal and figurative meanings. Students may find it helpful to keep this list in their writer's notebook or word study notebook. Students may wish to define and illustrate each word. They may also wish to record examples of how writers use the figurative meanings in various texts.

■ Have students fold back the sentences at the top of their two-column sorts, so that only the illustrations are visible. Have partners exchange sheets and attempt to figure out the word and meanings based on the illustrations. Partners can then reveal and read the sentences to see if they are right.

▶ Connect with Home

Ask students to share their illustrations and sentences with family members. Encourage them to talk about what they have learned about words with literal and figurative meanings.

Recognize That Some Words Have Literal and Figurative Meanings

Plan

▷ Consider Your Students

The concept of figurative language is challenging. Students may need to consider many examples over several days before they understand the principle sufficiently to apply their learning. You may find it helpful to teach and discuss the meanings of the words used in the sentence sort before students do the Apply activity. Be sure that students are familiar with the structure and components of dictionary entries, including multiple definitions and illustrative examples.

▷ Working with English Language Learners

English language learners understand that many words have multiple meanings. However, words that are used figuratively are likely to present a special challenge. Be sure that students understand the literal meanings of the words in the lesson. You may find it helpful to use picture cards, photographs, and videos to establish that students thoroughly understand the literal meaning of a word. Describe the figurative meaning of a word in simple terms. You may need to use the word in a variety of sentences over the course of several lessons to build adequate context for the figurative meaning.

YOU WILL NEED

Online Resources
- ▶ **WMV 21** Action Tags
- ▶ **WMV 21** Sentence Strips

Other Materials
- ▶ blank chart paper

Generative Lesson ✓

A generative lesson has a simple structure that you can use to present similar content or concepts. Use this lesson structure to teach students to recognize a variety of words that have both literal and figurative meanings.

UNDERSTAND THE PRINCIPLE

For comprehension and coherence, students need to know the meaning of the words in the texts they read and write. Even as they constantly expand their listening, speaking, reading, and writing vocabularies, it is important for them to develop more complex understandings of words they already know, including the fact that some words have a literal meaning but may also be used figuratively. The *literal* meaning of a word is its usual meaning, without exaggeration or imaginative use. *Figurative* language changes or goes beyond literal meaning.

EXPLAIN THE PRINCIPLE

Some words have a literal meaning and a figurative meaning.

Comprehensive Phonics, Spelling, and Word Study Guide

Refer to: page **47**, row **17**

INSTRUCTIONAL PROCEDURE

MAP WORDS

See page 32 for detailed descriptions of Instructional Procedures.

EXPLAIN THE PRINCIPLE

Some words have a literal meaning and a figurative meaning.

Comprehensive Phonics, Spelling, and Word Study Guide

Refer to: page **47**, row **17**

A toad <u>jumped</u> onto a log.

She <u>jumped</u> from book to book to find a story that she wanted to read.

Teach

1. On chart paper, write the following sentences with the word *jumped* underlined.

   A toad <u>jumped</u> onto a log.

   She <u>jumped</u> from book to book to find a story that she wanted to read.

2. Read the sentences with students. *What do you notice about the underlined words in these sentences?* • Guide students to think about the meanings of the word. *What do you notice about the meaning of* jumped *in each sentence?* • Allow time for students to explain the two meanings. Incorporate the principle into the discussion. *In the first sentence,* jumped *means "leaped." This is the literal meaning. In the second sentence,* jumped *means "moved or changed quickly, without a plan or an order." This is a figurative meaning. It's different from the literal meaning.*

3. Add the following sentences to the chart.

   My <u>heart</u> was beating fast by the end of the game.

   The park is in the <u>heart</u> of the city.

4. Read the sentences with students. *What do you notice about the words in these sentences?* • *Which sentence uses the literal meaning of the word, and which sentence uses a figurative meaning of the word?* • *The first sentence uses the literal meaning: "the organ that pumps blood through the body." The second sentence uses a figurative meaning: "the central part." The park is not in an actual heart. It's in the center of the city.*

5. Build on students' observations and ideas to reinforce the principle. *Some words have a literal meaning and a figurative meaning.* Invite students to name other words that have literal and figurative meanings. Guide them to use the words in sentences that provide context for the meanings.

6. Tell students that they are going to say and sort sentences based on the literal and figurative meanings of a word. Explain that students will read each pair of sentences with the same underlined word. One sentence uses the literal meaning of the word, and one sentence uses the figurative meaning of the word. Students sort the sentences under the correct heads. After completing the sort, students choose another word with literal and figurative meanings and write their own pair of sentences on blank sentence strips. They then add their sentences to the sort.

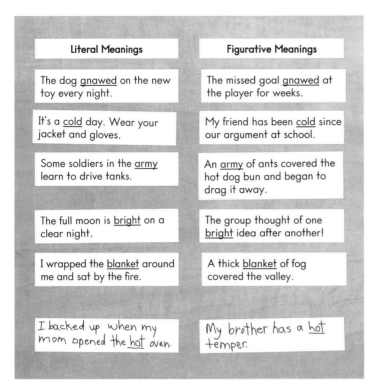

Literal Meanings	Figurative Meanings
The dog <u>gnawed</u> on the new toy every night.	The missed goal <u>gnawed</u> at the player for weeks.
It's a <u>cold</u> day. Wear your jacket and gloves.	My friend has been <u>cold</u> since our argument at school.
Some soldiers in the <u>army</u> learn to drive tanks.	An <u>army</u> of ants covered the hot dog bun and began to drag it away.
The full moon is <u>bright</u> on a clear night.	The group thought of one <u>bright</u> idea after another!
I wrapped the <u>blanket</u> around me and sat by the fire.	A thick <u>blanket</u> of fog covered the valley.
I backed up when my mom opened the <u>hot</u> oven.	My brother has a <u>hot</u> temper.

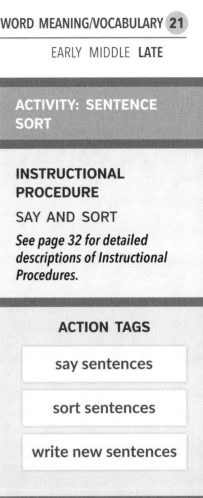

ACTIVITY: SENTENCE SORT

INSTRUCTIONAL PROCEDURE

SAY AND SORT

See page 32 for detailed descriptions of Instructional Procedures.

ACTION TAGS

say sentences

sort sentences

write new sentences

Apply

- If students find the sort challenging, you may wish to have them work with a partner or in a small group to complete the activity.
- As they prepare to write their own sentences, students may find it helpful to consult a dictionary. Most dictionaries provide example phrases and sentences that can help students understand the figurative use of a word.

Share

- Invite students to discuss the sort and to share the new sentences that they wrote. Encourage students to talk about what they have observed about the figurative meanings of words.
- Review the principle, and remind students to notice words that have literal and figurative meanings when they read and write.

Assess

- Have students sort a new pair of sentences and describe the literal meaning and a figurative meaning of a word.
- Have students read a short text and identify words that are used figuratively.

Word Meaning/Vocabulary: Recognize That Some Words Have Literal and Figurative Meanings

Connect Learning Across Contexts

Shared Reading You may wish to use the following Shared Reading title from *Fountas & Pinnell Classroom*™ to point out that some words have literal and figurative meanings.

SR *From Flower to Honey* by June Schwartz

Guided Reading During the discussion of a text, guide students to notice a writer's use of figurative meanings of words.

Shared Writing As you construct a text, point out instances in which you are using a figurative meaning of a word. You may wish to ask students to think of other ways to express the idea and to discuss whether the figurative meaning is most effective.

Independent Writing Draw students' attention to uses of figurative meanings in their writing. Encourage them to consider if the figurative expression is the most precise, clearest, and most effective way to express their idea.

Extend Learning

Provide a list of additional words that have both literal and figurative meanings, such as *beast, dry, cool, fire, fishy,* and *puzzle.* Have students use a dictionary to define and illustrate the literal meaning and at least one figurative meaning of each word.

▶ Connect with Home

Have students take home a set of sentence strips to say and sort with family members.

Understand the Concept of Suffixes and Recognize Their Use in Determining the Meaning of Some English Words

Plan

▶ Consider Your Students

Use this lesson after students have noticed suffixes in texts they are reading and have begun to use suffixes in their own writing. If students have significant experience with suffixes and have control of the concept, you may wish to expand this lesson by creating a larger chart that provides an overview of many more suffixes. Alternatively, if students are just becoming aware of word parts, you may wish to teach this lesson over several days, focusing on a single suffix each day. You may wish to tailor the lesson to review suffixes that students are experiencing regularly in their reading or to introduce suffixes that would be useful to students in their writing.

▶ Working with English Language Learners

The concept that many English words are made up of more than one meaning-bearing part is essential for English language learners to understand. To illustrate this concept, you may find it helpful to have students put together and break apart word cards containing base words and suffixes. Gaining control of the precise meanings of suffixes will likely be challenging for English language learners, because the meanings of suffixes are often abstract in isolation. Students will need many examples in a variety of rich contexts in order to gain control of the meanings of suffixes.

UNDERSTAND THE PRINCIPLE

Many English words contain one or more parts: a base word, a word root, and/or one or more affixes. A *base word* is a word in its simplest form (e.g., *home, meat*), which has a meaning, can stand on its own, and can have affixes added to it. A *word root* is a word part, usually from another language such as Greek or Latin, that carries the essential meaning of the word but that cannot stand alone (e.g., *-gen-, -ject-, -prim-*). An *affix* is a letter or group of letters added to the beginning or ending of a base word or a word root to change its meaning or function. An affix added to the end of a base word or a word root is a *suffix*. A suffix changes the function or meaning of a base word or word root. Understanding how suffixes contribute to the meaning or function of words helps students solve more complex words and expand their vocabulary with greater efficiency. This lesson focuses on suffixes that change the meaning–and often the part of speech–of a word (e.g., *-er* in *teacher, -ful* in *painful, -ist* in *artist,* and *-ment* in *movement.*)

YOU WILL NEED

Online Resources
- ▶ **WMV 22** Action Tags
- ▶ **WMV 22** Follow the Path Game Board
- ▶ **WMV 22** Four-Way Sort
- ▶ **WMV 22** Directions for Follow the Path

Other Materials
- ▶ blank chart paper

Generative Lesson

A generative lesson has a simple structure that you can use to present similar content or concepts. Use this lesson structure to teach students to recognize a variety of suffixes.

EXPLAIN THE PRINCIPLE

A suffix is a word part that can be found at the end of many English words.

A suffix may contain hints about the meaning of an English word.

Comprehensive Phonics, Spelling, and Word Study Guide

Refer to: page **48**, row **22**

Word Meaning/Vocabulary: Understand the Concept of Suffixes and Recognize Their Use in Determining the Meaning of Some English Words

333

ACTIVITY: WORD LISTS

INSTRUCTIONAL PROCEDURE

NOTICE PARTS

See page 32 for detailed descriptions of Instructional Procedures.

EXPLAIN THE PRINCIPLE

A suffix is a word part that can be found at the end of many English words.

A suffix may contain hints about the meaning of an English word.

Comprehensive Phonics, Spelling, and Word Study Guide

Refer to:
page **48**, row **22**

Teach

1. On chart paper, write a column of three or four words ending in the first suffix you would like to teach, such as *colorful, helpful, thankful,* and *beautiful.* Have students read the words with you. *What do you notice about all of the words? • Each word ends with the same group of letters or part,* -ful.

-ful "full of"	-less "without"	-ly "like" or "in this way"	-ment "resulting in doing this or being this way"
colorful	hopeless		
helpful	careless	nicely	excitement
thankful	fearless	safely	amazement
beautiful	homeless	friendly	agreement
careful	endless	easily	movement
wonderful	spotless	quietly	enjoyment
		sadly	judgement

2. Write *-ful* as a column head. *What do you call the word part "ful"? This group of letters is a* suffix. *A suffix is a word part that can be found at the end of many words.* Cover up the suffix in each of the example words, inviting students to notice the presence of the base words *color, help,* and *thank,* as well as the base word *beauty.*

3. Ask students to think about the meaning of the first word. *What do you notice about the meaning of this word? • If a drawing is colorful, it is full of color.* Guide students to note that the suffix *-ful* changes the noun *color* to an adjective. *The suffix* -ful *changes* color *to a different kind of word.* Color *is a thing. It is a noun. When I add the suffix* -ful, *I make an adjective.*

4. Invite students to talk about the meanings of *helpful, thankful,* and *beautiful.* Encourage them to use the words in sentences that provide context for the meanings and for their function as adjectives. You may wish to point out that the spelling of some words, such as *beauty,* changes slightly when a suffix is added.

5. Building on students' ideas, write a simple meaning for *-ful,* such as "full of," near the top of the column. *A suffix may contain hints about the meaning of a word. It may also contain hints about how the word is used with other words. Noticing suffixes can help you solve the meanings of longer words and see how they are used in sentences.*

6. Invite students to name other words that end with the suffix *-ful.* Add examples to the list. Repeat the process to create additional columns of words with suffixes that you want students to notice, compare, and think about, such as *-less, -ly,* and *-ment.*

7. Tell students that today they are going to play Follow the Path. Taking turns, students toss a die, move that number of spaces, read aloud the word in the new space, name the suffix, and use the word in a sentence. They go back to the space they were on if they can't read the word correctly and use it in a sentence. The first player to reach "finish" wins the game. After playing the game, students will use a four-way sort to write the words that appear on the game board.

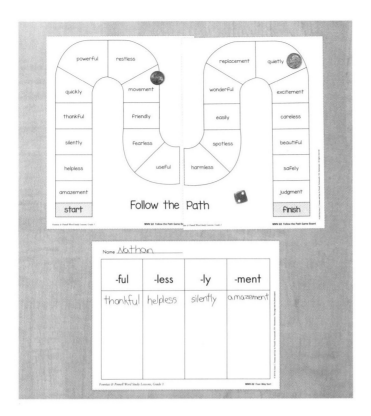

INSTRUCTIONAL PROCEDURE

NOTICE PARTS

See page 32 for detailed descriptions of Instructional Procedures.

ACTION TAGS

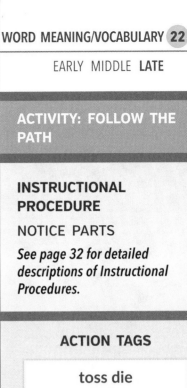

toss die
move
read word
name suffix
use in a sentence
sort and write

Apply

- The game board in Online Resources is based on the four suffixes presented in Teach. You can create a Follow the Path game board with other suffixes by using the blank template in Online Resources.

- Have students play Follow the Path in pairs or groups of three using a game board, a game die, and game pieces to mark their places on the board.

- Point out the suffixes at the top of the four-way sort. Encourage students to write words from the game board in the correct column.

Share

- Have students share a few words that they read on the game board. You may wish to add a few new words to the class chart.

- Review the principle, and remind students to notice suffixes and recognize their use in determining the function and/or meaning of some words when they read and write.

Assess

As you observe students reading, notice how efficient they are in recognizing and solving words that have suffixes.

Word Meaning/Vocabulary: Understand the Concept of Suffixes and Recognize Their Use in Determining the Meaning of Some English Words

Connect Learning Across Contexts

Shared Reading You may wish to use the following Shared Reading title from *Fountas & Pinnell Classroom*™ to point out the concept of suffixes and recognize their use in determining the function and/or meaning of some words.

SR *Exploring Underground* by Louis Petrone

Guided Reading During word work, have students identify words with suffixes. Prompt them to talk about the meanings of the words.

Shared Writing As you construct pieces of writing, point out examples of words with suffixes. Encourage students to talk about the meanings of the words and how the suffixes add to or change the function and/or meanings. You may wish to add new words to the class chart.

Independent Writing During conferences, draw writers' attention to their use of words with suffixes. Conversations around this topic may provide an opportunity to discuss word choice: e.g., *You used the word* wonderful *to describe this event. Does this description give your readers enough detail?*

Extend Learning

- Repeat the lesson with additional suffixes, such as ones that mean "person or thing that does something": e.g., *-er [teacher], -or [visitor], -ist [artist].*
- Distribute blank Follow the Path game boards, and have students work together to create boards with new sets of words with suffixes. Make the additional boards available for students to choose when playing the game.

▶ Connect with Home

Send Follow the Path game boards home so that students can play the game with family members.

Understand the Concept of Prefixes and Recognize Their Use in Determining the Meaning of Some English Words

Plan

▶ Consider Your Students

Use this lesson after students have noticed prefixes in texts they are reading and have begun to use prefixes in their own writing. If students have significant experience with prefixes and have control of the concept, you may wish to expand this lesson by creating a larger chart that provides an overview of many more prefixes. Alternatively, if students are just becoming aware of word parts, you may wish to teach this lesson over several days, focusing on a single prefix each day. You may wish to tailor the lesson to review prefixes that students are experiencing regularly in their reading or to introduce prefixes that would be useful to students in their writing.

▶ Working with English Language Learners

The concept that many English words are made up of more than one meaning-bearing part is essential for English language learners to understand. To illustrate this concept, you may find it helpful to have students put together and break apart word cards containing base words and prefixes. Gaining control of the precise meanings of prefixes will likely be challenging for English language learners, because the meanings of prefixes are often abstract in isolation. Students will need many examples in a variety of rich contexts in order to gain control of the meanings of prefixes.

UNDERSTAND THE PRINCIPLE

Many English words contain one or more parts: a base word, a word root, and/or one or more affixes. A *base word* is a word in its simplest form (e.g., *home, meat*), which has a meaning, can stand on its own, and can have affixes added to it. An *affix* is a letter or group of letters added to the beginning or ending of a base word or a word root to change its meaning or function. An affix added to the beginning of a base word is a *prefix* (e.g., *re-* in *refill*). A prefix changes the meaning of a base word. Understanding how prefixes contribute to meaning helps students solve more complex words and expand their vocabulary with greater efficiency.

YOU WILL NEED

PWS Ready Resources
- ▶ Blank Word Cards

Online Resources
- ▶ WMV 23 Action Tags
- ▶ WMV 23 Word Cards
- ▶ WMV 23 Three-Way Sort

Other Materials
- ▶ blank chart paper

Generative Lesson

A generative lesson has a simple structure that you can use to present similar content or concepts. Use this lesson structure to teach students to recognize a variety of prefixes.

EXPLAIN THE PRINCIPLE

A prefix is a word part that can be found at the beginning of many English words.

A prefix may contain hints about the meaning of an English word.

Comprehensive Phonics, Spelling, and Word Study Guide

Refer to: page **48**, row **23**

Word Meaning/Vocabulary: Understand the Concept of Prefixes and Recognize Their Use in Determining the Meaning of Some English Words

337

EARLY MIDDLE **LATE**

ACTIVITY: WORD LISTS

INSTRUCTIONAL PROCEDURE

NOTICE PARTS

See page 32 for detailed descriptions of Instructional Procedures.

EXPLAIN THE PRINCIPLE

A prefix is a word part that can be found at the beginning of many English words.

A prefix may contain hints about the meaning of an English word.

Comprehensive Phonics, Spelling, and Word Study Guide

Refer to: page **48**, row **23**

dis- "not"	mis- "wrong or poorly"	pre- "before"
dislike	mistake	precaution
disappear	mislead	prepay
dishonest	misunderstand	preheat
disobey	misspell	preview

Teach

1. On chart paper, write a column of three or four words that begin with the first prefix you would like to teach, such as *dislike, disappear,* and *dishonest.* Have students read the words with you. *What do you notice about all of the words?* • *Each word begins with the same group of letters,* dis.

2. Write *dis-* as a column head. *What do you call the word part* dis-*? This group of letters is a prefix. A prefix is a word part that can be found at the beginning of many words.* Cover up the prefix in each of the example words, inviting students to notice the presence of the base words *like, appear,* and *honest.*

3. Ask students to think about the meaning of the first word. *What do you notice about the meaning of this word?* • *If I dislike a type of food, I don't like it. I don't think it tastes good.* Guide students to note that the prefix *dis-* changes the meaning of the word *like.*

4. Invite students to talk about the meanings of *disappear* and *dishonest.* Encourage them to use the words in sentences that provide context for the meanings.

5. Building on students' ideas, write a simple meaning for *dis-* such as "not," near the top of the column. *A prefix may contain hints about the meaning of a word. Noticing prefixes and knowing their meanings can help you solve the meanings of longer words.*

6. Invite students to name other words that end with the prefix *dis-.* Add other examples to the list. Repeat the process to create additional columns of words with the prefixes *mis-* and *pre-.*

7. Tell students that today they are going to say and sort words by prefixes. After they complete the sort, students read each group of words to a partner. Students then choose a word with each prefix and write a sentence for each word on a three-way sort.

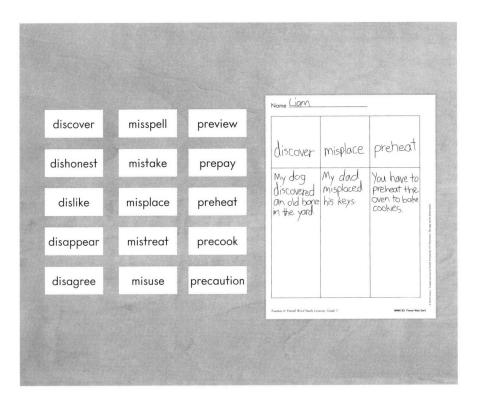

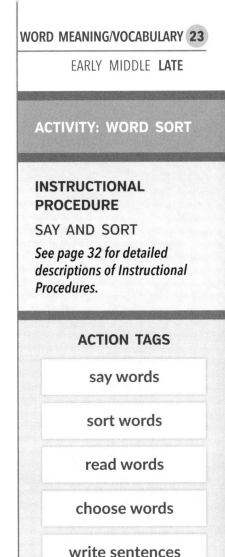

INSTRUCTIONAL PROCEDURE

SAY AND SORT

See page 32 for detailed descriptions of Instructional Procedures.

ACTION TAGS

say words

sort words

read words

choose words

write sentences

Apply

- The word cards provided in Online Resources are based on the three prefixes used in Teach. You can create word cards with other prefixes by using the blank cards in *Ready Resources*.

- Remind students to read the words they have sorted to a partner. Encourage partners to discuss the meanings of words and to consult a dictionary if a word is unfamiliar or its meaning is unclear.

- Have students write each of the words they choose at the top of a three-way sort and write a sentence in each column. Students may wish to illustrate their sentences as well.

Share

- Invite students to share the words they chose and to read their sentences. You may wish to add a few new words to the class chart.

- Review the principle, and remind students to notice prefixes and recognize their use in determining the meaning of some words when they read and write.

Assess

As you observe students reading, notice how efficient they are in recognizing and solving words that have prefixes.

Word Meaning/Vocabulary: Understand the Concept of Prefixes and Recognize Their Use in Determining the Meaning of Some English Words

Connect Learning Across Contexts

Shared Reading You may wish to use the following Shared Reading title from *Fountas & Pinnell Classroom*™ to point out prefixes and recognize their use in determining the meaning of some words.

> SR *Far Above Earth: A Day on the Space Station* by Jane Simon

Guided Reading During word work, have students identify words with prefixes. Prompt students to talk about the meanings of the words.

Shared Writing As you construct pieces of writing, point out examples of words with prefixes. Encourage students to talk about the meanings of the words and how the prefixes change the meanings of the base words. You may wish to add new words to the class chart.

Independent Writing During conferences, draw writers' attention to their use of words with prefixes. To encourage students to attend to word choice, ask them to talk about alternate ways to express the same idea. Students will often find that using a word with a prefix is the most concise option.

Extend Learning

- Repeat the lesson with additional prefixes, e.g., *non-* (*nonfiction,* "not"), *un-* (*unkind,* "not"), and *re-* (*refill,* "again").

- Encourage students to begin making a list of prefixes in their word study notebooks. For each prefix, they can record example words and sentences that they encounter in their reading.

▶ Connect with Home

Send sets of word cards home for students to say and sort with family members.

Word Structure

Looking at the structure of words will help students learn how words are related to each other and how words can be changed by adding letters. Being able to recognize syllables, for example, helps students break down words into smaller units that are easier to analyze. Students learn to identify distinct syllables in a word, and they can build on this useful information in reading and writing. Words often have *affixes*, parts added before or after a word to change its meaning or its function. Working with suffixes and prefixes will help students read, understand, and write words that use them. Other principles related to word structure include recognizing and using abbreviations and plurals accurately.

Connect to Assessment

See related (optional) WS Assessment tasks in Online Resources.

- Assessment A: Recognizing and Using Compound Words
- Assessment B: Recognizing and Using Contractions
- Assessment C: Recognizing Syllables in Words
- Assessment D: Writing Syllables in Words
- Assessment E: Recognizing and Using Plurals
- Assessment F: Recognizing and Using Words with Suffixes
- Assessment G: Recognizing and Using Word with Prefixes
- Assessment H: Individual Record (Recognizing and Using Compound Words)
- Assessment I: Individual Record (Recognizing and Using Contractions)
- Assessment J: Class Record (Recognizing and Writing Syllables in Words)
- Assessment K: Individual Record (Recognizing and Using Plurals)
- Assessment L: Class Record (Recognizing and Using Words with Suffixes)
- Assessment M: Individual Record (Recognizing and Using Words with Prefixes)

Develop Your Professional Understanding

See *The Fountas & Pinnell Comprehensive Phonics, Spelling, and Word Study Guide*. 2017. Portsmouth, New Hampshire: Heinemann. Related pages: 2-12, 51-73.

See *The Fountas & Pinnell Literacy Continuum: A Tool for Assessment, Planning, and Teaching*. 2017. Portsmouth, New Hampshire: Heinemann. Related pages: 357-397.

See *Word Matters: Teaching Phonics and Spelling in the Reading/Writing Classroom* by G.S. Pinnell and I.C. Fountas. 1998. Portsmouth, New Hampshire: Heinemann. Related pages: 97–98.

Recognize and Use Compound Words

Plan

▶ Consider Your Students

At this point in their learning, students have a great deal of experience with easy compound words and are ready to solve more complex examples. They can also think more analytically about how each word contributes to the meaning. Tailor the difficulty of the lesson by choosing harder or easier words, as needed.

▶ Working with English Language Learners

It can be challenging for English language learners to recognize compound words, notice their components, and think about the meaning of the components and the larger word. Gaps in any of this knowledge cause difficulty. Once students understand the principle, however, they will have acquired a powerful tool for acquiring new English vocabulary. Choose simple, concrete compound words, and provide picture support or demonstration as needed.

YOU WILL NEED

Online Resources
- ▶ WS 1 Action Tags
- ▶ WS 1 Word Cards
- ▶ WS 1 List Sheets

Other Materials
- ▶ chart paper

Generative Lesson
A generative lesson has a simple structure that you can use to present similar content or concepts. Use this lesson structure to teach students a variety of compound words.

UNDERSTAND THE PRINCIPLE

Compound words are made up of two whole words. In most compound words (for example, *haircut*), each smaller word contributes to the meaning of the whole word. Teaching students to look for the longer word parts can be a helpful technique for reading longer words.

EXPLAIN THE PRINCIPLE

The word parts in a compound word often give hints about the meaning of the compound word.

Comprehensive Phonics, Spelling, and Word Study Guide

Refer to:
Page **54**, row **16**

EARLY MIDDLE LATE

ACTIVITY: COMPOUND WORDS

INSTRUCTIONAL PROCEDURE

NOTICE PARTS

See page 32 for detailed descriptions of Instructional Procedures.

EXPLAIN THE PRINCIPLE

The word parts in a compound word often give hints about the meaning of the compound word.

Comprehensive Phonics, Spelling, and Word Study Guide

Refer to: page **54**, row **16**

starfish
barnyard
doorbell
wheelchair

Teach

1. Tell students that you are going to help them think about some longer words.

2. On chart paper, show a list of several compound words, such as *starfish, barnyard, doorbell,* and *wheelchair.*

3. Say the word *starfish,* and ask students to say and clap the word. *What do you notice about this word?* • Students will likely notice that it is made of two smaller words. *What is the first smaller word in this compound word?* • *What is the second smaller word in this compound word?*

4. *What do you think a* starfish *is? How do you know?* Listen for comments that show that students have put together the meanings of *star* and *fish* to arrive at a definition.

5. Repeat this procedure for *barnyard, doorbell,* and *wheelchair.*

6. Tell students that they are going to make compound words with two word cards and then write the compound words on a list sheet.

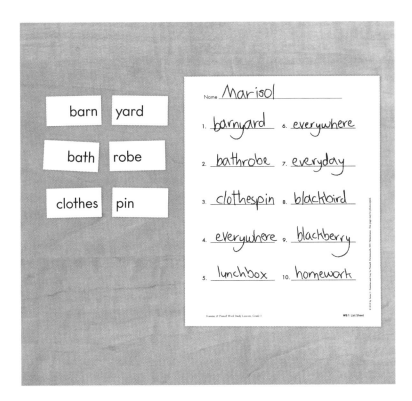

INSTRUCTIONAL PROCEDURE

MAKE WORDS

See page 32 for detailed descriptions of Instructional Procedures.

ACTION TAGS

take word cards

match words

write word

read

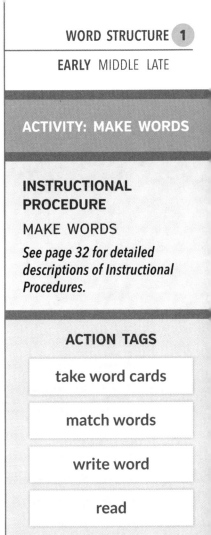

Apply

Instruct students to put together two word cards to make one word. Have them make at least ten. Remind them that the words must be real, and that they can use a word card more than once. Tell them to copy their words onto a list sheet.

Share

Have students read their list sheet to a partner. Add student examples to a class chart.

Assess

- Write four or five compound words on cards, and have students tell what they mean.
- Observe students' ability to take apart compound words while reading.
- You may wish to use Word Structure Assessment A or H.

Word Structure: Recognize and Use Compound Words

Connect Learning Across Contexts

Shared Reading After reading books together, quickly write down a few compound words on a whiteboard. Have students use the word parts to determine the words' meanings. You may wish to use the following Shared Reading title from *Fountas & Pinnell Classroom*™ to gain more practice locating compound words after reading.

> SR *From Flower to Honey* by June Schwartz

Guided Reading Encourage students to notice and identify one or two compound words after reading and discussing a book. Add new examples to the class list.

Shared Writing When working with a small group of writers, point out places where there are compound words.

Independent Writing When conferring with writers, help them notice compound words.

Extend Learning

- Repeat this lesson with a different variety of compound words.
- Ask students to select eight compound words and illustrate their meanings on a four-box sheet.

▶ Connect with Home

Send home a deck of game cards with compound words and game directions from Online Resources so students can play Battle with family members. As an alternative, have students choose two or three compound words to illustrate. These illustrations can be compiled into a class book.

Recognize and Use Compound Words That Have Frequently Used Words

Plan

▶ Consider Your Students

At this point in their learning, students will have a strong understanding of compound words and will be able to quickly call up many examples, such as *goldfish, everyone,* and *afternoon.* In this lesson, they develop flexibility using parts of words that appear in several different compound words.

▶ Working with English Language Learners

Compound words can be confusing to English language learners; some of the most common examples (e.g., *anyway, everywhere, somehow*) have meanings that are not easy to discern from analyzing the component parts. Help students increase their ability to recognize and understand compound words by using magnetic letters to make them and take them apart, by using them in sentences, and by discussing their meanings and the contexts in which they might be used.

YOU WILL NEED

Online Resources
- ▶ WS 2 Action Tags
- ▶ WS 2 Word Cards
- ▶ WS 2 Word and Sentence Sheets

Other Materials
- ▶ chart paper

Generative Lesson
A generative lesson has a simple structure that you can use to present similar content or concepts. Use this lesson structure to teach students a variety of compound words that combine frequently used words.

UNDERSTAND THE PRINCIPLE

Some words appear often in compound words. Identifying one or more frequently used words within a compound word will help students decode or take apart the compound word. Many of these frequently used words appear usually at the beginning of compound words (e.g., *anybody, anyplace*), whereas other frequently used words appear usually at the end of compound words (e.g., *anything, something*). Learning to look at parts helps students read and write many words.

EXPLAIN THE PRINCIPLE

Some frequently used words appear often in compound words

Make connections among compound words that have the same word parts.

Comprehensive Phonics, Spelling, and Word Study Guide

Refer to:
Page **54**, row **17**

EARLY MIDDLE LATE

ACTIVITY: COMPOUND WORDS WITH *ANY, EVERY,* AND *SOME*

INSTRUCTIONAL PROCEDURE

NOTICE PARTS

See page 32 for detailed descriptions of Instructional Procedures.

EXPLAIN THE PRINCIPLE

Some frequently used words appear often in compound words.

Make connections among compound words that have the same word parts.

Comprehensive Phonics, Spelling, and Word Study Guide

Refer to: page **54**, row **17**

anyone
anywhere
anything

everybody
everyone
everything

someday
somehow
someone

Teach

1. Tell students that they are going to learn more about words.

2. Write the words *anyone, anywhere,* and *anything* on chart paper. *What do you notice about all of these words?* • Students may observe that they are all compound words or that they all include the word *any.*

3. *There are other compound words that begin with* any. *What other ones can you think of?* • Write words such as *anybody, anyplace,* and *anytime* as students suggest them.

4. Repeat the procedure with words such as *everybody, everything, everyone* and *someday, somehow, someone.*

5. Tell students that they will make twenty compound words with word cards, write the words on a word and sentence sheet, and then use the words in sentences.

Name _____

Word	Sentence
anywhere	I can't find my book anywhere!
inside	It's raining, so we have to stay inside.
outdoors	Let's play outdoors in the sun.

WS 2 Word and Sentence Sheet

Pinnell & Fountas Word Study Lessons, Grade 1

ACTIVITY: WORD AND SENTENCE SHEETS

INSTRUCTIONAL PROCEDURE

MAKE WORDS

See page 32 for detailed descriptions of Instructional Procedures.

ACTION TAGS

make compound word

write compound word

use in a sentence

Apply

Have students use the word cards to make the compound words. Tell them that they can use word cards more than once. Then have them record their words on a word and sentence sheet to make a sentence for each.

Share

Have students share some of their compound words and sentences with a partner.

Assess

- Have students read a list of five to ten compound words.
- Observe students' ability to take apart compound words while reading.
- You may wish to use Word Structure Assessment A or H.

Word Structure: Recognize and Use Compound Words that Have Frequently Used Words

Connect Learning Across Contexts

Shared Reading After rereading books aloud, quickly write down one or two compound words on a whiteboard. Have students use the word parts to determine the words' meanings. You may wish to use the following Shared Reading title from *Fountas & Pinnell Classroom*™ to locate more compound words after reading.

SR *From Flower to Honey* by June Schwartz

Guided Reading Encourage students to notice and identify one or two compound words after discussing the book. Add new examples to the class list.

Shared Writing When working with a small group of writers, point out places where there are compound words.

Independent Writing When conferring with writers, help them notice compound words.

Extend Learning

- Repeat this lesson with a different variety of compound words.
- Give students a set of compound words that include common words, and have them sort them by word part.

▶ ## Connect with Home

Give students word cards to take home and make compound words with family members.

Recognize and Use Contractions with *not*

Plan

▶ Consider Your Students

Your students will have encountered many contractions in reading and writing and will likely be familiar with the concept from their work in previous grades. They will probably be able to read most of the words in the lesson easily and will therefore be able to focus on the principle of how contractions are constructed. This lesson will have the most impact if students also encounter contractions with *will* throughout other instructional contexts.

▶ Working with English Language Learners

Once English language learners understand the idea of contractions and are familiar with many examples and their component words, they will be able to use this knowledge to solve new contractions or to form them in writing. If English language learners do not understand the meanings of contractions, use the contrasting forms in simple sentences. Making a summary chart and stating the principle will also help students recognize and solve new contractions.

UNDERSTAND THE PRINCIPLE

When two words are put together in a shortened form, one or more letters are left out and an apostrophe is put in. This shortened, or contracted, form is called a *contraction*. Contractions appear frequently in oral and written language. Knowing how contractions with *not* are constructed will help students understand what these words mean when they read them and will help students spell them conventionally when they write them. As students add to their knowledge of contractions, they will form mental categories for different types of contractions that will aid them in efficiently identifying, reading, and writing various contractions.

YOU WILL NEED

Online Resources
- ▶ **WS 3** Action Tags
- ▶ **WS 3** Game Cards
- ▶ **WS 3** Directions for Concentration

Other Materials
- ▶ chart paper

Generative Lesson
A generative lesson has a simple structure that you can use to present similar content or concepts. Use this lesson structure to teach students a variety of contractions.

EXPLAIN THE PRINCIPLE

Some contractions are made with not.

To write a contraction with not, *leave out the letter* o *and put an apostrophe in its place.*

Comprehensive Phonics, Spelling, and Word Study Guide

Refer to:
Page **54**, row **20**

didn't   did not

don't   do not

can't   can not

ACTIVITY: CONTRACTIONS WITH *NOT*

INSTRUCTIONAL PROCEDURE

SEE AND SAY

See page 32 for detailed descriptions of Instructional Procedures.

EXPLAIN THE PRINCIPLE

Some contractions are made with not.

To write a contraction with not, *leave out the letter* o *and put an apostrophe in its place.*

Comprehensive Phonics, Spelling, and Word Study Guide

Refer to: page **54**, row **20**

Teach

1. On chart paper, write the words *didn't, don't,* and *can't. What do you notice about all of these words?*

2. *Using what you know about contractions, what two words do you think were put together to make* didn't? • Students will likely be familiar with this word from their reading, or they may use the key word *not* to infer that the contraction is formed by the words *did* and *not.* Write the words *did not* beside the contraction.

3. Write the word *don't* on chart paper. *What two words do you think were put together to make* don't? • Do not *makes* don't. Write *do not* on the chart paper next to *don't. What letter did I remove to make the contraction* don't? • *What did I put in its place?*

4. *Can you think of other contractions with the word* not? • Write each contraction that students suggest and the two words that were joined to form it. Examples may include *aren't, couldn't, doesn't, hadn't, hasn't, haven't, isn't, shouldn't, wasn't, weren't,* and *wouldn't.*

5. Use students' observations to restate the principle: *Some contractions are made with* not. *To write a contraction with* not, *leave out the letter* o *and put an apostrophe in its place.*

6. Explain that students will play Concentration by matching a two-word phrase with the appropriate contraction. Have students demonstrate with a pair of game cards, if helpful.

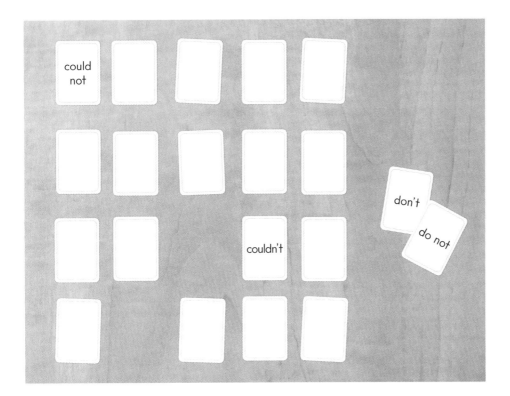

**ACTIVITY:
CONCENTRATION**

**INSTRUCTIONAL
PROCEDURE**

FIND AND MATCH

*See page 32 for detailed
descriptions of Instructional
Procedures.*

ACTION TAGS

| turn over card |
| read word or words |
| match pairs |

Apply

Have students play Concentration in groups of two or three.

Share

Have students share some of the contractions they learned from the game. They can state the contraction and the two words that were joined together to form it.

Assess

- Dictate four or five contractions with *not* for children to write, such as *aren't, don't, hasn't,* and *wouldn't.*

- Notice whether children can locate contractions and state the two words that make up each contraction.

- You may wish to use Word Structure Assessment B or I.

Connect Learning Across Contexts

Shared Reading After rereading books aloud, quickly write down one or two contractions on a whiteboard. Have students tell what words make them up. You may wish to use the following Shared Reading title from *Fountas & Pinnell Classroom™* to locate more contractions after reading.

SR *Saving Cranes* by Brenda Iasevoli

Guided Reading Encourage students to notice and identify one or two contractions after they read and discuss a book. Add new examples to the class list.

Shared Writing As students write contractions, help them notice where the letters are left out and an apostrophe is inserted.

Independent Writing Have students reread and edit their writing for correct spelling of contractions.

Extend Learning

- Continue to help students notice contractions during shared reading.
- Have students play Lotto. Write two-word phrases in some boxes on the game card and contractions in others. Place the same phrases and contractions on the word cards. Have students say and look for the contraction if the word card contains a two-word phrase or say and look for the two-word phrase if the word card contains a contraction.

▶ Connect with Home

Send home a set of word cards so that students can cut them apart and match words with the corresponding contractions.

Recognize and Use Syllables in Words with Double Consonants

Plan

▶ Consider Your Students

In order to benefit most from this lesson, students will need to have good control of simple one-syllable word patterns such as CVC and CVC*e*. They should also have strong control of basic phonogram patterns so they can notice and use word parts in longer words. In this lesson, students will work with two-syllable words that have a short vowel sound in the first syllable (CVC).

▶ Working with English Language Learners

Taking apart multisyllable words is basic to solving them. Provide very explicit demonstrations using magnetic letters, and also let students say and take apart the words themselves. After looking at the words, students will likely find it quite easy to divide them between the double consonants. However, it is also important for them to know the meaning of each word and to say the word, emphasizing the syllable break.

YOU WILL NEED

Online Resources
- ▶ WS 4 Action Tags
- ▶ WS 4 Word Cards
- ▶ WS 4 List Sheets

Other Materials
- ▶ magnetic letters
- ▶ magnetic whiteboard

Generative Lesson
A generative lesson has a simple structure that you can use to present similar content or concepts. Use this lesson structure to teach students a variety of syllable patterns.

UNDERSTAND THE PRINCIPLE

A *syllable* is a word part or unit of pronunciation that helps readers and writers use parts larger than individual letters. Students can use word parts to take apart or write longer words. Many two-syllable words have two consonants in the middle. In this lesson, the two consonants are the same letter (e.g., *better*). When students learn that they can divide a word between its two consonants, they can solve two-syllable words more easily.

EXPLAIN THE PRINCIPLE

When a word has double consonants in the middle, divide the syllables between the consonants.

 Comprehensive Phonics, Spelling, and Word Study Guide

Refer to: Page **52**, row **4**

**INSTRUCTIONAL
PROCEDURE**

MAKE WORDS

*See page 32 for detailed
descriptions of Instructional
Procedures.*

EXPLAIN THE PRINCIPLE

*When a word has double
consonants in the middle, you
divide the words between the
consonants.*

Comprehensive
Phonics, Spelling,
and Word Study
Guide

Refer to:
page **52**, row **4**

Teach

1. Use magnetic letters to build the following words: *kitten, pepper, sudden, suggest,* and *cottage.* Have students read the words with you and clap the syllables.

2. *What do you notice about all of the words on the whiteboard?* • Students may observe that they all have two syllables or double letters in the middle. *Clap the word* kitten. • *Can you show me where the word* kitten *breaks into two syllables?* • Invite a student to the board to break apart the word. *Clap the word* pepper. *Where does the word* pepper *break into two syllables?* • Invite student(s) to clap the syllables and break apart each of the remaining words.

3. *What do you notice about where all of the words break apart?* • *The words break between the double consonant letters.* Move the two parts together again to remake the word.

4. Invite students up to the whiteboard to write a few more two-syllable words with double consonants in the middle. Ask them to divide the words into syllables by making a slash mark to signify the syllable break in the word.

5. Tell students that now they are going to put together two word parts to make a whole word (for example, *col + lar = collar*). Explain that they will take one word card and look for another word card to put together with the first card to make a real word. Once students make a real word by putting together two word parts, they will write the word on a list sheet.

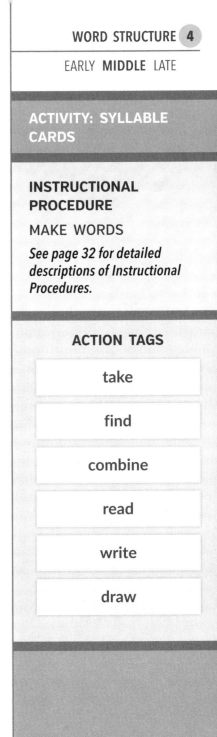

The syllable cards shown:

chan	nel
slip	per
traf	fic
splat	ter
siz	zle
of	fice
pil	low
cher	ry
gig	gle
at	tic

Name _Reese_

1. channel
2. slipper
3. traffic
4. splatter
5. sizzle
6. office
7. pillow
8. cherry
9. giggle
10. attic

Fountas & Pinnell Word Study Lessons, Grade 1   **WS 4** List Sheet

ACTIVITY: SYLLABLE CARDS

INSTRUCTIONAL PROCEDURE

MAKE WORDS

See page 32 for detailed descriptions of Instructional Procedures.

ACTION TAGS

take
find
combine
read
write
draw

Apply

Give students a collection of word cards. Instruct each student to take one card (for example, with the syllable *bit*) and look for a second card with a part (i.e., *ten*) that would complete a real word (*bitten*). The student will combine the parts to make a word, read it, and write it on a list sheet. Tell students to draw a line between the double consonants to show the separate syllables in the word (*bit/ten*).

Share

Have students read some of their words and share where they divided them.

Assess

■ Dictate four to six words with double consonants in the middle. Have students write them and draw a line to divide them between the syllables.

■ Have students read a few words with double consonants in the middle, and notice how easily they read them.

■ You may wish to use Word Structure Assessment C, D, or J.

Word Structure: Recognize and Use Syllables in Words with Double Consonants

Connect Learning Across Contexts

Shared Reading On a whiteboard, write a few two-syllable words for students to read quickly after reading a book. You may wish to use the following Shared Reading title from *Fountas & Pinnell Classroom*™ to locate more syllables with double medial consonant letters after reading.

SR *Trapped in Tar* by Hannah Cales

Guided Reading When students encounter longer words with double consonants, remind them to look at the first part and to break the words between the two consonants to solve them more easily.

Shared Writing When students are going to write words with double consonants in the middle, have them clap and listen for middle sounds and then write the first and last parts.

Independent Writing Remind students to recognize the pattern of double consonants in the middle when they edit their writing for spelling.

Extend Learning

- Repeat the lesson with other words that have double consonants in the middle.
- Small groups of students can play the game Concentration with one syllable of a word on one card and the other syllable on a second card. Players put together two syllables to make a real word.

▶ Connect with Home

Have students look for words with double consonants in books, magazines, newspapers, or labels around their house. Give them a goal of finding ten to bring to school.

Identify Syllables in Words with Three or More Syllables

Plan

▶ Consider Your Students

Teach this lesson once students have strong control of syllable juncture in two-syllable words. Students should also be familiar with compound words, words with double consonants, and common affixes such as *-ing* and *-ed*. In this lesson, they develop flexibility in noticing parts in three- and four-syllable words so that they can solve multisyllable words easily and quickly.

▶ Working with English Language Learners

Being able to break down words into syllables is very helpful to English language learners as they develop their ability to use standard pronunciation of words. Multisyllable words will not be so daunting when students know how to look for the parts. Have them work with cut-up words that they put together and take apart. Be sure students understand the meaning of the words you select.

UNDERSTAND THE PRINCIPLE

Syllables are basic units of words that are easy to hear. They make it possible to break down words into manageable parts. Knowing that each syllable has a vowel is helpful to spellers in structuring words and making more complete attempts at spelling words. This lesson will help students generalize their knowledge and see the syllable as a unit that they can identify and use to decode or spell multisyllable words.

YOU WILL NEED

Online Resources
- ▸ **WS 5** Action Tags
- ▸ **WS 5** Word Cards
- ▸ **WS 5** Three-Way Sort

Other Materials
- ▸ chart paper

Generative Lesson ✓

A generative lesson has a simple structure that you can use to present similar content or concepts. Use this lesson structure to teach students a variety of words with three or more syllables.

EXPLAIN THE PRINCIPLE

Listen for the syllables in words.

Look at the syllables in a word to read it.

Say and clap the syllables to identify them in a word.

Comprehensive Phonics, Spelling, and Word Study Guide

Refer to: Page **52**, row 5

5 WORD STRUCTURE

EARLY **MIDDLE** LATE

**ACTIVITY:
MULTISYLLABLE WORDS**

INSTRUCTIONAL PROCEDURE

NOTICE PARTS

See page 32 for detailed descriptions of Instructional Procedures.

EXPLAIN THE PRINCIPLE

Listen for the syllables in words.

Look at the syllables in a word to read it.

Say and clap the syllables to identify them in a word.

Comprehensive Phonics, Spelling, and Word Study Guide

Refer to:
page **52**, row **5**

en/ter
pen/cil

ic/i/cle
cu/cum/ber
tor/na/do

al/li/ga/tor
a/dor/a/ble
wa/ter/mel/on

Teach

1. Write the words *enter* and *pencil* on chart paper. Have students read the words with you and clap the syllables in each word. *What do you notice about the first part in both of these words?* • Help students notice that the first syllable ends with a consonant. *Where do you think you break the word* enter *to make two syllables?* • Draw a slash line to show *en/ter. Where do you think you break the word* pencil *to make two syllables?* Draw a slash line to show *pen/cil.*

2. Then write some three- and four-syllable words on the chart paper, such as *icicle, cucumber, tornado, alligator, adorable,* and *watermelon. Read each word with me and clap the syllables.* • *How many syllables does the word* icicle *have?* • Invite a student to break apart the word *icicle* on the chart paper by inserting slash marks. Repeat the process with other three- and four-syllable words.

3. During this process, guide students to notice that in each syllable you can hear a vowel sound. *In the -ble syllable, there is a shortened vowel sound between the sound of* b *and the sound of* l.

4. Tell students that they are going to sort some words by the number of syllables. They will read each word, clap the syllables, and sort by the number of syllables: two, three, or four. Then they will write each word, with slash lines representing the syllables, in the correct column on a three-way sort.

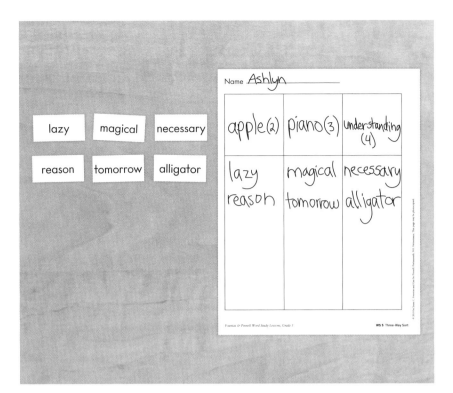

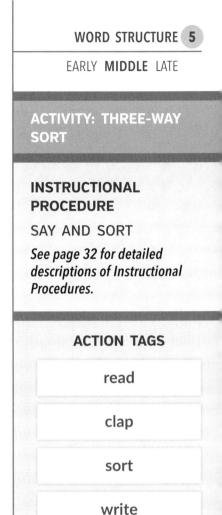

ACTIVITY: THREE-WAY SORT

INSTRUCTIONAL PROCEDURE

SAY AND SORT

See page 32 for detailed descriptions of Instructional Procedures.

ACTION TAGS

| read |
| clap |
| sort |
| write |

Apply

Have students sort the words, write them, and draw slash lines that represent each syllable, on a three-way sort. Remind them that each syllable in a word has one vowel sound.

Share

Have students compare their three-way sort with a partner. Ask them to clap the syllables again for any words they disagree about.

Assess

- Ask students to read four or five multisyllable words. Note their ability to solve each syllable.
- Using a list of six to ten words, read a word and write it on a whiteboard. Have students look at each word as you say it. Then have them draw a slash to show how syllables are divided.
- You may wish to use Word Structure Assessment C, D, or J.

Word Structure: Identify Syllables in Words with Three or More Syllables

Connect Learning Across Contexts

Shared Reading After rereading books or poems, write a few three- or four-syllable words for students to read quickly. You may wish to use the following Shared Reading title from *Fountas & Pinnell Classroom*™ to clap three- or four-syllable words after reading.

　　SR *Exploring Underground* by Louis Petrone

Guided Reading When students encounter longer words with multiple syllables, remind them to look at the parts and break the words into syllables to solve them more easily.

Shared Writing As students attempt to write new words, encourage them to think about how to listen for and write each syllable.

Independent Writing Prompt students to look carefully at each syllable in the multisyllable words they write and be sure that each syllable has a vowel sound.

Extend Learning

■ Repeat this lesson with a variety of other three- or four-syllable words.

■ Have students complete a four-way sort with one-, two-, three-, and four-syllable words or a two-way sort with three- and four-syllable words.

▶ **Connect with Home**

■ Send home a word grid (see Online Resources) with three- and four-syllable words for students to read to family members.

■ Challenge students to find three- and four-syllable words in print around their house or neighborhood. Have them record the words they find and share them with the class.

Recognize and Use Open Syllables

Plan

▶ Consider Your Students

In order to read longer words, it is helpful for students to be able to break words into syllables. By now, students will have experience with syllabication and many common syllable patterns. In this lesson, students focus on syllables that end in a vowel. Be sure to use words that students have in their oral vocabularies so that they can quickly and automatically hear the breaks in a multisyllable word.

▶ Working with English Language Learners

Once English language learners have internalized the concept of syllable breaks in words, teach them how to use this information to solve words. Provide explicit demonstrations of how to take apart two-syllable words with a single consonant in the middle. Open syllables will be more natural for many learners because in languages such as Spanish and Chinese, syllables typically end with a vowel. Have students work with magnetic letters to divide words into syllables and say each syllable as they do so. Blending syllables produces an approximate pronunciation, so it is important that the words that you use are already part of students' oral vocabulary.

YOU WILL NEED

Online Resources
- ▶ **WS 6** Action Tags
- ▶ **WS 6** Word Cards
- ▶ **WS 6** List Sheets

Other Materials
- ▶ chart paper
- ▶ scissors

Generative Lesson

A generative lesson has a simple structure that you can use to present similar content or concepts. Use this lesson structure to teach students to recognize and use a variety of syllable patterns.

UNDERSTAND THE PRINCIPLE

A *syllable* is a word part or a unit of pronunciation. Students need to understand the concept of a syllable as a unit of pronunciation with *one* vowel sound. Students can notice and use the syllable patterns to help them read and write words. When students pronounce an open syllable, the vowel sound is long and their mouths are open at the end.

EXPLAIN THE PRINCIPLE

When a syllable ends with a single vowel, the vowel sound is usually long.

Comprehensive Phonics, Spelling, and Word Study Guide

Refer to:
Page **53**, row **6**

EARLY **MIDDLE** LATE

ACTIVITY: OPEN SYLLABLES

INSTRUCTIONAL PROCEDURE

NOTICE PARTS

See page 32 for detailed descriptions of Instructional Procedures.

EXPLAIN THE PRINCIPLE

When a syllable ends with a single vowel, the vowel sound is usually long.

Comprehensive Phonics, Spelling, and Word Study Guide

Refer to: page **53**, row **6**

---

music   mu/sic
photo   pho/to
pilot   pi/lot
open   o/pen
recent   re/cent

Teach

1. Write *music, photo, pilot, open,* and *recent* on the chart, and ask students to read and clap the words. *What do you notice about the first part in all of the words?* • Help them notice that when they pronounce each word their mouths are open at the end of the first syllable. Ask students to describe the vowel sound. (It is long.)

2. Rewrite the word *music* with a slash mark to show the syllable division (*mu/sic*). *What do you notice about how this word is broken apart?* • Students may notice that there are two syllables. *What sound do you hear at the end of the first syllable?* • Encourage them to identify the long *u* sound and conclude that it is long.

3. Repeat this procedure with the words *photo* (*pho/to*); *pilot* (*pi/lot*); *open* (*o/pen*); and *recent* (*re/cent*). *What do you notice about how this word is broken apart?*

4. Use students' observations to summarize the principle: *When a syllable ends with a vowel, the vowel sound is usually long.*

5. Tell students that they are going to practice breaking apart words into syllables and reading them. Explain that they will take a word card, read it, cut it into two syllables, and write the divided word on a list sheet. They then will draw slash marks to indicate the syllable break in each word on the list sheet.

Name Julia

1. bo/nus
2. rhi/no
3. si/lent
4. hu/man
5. spi/der
6. co/zy
7. lo/cal
8. le/gal
9. fu/ture
10. glo/bal

11. ___
12. ___
13. ___
14. ___
15. ___
16. ___
17. ___
18. ___
19. ___
20. ___

Fountas & Pinnell Word Study Lessons, Grade 1   **WS 6** List Sheet

bo	nus
rhi	no
si	lent
hu	man
spi	der

INSTRUCTIONAL PROCEDURE

NOTICE PARTS

See page 32 for detailed descriptions of Instructional Procedures.

ACTION TAGS

take word

read word

cut word into syllables

write divided word

Apply

Distribute word cards, scissors, and list sheets. Have students divide and write twenty words, each time drawing a slash mark to indicate the syllable break on the sheet.

Share

Have students choose three or four words and tell how they divided them.

Assess

- Have students read four to six words with open and closed syllables.
- Dictate three to five words with open syllables, and note students' control of syllables in writing.
- You may wish to use Word Structure Assessment C, D, or J.

Connect Learning Across Contexts

Shared Reading After rereading books or poems, quickly write one or two words with syllables that end in a long vowel sound for students to read. You may wish to use the following Shared Reading title from *Fountas & Pinnell Classroom*™.

SR *Tiny but Fierce* by Cheri Colburn

Guided Reading When students come to an unknown word with an open syllable, teach them how to cover the last part and focus on the first part or the open syllable.

Shared Writing After you have written a text together, have students point out two or three words with open first syllables that end with a long vowel sound (CV).

Independent Writing Prompt students to say words and write the letters representing consecutive sounds. Point out words in their writing that have open (CV) syllables.

Extend Learning

- Repeat this lesson with a variety of other words with open syllables.
- Have students play Follow the Path with words that have open syllables (see Online Resources for blank game boards).

▶ Connect with Home

Have students take home a set of word cards to read with family members. Encourage them to clap the syllables as they read the words aloud.

Recognize and Use Closed Syllables

Plan

▶ Consider Your Students

In order to read longer words, it is helpful for students to be able to break words into syllables. By now, students will have experience with syllabication and many common syllable patterns. In this lesson, students focus on syllables that end in a consonant. Be sure to use words that students have in their oral vocabularies so that they can quickly and automatically hear the breaks in a multisyllable word.

▶ Working with English Language Learners

Once English language learners have internalized the concept of syllable breaks in words, teach them how to use this information to solve words. Provide explicit demonstrations of how to take apart two-syllable words with a single consonant in the middle. Closed syllables will be more challenging for many learners because in languages such as Spanish and Chinese, syllables typically end with a vowel rather than a consonant. Have students work with magnetic letters to divide words into syllables and say each syllable as they do so. Blending syllables produces an approximate pronunciation, so it is important that the words that you use are already part of students' oral vocabulary.

YOU WILL NEED

Online Resources
- ▶ **WS 7** Action Tags
- ▶ **WS 7** Word Cards
- ▶ **WS 7** List Sheets

Other Materials
- ▶ chart paper
- ▶ magnetic letters

Generative Lesson

A generative lesson has a simple structure that you can use to present similar content or concepts. Use this lesson structure to teach students to recognize and use a variety of syllable patterns.

UNDERSTAND THE PRINCIPLE

A *syllable* is a word part or a unit of pronunciation. Students need to understand the concept of a syllable as a unit of pronunciation with *one* vowel sound. Students can notice and use the syllable patterns to help them read and write words. Closed syllables end with a consonant sound and are pronounced with a short vowel sound. The syllable break is after the consonant.

EXPLAIN THE PRINCIPLE

When a syllable ends with a vowel and a consonant, the vowel is usually short.

Comprehensive Phonics, Spelling, and Word Study Guide

Refer to: Page **53**, row **7**

ACTIVITY: CLOSED
SYLLABLES

INSTRUCTIONAL PROCEDURE

NOTICE PARTS

See page 32 for detailed descriptions of Instructional Procedures.

EXPLAIN THE PRINCIPLE

When a syllable ends with a vowel and a consonant, the vowel sound is usually short.

Comprehensive Phonics, Spelling, and Word Study Guide

Refer to:
page **53**, row **7**

robin   rob/in

panic   pan/ic

cabin   cab/in

Teach

1. Explain to students that they are going to think more about syllables.

2. Write *robin, panic,* and *cabin* on the chart, and ask students to read and clap the words. *What do you notice about the first part in all of the words? •* Students may observe that there are two syllables and the first part ends in a consonant. *What do you notice about the vowel sounds in all of the words? •* The vowel sounds are short.

3. Draw a slash to represent the syllable break in the word *robin* (*rob/in*). *Why did I draw a slash in the word robin? • The slash stands for where we break the word.* Invite a student up to the board to break apart the words *panic* and *cabin* by drawing a slash to represent the syllable break.

4. Use students' observations to summarize the principle: *When a syllable ends with at least one consonant, the vowel sound is usually short.*

5. Tell students that they are going to practice breaking apart words into syllables and reading them. Explain that they will take a word card, read it, and clap the parts. They then will write the word with a slash (to show the syllable break) on a list sheet or in their word study notebook.

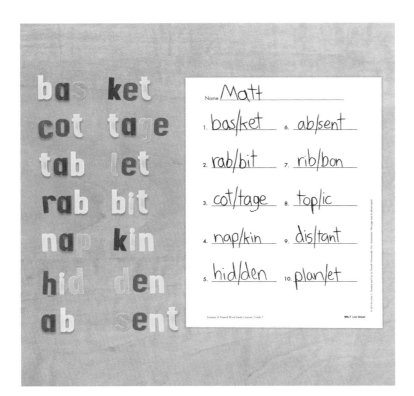

ACTIVITY: MAKE AND DIVIDE WORDS

INSTRUCTIONAL PROCEDURE

NOTICE PARTS

See page 32 for detailed descriptions of Instructional Procedures.

ACTION TAGS

take card

read word

make word

divide word

write word

Apply

Distribute word cards, magnetic letters, and list sheets. Have students divide and write approximately ten words.

Share

Have students choose three or four words and tell how they divided them. Invite them to use the magnetic letters if they wish.

Assess

- Have students read four to six words with open and closed syllables.
- Dictate three to five words with closed syllables, and note students' control of syllables in writing.
- You may wish to use Word Structure Assessment C, D, or J.

Connect Learning Across Contexts

Shared Reading After rereading books or poems, quickly write one or two words with closed syllables for students to read and to identify the parts. You may also wish to use the following Shared Reading title from *Fountas & Pinnell Classroom*™ to locate more words with closed syllables.

> SR *Exploring Underground* by Louis Petrone

Guided Reading When students come to an unknown word with a closed syllable, teach them how to cover the last part and focus on the first part.

Shared Writing After you have written a text together, have students point out two or three words with syllables that end with a consonant (CVC).

Independent Writing Prompt students to say words and write the letters representing consecutive sounds. Point out words in their writing that have syllables ending with a consonant (CVC).

Extend Learning

- Repeat this lesson with a variety of other words with closed syllables.
- Give students a set of word cards with both open and closed syllables. Have them sort the cards by open or closed first syllables.

▶ Connect with Home

Send home a set of word cards with closed syllables for students to cut apart into syllables. They can glue them on a sheet and bring them to school to share.

Recognize and Use
r-Influenced Syllables

Plan

▶ Consider Your Students

Students should have experience with single-syllable words that have a vowel influenced by the letter *r* (e.g., *fern, shirt, park, form, turn*). In this lesson, students learn to notice and use two-syllable words that have the five vowels influenced by *r*. Be sure to select words children understand. If students are less experienced, then select only words with one or two of the vowels at first.

▶ Working with English Language Learners

In English, when a vowel is followed by *r,* the pronunciation of the vowel is different from the pronunciation of that same vowel in words in which it is not followed by *r*. Many English language learners may find words with *r* difficult to pronounce, and figuring out the vowel sound can present a challenge. Be sure students know simple one-syllable words before working with multisyllable words. Work with a small group to explore examples on a whiteboard, or make a chart that provides them with one or two very clear examples of each kind of *r*-controlled vowel.

YOU WILL NEED

Online Resources
- ▶ **WS 8** Action Tags
- ▶ **WS 8** Word Cards
- ▶ **WS 8** Blank Word Strips

Other Materials
- ▶ scissors
- ▶ plastic or paper baggies (optional)

Generative Lesson

A generative lesson has a simple structure that you can use to present similar content or concepts. Use this lesson structure to teach students to recognize and use a variety of syllable patterns.

UNDERSTAND THE PRINCIPLE

The letter *r* is often part of a syllable and influences the sound of the vowel in that syllable. The vowel sound is usually neither long nor short, but unique. The syllable with *r* can be the first or second syllable of two-syllable words. Giving specific attention to syllables with *r* will help students understand the changes in vowel sounds and move to conventional spelling.

EXPLAIN THE PRINCIPLE

Some words have one or two vowels followed by the letter r. *The letter* r *changes the vowel sound. The vowel(s) and the letter* r *stay together in the same syllable.*

Comprehensive Phonics, Spelling, and Word Study Guide

Refer to:
Page **53**, row 8

ACTIVITY: *R*-INFLUENCED SYLLABLES

INSTRUCTIONAL PROCEDURE

NOTICE PARTS

See page 32 for detailed descriptions of Instructional Procedures.

EXPLAIN THE PRINCIPLE

Some words have one or two vowels followed by the letter r. *The letter* r *changes the vowel sound. The vowel(s) and the letter* r *stay together in the same syllable.*

Comprehensive Phonics, Spelling, and Word Study Guide

Refer to: page **53**, row **8**

artist	art / ist
carton	car / ton
perfect	per / fect
person	per / son
order	or / der
formal	for / mal
furry	fur / ry
urgent	ur / gent
birthday	birth / day
thirty	thir / ty

Teach

1. Explain to students that they will be noticing more about syllables.

2. Write *artist* and *carton* on the chart, and ask students to read and clap the words. *What do you notice about both of these words?* • Students may observe that there are two syllables or that they both have the /ar/ vowel sound.

3. *Where should I break apart the two-syllable word* artist? • Draw a slash in between the letters *r* and *t* in the word *artist. What do you notice about where this word is broken apart?* • Guide students to notice that the vowel and the *r* stay together when the syllables are divided. *Where would you break the word* carton? • Draw a slash in between the letters *r* and *t* in *carton. What do you notice about where this word is broken apart?* • Like in *artist, the vowel,* a, *and the letter* r *stay together in the first syllable.*

4. *What vowel sound do you hear in the first syllable in both of these words?* Encourage the class to notice that the vowel sound is different from the long or short sound of *a* because it is blended with *r.*

5. Repeat this procedure with the words *perfect, person; order, formal; furry, urgent;* and *birthday, thirty. What do you notice about how this word is broken apart? What vowel sound do you hear in the first syllable?*

6. Use students' observations to summarize the principle: *Some words have a vowel followed by the letter* r. *The letter* r *changes the vowel sound. The vowel and the letter* r *stay together in the same syllable.*

7. Tell students that they are going to play Cut and Connect. Have them take ten word cards. Then have them write each word on a blank word strip. Tell them to divide each word into syllables by cutting it apart between syllables. Children will trade cut-up words with a partner. Partners must rebuild the words and then blend the syllables to read them aloud.

ACTIVITY: CUT AND CONNECT

INSTRUCTIONAL PROCEDURE

NOTICE PARTS

See page 32 for detailed descriptions of Instructional Procedures.

ACTION TAGS

take
write
cut apart
trade
rebuild
blend

Apply

- You may wish to remind students that the vowel and the *r* stay together in an *r*-influenced syllable.

- As you observe students cutting apart their words, make sure they keep the syllables for each word separate. You may wish to provide plastic or paper bags for students to put their syllables in.

- Encourage students to check their reassembled words by comparing them to the word cards.

Share

Have students choose three or four words and tell how they divided them. Invite them to explain how they knew which letters to keep together.

Assess

- Have students read four to six words with *r*-influenced syllables.

- Dictate three to five words with *r*-influenced syllables, and note students' control of syllables in writing.

- You may wish to use Word Structure Assessment C, D, or J.

Connect Learning Across Contexts

Shared Reading After rereading books or poems, quickly write one or two words with *r*-influenced syllables for students to read. You may also wish to use the following Shared Reading title from *Fountas & Pinnell Classroom*™ to locate more words with *r*-influenced syllables.

SR *A Meerkat Day* by Geerhardt Heever

Guided Reading When students come to unfamiliar multisyllable words with a vowel and *r*, encourage them to notice and use the syllables to take the word apart.

Shared Writing After you have written a text together, have students point out words with *r*-influenced syllables.

Independent Writing As students write unfamiliar multisyllable words, help them notice and use syllable parts to help them spell the words correctly.

Extend Learning

- Repeat this lesson with a variety of other words with *r*-influenced syllables.
- Have students play Concentration with pairs of similar words that have two syllables and *r*-influenced vowels.

▶ Connect with Home

Send home word cards and blank word strips so students can cut apart words and reassemble them with family members.

Recognize and Use Vowel Combination Syllables

Plan

▶ **Consider Your Students**

This lesson focuses on two-syllable words with vowel combinations. Before participating in this lesson, students should have strong control of common spelling patterns with vowel combinations in single-syllable words. Be sure students understand all the words you select.

▶ **Working with English Language Learners**

Vowel combinations within words, especially those with multiple syllables, often challenge spellers of any age. English language learners need to learn to recognize vowel pairs. It will be helpful if they divide words into syllables and understand that the vowel pairs usually stay together, forming a pattern. Have students work with magnetic letters during word work. They can build the words and then physically divide them, noticing the vowel pairs.

YOU WILL NEED

Online Resources
- ▶ **WS 9** Action Tags
- ▶ **WS 9** Word Cards
- ▶ **WS 9** List Sheets

Other Materials
- ▶ chart paper

Generative Lesson

A generative lesson has a simple structure that you can use to present similar content or concepts. Use this lesson structure to teach students to recognize and use a variety of syllable patterns.

UNDERSTAND THE PRINCIPLE

Many vowel sounds are represented by vowel combinations such as *ai, ee, ow, ea, ay, oo,* and *ou.* Sometimes *y* and *w* represent a vowel sound when paired with a vowel. The vowel combinations appear in the same syllable. Sometimes the vowel sound is the same as the name of the first vowel (e.g., *meet*), and sometimes it represents a unique sound (e.g., *house, moon*). When students become comfortable dividing words between syllables, they can solve two-syllable words more easily.

EXPLAIN THE PRINCIPLE

Some words have two or more letters together that represent one vowel sound. The letters usually stay together in the same syllable.

Comprehensive Phonics, Spelling, and Word Study Guide

Refer to: Page **53**, row **9**

ACTIVITY: VOWEL COMBINATION SYLLABLES

INSTRUCTIONAL PROCEDURE

NOTICE PARTS

See page 32 for detailed descriptions of Instructional Procedures.

EXPLAIN THE PRINCIPLE

Some words have two or more letters together that represent one vowel sound. The letters usually stay together in the same syllable.

Comprehensive Phonics, Spelling, and Word Study Guide

Refer to: page **53**, row **9**

---

rain
play
meet
house

beneath   be/n<u>ea</u>th
explain   ex/pl<u>ai</u>n
hockey   hock/<u>ey</u>
railroad   r<u>ai</u>l/r<u>oa</u>d

Teach

1. Explain to students that they are going to be noticing more about syllables.

2. Write *rain, play, meet,* and *house* on a chart. Ask students to read each word and think about the letters that stand for the vowel sound. Guide them to conclude that the vowel combinations *ai, ay, ee,* and *ou* represent one vowel sound in these single-syllable words.

3. Next write *beneath, explain, hockey,* and *railroad.* Have students read the words, clap the syllables they hear, and tell you where to draw a slash mark that represents the syllable break in each word. *What do you notice about all of these words?* • *They each have two syllables.* In each syllable, help them notice and underline the letters that stand for the vowel sound [*beneath, explain, hockey, railroad*]. *What letters stand for the vowel sound?* • *All of the words have a syllable with a vowel combination that stands for one sound.*

4. Review several additional words, using the same process, such as *enjoy, nighttime,* and *between.*

5. Tell students they will select one word card at a time, read it, write the word in parts on a list sheet, and underline the letters that stand for the vowel sound. Demonstrate with two words. They will select twenty different words.

Fountas & Pinnell Word Study Lessons, Grade 3

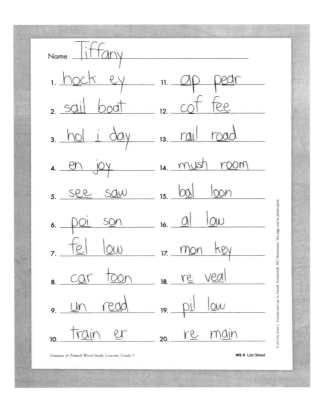

Name Tiffany

1. hock ey
2. sail boat
3. hol i day
4. en joy
5. see saw
6. poi son
7. fel low
8. car toon
9. un read
10. train er
11. ap pear
12. cof fee
13. rail road
14. mush room
15. bal loon
16. al low
17. mon key
18. re veal
19. pil low
20. re main

Fountas & Pinnell Word Study Lessons, Grade 3   **WS 9** List Sheet

© 2013 by Irene C. Fountas and Gay Su Pinnell. Portsmouth, NH: Heinemann. This page may be photocopied.

ACTIVITY: LIST SHEET

INSTRUCTIONAL PROCEDURE

NOTICE PARTS

See page 32 for detailed descriptions of Instructional Procedures.

ACTION TAGS

take card

read word

divide word

write word

underline vowel sound

Apply

Have students work with twenty words. Remind them to leave a space between syllables when they write the words on their list sheet and underline the combination of letters that stand for the vowel sound.

Share

Invite students to share a few words that are not yet on the chart, and tell or demonstrate how to divide them.

Assess

- Give students a list of five words with vowel combinations, and ask them to divide them.
- Notice how easily students use word parts to solve words they encounter in texts.
- You may wish to use Word Structure Assessment C, D, or J.

Word Structure: Recognize and Use Vowel Combination Syllables

Connect Learning Across Contexts

Guided Reading Prompt students to notice and use syllables to take apart words. During word work, students can focus on families of words with the same vowel combinations.

Independent Reading As you meet with individual readers, prompt them to use what they know about syllables with vowel combinations to take apart and read longer words.

Shared Writing After you have written a text together, have students point out two or three words that have syllables with vowel combinations. Invite them to underline the vowel combinations.

Independent Writing As students write new words, have them think of each syllable and the vowel sound they hear in it.

Extend Learning

- Repeat this lesson with a different variety of words.
- Have students play Follow the Path with two-syllable words with vowel combinations. When they land on a space, they say the word in parts. To increase the challenge, try a few three-syllable words.

▶ Connect with Home

Send home a sheet of two-syllable words for students to cut into syllables and glue on a sheet of paper.

Recognize and Use VCe Syllables

Plan

▶ Consider Your Students

Before using this lesson, be sure that students have good control of the silent *e* pattern in single-syllable words. In this lesson, students focus on two-syllable words that have a syllable with the vowel-consonant-*e* pattern. Be sure to use words that students have in their oral vocabularies so that they can quickly and automatically hear the breaks in a multisyllable word.

▶ Working with English Language Learners

Some languages have very few silent letters. It will be helpful for English language learners to understand that in English, some letters in a word may not be associated with an audible sound. Seeing silent letters as part of a commonly occurring pattern will turn their attention to other aspects of words. They will be able to understand that looking for these larger patterns will help them solve words and that these patterns exist in simple words and in multisyllable words.

UNDERSTAND THE PRINCIPLE

Many single-syllable words have a vowel-consonant-silent *e* pattern (e.g., *home, name*). In this lesson, students learn how to notice and apply this VCe pattern in words with two syllables. The pattern can form the first syllable (e.g., *hopeless*) or the second syllable (e.g., *compete*). The vowel-consonant-silent *e* pattern is one of several common patterns that are helpful in solving multisyllable words.

YOU WILL NEED

Online Resources
- ▶ WS 10 Action Tags
- ▶ WS 10 Word Cards
- ▶ WS 10 Five-Way Sorts

Other Materials
- ▶ chart paper

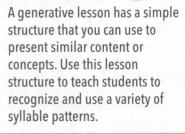

Generative Lesson

A generative lesson has a simple structure that you can use to present similar content or concepts. Use this lesson structure to teach students to recognize and use a variety of syllable patterns.

EXPLAIN THE PRINCIPLE

Some words have a vowel followed by a consonant and then a silent e. *The pattern stays together in a syllable, and the vowel sound is long.*

Comprehensive Phonics, Spelling, and Word Study Guide

Refer to:
Page **53**, row **10**

ACTIVITY: VOWEL-CONSONANT-*E* (VC*E*) SYLLABLES

INSTRUCTIONAL PROCEDURE

NOTICE PARTS

See page 32 for detailed descriptions of Instructional Procedures.

EXPLAIN THE PRINCIPLE

Some words have a vowel followed by a consonant and then a silent e. The pattern stays together in a syllable, and the vowel sound is long.

Comprehensive Phonics, Spelling, and Word Study Guide

Refer to: page **53**, row **10**

---

name
home
line
cute
Pete

hopeful	hope/ful
basement	base/ment
lonely	lone/ly

athlete	ath/lete
erase	e/rase
reptile	rep/tile

Teach

1. Explain to students that they will be noticing more about syllables.

2. Write *name, home, line, cute,* and *Pete* (or another name) on a chart. Have students read the words aloud. *What do you notice about the vowel sounds in all of the words?* Guide them to conclude that each word has one syllable that consists of a long vowel sound and a silent *e* (VC*e* pattern).

3. Next write *hopeful, basement,* and *lonely* on the chart. Have students read the words and clap the syllables they hear. *What do you notice about the vowel sound in the first syllable in these words?* ● *It has the long vowel sound. It has the VCe pattern.* Rewrite each word to show the syllable division, and have volunteers underline the VC*e* syllable.

4. Repeat with *athlete, erase,* and *reptile,* guiding students to notice that in these words, the second syllable has the VC*e* pattern.

5. Use students' observations to summarize the principle: *Some words have a vowel followed by a consonant and then a silent* e. *The pattern stays together in a syllable, and the vowel sound is long.*

6. Tell students they will complete a five-way sort, based on the vowel patterns *a_e, e_e, i_e, o_e,* and *u_e.* They will sort the word cards and then write them on a five-way sort. Instruct students to draw a slash mark to represent the syllables they hear in the words.

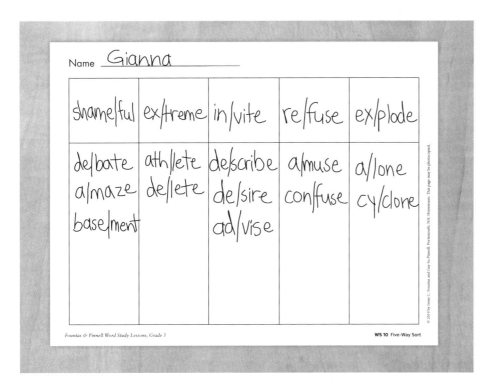

Name _Gianna_

shame/ful	ex/treme	in/vite	re/fuse	ex/plode
de/bate a/maze base/ment	ath/lete de/lete	de/scribe de/sire ad/vise	a/muse con/fuse	a/lone cy/clone

Fountas & Pinnell Word Study Lessons, Grade 3

© 2019 by Irene C. Fountas and Gay Su Pinnell. Portsmouth, NH: Heinemann. This page may be photocopied.

WS 10 Five-Way Sort

INSTRUCTIONAL PROCEDURE

NOTICE PARTS

See page 32 for detailed descriptions of Instructional Procedures.

ACTION TAGS

read words

sort words

write words

Apply

Have students sort their words, write them on a five-way sort, and draw slash marks to separate the syllables. Then have the students write two examples of words that have a syllable with a long vowel sound and a silent *e* in their word study notebook or on an index card.

Share

Invite students to share one new multisyllable word with the VC*e* pattern as you add it to the chart.

Assess

- Dictate three to five words with a VC*e* pattern. Notice whether students quickly write word parts.
- Notice how easily students read multisyllable words with the VC*e* pattern that they encounter in texts.
- You may wish to use Word Structure Assessment C, D, or J.

Word Structure: Recognize and Use VCe Syllables

Connect Learning Across Contexts

Guided Reading Prompt students to notice and use syllables to take apart words.

Independent Reading As you meet with individual readers, prompt them to use what they know about VCe syllables to take apart and read longer words.

Shared Writing After you have written a text together, have students point out two or three multisyllable words that have a VCe syllable. Invite them to underline the vowel combination.

Independent Writing As students write new words, have them think of each syllable and the vowel sound they hear in it.

Extend Learning

- Have students complete a two-way sort with the words, based on whether they have a VCe pattern in the first syllable or the second syllable.

- Have students play Lotto with words with VCe syllables. Blank Lotto boards are available in Online Resources.

▶ Connect with Home

Send home the word cards and have students sort them with family members. Encourage them to do both five-way and two-way sorts.

Recognize and Use Syllables in Words with the VCCV Pattern

Plan

▶ Consider Your Students

Before using this lesson, make sure students understand the concept of syllables and how to identify vowels, consonants, and consonant digraphs. Students should also have worked with open syllables (syllables ending with a vowel sound) and closed syllables (syllables ending with a consonant sound) and be familiar with their pronunciation. In this lesson, students will focus on breaking words with consonants in the middle. You may wish to start with double consonants and consonant blends before moving on to words with digraphs.

▶ Working with English Language Learners

Longer words challenge English language learners, especially if students lack full control of the words in their speaking vocabularies. Being able to break words into syllables will help. Nonetheless, students may have difficulty pronouncing the words, which makes it more difficult to make connections. Say words and syllables clearly, and have students repeat them several times. Consider having students manipulate the syllables by using magnetic letters or by cutting apart word cards.

YOU WILL NEED

Online Resources
- ▶ **WS 11** Action Tags
- ▶ **WS 11** Word Cards
- ▶ **WS 11** List Sheets

Other Materials
- ▶ chart paper
- ▶ magnetic letters

Generative Lesson

A generative lesson has a simple structure that you can use to present similar content or concepts. Use this lesson structure to teach students to recognize and use a variety of syllable patterns.

UNDERSTAND THE PRINCIPLE

In this lesson, students learn more about syllable units and the VCCV (vowel-consonant-consonant-vowel) pattern. The VCCV pattern indicates that a word has more than one syllable. The two consonants form the syllable juncture, or the place where the syllables are joined. Words can have the same letters at the juncture (e.g., *kitten*), or they can have different letters (e.g., *winter*). In either case, syllables are formed by dividing the two consonants. When there is a consonant digraph (consonants representing one sound) at the juncture, then the word is divided after the digraph. Recognizing the VCCV pattern and the basic rules for syllable division makes it easier for students to quickly divide words into smaller, more manageable parts.

EXPLAIN THE PRINCIPLE

When there are two consonants in the middle of a word, break the word between the consonants, but keep digraphs together.

Comprehensive Phonics, Spelling, and Word Study Guide

Refer to:
Page **53**, row **12**

ACTIVITY: SYLLABLE DIVISION

INSTRUCTIONAL PROCEDURE

NOTICE PARTS

See page 32 for detailed descriptions of Instructional Procedures.

EXPLAIN THE PRINCIPLE

When there are two consonants in the middle of a word, break the word between the consonants, but keep digraphs together.

Comprehensive Phonics, Spelling, and Word Study Guide

Refer to:
page **53**, row **12**

dinner	din/ner
basket	bas/ket
picnic	pic/nic
rabbit	rab/bit
chicken	chick/en
brother	broth/er
gopher	go/pher

Teach

1. Explain to students that they will be learning more about syllables.

2. Write *dinner, basket, picnic,* and *rabbit* on chart paper. Ask the class to read and clap the words with you. *What do you notice about all of these words?* • Students may notice that the words have two syllables or that that they have short vowel sounds. If necessary, draw their attention to the VCCV pattern, or the fact that all of the words have two consonants in the middle of each word.

3. Ask the students to identify the syllable break and make a slash mark in each of the words: *din/ner, bas/ket, pic/nic, rab/bit.*

4. Now repeat the procedure with the words *chicken, brother,* and *gopher.* Have the students identify the syllable break and use a slash mark to show the syllable division: *chick/en, broth/er, goph/er. What do you notice about where these words are divided?*

5. Use students' observations to summarize the principle: *When there are two consonants in the middle of a word, break the word between the consonants, but keep digraphs together.*

6. Tell students that they are going to practice dividing words into syllables. Explain that they will take a word card, read it, make the word with magnetic letters, divide it into syllables, and then write the divided word on a list sheet or in their word study notebook.

Name Nathan
1. crash/es   6. hid/den
2. munch/ling   7. for/get
3. ad/mit   8. vel/vet
4. thun/der   9. fos/sil
5. trick/y   10. tid/bit

Fountas & Pinnell Word Study Lessons, Grade 3   WS 11 List Sheet

INSTRUCTIONAL PROCEDURE

NOTICE PARTS

See page 32 for detailed descriptions of Instructional Procedures.

ACTION TAGS

take card
read word
make word
divide word
write word
draw slash mark

Apply

Distribute word cards, magnetic letters, and list sheets. Have students divide and write approximately ten words with slash marks to represent syllable breaks.

Share

Have students choose three or four words and tell how they divided them. Invite them to use the magnetic letters if they wish.

Assess

- Have students read four to six words with the VCCV pattern.
- Dictate three to five words with the VCCV pattern, and note students' ability to divide them.
- You may wish to use Word Structure Assessment C, D, or J.

Word Structure: Recognize and Use Syllables in Words with the VCCV Pattern

Connect Learning Across Contexts

Guided Reading Prompt students to notice and use syllables to take apart words.

Independent Reading As you meet with individual readers, prompt them to use what they know to take apart words with consonants in the middle.

Shared Writing After you have written a text together, have students point out two or three words that have consonants in the middle. Prompt them to mark the syllables.

Independent Writing As students write new words, have them think of each syllable to figure out the spelling.

Extend Learning

Repeat this lesson with a different variety of two-syllable words.

▶ Connect with Home

Send home the word cards and have students divide and read the words with family members.

Understand That the Ending -ed Can Represent Several Different Sounds

Plan

▶ Consider Your Students

Your students should have read many words with the -ed ending and used the past tense of verbs both in their speech and in their writing. Students should already be able to add -ed to words and change the spelling, if necessary. This lesson will help them focus on the sound of the ending.

▶ Working with English Language Learners

Inflectional endings can be challenging for English language learners. Encourage students to make links to their own languages to help them understand the concept. Be sure they know the meaning of the words you are using. Model using the words in sentences, and at the same time, provide the visual example. Students will need many opportunities to say the different verb forms slowly and to think about how the word endings *sound* and *look*.

Generative Lesson
A generative lesson has a simple structure that you can use to present similar content or concepts. Use this lesson structure to present other inflectional endings.

UNDERSTAND THE PRINCIPLE

In their reading and writing, students will frequently encounter words that end in the suffix -ed. Students need to learn that there are three different sounds for the suffix -ed: /t/, /d/, and /ed/. If the base verb ends in an unvoiced sound, such as /p/, /k/, or /sh/, the -ed sounds like /t/. If the base verb ends in a voiced sound, such as /b/ or /g/, the -ed sounds like /d/. If the base verb ends in a /t/ or /d/ sound, the -ed ending sounds like /ed/. Recognizing the different sounds for -ed will help students standardize their pronunciation and spelling of words in the past tense.

EXPLAIN THE PRINCIPLE

When -ed is added to a verb, sometimes it sounds like /d/.

When -ed is added to a verb, sometimes it sounds like /ed/.

When -ed is added to a verb, sometimes it sounds like /t/.

Comprehensive Phonics, Spelling, and Word Study Guide

Refer to:
Page **60**, row **48**

ACTIVITY: ENDING SOUNDS

INSTRUCTIONAL PROCEDURE

SEE AND SAY

See page 32 for detailed descriptions of Instructional Procedures.

EXPLAIN THE PRINCIPLE

When -ed is added to a verb, sometimes it sounds like /d/.

When -ed is added to a verb, sometimes it sounds like /ed/.

When -ed is added to a verb, sometimes it sounds like /t/.

Comprehensive Phonics, Spelling, and Word Study Guide

Refer to: page **60**, row **48**

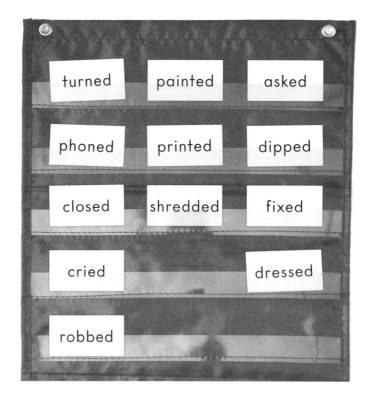

Teach

1. Place *turned, painted,* and *asked* at the top of three columns in the pocket chart. Have students read each word. *What do you notice about all of these words?* • Students may observe that they all end in *-ed. What else do you notice when thinking about the ending in each of the words?* • Guide students to notice that sometimes the letters *-ed* make different sounds, and sometimes the letters can make up a syllable.

2. Invite a student to say *turned. What sound do you hear at the end of the word* turned? • *You hear the /d/ sound.* Invite a student to say *painted. What sound do you hear at the end of the word* painted? • Help students to notice that when you add *-ed* to *paint,* you hear a whole syllable. Have them clap the parts: paint/ed.

3. Now say *asked. What sound do you hear at the end of* asked? • Asked *ends with the /t/ sound.*

4. Then display the cards *phoned, printed, dipped, closed, shredded, fixed,* and *cried,* and as you show each, have students read the word and place it in the column with other words that have the same ending sound. Guide them to observe that the letters *-ed* can stand for three different sounds at the end of a word.

5. Tell students to place the key words *turned, painted,* and *asked* at the top of a three-way sort. Ask them to take a word card, read it, and place it under the key word that has the same sound at the end. After they have sorted all the word cards, have them read their three columns to a partner. Finally, ask them to copy the three columns on a three-way sort. As the students write the words, instruct them to insert slash marks to represent the syllables.

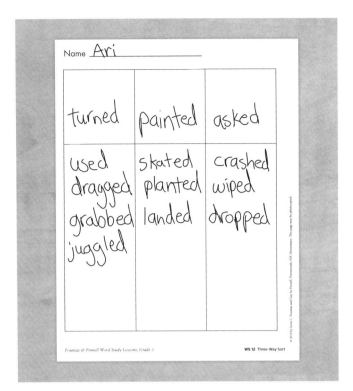

INSTRUCTIONAL PROCEDURE

SAY AND SORT

See page 32 for detailed descriptions of Instructional Procedures.

ACTION TAGS

take card

read card

sort card

read columns

write words

draw slash marks

Apply

Have students say and sort the word cards, read their columns of words to a partner, and write the words, with slash marks, on a three-way sort.

Share

Have students give one more example for each column on the class chart.

Assess

- Dictate seven or eight words, and have students add the *-ed* ending.
- Notice whether students read words with *-ed* endings correctly and spell the words correctly when they write them.

Connect Learning Across Contexts

Guided Reading After discussing a book, ask students to point out one or two words with the *-ed* ending, and have students tell whether it sounds like /d/, /t/, or /ed/.

Independent Reading As you meet with individual readers, prompt them to use what they know about the different sounds of *-ed* to read words that are in the past tense.

Shared Writing In texts students write with you, words with the *-ed* ending will often be included. Prompt students to think about how the ending looks and sounds when they write it.

Independent Writing Teach students how to check the spelling of words with the *-ed* ending when they edit their work.

Extend Learning

- Repeat the lesson with a variety of other verbs to give students more practice.
- Have students suggest more words that have the different sounds of the *-ed* ending, and add them to a class chart.

▶ ## Connect with Home

Give students a sheet of word cards with verbs that have the *-ed* ending to take home and sort on a three-way sort.

Recognize and Use Common Abbreviations

Plan

▶ Consider Your Students

Use this lesson after students have encountered abbreviations in reading and interactive or shared writing. *In this lesson the focus is on common abbreviations:* Mr., Mrs., Dr., Ave., Rd., Ln., St., Sun., Mon., Tues., Wed., Thurs., Fri., Sat., Jan., Feb., Mar., Apr., Aug., Sept., Oct., Nov., Dec. Once students understand the concept, it will be easy for them to learn a whole collection of abbreviations.

▶ Working with English Language Learners

While English language learners are still learning many new English words and their meanings, they still may struggle with the concept of abbreviations. Start with abbreviations they may have seen before. Place abbreviations in appropriate places for students to become familiar with them, such as on calendars and maps.

UNDERSTAND THE PRINCIPLE

Abbreviations are shortened forms of particular words. They are used often in reading and writing. Students will encounter abbreviations in many texts. Understanding the concept of abbreviations and how they are formed will help students understand their meaning and promote correct and conventional use of abbreviations.

YOU WILL NEED

Online Resources
- ▶ **WS 13** Action Tags
- ▶ **WS 13** Game Cards
- ▶ **WS 13** List Sheets
- ▶ **WS 14** Directions for Concentration

Other Materials
- ▶ chart paper

✓ Generative Lesson

A generative lesson has a simple structure that you can use to present similar content or concepts. Use this lesson structure to present other abbreviations.

EXPLAIN THE PRINCIPLE

Some words have a shortened form that uses some of the letters. They are abbreviations.

Abbreviations are usually pronounced the same as the longer form of the word.

Many abbreviations begin with an uppercase letter, and most are followed by a period.

Comprehensive Phonics, Spelling, and Word Study Guide

Refer to: Page **71**, row **88**

ACTIVITY: ABBREVIATION LIST

INSTRUCTIONAL PROCEDURE

NOTICE PARTS

See page 32 for detailed descriptions of Instructional Procedures.

EXPLAIN THE PRINCIPLE

Some words have a shortened form that uses some of the letters. They are abbreviations.

Abbreviations are usually pronounced the same as the longer form of the word.

Many abbreviations begin with an uppercase letter, and most are followed by a period.

Comprehensive Phonics, Spelling, and Word Study Guide

Refer to: page **71**, row **88**

Mister Mr.	January Jan.
Doctor Dr.	February Feb.
	March Mar.
Street St.	
Avenue Ave.	
Road Rd.	August Aug.
	September Sept.
Sunday Sun.	December Dec.
Monday Mon.	
Friday Fri.	
Saturday Sat.	

Teach

1. On a piece of chart paper, write the words *Mister* and *Doctor*. Next to each word, write the abbreviations *Mr.* and *Dr.* Have students read the word pairs. *What do you notice about these word pairs?* • Students may observe that the abbreviations start with a capital letter and end with a period, or that they have the first and last letters of the longer words, or that the words and their abbreviations sound very similar or the same.

2. Have students underline the letters in *Mister* and *Doctor* that are used in the abbreviations.

3. Continue the procedure with other common abbreviations, such as *Street (St.)*, *Avenue (Ave.)*, *Road (Rd.)*, days of the week, and months of the year.

4. *How are the abbreviations for the days of the week and the months of the year different from other common abbreviations?* • Help students notice that common abbreviations are usually formed with the first and last letters of the word, plus a period. Abbreviations for months and days are usually formed with the first three or four letters of the word, plus a period.

5. *What are some abbreviations you use all the time?* • *What are some abbreviations you use when you need to save space?*

6. Tell students they will play Concentration, trying to match an abbreviation with its whole word. The player with the most matched pairs wins the game. Students then make a list of twenty different abbreviations on a list sheet.

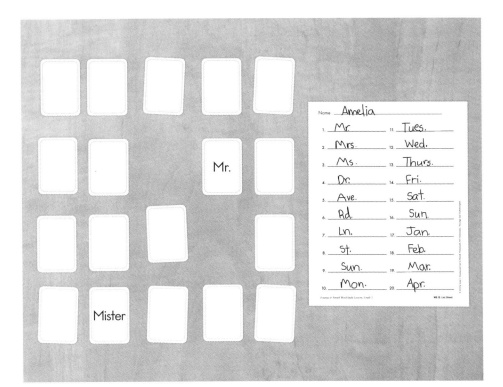

INSTRUCTIONAL PROCEDURE

FIND AND MATCH

See page 32 for detailed descriptions of Instructional Procedures.

ACTION TAGS

turn card

read word or abbreviation

match word or abbreviation

write list

Apply

Have students play Concentration in groups of two to four. Then have them make a list of twenty different abbreviations on a list sheet.

Share

Invite a few students to write an abbreviation on the board while the other students tell the complete word.

Assess

- Dictate six to ten words for children to abbreviate.
- Notice whether students form abbreviations correctly in their writing and pronounce them correctly in their reading.

Connect Learning Across Contexts

Guided Reading After reading and discussing a text, have students find one or two abbreviations or words that can be abbreviated.

Independent Reading As you meet with individual readers, prompt them to notice abbreviations and pronounce them correctly.

Shared Writing Look for opportunities for students to use abbreviations in the texts that you compose together.

Independent Writing Have students edit their writing to be sure that abbreviations start with a capital letter and end with a period, if needed.

Extend Learning

Repeat this lesson with other more challenging abbreviations, such as state names that are shortened and written in capital letters without a period.

▶ Connect with Home

Send home the game cards with words and abbreviations for students to play Concentration with family members.

Recognize and Use Plurals That Add -es to Words That End with the Letters ch, sh, s, x, or z

Plan

▶ Consider Your Students

Use this lesson after students are familiar with the concept of plural and have worked with plurals by adding -s. You may wish to briefly review this concept before teaching this lesson. They should also be skilled in hearing sounds in words and be able to hear the syllable breaks by saying and clapping words.

▶ Working with English Language Learners

Be sure that English language learners have worked enough with simple plurals to understand the concept and are familiar with plenty of common examples. This lesson will expand their knowledge of plurals. Use pictures and objects to illustrate the meanings of words, and work with a small group to be sure that the students can read and talk about the plurals they are making. Encourage them to talk about what they notice about words.

UNDERSTAND THE PRINCIPLE

Students need to understand that there are different forms for plural nouns. This lesson focuses on the ending -es, which is added as a suffix to nouns ending with the letters ch, sh, s, x, and z to indicate plurality (i.e., more than one number). Students can improve their spelling by saying the word and making a connection between the sound of the ending and the word they are spelling.

YOU WILL NEED

Online Resources
- ▶ **WS 14** Action Tags
- ▶ **WS 14** Word Cards
- ▶ **WS 14** List Sheets

Other Materials
- ▶ pocket chart

Generative Lesson ✓

A generative lesson has a simple structure that you can use to present similar content or concepts. You can use this lesson structure to teach students to form a variety of plurals.

EXPLAIN THE PRINCIPLE

Add -es to words that end with ch, sh, s, x, and z to make them plural.

Comprehensive Phonics, Spelling, and Word Study Guide

Refer to: Page **72**, row **88**

EARLY **MIDDLE** LATE

ACTIVITY: SINGULAR AND PLURAL FORMS

INSTRUCTIONAL PROCEDURE

NOTICE PARTS

See page 32 for detailed descriptions of Instructional Procedures.

EXPLAIN THE PRINCIPLE

Add -es to words that end with ch, sh, s, x, and z to make them plural.

Comprehensive Phonics, Spelling, and Word Study Guide

Refer to: page **56**, row **29**

---

dress	dresses
bush	bushes
box	boxes
wrench	wrenches
buzz	buzzes

Teach

1. On chart paper, write the following words in a column: *dress, bush, box, wrench, buzz.* Read the words, and have students say them and clap them with you. *How would you make the first word,* dress, *plural?* • *You would add -es to the end of the word.* Add the *-es* to the word *dress,* and underline the base word. *Let's read and clap the word* dress. • *Now, let's read and clap the word* dresses. • How *would you make the word* bush *plural?* • *You would add an -es to the end of the word.* Add *-es* to the word *bush,* and underline the base word. *Let's read and clap the word* bush. • *Now, let's read and clap the word* bushes. • Continue asking the class how to make the rest of the words plural, and then read and clap the words.

2. *What do you notice about all of these words?* • *The plural words all end in* -es. *Each word that ends in* -es *has two syllables.*

3. *Let's look at a few more words.* Write the words *fox, box, glass, dish, bus,* and *church* on the board. Repeat the procedure.

4. Emphasize that adding *-es* also adds a syllable by having students read and clap the plural words one more time, if necessary.

5. *Take a look at the ending letters of the words in the left column. What are some ways you can tell you write -es to make the word plural?* • *When you say words like* foxes *or* dresses, *you can hear the added syllable,* -es. *When you make these words plural, you need* -es *to pronounce the word.* Guide students to understand the principle: *Add -es to words that end with* ch, sh, s, x, *and* z *to make them plural.*

6. Tell students they will choose twenty word cards and write the plural form of each word on a list sheet.

INSTRUCTIONAL PROCEDURE

NOTICE PARTS

See page 32 for detailed descriptions of Instructional Procedures.

ACTION TAGS

take card

write plural

read plural

Name Maya

1.	glasses	11.	bushes
2.	batches	12.	guesses
3.	axes	13.	riches
4.	faxes	14.	messes
5.	wishes	15.	pitches
6.	patches	16.	circuses
7.	classes	17.	dishes
8.	inches	18.	passes
9.	buses	19.	buzzes
10.	lunches	20.	crutches

Fountas & Pinnell Word Study Lessons, Grade 3   **WS 14** List Sheet

Apply

Have students write the plural form of at least twenty words. You may wish to have them underline the ending letter or letter cluster in the base word.

Share

Have students share two plurals from their list. Then have them suggest additional examples to add to the class chart.

Assess

- Notice whether students are using conventional plural forms for nouns in their writing.
- Include four to six plural nouns on a quick spelling test.
- You may wish to use Word Structure Assessment E or K.

Word Structure: Recognize and Use Plurals That Add -es to Words That End with the Letters ch, sh, s, x, or z

Connect Learning Across Contexts

Guided Reading After reading and discussing a text, have students locate one or two plural forms that add -es.

Independent Reading As you meet with individual readers, remind them that the letters -es are usually pronounced as an extra syllable at the end of words.

Shared Writing If students have difficulty forming plurals, have them say the plural form of the word aloud and clap the syllables. If a syllable is added to the word, remind students that this means to add -es.

Independent Writing Have students check their spelling of plural forms when they reread and edit their work.

Extend Learning

- Have students play Concentration with pairs of singular and plural forms of words. You will need to use the blank game cards (see Online Resources) to make singular and plural forms.

- Have students find ten plural words in print around the room and make a list.

▶ Connect with Home

Send home word cards containing the singular and plural forms of another set of simple nouns that end with *sh, ch, s, x,* and *z.* Have students match the singular and plural forms of words.

Recognize and Use Plurals That Add *-es* to Words That End with a Consonant and *y*

Plan

▶ Consider Your Students

Use this lesson after students are familiar with the concept of plural and can easily form simple plurals by adding *-s* and *-es*. In this lesson, they learn that they need to look at the last two letters to help them know how to change the spelling. The lesson focuses on words ending in a consonant and *y*.

▶ Working with English Language Learners

Making words plural can be challenging for English language learners because there are many plural forms in English. Once they learn the most regular plurals (*-s* and *-es*), which are themselves a challenge, they need to expand the way they look at words to include other variations. Be sure your English language learners have had a chance to see and read the words you use in this lesson. Use shared reading and interactive writing to help them meet and notice these word structures in a meaningful context before they work with them more directly in this lesson. For example, you could have a small group compose and write sentences about their families or any other topic that would incorporate these words. Show students how to change the *y* to *i* and add *-es*. Then have them take turns writing the plural on the chart.

YOU WILL NEED

Online Resources
▸ **WS 15** Action Tags
▸ **WS 15** Two-Way Sorts
▸ **WS 15** Word Cards

Other Materials
▸ chart paper
▸ magnetic letters

Generative Lesson ✅
A generative lesson has a simple structure that you can use to present similar content or concepts. You can use this lesson structure to teach students to form a variety of plurals.

UNDERSTAND THE PRINCIPLE

Students need to understand that there are different processes for making nouns plural. Some nouns, such as those that end in a consonant and *y*, require a spelling change before the plural is added. When there is a consonant and *y*, they change the *y* to *i* and add *-es*. This widely applicable rule is one that will help students spell the plural forms of a large number of nouns that end in *y*.

EXPLAIN THE PRINCIPLE

When a word ends with a consonant and y, *change the* y *to* i *and add* -es *to make the word plural.*

Comprehensive Phonics, Spelling, and Word Study Guide

Refer to:
Page **56**, row **31**

EARLY **MIDDLE** LATE

ACTIVITY: SINGULAR AND PLURAL FORMS

INSTRUCTIONAL PROCEDURE

NOTICE PARTS

See page 32 for detailed descriptions of Instructional Procedures.

EXPLAIN THE PRINCIPLE

When a word ends with a consonant and y, change the y to i and add -es to make the word plural.

Comprehensive Phonics, Spelling, and Word Study Guide

Refer to: page **56**, row **31**

---

city   cities
trophy   trophies
party   parties

baby   babies
puppy   puppies

Teach

1. On chart paper, write the word pairs *city, cities; trophy, trophies;* and *party, parties.* Invite students to read the words with you. *What do you notice about all of these words?* ● Students may notice that the spelling of the base word differs or that the words on the left are singular and the words on the right are plural.

2. *Take a look at the ending letters of the words in the left column. What do you notice about the spelling of all of the words?* ● *All of the words end in the letter* y. *What do you notice about the letter in each of the words that comes just before the* y? ● *They are all consonant letters.*

3. Write the words *baby* and *puppy* on the chart, and have students form the plural of each word. Ask them to explain why they formed it that way. Guide students to understand the principle: *When the letter before* y *is a consonant, change the* y *to* i *and add* -es.

4. Explain to students that they will be making and writing plural forms of words. Students will take a word card, make it with magnetic letters, and then write it in the first column of a two-way sort. Then they will make the word plural by changing *y* to *i* and adding *-es* with magnetic letters. Finally, they will write the plural form in the second column.

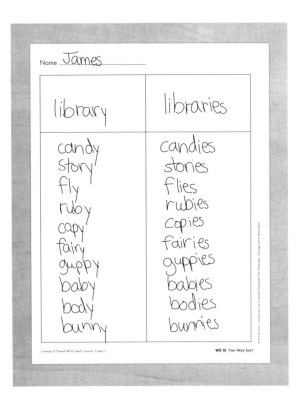

INSTRUCTIONAL PROCEDURE

NOTICE PARTS

See page 32 for detailed descriptions of Instructional Procedures.

ACTION TAGS

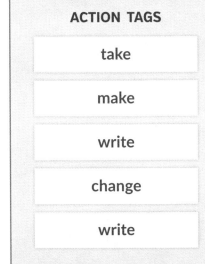

take
make
write
change
write

Apply

Distribute copies of the two-way sort, magnetic letters, and one set of word cards to each student. Have them make and write at least ten word pairs. Then have them read their word pairs to a partner.

Share

- Ask students to share a pair of words from their sheet.
- Ask students to discuss what they have learned about plurals. They can describe the process of making a word such as *lady* plural.

Assess

- Give students a list of five words that end in *y*, and have them write the plural form. You can increase the difficulty of this task by dictating the list of words.
- Notice how easily students read plural forms in text.
- You may wish to use Word Structure Assessment E or K.

Word Structure: Recognize and Use Plurals That Add -es to Words That End with a Consonant and y

Connect Learning Across Contexts

Guided Reading After reading and discussing a text, quickly write one or two plural words. Have students tell how the plural was formed.

Independent Reading As you meet with individual readers, remind them that the *s* in the *-ies* ending usually sounds like /z/.

Shared Writing As you write together, draw attention to plurals that are formed by changing *y* to *i* and adding *-es*.

Independent Writing During the editing process, have students check their spelling of plural forms. They can use the class chart as a reference.

Extend Learning

Have students play Lotto with pairs of singular and plural forms of words. Give students a mix of words that end with a vowel and *y* and a consonant and *y* and have them form plurals.

▶ Connect with Home

Give students a sheet of singular and plural words to take home, cut out, and match with family members. Alternatively, send home only the singular forms, and have them make and write the plural forms.

Recognize and Use Plurals That Add *-es* to Words After Changing the Final *f* or *fe* to *v*

Plan

▶ Consider Your Students

Use this lesson after your students have become familiar with the concept of plural and can form simple plurals by adding *-s* and *-es* as well as plurals for words that end in *y*. It is important for students to be able to recognize plural forms in oral language and have significant experience identifying examples in texts before learning to spell them.

▶ Working with English Language Learners

Be sure that English language learners understand simpler forms of plurals before they attempt plurals for words ending in *f* or *fe*. The words you use in the lesson should be part of students' speaking and listening vocabularies, and it will help a great deal if they have previously experienced the words in shared reading and shared writing. If students are unfamiliar with such words, you may wish to provide additional support to a small group using interactive writing, a very supportive environment for scaffolding the concept.

YOU WILL NEED

Online Resources
- ▸ **WS 16** Action Tags
- ▸ **WS 16** Word Cards
- ▸ **WS 16** Two-Way Sorts

Other Materials
- ▸ blank chart paper
- ▸ magnetic letters

Generative Lesson

A generative lesson has a simple structure that you can use to present similar content or concepts. Use this lesson structure to teach students to recognize a variety of words in which the final *f* or *fe* is changed to *v* when making a plural.

UNDERSTAND THE PRINCIPLE

Students need to understand that there are different processes for making nouns plural. Some nouns, such as those that end in *f* or *fe*, require a spelling change before the plural is added. When words end in these letters, the plural is often formed by changing *f* or *fe* to *v* and adding *-es*. This rule will help students spell the plural forms of a large number of nouns that end in *f* or *fe*. Common exceptions to this rule include *roofs* and *chiefs*.

EXPLAIN THE PRINCIPLE

For most words ending with f *or* fe, *change the* f *or* fe *to* v *and add* -es *to make the words plural.*

Comprehensive Phonics, Spelling, and Word Study Guide

Refer to: page **56**, row **32**

ACTIVITY: SINGULAR AND PLURAL FORMS

INSTRUCTIONAL PROCEDURE

NOTICE PARTS

See page 32 for detailed descriptions of Instructional Procedures.

EXPLAIN THE PRINCIPLE

For most words ending with f or fe, change the f or fe to v and add -es to make the words plural.

Comprehensive Phonics, Spelling, and Word Study Guide

Refer to: page **56**, row **32**

life   lives

calf   calves

hoof   hooves

knife   knives

Teach

1. Tell students that they are going to learn more about making words plural.

2. On chart paper, write the word *life*, and have students read it with you. *What is the plural of* life*?* ● Write the word *lives*, and have students read it with you. *Use* lives *in a sentence. You also might know this word pronounced as* lives, *such as, "lives in Boston."* Write the word *calf*. *What is the plural of the word* calf*?* ● Write the word *calves*, and have students read it with you. Use *calves* in an example sentence to ensure understanding.

3. *What do you notice about the singular and plural forms of these words?* ● *You changed the letters* fe *to* v *and added the letters* es *to make these words plural.*

4. Repeat the process with the words *hoof/hooves.* Prompt students to describe how the words changed to form the plural. ● *The plural of these words is formed by changing the letter* f *to* v *and adding* -es*.* You may wish to write more singular words that fit the principle and have students say and help you write the plurals. Possible words include *knife, scarf, shelf,* and *thief.* You may also wish to point out two common exceptions: *roof/roofs* and *chief/chiefs.*

5. Guide students to understand the principle: *For most words ending with f or fe, change the* f *or* fe *to* v *and add* -es *to make the words plural.*

6. Explain to students that they will be making and writing plural forms of words. Students will take a word card, make it with letter cards or magnetic letters, and write it in the first column of a two-way sort. Students then use letter cards or magnetic letters to make the plural form of the word and write it in the second column of the sheet.

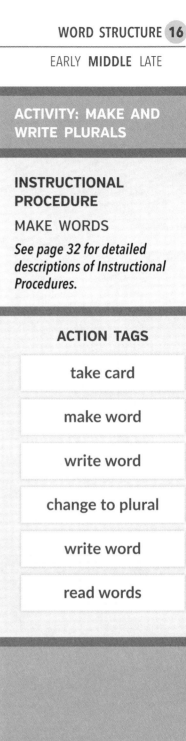

ACTIVITY: MAKE AND WRITE PLURALS

INSTRUCTIONAL PROCEDURE

MAKE WORDS

See page 32 for detailed descriptions of Instructional Procedures.

ACTION TAGS

take card

make word

write word

change to plural

write word

read words

Apply

Distribute copies of the two-way sorts, sets of word cards, and magnetic letters. Have students make and write at least twelve word pairs. Then have them read their word pairs to a partner.

Share

Ask students to share one pair of words that they wrote and talk about what they learned about forming plurals.

Assess

■ Notice whether students, in their writing, are using conventional plural forms of nouns that end in *f* and *fe.*

■ Dictate five to seven words that end in *f* or *fe,* and have students write the singular and plural forms.

■ You may wish to use Word Structure Assessment E or K.

Word Structure: Recognize and Use Plurals That Add -es to Words After Changing the Final f *or* fe *to* v

Connect Learning Across Contexts

Shared Reading You may wish to display the Shared Reading book *Wolf Pack* from *Fountas & Pinnell Classroom*™. After rereading the book with students, have them use highlighter tape to locate the singular and plural forms of the noun *wolf.*

　　SR *Wolf Pack* by Annette Bay Pimentel

Independent Reading As you confer with an individual reader, skim the pages of the book she is reading for one or two examples of plurals that are formed by changing *f* or *fe* to *v* and adding *-es.* If examples appear in the book, ask the student to locate the words. Use the opportunity to reinforce the principle.

Shared Writing Call attention to the principle when you are writing the plural form of a word that ends in *f* or *fe.*

Independent Writing Draw attention to the principle for forming plurals of words that end in *f* or *fe* while conferring with students about their editing.

Extend Learning

Have students play Concentration with singular and plural forms of nouns that are examples of the principle. Blank game cards are available in Online Resources.

▶ **Connect with Home**

Send home the word cards, and have students work with a family member to write the plurals.

Recognize and Use Plurals That Add -*s* to Words That End with *o*

Plan

▶ Consider Your Students

Teach this lesson after students have had extensive experience with more common plural forms and can write them correctly. This lesson will be particularly helpful if students have been attempting to spell the plural form of words that end with *o* during independent writing and if they are regularly encountering words that end with *o* in their reading. It is important for students to be able to recognize plural forms in oral language and have significant experience identifying examples in texts before learning to spell them.

▶ Working with English Language Learners

The words you use in the lesson should be part of students' speaking and listening vocabularies, and it will help a great deal if they have previously experienced the words in shared reading and shared writing. Consider working with small groups to help students understand the many different ways that plurals are formed in English. Seeing and connecting several examples help them establish categories of plural formations.

YOU WILL NEED

Online Resources
- ▶ **WS 17** Action Tags
- ▶ **WS 17** Word Cards
- ▶ **WS 17** Three-Way Sorts

Other Materials
- ▶ blank chart paper
- ▶ dictionaries
- ▶ magnetic letters

UNDERSTAND THE PRINCIPLE

Students need to understand that there are different processes for making nouns plural. The plural of a noun that ends with *o* is usually formed by adding -*s* to the end of the word. However, some words that end with *o*, such as *zero*, may end with -*s* or with -*es* in the plural form. This principle applies to a relatively small number of words.

EXPLAIN THE PRINCIPLE

Add -s to most words that end with o to make them plural.

Some words that end in o have two plural forms—e.g., zeros, zeroes.

Comprehensive Phonics, Spelling, and Word Study Guide

Refer to: page **56**, row **35**

ACTIVITY: SINGULAR AND PLURAL FORMS

INSTRUCTIONAL PROCEDURE

NOTICE PARTS

See page 32 for detailed descriptions of Instructional Procedures.

EXPLAIN THE PRINCIPLE

Add -s to most words that end with o to make them plural.

Some words that end in o have two plural forms—e.g., zeros, zeroes.

Comprehensive Phonics, Spelling, and Word Study Guide

Refer to: page **56**, row **35**

piano	pianos	
video	videos	
radio	radios	
kangaroo	kangaroos	
zero	zeros	zeroes

Teach

1. Tell students that they are going to learn more about making words plural.

2. On chart paper, write the words *piano, video, radio,* and *kangaroo.* Have students read them with you. *What do you notice about the words?* • *Each word ends with the letter* o.

3. Write the plural form of each word beside the singular form. Have students read the words with you. *What do you notice about the plural of each word?* • *The plurals end with* -s.

4. Guide students to generalize the principle. *Based on these four words, what have you learned about making words plural?* • Build on students' responses to summarize the principle. *You add* -s *to most words that end with* o *to make them plural.*

5. Write the singular and two plural forms of the word *zero.* Have students read the words with you. *A few words that end with* o, *such as* zero, *have two plural forms:* -s *at the end and* -es *at the end. Either form is correct.* [This idea may be a new concept for some students.] As *you are learning the plurals of words that end with* o, *it is helpful to check the spellings in a dictionary.*

6. Explain to students that they will be making and writing plural forms of words. Students will take a word card, make it with magnetic letters, and write it in the first column of a three-way sort. Students then use magnetic letters to make the plural form (-s) and write it in the second column. If the word has a second plural form (-es), students use letter cards or magnetic letters to make the word a third time and write it in the third column. Encourage students to check the spelling of plural forms in the dictionary.

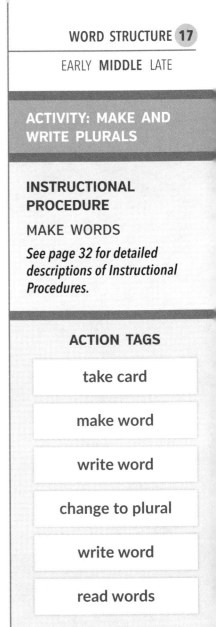

ACTIVITY: MAKE AND WRITE PLURALS

INSTRUCTIONAL PROCEDURE

MAKE WORDS

See page 32 for detailed descriptions of Instructional Procedures.

ACTION TAGS

take card
make word
write word
change to plural
write word
read words

Apply

- Distribute copies of the three-way sort, sets of word cards, and magnetic letters. Have students make and write at least five words (the singular form and up to two plural forms).

- You may wish to point out to students where they can find plural forms of nouns within entries in your classroom dictionary. Encourage them to consult a dictionary to confirm the spelling or spellings of the words they choose.

- Have students read their words to a partner.

Share

Ask students to share one word that they wrote. Invite students to talk about what they learned about forming plurals.

Assess

- Notice whether students, in their writing, are using conventional plural forms of nouns that end with *o*.

- Dictate five to seven words that end with *o*, and have students write the singular and plural forms.

- You may wish to use Word Structure Assessment E or K.

Connect Learning Across Contexts

Guided Reading During word work, display the singular form of four to six words that end with *o*, and have students explain how to form the plurals.

Independent Reading As you confer with an individual reader, notice any examples of words that end with *o* in the text. If examples appear, have the student locate the words and explain how to form the plural. Use the opportunity to reinforce the principle.

Shared Writing Call attention to the principle when you are writing the plural form of a word that ends with *o*.

Independent Writing Draw attention to the principle for forming plurals of words that end with *o* while conferring with students about their editing.

Extend Learning

Have students play Go Fish with singular and plural forms of nouns that are examples of the principle. Blank game cards are available in Online Resources.

▷ Connect with Home

Send home the word cards, and have students work with a family member to write the plurals.

Recognize and Use Plurals That Add -es to Words That End with a Consonant and o

Plan

▶ Consider Your Students

Teach this lesson after teaching WS 17, which presents the principle that -s is added to most words that end with o. To help students relate the principle in this lesson to other categories of plurals, students should have extensive experience with more common plural forms. This lesson will be particularly helpful if students have been attempting to spell the plural form of words that end with o during independent writing and if they are regularly encountering words that end with o in their reading. For this lesson to be effective, students will need to be familiar with the format of dictionary entries (WSA 9).

▶ Working with English Language Learners

The words you use in the lesson should be part of students' speaking and listening vocabularies, and it will help a great deal if they have previously experienced the words in shared reading and shared writing. Consider working with small groups to help students understand the many different ways that plurals are formed in English. Seeing and connecting several examples help them establish categories of plural formations.

UNDERSTAND THE PRINCIPLE

Students need to understand that there are different processes for making nouns plural. The plural of a noun that ends with a consonant and o is sometimes formed by adding -es to the end of the word. However, some words that end with a consonant and o, such as *volcano,* may end with -es or just with -s in the plural form. This principle applies to a small number of words.

YOU WILL NEED

Online Resources
- ▶ **WS 18** Action Tags
- ▶ **WS 18** Three-Way Sorts

Other Materials
- ▶ blank chart paper
- ▶ dictionaries

EXPLAIN THE PRINCIPLE

Add -es to a few words that end in a consonant and o to make them plural.

Some words that end with o have two plural forms–e.g., volcanoes, volcanos.

Comprehensive Phonics, Spelling, and Word Study Guide

Refer to: page **56**, row **36**

ACTIVITY: SINGULAR AND PLURAL FORMS

INSTRUCTIONAL PROCEDURE

NOTICE PARTS

See page 32 for detailed descriptions of Instructional Procedures.

EXPLAIN THE PRINCIPLE

Add -es to a few words that end in a consonant and o to make them plural.

Some words that end with o have two plural forms—e.g., volcanoes, volcanos.

Comprehensive Phonics, Spelling, and Word Study Guide

Refer to: page **56**, row **36**

echo	echoes	
hero	heroes	
potato	potatoes	
tomato	tomatoes	
volcano	volcanoes	volcanos
mosquito	mosquitoes	mosquitos

Teach

1. Tell students that they are going to learn more about making words plural.

2. On chart paper, write the words *echo, hero, potato,* and *tomato* in a column. Have students read each of the words with you, and ask what the plural form is. Write the answers on the right side of the chart.

3. Point to the left side of the chart. *What do you notice about all of these words?* • *Each word ends with the letter* o. *What do you notice about the letter before the* o *in all of the words?* • *A consonant comes before the letter* o *in each of the words.*

4. Point to the right side of the chart. *What do you notice about the plural of each word?* • *The plurals end with -es, not just -s.*

5. Guide students to generalize the principle from their observations. Build on students' responses to state the first part of the principle. *Add -es to a few words that end in a consonant and o to make them plural.*

6. Write the singular and two plural forms of the words *volcano* and *mosquito.* Have students read the words with you. *Some words that end with o, such as* volcano *and* mosquito, *have two plural forms: -es at the end and -s at the end. Either form is correct. As you are learning the plurals of words that end in a consonant and o, it is helpful to check the spellings in a dictionary.*

7. Tell students that they will be checking the dictionary and writing plural forms of words. Display the three-column sort. Explain that students say each word in the first column and look it up in a dictionary. They write the plural form of the word (*-es*) in the second column. If the word has a second plural form (*-s*), students write it in the third column. Students then read the words to a partner and compare spellings.

Name Savannah

volcano	volcanoes	volcanos
hero	heroes	
potato	potatoes	
domino	dominoes	dominos
echo	echoes	
torpedo	torpedoes	
tomato	tomatoes	

Fountas & Pinnell Word Study Lessons, Grade 3

WS 18 Three-Way Sort

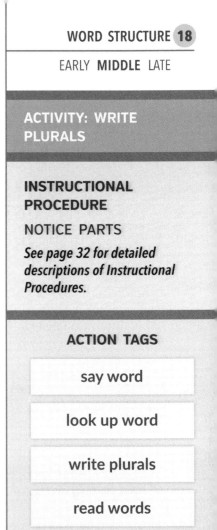

ACTIVITY: WRITE PLURALS

INSTRUCTIONAL PROCEDURE

NOTICE PARTS

See page 32 for detailed descriptions of Instructional Procedures.

ACTION TAGS

say word

look up word

write plurals

read words

Apply

- Distribute copies of the three-way sort and dictionaries. Remind students to say each word as they look carefully at the letters before looking up the word in the dictionary.

- If partners notice differences in spellings when they read and compare their lists, encourage them to look up the words again in the dictionary.

Share

Ask students to name the words that have only one plural form (*hero, potato, echo, torpedo, tomato*). Invite students to talk about what they have learned about forming plurals.

Assess

- Notice whether students, in their writing, are using conventional plural forms of nouns that end with *o*.

- Dictate five to seven words that end with *o*, and have students write the singular and plural forms.

- You may wish to use Word Structure Assessment E or K.

Word Structure: Recognize and Use Plurals That Add -es to Words That End with a Consonant and o

Connect Learning Across Contexts

Shared Reading Reread texts that the class has composed together. Have students use highlighter tape to identify words that end in a consonant and o. Use the opportunity to reinforce the principle.

Guided Reading During word work, ask students to write the plural form of several words that end in a consonant and the letter o. Have the group compare spellings and talk about the principle.

Independent Reading As you confer with an individual reader, notice any examples of words that end with o in the text. If examples appear, have the student locate the words and discuss the singular and plural forms.

Independent Writing While conferring with a writer, point out words within the writing that end with o. As needed, guide the student to recall and apply the principle.

Extend Learning

■ Have students play Follow the Path with singular and plural forms of nouns that are examples of the principle. Blank game boards are available in Online Resources.

■ Singular forms of nouns can be printed on each space of the game board. When a player lands on a space, she spells the plural form of the noun on a sheet of paper. Other players can check a dictionary, if needed, to confirm the spelling. If the player doesn't spell the plural correctly, she must go back to the space she was previously on. The first player to reach "finish" wins the game.

▶ Connect with Home

Ask students to work with a family member to find examples of words that end with o in the print around their home. Encourage students to share their findings during a group share.

Recognize and Use the Suffixes -*er* and -*est* to Show Comparison

Plan

▶ Consider Your Students

Use this lesson if your students are encountering comparative adjectives regularly in their reading and have begun to notice the ending forms. The principles in this lesson will also be useful to students who are exploring a greater variety of adjectives in their independent writing and are attempting to gain control of conventional spellings. The lesson incorporates changing the spelling of words that end in *y* or that end in a short vowel followed by a single consonant. When possible, use words that are part of students' oral vocabularies to help them understand the comparisons.

▶ Working with English Language Learners

Use pictures or concrete objects, and role play whenever possible to help English language learners understand the concept of comparison. Simple sentences that use comparative adjectives can help students understand the meanings of the words through context. During small-group work, have students use whiteboards to write the base words and suffixes; you can focus students' attention on how the words are constructed, as well as any changes in spelling.

UNDERSTAND THE PRINCIPLE

Understanding the role of affixes helps students analyze words. *Affixes* are groups of letters added to a base word or a word root to change its function or meaning. Affixes added to the end of base words or word roots are called *suffixes*. The suffix -*er* can be added to adjectives to compare two or more things, and the suffix -*est* can be added to adjectives to compare three or more things. Understanding how suffixes contribute to meaning helps students solve more complex words and expand their vocabulary with greater efficiency.

YOU WILL NEED

Online Resources
- ▶ **WS 19** Action Tags
- ▶ **WS 19** Word Cards
- ▶ **WS 19** Three-Way Sorts

Other Materials
- ▶ blank chart paper

Generative Lesson ✓

A generative lesson has a simple structure that you can use to present similar content or concepts. Use this lesson structure to present a variety of words with comparative endings.

EXPLAIN THE PRINCIPLE

Add the suffix -er to the end of a base word to show comparison between two things.

Add the suffix -est to the end of a base word to show comparison among three or more things.

Use the basic rules to spell words correctly when adding suffixes -er and -est.

 Comprehensive Phonics, Spelling, and Word Study Guide

Refer to: page **61**, row **53**

ACTIVITY: SUFFIXES -ER AND -EST CHART

INSTRUCTIONAL PROCEDURE

NOTICE PARTS

See page 32 for detailed descriptions of Instructional Procedures.

EXPLAIN THE PRINCIPLE

Add the suffix -er to the end of a base word to show comparison between two things.

Add the suffix -est to the end of a base word to show comparison among three or more things.

Use the basic rules to spell words correctly when adding suffixes -er and -est.

Comprehensive Phonics, Spelling, and Word Study Guide

Refer to: page **61**, row **53**

Teach

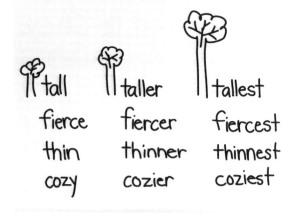

1. Tell students that they are going to work with word parts.

2. On chart paper, write the word *tall*, and draw a simple picture that represents the concept, such as a tree. Have students read the word with you. Draw another tree, taller than the first. *What would you say about this tree? •* *This tree is taller than the first tree.* Write the word *taller*, and have students read it with you. *What ending is added to* tall *to make* taller? • *The ending* -er *is added to* tall *to make* taller. Underline *-er*. Draw a third tree, taller than the other two. *This tree is tallest.* Write the word *tallest,* and have students read it with you. *What ending is added to* tall *to make* tallest? • *The ending* -est *is added to* tall *to make* tallest. Underline *-est*.

3. Tell students that the endings *-er* and *-est* are suffixes. *Tell what you know about suffixes. •* Build on students' responses to explain the concept. *A suffix is a word part that can be found at the end of many words. A suffix may change the meaning of a word. The suffixes* -er *and* -est *show how things compare.*

4. Using a sheet of paper, temporarily cover the word *tallest* and the drawing of the tallest tree. *How many trees did we compare with the word* taller? • *We compared two trees.* Remove the sheet of paper. *How many trees did we compare with the word* tallest? • *We compared three trees.*

5. State the principle simply. *Add* -er *to the end of a word when comparing two things. Add* -est *to the end of a word when comparing three or more things.*

6. Add the words *fierce, fiercer,* and *fiercest.* Have students read the words with you. *What do you notice about the words? •* If needed, prompt students to think about the spelling of the words. • *When a word ends with the letter* e, *you add only the letter* -r *to compare two things and only the letters* -st *to compare three things.*

7. Add the words *thin, thinner,* and *thinnest.* Have students read the words with you. *What do you notice? •* *When a word ends in a short vowel and a consonant, you double the final consonant before adding* -er *or* -est.

8. Add the words *cozy, cozier,* and *coziest.* Have students read the words with you. *What do you notice? •* *When a word ends in* y, *you change the* y *to* i *before adding* -er *or* -est.

9. Explain to students that they will be adding *-er* and *-est* to words. Students will take a word card, read it aloud, and write it in the first column of a three-way sort. They then write the word with the suffix *-er* in the second column and the word with the sufffix *-est* in the third column. Remind students that they will sometimes need to make a spelling change before adding each ending.

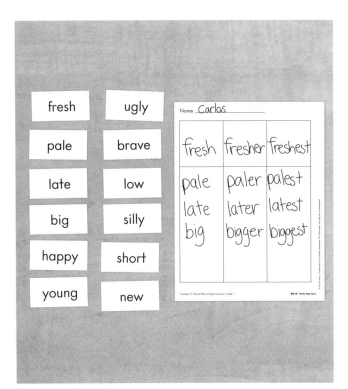

ACTIVITY: SUFFIXES *-ER* AND *-EST*

INSTRUCTIONAL PROCEDURE

NOTICE PARTS

See page 32 for detailed descriptions of Instructional Procedures.

ACTION TAGS

take card
read word
write word
add *-er*
add *-est*

Apply

- Distribute copies of the three-column sort and sets of word cards. Have students choose and add endings to at least twelve words.
- Encourage students to refer to the class chart to recall the spelling principles.

Share

Have students, in turn, share a set of words from their sheet. Ask them to tell what spelling change they made, if any, before adding the ending.

Assess

- Dictate eight to ten words (representing the different types of spelling changes), and ask students to add *-er* and *-est* to each word. Notice whether students are adding only *-r* and *-st,* doubling consonants, and changing *y* to *i* appropriately.
- You may wish to use Word Structure Assessment F or L.

Word Structure: Recognize and Use the Suffixes -er *and* -est *to Show Comparison*

Connect Learning Across Contexts

Shared Reading Enlarge or project poems that include adjectives with comparative endings. After reading and talking about the poems, have students use highlighter tape to identify the words with *-er* and *-est*. Ask students to describe any changes to the spelling of the base words.

Guided Reading During word work, display several adjectives, such as *blue, lazy, sweet,* and *big*. Ask students to explain how to change the spelling of each word, if at all, when adding *-er* and *-est*.

Shared Writing As you edit a piece of writing that the class has composed together, look for opportunities to include comparisons. Encourage students to suggest words that end with *-er* or *-est*. As you write, have students talk through any changes to the spelling of the base words.

Independent Writing Encourage students to include descriptions and comparisons in their writing. During conferences, prompt writers to use the class chart as a resource to remind them of the spelling principles.

Extend Learning

- Repeat the lesson with other adjectives. You may wish to expand the chart to include more examples of each type of spelling change.
- Have students sort the word cards into four groups according to the type of spelling change: 1) add *-er* or *-est* with no change to the base word; 2) add only *-r* or *-st* (because the base word ends with *e*); 3) double the final consonant before adding *-er* or *-est*; 4) change the *y* to *i* before adding *-er* or *-est*.

▶ Connect with Home

Send home the word cards. Encourage students to work with a family member to find objects around their home to compare using one or more of the words.

Recognize and Use the Suffixes *-er, -or, -ar,* and *-ist* to Form a Noun

Plan

▶ Consider Your Students

This lesson will be most effective if students have already worked with adding other suffixes, including those that require a spelling change to the base word. Students will also need to be familiar with the concepts of nouns and verbs in order to understand how the suffixes change the meaning and function of the base words. This lesson focuses on all four endings (*-er, -or, -ar,* and *-ist*) and the related spelling changes. Depending on your students' level of experience with suffixes, you may wish to focus on just one or two endings at a time, or you may wish to teach the basic principles in the initial lesson and then later teach the various spelling rules.

▶ Working with English Language Learners

English language learners may have difficulty understanding that not only does a word's spelling (and pronunciation) change when you add the suffixes *-er, -or, -ar,* and *-ist,* but the part of speech and the meaning change as well. Use words in sentences to provide context for the change in meaning and function. It may also be helpful to put an article (such as *the* or *a*) in front of the word to signal that it is now a noun. To draw students' attention to the added endings, have students highlight the suffixes or use letter cards or magnetic letters to build the words.

UNDERSTAND THE PRINCIPLE

Understanding the role of affixes helps students analyze words. *Affixes* are groups of letters added to a base word or a word root to change its function or meaning. Affixes added to the end of base words or word roots are called *suffixes.* The suffixes *-er, -or, -ar,* and *-ist* can be added to base words to create nouns that name a person or thing that does something. Understanding how suffixes contribute to meaning helps students solve more complex words and expand their vocabulary with greater efficiency.

YOU WILL NEED

Online Resources
- ▶ **WS 20** Action Tags
- ▶ **WS 20** Word Cards
- ▶ **WS 20** List Sheets

Other Materials
- ▶ blank chart paper
- ▶ magnetic letters

Generative Lesson ✓

A generative lesson has a simple structure that you can use to present similar content or concepts. Use this lesson structure to teach students to recognize and add a variety of suffixes to words.

EXPLAIN THE PRINCIPLE

Add the suffixes -er, -or, -ar, *or* -ist *to the end of a base word to name a person or thing that does something.*

Use the basic rules to spell words correctly when adding the suffixes -er, -or, -ar, *and* -ist.

Sometimes the suffixes -er, -or, -ar, *and* -ist *require the use of additional spelling rules:*

- *For words that end with a hard c, add k before adding* -er.

- *For some words that end with a consonant and y, drop the y and add* -ist.

- *For some words that end with an o, drop the o and add* -ist.

Comprehensive Phonics, Spelling, and Word Study Guide

Refer to: page **65**, row **65**

ACTIVITY: WORD PAIRS

INSTRUCTIONAL PROCEDURE

NOTICE PARTS

See page 32 for detailed descriptions of Instructional Procedures.

EXPLAIN THE PRINCIPLE

Add the suffixes -er, -or, -ar, or -ist to the end of a base word to name a person or thing that does something.

Use the basic rules to spell words correctly when adding the suffixes -er, -or, -ar, and -ist.

Sometimes the suffixes -er, -or, -ar, and -ist require the use of additional spelling rules:

* *For words that end with a hard c, add k before adding -er.*

* *For some words that end with a consonant and y, drop the y and add -ist.*

* *For some words that end with an o, drop the o and add -ist.*

Comprehensive Phonics, Spelling, and Word Study Guide

Refer to: page **65**, row **65**

Teach

1. Tell students that they are going to learn more about word parts.

2. On chart paper, write the words *help, visit, beg,* and *art* in a column to the left, and the words *helper, visitor, beggar,* and *artist* in a column to the right. Have students read the words aloud with you and invite students to use each word in a sentence. Provide a sentence if the class struggles with the meaning.

help	helper
visit	visitor
beg	beggar
art	artist

3. *What do you notice about the meaning of all of the words in the second column?* • Some student responses might be:

   "All of the words are nouns."

   "The words are all about something or someone who does something."

   "The meaning is different from the first word."

   What do you notice about each word part that was added to each word on the left? • Underline each suffix if needed. *How did the spelling change when the suffix was added?*

4. Continue to add words that reflect the principle and the spelling rules you wish to teach in the lesson. Give students the opportunity to make observations and to use words in context before reinforcing the principle and the spelling rules, including two additional spelling rules below:

   ■ *When a word ends with the letter* e, *you add only the letter -r to name a person or thing that does something: e.g.,* dive, diver.

   ■ *When a word ends in a short vowel and a consonant, you need to double the final consonant before adding the ending: e.g.,* drum, drummer.

5. Explain to students that they are going to make twenty words that name a person or thing that does something. They will take a word card, make the word with magnetic letters, and add the suffix *-er, -or, -ar,* or *-ist.* Point out that they will sometimes need to change the spelling of the base word. They then write each word on a list sheet.

ACTIVITY: WORD LIST

INSTRUCTIONAL PROCEDURE

MAKE WORDS

See page 32 for detailed descriptions of Instructional Procedures.

ACTION TAGS

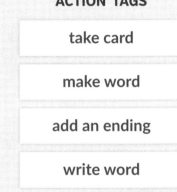

take card

make word

add an ending

write word

Apply

- Distribute the word cards, magnetic letters, and list sheets. Remind students to make and write twenty words.
- Prompt students to refer to the class chart or a dictionary, as needed, to confirm spellings.

Share

Have students read their lists to a partner. Then encourage students to share what they have learned about forming words that name a person or thing that does something.

Assess

- Dictate seven to ten words, some of which require a spelling change when the suffix is added, to assess students' control of the principle.
- You may wish to use Word Structure Assessment F or L.

Word Structure: Recognize and Use the Suffixes -er, -or, -ar, *and* -ist *to Form a Noun*

Connect Learning Across Contexts

Guided Reading During word work, write four to five words that have the suffixes -*er*, -*or*, -*ar*, and -*ist*. Have students read the words and then identify the base words and any spelling changes that occurred.

Independent Reading During conferences, draw readers' attention to words in the text that name a person or thing that does something. Guide them to talk about the structure of the words.

Shared Writing When writing a word that names a person or thing that does something, invite students to identify the suffix and to describe any necessary change to the spelling of the base word.

Independent Writing When students attempt to write a word with the suffix -*er*, -*or*, -*ar*, or -*ist*, demonstrate how to change the spelling of the base word, if needed.

Extend Learning

Repeat the lesson with additional words that include the suffixes -*er*, -*or*, -*ar*, and -*ist*. You may wish to create an expanded summary chart that groups words by suffix and spelling rule.

▶ Connect with Home

Send home word cards and a set of letter cards. (Printable lowercase letters are available in Online Resources.) Have students use the letter cards to make the words and add the correct suffix to name a person or thing that does something. Invite them to read the words to a family member.

Recognize and Use the Prefix *re-*, Meaning "again"

Plan

▶ Consider Your Students

Use this lesson after students have noticed words with prefixes in texts they are reading and have begun to use prefixes in their own writing. If students have significant experience with the prefix *re-* and have control of the concept, you may wish to expand this lesson by discussing a few word histories and word relationships in greater depth, such as the relationship between *remember* and *memory* connected to the word root *-mem-*. As students begin to attempt deeper word analysis, it is important to point out that it is not always easy to tell whether a particular group of letters is really a prefix. For example, the *re* in *react* is a prefix, but the *re* in *read* is not. The analysis of word structure needs to be used flexibly and in combination with other word-solving actions.

▶ Working with English Language Learners

The concept that many English words are made up of more than one meaning-bearing part is essential for English language learners to understand. To illustrate this concept, you may find it helpful to have students work in a small group to put together and break apart word cards containing base words and the prefix *re-*. Be sure that students know the meanings of the base words used in the lesson and on the game board.

UNDERSTAND THE PRINCIPLE

Many English words can be divided into parts: base words, roots, and affixes. A *base word* is a word in its simplest form, which can be modified by adding affixes (e.g., *harm, act*). A *word root* is a word part, often from Greek or Latin, that carries the essential meaning of and is the basis for an English word (e.g., *-gen-, -ject-, -prim-*). *Affixes* are groups of letters added to a base word or a word root to change its function or meaning. Affixes added to the beginning of base words or word roots are called *prefixes.* A prefix adds to or changes the meaning of a base word or word root. A prefix may have more than one meaning. Understanding how prefixes contribute to meaning helps students solve more complex words and expand their vocabulary with greater efficiency.

YOU WILL NEED

PWS **Ready Resources**
- ▶ **WS 21** Pocket-Chart Cards

Online Resources
- ▶ **WS 21** Action Tags
- ▶ **WS 21** Follow the Path Game Board
- ▶ **WS 21** Directions for Follow the Path

Other Materials
- ▶ pocket chart

Generative Lesson

A generative lesson has a simple structure that you can use to present similar content or concepts. Use this lesson structure to teach students to recognize a variety of words with the prefix *re-*.

EXPLAIN THE PRINCIPLE

Add the prefix re- *to the beginning of a word root or base word to mean "again."*

Comprehensive Phonics, Spelling, and Word Study Guide

Refer to: page **67**, row **75**

ACTIVITY: POCKET-CHART CARDS

INSTRUCTIONAL PROCEDURE

NOTICE PARTS

See page 32 for detailed descriptions of Instructional Procedures.

EXPLAIN THE PRINCIPLE

Add the prefix re- to the beginning of a word root or base word to mean "again."

Comprehensive Phonics, Spelling, and Word Study Guide

Refer to: page **67**, row **75**

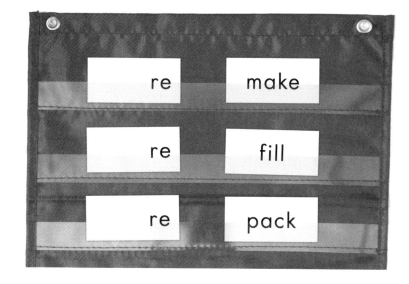

Teach

1. Tell students that they are going to notice more about word parts.

2. Using the *re* cards and base word cards, make the following words in the pocket chart: *remake, refill, repack.* Read the words with students.

3. *What do you notice about all of the words?* • *Each word begins with the prefix re-. Tell what you know about prefixes.* • *A prefix is a word part that can be found at the beginning of many words. A prefix changes the meaning of a word.*

4. Ask students to explain the meaning of each word. *What do you notice?* • *In each word, the prefix* re- *means "again": to make again, to fill again, to pack again.*

5. Remove the *re* cards, leaving just the base words. *What do you notice?* • *When the prefix is removed, the words are still complete and meaningful.* Replace the *re* cards.

6. Invite students to name other words with the prefix *re-.* You may wish to use blank pocket-chart cards to add new words that illustrate the principle, such as *replay, resale,* and *reuse.*

7. Students are also likely to name words that do not fit the principle, including words in which the letters *re* are not a prefix, e.g., *reason;* words in which the prefix *re-* means "back," e.g., *repay* and *recall;* and words in which the prefix *re-* is attached to a word root with an unfamiliar meaning, e.g., *remember* ("to call back to mind," *-member* being related to *memory*) or *repair* ("to make good again by fixing," *-pair* originating from a Latin word that means to "make ready"). Use the opportunity to build excitement for word study. Explain that words are often related in fascinating and unexpected ways. Encourage students to use a dictionary to investigate word histories and relationships.

8. Tell students that they are going to play Follow the Path. Taking turns, students toss a die, move that number of spaces, read aloud the word in the new space, and use the word in a sentence. They go back to the space they were on if they can't read the word correctly and use it in a sentence. The first player to reach "finish" wins the game.

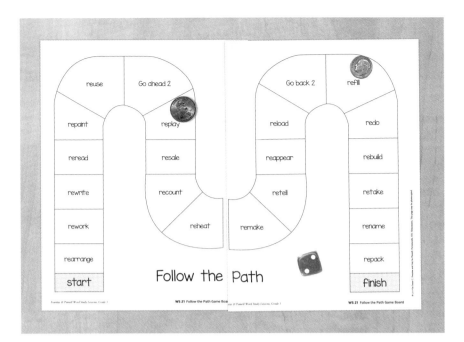

ACTIVITY: FOLLOW THE PATH

INSTRUCTIONAL PROCEDURE

NOTICE PARTS

See page 32 for detailed descriptions of Instructional Procedures.

ACTION TAGS

> toss die

> move

> read word

> use in a sentence

Apply

- Have students play Follow the Path in pairs or groups of three using a game board, a game die, and game pieces to mark their places on the board.
- If needed, point out and explain the spaces labeled "Go ahead 2" and "Go back 2."

Share

Have students share words that they read on the game board and use them in sentences. You may wish to add a few new words to the class chart.

Assess

- As you observe students reading, notice how efficient they are in recognizing and solving words that have the prefix *re-*.
- You may wish to use Word Structure Assessment G or M.

Word Structure: Recognize and Use the Prefix re-, *Meaning "again"*

Connect Learning Across Contexts

Shared Reading After rereading a text, draw students' attention to words featuring the prefix *re-*. Discuss the meanings of the words with and without the prefix.

Guided Reading Guide students to identify the base word and the prefix when they are attempting to solve unknown words with the prefix *re-*.

Shared Writing As you construct pieces of writing, point out words with the prefix *re-*. Encourage students to talk about how the prefix changes the meanings of the words. You may wish to add new words to the class chart.

Independent Writing During conferences, draw writers' attention to their use of words with the prefix *re-*. Discuss the meanings of the words with students, and encourage them to talk about why they chose the words.

Extend Learning

■ Encourage students to be a "word detective" and research the history of a word with the prefix *re-*, such as *remember, repair,* or *report*. You may wish to have students compare multiple sources, including at least one print dictionary and one online dictionary or related website. Students may also wish to create a list or web of related words. They can record their findings in their word study notebook.

■ Distribute blank Follow the Path game boards (found in Online Resources), and have students work together to create boards with new sets of words with the prefix *re-*. Make the additional boards available for students to choose when playing the game.

▷ **Connect with Home**

Send Follow the Path game boards home so that students can play the game with family members.

Recognize and Use the Prefixes That Mean "not"

Plan

▶ Consider Your Students

Use this lesson after students have noticed words with prefixes in texts they are reading and have begun to use prefixes in their own writing. If the students do not have much experience recognizing prefixes, you may wish to focus on only one or two prefixes at a time. The summary chart can be created over several lessons.

▶ Working with English Language Learners

The concept that many English words are made up of more than one meaning-bearing part is essential for English language learners to understand. To illustrate this concept, you may find it helpful to have students work in a small group to put together and break apart word cards containing base words and the prefixes *un-*, *in-*, *dis-*, and *non-*. Be sure that students know the meanings of the base words used in the lesson and in the sort.

UNDERSTAND THE PRINCIPLE

Many English words can be divided into parts: base words, roots, and affixes. A *base word* is a word in its simplest form, which can be modified by adding affixes (e.g., *harm*, *act*). A *word root* is a word part, often from Greek or Latin, that carries the essential meaning of and is the basis for an English word (e.g., *-gen-*, *-ject-*, *-prim-*). *Affixes* are groups of letters added to a base word or a word root to change its function or meaning. Affixes added to the beginning of base words or word roots are called *prefixes*. A prefix adds to or changes the meaning of a base word or word root. A prefix may have more than one meaning. Understanding how prefixes contribute to meaning helps students solve more complex words and expand their vocabulary with greater efficiency.

YOU WILL NEED

Online Resources
- ▶ **WS 22** Action Tags
- ▶ **WS 22** Word Cards
- ▶ **WS 22** Four-Way Sorts

Other Materials
- ▶ blank chart paper

Generative Lesson ✓

A generative lesson has a simple structure that you can use to present similar content or concepts. Use this lesson structure to teach students to recognize a variety of words with the prefixes *un-*, *in-*, *dis-*, and *non-*.

EXPLAIN THE PRINCIPLE

Add the prefix un- *to the beginning of a word root or base word to mean "not" or "opposite of."*

Add the prefix in- *to the beginning of a word root or base word to mean "not."*

Add the prefix dis- *or* non- *to the beginning of a word root or base word to mean "not," "lack of," or "opposite of."*

Comprehensive Phonics, Spelling, and Word Study Guide

Refer to: page **67**, row **76**

ACTIVITY: SUMMARY CHART

INSTRUCTIONAL PROCEDURE

NOTICE PARTS

See page 32 for detailed descriptions of Instructional Procedures.

EXPLAIN THE PRINCIPLE

Add the prefix un- *to the beginning of a word root or base word to mean "not" or "opposite of."*

Add the prefix in- *to the beginning of a word root or base word to mean "not."*

Add the prefix dis- *or* non- *to the beginning of a word root or base word to mean "not," "lack of," or "opposite of."*

Comprehensive Phonics, Spelling, and Word Study Guide

Refer to: page **67**, row **76**

Prefixes That Mean "Not"

un- "not" "opposite of"	in- "not"
unhappy unfair	incomplete independent
dis- "not" "lack of" "opposite of"	non- "not" "lack of" "opposite of"
dislike displease	nonfiction nonstop

Teach

1. Tell students that today they are going to learn more about word parts.

2. Divide a sheet of chart paper into four parts. In the first part, write the words *happy* and *fair*, leaving space before the words to add a prefix and space above the words to add a heading. *What do each of these words mean?* • Write the prefix *un-* before both of the words to make *unhappy* and *unfair*. *What do you notice about these words?* • *How does the prefix change the meaning?* • Point out the prefix *un-* if needed. *In* happy *and* fair, *the prefix* un- *means "not" or "opposite of." The meaning changes from happy to not happy and from fair to not fair.* Write *un-* and "not" or "opposite of" as a heading.

3. Repeat the process for the prefixes *in-*, *dis-*, and *non-*, filling in the other three sections of the chart.

4. Ask students to reread the words in each section, and then reinforce the principle. *Add the prefix* un- *to the beginning of a word root or base word to mean "not" or "opposite of." Add the prefix* in- *to the beginning of a word root or base word to mean "not." Add the prefix* dis- *or* non- *to the beginning of a word root or base word to mean "not," "lack of," or "opposite of."* You may wish to add a heading for the entire chart.

5. Tell students that they are going to say and sort words by prefixes. After they complete the sort, students read each group of words to a partner. Students then choose a word with each prefix and write a sentence for each word on a four-way sort.

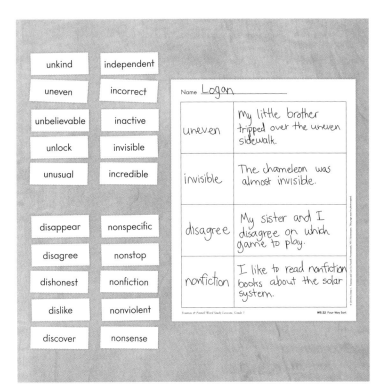

unkind	independent
uneven	incorrect
unbelievable	inactive
unlock	invisible
unusual	incredible
disappear	nonspecific
disagree	nonstop
dishonest	nonfiction
dislike	nonviolent
discover	nonsense

Name Logan

uneven	My little brother tripped over the uneven sidewalk.
invisible	The chameleon was almost invisible.
disagree	My sister and I disagree on which game to play.
nonfiction	I like to read nonfiction books about the solar system.

ACTIVITY: WORD SORT

INSTRUCTIONAL PROCEDURE

SAY AND SORT

See page 32 for detailed descriptions of Instructional Procedures.

ACTION TAGS

say words

sort words

read words

choose words

write sentences

Apply

- Remind students to read the words they have sorted to a partner. Encourage partners to discuss the meanings of words and to consult a dictionary if a word is unfamiliar or if its meaning is unclear.

- To give students room to write their sentences, have them turn the four-way sort sideways to create four rows. They write the words they choose along the side and write a sentence in each row. Students may wish to illustrate their sentences as well.

Share

Invite students to share the words they chose and to read their sentences. You may wish to add a few new words to the class chart.

Assess

- As you observe students reading, notice how efficient they are in recognizing and solving words that have the prefixes *un-*, *in-*, *dis-*, and *non-*.

- You may wish to use Word Structure Assessment G or M.

Word Structure: Recognize and Use the Prefixes That Mean "not"

Connect Learning Across Contexts

Guided Reading Guide students to identify the base word and the prefix when they are attempting to solve unknown words with the prefixes *un-*, *in-*, *dis-*, and *non-*.

Independent Reading As you confer with individual readers, notice words with the prefixes *un-*, *in-*, *dis-*, and *non-* in the text. Ask the student to identify the words and describe their meanings. Use the opportunity to prompt the reader to recall and apply the principle.

Shared Writing As you construct pieces of writing, point out words with the prefixes *un-*, *in-*, *dis-*, and *non-*. Encourage students to talk about how each prefix changes the meanings of the words. You may wish to add new words to the class chart.

Independent Writing During conferences, draw writers' attention to their use of words with the prefixes *un-*, *in-*, *dis-*, and *non-*. Discuss the meanings of the words with students, and encourage them to talk about why they chose the words.

Extend Learning

- Encourage students to begin (or continue to add to) a list of prefixes in their word study notebook. For each prefix, they can record example words and sentences that they encounter in their reading.
- Distribute blank game cards (found in Online Resources), and have students work together to create a deck of words with the prefixes *un-*, *in-*, *dis-*, and *non-*. Students can use the game cards to play Concentration.

▶ Connect with Home

Send sets of word cards home for students to say and sort with family members.

Word-Solving Actions

Word-solving actions are the strategic moves readers and writers make when they use their knowledge of the language system to solve words. These strategies are "in-the-head" actions that are invisible, although we can infer them from some overt or observable behavior. The principles listed in this section represent students' ability to use the principles in all previous sections of the *The Fountas & Pinnell Literacy Continuum*.

Classroom lessons developed around these principles should provide opportunities for students to apply concepts in active ways–for example, through sorting, building, locating, reading, or writing. Lessons related to word-solving actions demonstrate to students how they can problem-solve by working on words in isolation or while reading or writing continuous text. The more students can integrate these strategies into their reading and writing systems, the more flexible they will become in solving words. The reader/writer may use knowledge of letter-sound relationships, for example, either to solve an unfamiliar word or to check that the reading is accurate. Rapid, automatic word solving is a basic component of fluency and important for comprehension because it frees students' attention to focus on the meaning and language of the text.

Connect to Assessment

See related (optional) WSA Assessment tasks in Online Resources.

- Assessment A: Recognizing and Using Onsets and Rimes
- Assessment B: Sorting Words
- Assessment C: Recognizing and Using Word Parts to Solve Words and Monitor Reading
- Assessment D: Using Sound and Letter Sequence to Read and Spell Unknown Words
- Assessment E: Individual Record (Reading)
- Assessment F: Individual Record (Word Solving Actions)

Develop Your Professional Understanding

See *The Fountas & Pinnell Comprehensive Phonics, Spelling, and Word Study Guide*. 2017. Portsmouth, New Hampshire: Heinemann. Related pages: 2-12, 76-83.

See *The Fountas & Pinnell Literacy Continuum: A Tool for Assessment, Planning, and Teaching*. 2017. Portsmouth, New Hampshire: Heinemann. Related pages: 357-397.

See *Word Matters: Teaching Phonics and Spelling in the Reading/ Writing Classroom* by G.S. Pinnell and I.C. Fountas. 1998. Portsmouth, New Hampshire: Heinemann. Related pages: 46–47, 63–64, 90–93, 95, 222–228, 237–244.

v | a | n | d | e

| | | |

o | r | o | b | a

wander

probably

Recognize and Use Onsets and Rimes to Read Words

Plan

▶ Consider Your Students

This lesson draws students' attention to the structure of words, both by saying them and by noticing the letters that represent the sounds in certain parts of words. Even though students will already be able to identify initial letter clusters and word endings, they still need continued practice using these elements in flexible ways to solve words. It is not necessary to use the technical words *onset* and *rime*; rather, you will want students to be able to recognize and talk about the first and last part of a word.

▶ Working with English Language Learners

Developing the ability to take words apart to solve them gives English language learners power over words and helps them notice the details of written language. If necessary, have students work with magnetic letters so they will see explicitly how letter clusters work. You may want to repeat this lesson for your English language learners using different examples.

UNDERSTAND THE PRINCIPLE

In a one-syllable word, the *onset* is the consonant letter or letters that come before the vowel. The *rime* is the vowel and all of the letters that come after it. Noticing onsets and rimes helps students break words apart and think about the sounds of vowels and various letter sequences. Working with word parts (such as onsets and rimes) in a flexible way helps students build the automatic word-solving skills that they need to use when reading.

YOU WILL NEED

Online Resources
- ▶ **WSA 1** Action Tags
- ▶ **WSA 1** Word Grids
- ▶ **WSA 1** Game Dice
- ▶ **WSA 1** Directions for Word Grids

Other Materials
- ▶ magnetic letters
- ▶ magnetic whiteboard
- ▶ marker for whiteboard

Generative Lesson
A generative lesson has a simple structure that you can use to present similar content or concepts. Use this lesson structure to teach students a variety of onsets and rimes.

EXPLAIN THE PRINCIPLE

Look at the first part and the last part of a word to read the word.

Use parts of words you know to read an unknown word.

Comprehensive Phonics, Spelling, and Word Study Guide

Refer to: page **78**, row **19**

ACTIVITY: WORD PARTS

**INSTRUCTIONAL
PROCEDURE**

NOTICE PARTS

*See page 32 for detailed
descriptions of Instructional
Procedures.*

EXPLAIN THE PRINCIPLE

*Look at the first part and the last
part of a word to read the word.*

*Use parts of words you know to
read an unknown word.*

**Comprehensive
Phonics, Spelling,
and Word Study
Guide**

Refer to:
page **78**, row **19**

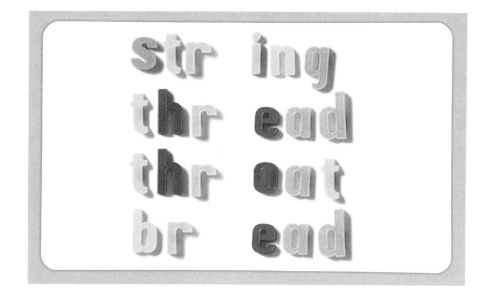

Teach

1. Make *string* with magnetic letters on a magnetic surface. Listen to this word: *string*. Move the letters to create a space between the onset *str* and the rime *ing*. *What is the first part of this word?* ● Students may say *s*, *t*, or *str*. *String begins with a consonant cluster. Remember that consonant clusters can have two or three letters. When you have a consonant cluster like* str *at the beginning of the word, the group of consonant letters is the first part of the word. So the first part of* string *is* str.

2. *What is the last part of the word?* ● *The letters* ing, *which stand for /ĭ/ /ng/, is the last part. The last part of a word starts with a vowel and includes all of the letters after it.*

3. Demonstrate the same concept by making the words *thread, throat, bread*. *Which two words start the same way?* ● Thread *and* throat *both start with* thr. *Which two words end the same way?* ● Thread *and* bread *both end with* ead.

4. Write the consonant cluster *scr*, and challenge students to suggest words that begin with this part. Write the words they suggest, and read each one as a group. Repeat for the ending *ow*.

5. Have students summarize how they used word parts to think about and read new words. Restate the principle to synthesize their thinking: *Look at the first and last part of a word to read it. Use parts of words you know to read an unknown word.*

6. Tell students they will play a game called Word Grid, looking for different word parts shown on a die. They will look for beginning letter clusters or word endings. The word part will always have more than one letter.

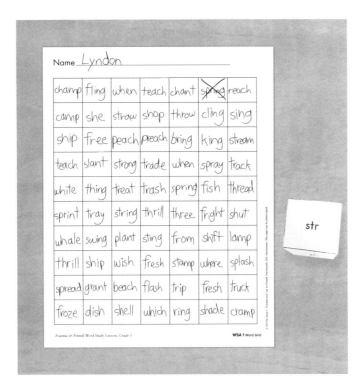

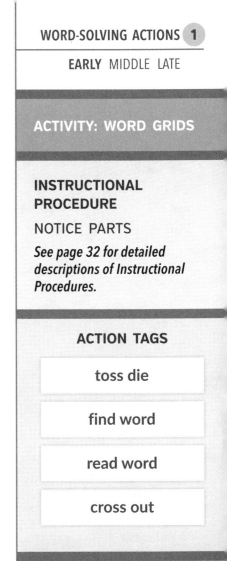

INSTRUCTIONAL PROCEDURE

NOTICE PARTS

See page 32 for detailed descriptions of Instructional Procedures.

ACTION TAGS

| toss die |
| find word |
| read word |
| cross out |

Apply

Give each player a word grid. Each group has a pair of dice, which players use one at a time. Taking turns, each player tosses a die, looks for a word on the grid that has the same letter cluster or ending, says the word, and crosses it out. After each player has tossed the first die, players switch to the second die and toss again. Players continue to switch the dice back and forth. The first player to cross out all words wins the game.

Share

- Ask students to read their grids to a partner. Invite them to record some interesting words in their word study notebooks or on a sheet of paper.
- Review the principle, and remind students to recognize and use onsets and rimes when they read and write.

Assess

- Notice students' abilities to take words apart while reading text.
- Show students a list of four or five new words, and observe students' ability to separate the words into onsets and rimes and then to read the words.
- You may wish to use Word-Solving Actions Assessment A, B, C, E, or F.

Connect Learning Across Contexts

Interactive Read-Aloud After you reread a book aloud, select one or two new or more challenging one-syllable words and quickly write them on the whiteboard. Have students tell how to separate each one into onset and rime and then blend the parts to read the words.

> IRA *Puss in Boots* by Jerry Pinkney

> IRA *Sky Sisters* by Jan Bourdeau Waboose

Shared Reading You may wish to use the following Shared Reading title from *Fountas & Pinnell Classroom™* to point out onsets and rimes.

> SR *From Beans to Chocolate* by June Schwartz

Shared Writing Prompt students to break words into parts so that they can spell the words.

Independent Writing When conferring with students, guide students to separate one-syllable words into onsets and rimes to help them spell them with greater accuracy.

Extend Learning

Repeat this lesson, using a different grid and set of dice to focus on other word parts: e.g., *-and, -end, -eam, cr-, ser-*.

▶ Connect with Home

Send home a word grid and dice. Have students set a timer for five minutes and go through the card, crossing out matches on the word grid.

Recognize and Use Onsets and Rimes to Read Words

Plan

▶ Consider Your Students

Throughout word study lessons and applications, as well as across reading and writing activities, students have learned to make connections between words. Use this lesson when students have had plenty of practice connecting words that start the same or end the same. In this lesson, they will make both of these kinds of connections. You can adjust the difficulty by focusing on word beginnings only or word endings only.

▶ Working with English Language Learners

English language learners will benefit from learning to connect words. These actions help them build categories for word patterns and letter clusters rather than trying to learn words in isolation. Use words that students understand and, for the most part, can read. The important learning here is to make the connections quickly, not necessarily to learn new words.

UNDERSTAND THE PRINCIPLE

In a one-syllable word, the *onset* is the consonant letter or letters that come before the vowel. The *rime* is the vowel and all of the letters that come after it. Noticing onsets and rimes helps students break words apart and think about the sounds represented by vowels and by various letter sequences. Working with word parts (such as onsets and rimes) in a flexible way helps students build the automatic word-solving skills that they need to use when reading.

YOU WILL NEED

PWS Ready Resources
- ▶ WSA 2 Pocket-Chart Cards

Online Resources
- ▶ WSA 2 Action Tags
- ▶ WSA 2 Word Cards

Other Materials
- ▶ chart paper

Generative Lesson
A generative lesson has a simple structure that you can use to present similar content or concepts. Use this lesson structure to teach students a variety of onsets and rimes.

EXPLAIN THE PRINCIPLE

Look at the first part and the last part of a word to read the word.

Use parts of words you know to read an unknown word.

Comprehensive Phonics, Spelling, and Word Study Guide

Refer to:
page **78**, row **19**

ACTIVITY: WORD PARTS

INSTRUCTIONAL PROCEDURE

NOTICE PARTS

See page 32 for detailed descriptions of Instructional Procedures.

EXPLAIN THE PRINCIPLE

Look at the first part and the last part of a word to read the word.

Use parts of words you know to read an unknown word.

Comprehensive Phonics, Spelling, and Word Study Guide

Refer to:
page **78**, row **19**

three

small

plant

slam

Teach

1. Write the words *three, small, plant,* and *slam* on chart paper.

2. Hold up a pocket-chart card with *-ant* written on it. *Does anyone see a word on the chart that has this word part?* ● Plant *ends with* -ant. Have a volunteer underline the part.

3. Discuss the first part of the word, *pl-. We can put the beginning sounds, /pl/, together with the ending sounds, /ant/, to read the word* plant.

4. Invite students to name other words that start or end like *plant.*

5. Repeat with parts *thr-, -all,* and *sl-.* Each time, have students underline the part, identify the other part, and then read the whole word.

6. Have students summarize how they used word parts to think about and read words. Restate the principle to synthesize their thinking: *Look at the first and last part of a word to read it. Use parts of words you know to read an unknown word.*

7. Tell students that today they are going to sort words by the first part and then read the words in each pile. Then they will sort the words by their last part and read the words in each pile.

stop
chop
shop

brick
bring
bright

chop
chip
chick

INSTRUCTIONAL PROCEDURE

NOTICE PARTS

See page 32 for detailed descriptions of Instructional Procedures.

ACTION TAGS

sort by first part
read
sort by last part
read

Apply

Have students sort the words by first part and then read the words in each pile to a partner. Then have students sort the words by last part and read the words in each pile to a partner.

Share

- Invite students to name more words that start or end the same as the words in their piles.
- Review the principle, and remind students to use word parts to read unfamiliar words they encounter when they read.

Assess

- Notice students' ability to take words apart while reading text. Observe their speed and success.
- Observe how students approach writing or reading unfamiliar words. Are they able to use onsets and rimes to help them spell and decode?
- You may wish to use Word-Solving Actions Assessment A, B, C, E, or F.

Connect Learning Across Contexts

Shared Reading You may wish to use the following Shared Reading title from *Fountas & Pinnell Classroom*™ to point out onsets and rimes.

> SR *From Buds to Bananas* by Betty Riggs

Guided Reading When students encounter an unfamiliar word, remind them to make connections with known words using prompts such as: *Do you see a part you know? Do you know a word like that? The last part of the word is like* _____.

Shared Writing Prompt students to break words into parts so that they can spell them.

Independent Writing Have students use known words as resources for writing new words. Encourage them to use word study charts as a resource.

Extend Learning

Repeat this lesson, using a different set of words for students to sort.

▶ Connect with Home

Send home word cards and have students sort them by onset and rime with a family member.

Recognize and Use Onsets and Rimes to Read Words

Plan

▶ Consider Your Students

Before using this lesson, be sure that students have had experience connecting words and noticing patterns and parts. They should have knowledge of many phonogram patterns and be able to connect words by their beginning and ending parts. If the words provided for this are not appropriate (too easy or too challenging), use any list of words that is suitable.

▶ Working with English Language Learners

Learning to connect words will help English language learners build categories for word patterns and letter clusters rather than trying to learn words in isolation. Be sure to use words with which students are familiar. The important learning here is to make the connections quickly, not necessarily to learn new words.

YOU WILL NEED

Online Resources
- ▶ **WSA 3** Action Tags
- ▶ **WSA 3** Follow the Path Game Boards
- ▶ **WSA 3** Game Die
- ▶ **WSA 3** Directions for Follow the Path

Other Materials
- ▶ chart paper
- ▶ game markers

Generative Lesson

A generative lesson has a simple structure that you can use to present similar content or concepts. Use this lesson structure to teach students a variety of onsets and rimes.

UNDERSTAND THE PRINCIPLE

In a one-syllable word, the *onset* is the consonant letter or letters that come before the vowel. The *rime* is the vowel and all of the letters that come after it. Noticing onsets and rimes helps students break words apart and think about the sounds represented by vowels and by various letter sequences. Working with word parts (such as onsets and rimes) in a flexible way helps students build the automatic word-solving skills they need to use when reading. In this lesson, students apply what they have learned about word beginnings and endings to solve new words.

EXPLAIN THE PRINCIPLE

Look at the first part and the last part of a word to read the word.

Use parts of words you know to read an unknown word.

Comprehensive Phonics, Spelling, and Word Study Guide

Refer to: page **78**, row **19**

ACTIVITY: WORD PARTS

INSTRUCTIONAL PROCEDURE

NOTICE PARTS

See page 32 for detailed descriptions of Instructional Procedures.

EXPLAIN THE PRINCIPLE

Look at the first part and the last part of a word to read the word.

Use parts of words you know to read an unknown word.

Comprehensive Phonics, Spelling, and Word Study Guide

Refer to: page **78**, row **19**

fr	ame	=	frame
fr	iend	=	friend
st	ir	=	stir
sm	ooth	=	smooth
sh	eep	=	sheep
wh	ich	=	which

Teach

1. Write *fr* on chart paper and tell students that it is the first part of a word. Then add *ame* and tell students that it is the last part of the word. *What is the whole word?*

2. Repeat the process with *friend, stir, smooth, sheep, which,* and any other words that you wish to use.

3. Have students name five or six other words that begin or end like the words already on the chart. Invite volunteers to take turns underlining either the beginning or ending part of the word. Ask students to refrain from saying the word until after they have underlined the part. Then the whole group can be invited to say the word.

4. You may wish to continue the lesson with words containing the parts *thr-, -all,* and *sl-*. Each time, have students underline the part, identify the other part, and then read the whole word.

5. Tell students that they will play Follow the Path. Players will think about the beginnings and endings of words to quickly read whole words.

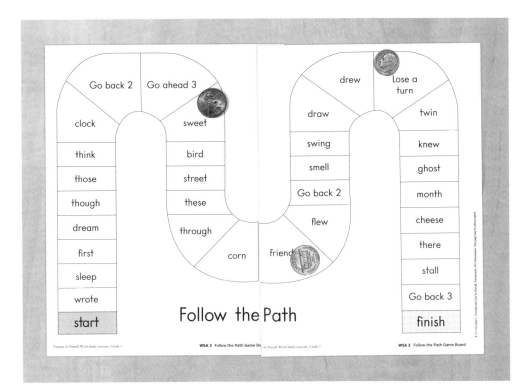

INSTRUCTIONAL PROCEDURE

NOTICE PARTS

See page 32 for detailed descriptions of Instructional Procedures.

ACTION TAGS

throw die

move marker

read word

tell part

Apply

Have students play Follow the Path in groups of two to four. Players take turns tossing a die and moving the number of spaces shown (you may wish to use the provided die in Online Resources, or you can use your own). The player reads the word in the space and identifies two parts that help him read it. If a player cannot read the word or identify two parts, he passes, and another player gives the answer. If no one in the group can read and/or break apart the word, one student writes it on a card and brings it to group share to ask for help from the whole group. The first player to reach the end wins the game.

Share

Point to a few words from the game, and have students read them and tell the beginning or ending part. Guide students to identify word parts that appear in many words and to talk about how knowing word parts helps them read words. They can bring to the group's attention any words they found tricky.

Assess

■ Ask students to read four or five words that you know will be new to them. After reading, have them highlight a part that was helpful. Notice whether they are attempting to use word parts even if they do not read the word accurately.

■ Observe how students approach writing or reading unfamiliar words. Are they able to use onsets and rimes to help them spell and decode?

■ You may wish to use Word-Solving Actions Assessment A, B, C, E, or F.

Connect Learning Across Contexts

Shared Reading You may wish to use the following Shared Reading title from *Fountas & Pinnell Classroom™* to point out onsets and rimes.

 *Exploring Underground* by Louis Petrone

Guided Reading When students encounter an unfamiliar word, remind them to make connections with known words using prompts such as: *Do you see a part you know? Do you know a word like that? The last part of the word is like* _____.

Shared Writing Prompt students to break words into parts so that they can spell them.

Independent Writing Have students use known words as resources for writing new words. Encourage them to use word study charts as a resource.

Extend Learning

Repeat this lesson, using different words on the game board.

▶ Connect with Home

Send home a game board and the lesson's game die (see Online Resources) so that children can play Follow the Path with family members. When students read books aloud to family members, encourage them to use the beginnings and endings of words to help them solve unknown words.

Plan

▶ Consider Your Students

Use this lesson after students have had experience adding or substituting letters to make words. This lesson reinforces using word knowledge to search for connections. In this lesson, students will substitute the beginnings or endings of words. If this is challenging for some students, you may want to focus on substituting just beginnings or just endings.

▶ Working with English Language Learners

You may want to work with English language learners in a small group first so that you can give them more support. Also observe how they solve words. If they have difficulty, focus on just word beginnings or just word endings. Also, be sure to use words that are in students' listening vocabularies.

UNDERSTAND THE PRINCIPLE

When effective readers and writers solve words, they make connections to what they already know about words. This helps them build categories of words and principles for how words work.

YOU WILL NEED

Online Resources
▶ WSA 4 Action Tags
▶ WSA 4 Word Cards
▶ WSA 4 Word Ladders

Other Materials
▶ chart paper

Generative Lesson ✓
A generative lesson has a simple structure that you can use to present similar content or concepts. Use this lesson structure to teach students a variety of new words using onsets and rimes in known words.

EXPLAIN THE PRINCIPLE

Sometimes a part of a word you know can be found in another word.

Use parts of words you know to read or write another word with the same parts.

Comprehensive Phonics, Spelling, and Word Study Guide

Refer to: page **77**, row **11**

chase   treat

choose   beat

chair   seat

chisel   feat

ACTIVITY: WORD CONNECTIONS

INSTRUCTIONAL PROCEDURE

NOTICE PARTS

See page 32 for detailed descriptions of Instructional Procedures.

EXPLAIN THE PRINCIPLE

Sometimes a part of a word you know can be found in another word.

Use parts of words you know to read or write another word with the same parts.

Comprehensive Phonics, Spelling, and Word Study Guide

Refer to: page **77**, row **11**

Teach

1. Write the words *chase, choose,* and *chair* on chart paper. *What do you notice about all of these words?* • *They all begin with the letters* ch.

2. Then write a word that students are less likely to know, such as *chisel,* and use it in a sentence. *How is this word like* chase, choose, *and* chair? • *It starts with* ch, *too. How do you think you might say this word?* Students may or may not pronounce it correctly, but listen for them to start it with a /ch/ sound. *You can use what you know about the beginnings of words to help you read new words.*

3. If students quickly grasp beginning sounds, move on to ending sounds by writing a group of words such as *treat, beat,* and *seat. What do you notice about all of these words?* • *They all end in /ē/ /t/.*

4. Write another word that may be unfamiliar, such as *feat. How is this word like* treat, beat, *and* seat? • *It ends with the letters* eat. *How do you think you might say this word?* Listen for students' pronunciation. *You can use what you know about the endings of words to help you read new words.*

5. Tell students that they will make word ladders by changing the beginnings or endings of words. Demonstrate how to make word ladders: write one word, and change the beginning or ending to write another word. The letters added, removed, or changed must be consecutive in the words. For example, *blast, black, blew, flew, flight, bright, slight, slip.*

Name Randy   Date

free	treat
see	seat
bee	beat
tree	wheat
trip	while
sip	smile
snip	smell
snap	shell

drink	name
drop	tame
pop	same
bop	shame
stop	ship
step	flip
stay	flop
way	flee

Fountas & Pinnell Word Study Lessons, Grade 3   **WSA 4** Word Ladders

ACTIVITY: WORD
LADDERS

INSTRUCTIONAL PROCEDURE

NOTICE PARTS

See page 32 for detailed descriptions of Instructional Procedures.

ACTION TAGS

choose word card

write word

change letters

write new word

underline similar parts

Apply

Distribute word ladder sheets, and have students make word ladders on them. Ask students to choose a word card and write it in one of the boxes on the sheet. Then they change, add, or remove one to three letters and write the new word under the first word. The letters students add, remove, or change must be consecutive within the words (e.g., beginning or ending). When students finish a ladder, have them underline in each word the word part that they used from the word above to make the new word.

Share

Have students read one word ladder to a partner. Show two or three ladders so that students can see a variety of connections.

Assess

- Notice whether students are using words they know to solve words when they are reading.
- Notice whether students are using words they know to spell words when they are writing.
- You may wish to use Word-Solving Actions Assessment A, B, C, E, or F.

Word-Solving Actions: Use Onsets and Rimes in Known Words to Read and Write Other Words with the Same Parts

Connect Learning Across Contexts

Shared Reading You may wish to use the following Shared Reading title from *Fountas & Pinnell Classroom™* to point out onsets and rimes in known words in order for students to read and write other words with the same parts.

 *Saving Cranes* by Brenda Iasevoli

Guided Reading When students encounter an unfamiliar word, remind them to make connections with known words using prompts such as: *Do you see a part you know? Do you know a word like that? The last part of the word is like _____.*

Shared Writing As students work to solve a new word, help them connect it to a word they already know.

Independent Writing Encourage students to use familiar word parts to help them spell new words.

Extend Learning

Repeat this lesson with different words. You can adjust the difficulty of this lesson with the words you select.

▶ Connect with Home

Send home a word ladder sheet (see Online Resources), and have students make word ladders with family members.

Break a Word into Syllables to Decode Manageable Units

Plan

▶ Consider Your Students

Most students are now familiar with word components and can divide multisyllable words into the parts they hear. However, students may not automatically use their syllabication strategies to take apart longer words when reading them or constructing them in spelling. This lesson builds this skill. It includes words with two, three, and four syllables. If students are not ready for four-syllable words, adjust the words to include two- and three-syllable words only.

▶ Working with English Language Learners

Breaking apart words into syllables helps English language learners focus on the details of English words. They hear clear, slowed-down pronunciations, as well as the breaks indicating different parts. Use pictures, gestures and actions, or sentences to indicate or clarify the meanings of the words you've chosen. Provide repeated opportunities for students to work with syllables, and accept approximate pronunciations.

UNDERSTAND THE PRINCIPLE

One determinant of text difficulty is the number of multisyllable words that readers are required to process. The texts that third-grade students read have many more two-, three-, and four-syllable words than do texts from earlier grades. Students need to know that when they encounter a lengthy unfamiliar word, they should break it into syllables. It will help students to keep in mind that each syllable has one vowel sound. If this kind of analysis of multisyllable words is performed with efficiency, less attention is needed for word solving.

YOU WILL NEED

Online Resources
- ▶ **WSA 5** Action Tags
- ▶ **WSA 5** Game Cards
- ▶ **WSA 5** Syllable Race Game Boards

Other Materials
- ▶ whiteboard
- ▶ game markers

Generative Lesson

A generative lesson has a simple structure that you can use to present similar content or concepts. Use this lesson structure to teach students to break into syllables and then decode a variety of words.

EXPLAIN THE PRINCIPLE

You can listen for the syllables in words.

Some words have one syllable. Some words have more than one syllable.

Each syllable in a word has a vowel sound.

You can break a word into syllables.

Look at the syllables in a word to read it.

Comprehensive Phonics, Spelling, and Word Study Guide

Refer to:
page **80**, row **30**

EARLY MIDDLE LATE

ACTIVITY: SYLLABLES

INSTRUCTIONAL PROCEDURE

NOTICE PARTS

See page 32 for detailed descriptions of Instructional Procedures.

EXPLAIN THE PRINCIPLE

You can listen for the syllables in words.

Some words have one syllable. Some words have more than one syllable.

Each syllable in a word has a vowel sound.

You can break a word into syllables.

Look at the syllables in a word to read it.

Comprehensive Phonics, Spelling, and Word Study Guide

Refer to: page **80**, row **30**

---

kind
unkind
unkindly

cantaloupe	can ta loupe
crocodile	croc o dile
balloon	bal loon
terrible	ter ri ble
motorcycle	mo tor cy cle
watermelon	wa ter mel on
rainbow	rain bow
catastrophe	ca tas tro phe

Teach

1. Start with examples that have the same base word. Write the words *kind, unkind,* and *unkindly* on a whiteboard. Read the words with students.

2. *What do you notice about all of these words?* • Students may observe that all of the words have the base word *kind* or that they have different numbers of syllables.

3. Have students read each word again, this time clapping as they say the words. *What do you notice about how many syllables each word has?* • As needed, review with students that every syllable has a vowel sound.

4. *You know that some words have one syllable and some have more syllables. When you divide a word into syllables, it helps you take it apart to read it. When you read a long word, it helps to say the syllables, then look at them and connect them with other words or parts of words you know. Let's try to say and take apart these longer words.*

5. Have students say the words you have written on the whiteboard and clap a few of them. Then ask students to divide each word without clapping. Call on students to say the syllables with a slight break between parts.

6. On the whiteboard (or with magnetic letters), create visual space between the parts of a word. *Look at the parts of* cantaloupe *[can/ta/loupe]. Do you see any parts that you know?* Students may respond by noticing the word *can,* pronouncing the letters *ta,* or even noticing that the ending syllable looks a little like the word *loop.* You do not need to make these connections directly. Let students use their own thinking to figure out the parts of words.

7. Tell students that they will play Syllable Race. Each player places her marker at the start point, takes a game card, reads the word, tells the number of syllables, and pronounces the word again slowly so that each syllable can be heard (for example, *"happening,* three, *hap/pen/ing"*). The player then moves her piece the number of syllables that are in the word. The first player to reach the end wins the game.

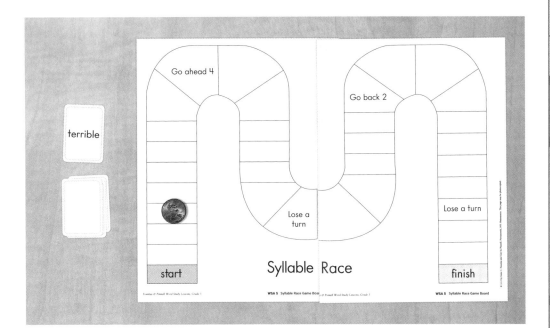

ACTIVITY: SYLLABLE RACE

INSTRUCTIONAL PROCEDURE

NOTICE PARTS

See page 32 for detailed descriptions of Instructional Procedures.

ACTION TAGS

take card

read word

tell syllables

move marker

Apply

Have students play Syllable Race in groups of two to four players. Remind them that they will take a card, read it, tell the number of syllables, and say the word in syllable parts. They will move their marker the same number of spaces as syllables in the word.

Share

Have students read aloud a few of the words they selected during the game and tell how many syllables each word has.

Assess

- Observe students' ability to break longer words into syllables and decode them as they read texts.

- Have students read three- and four-syllable words; note how successfully they are able to divide the words into manageable units.

- You may wish to use Word-Solving Actions Assessment B, C, E, or F.

Word-Solving Actions: Break a Word into Syllables to Decode Manageable Units

Connect Learning Across Contexts

Shared Reading You may wish to use the following Shared Reading title from *Fountas & Pinnell Classroom*™ to point out multisyllable words that can be decoded into manageable units.

SR *A Meerkat Day* by Geerhardt Heever

Guided Reading Observe students' ability to take apart longer words as they read texts. Have students read four or five multisyllable words, and notice how efficiently they approach them and whether they use parts appropriately.

Shared Writing As students write new words, have them say the parts. They can also say the parts to check their spelling.

Independent Writing As students write new words, have them say each syllable by itself before writing it.

Extend Learning

Repeat this lesson with different words, and provide a different set of word cards for Syllable Race. Increase the challenge by including more three- and four-syllable words.

▶ Connect with Home

Send home Syllable Race and game cards so students can play the game with family members. Students can work with a family member to search newspapers and magazines for words with more than four syllables.

Recognize and Use Word Parts to Solve an Unknown Word and Understand Its Meaning

Plan

▶ Consider Your Students

Use this lesson after students have good control over base words and common prefixes and suffixes. Students will already be familiar with some words with prefixes, such as *unhappy*, or with suffixes, such as *careful*, but now you will be using these words to explain the concept in more depth. If students are experienced at recognizing and using word parts, you may wish to include words that have both prefixes and suffixes, such as *unwisely*.

▶ Working with English Language Learners

Learning some basic word parts helps English language learners rapidly expand their knowledge of English. Begin with simple examples, making sure students know the base words you use. Demonstrate segmenting words into word parts using magnetic letters or cut-up words. Point to each word part as you explain its meaning.

UNDERSTAND THE PRINCIPLE

Words often have affixes, parts added before or after a word to change its meaning. An affix can be a prefix or a suffix. The word to which affixes are added can be a base word or a word root. A *base word* is a word in its simplest form. A *word root* is a word part, usually from another language, that carries the essential meaning of and is the basis for an English word (e.g., the Greek word root *phon* and the English word *telephone*). Breaking longer words into word parts makes them easier to understand and to decode. Knowing even one part of a longer word can help a reader arrive at an approximation of the word's meaning.

YOU WILL NEED

Online Resources
- ▶ WSA 6 Action Tags
- ▶ WSA 6 Word Strips

Other Materials
- ▶ magnetic letters

Generative Lesson ✓

A generative lesson has a simple structure that you can use to present similar content or concepts. Use this lesson structure to teach students to recognize and use a variety of word parts to solve an unknown word.

EXPLAIN THE PRINCIPLE

An unknown word may contain one or more word parts–word root, base word, prefix, or suffix.

Any word root, base word, or affix may contain hints about the meaning of an unknown word.

Comprehensive Phonics, Spelling, and Word Study Guide

Refer to:
page **80**, row **33**

ACTIVITY: WORD PARTS

INSTRUCTIONAL PROCEDURE

NOTICE PARTS

See page 32 for detailed descriptions of Instructional Procedures.

EXPLAIN THE PRINCIPLE

An unknown word may contain one or more word parts—word root, base word, prefix, or suffix.

Any word root, base word, or affix may contain hints about the meaning of an unknown word.

Comprehensive Phonics, Spelling, and Word Study Guide

Refer to: page **80**, row **33**

Teach

1. Using magnetic letters, build the word *unfair* on a magnetic surface. Ask students to read the word with you.

2. *Do you see any parts that you know in this word?* • Slide the magnetic letters apart to show *un* and *fair. What do you notice about the meaning of this word?*

3. Repeat with the words *redo, reread,* and *preview.*

4. Now build the word *careful.* Ask students to read the word with you.

5. *Do you see any parts that you know in this word?* • Slide the magnetic letters apart to show *care* and *ful. What do you notice about the meaning of this word?*

6. Repeat with *sweetly* and *artist.*

7. Read each group of words with students again, this time having them clap each word part as they read the words. Encourage them to generalize the principle. *What have you noticed about word parts and word meaning from working with these words?* • Build on students' observations to summarize the principle. *Words can contain one or more word parts. Any word parts may give information about the meaning of the word.*

8. Explain to students that they will practice taking apart and putting together words that have prefixes and suffixes. Tell students that they will write a word in big letters on a sentence strip. Then they will segment the word into parts by cutting the word into pieces. Finally, they will trade cut-up words with a partner, reassemble the words they receive, read them aloud, and tell what they mean.

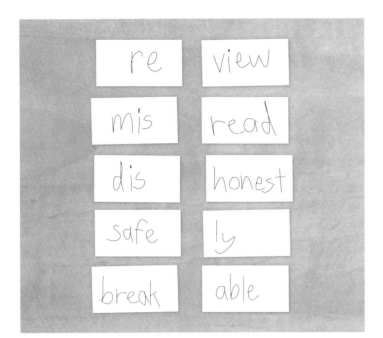

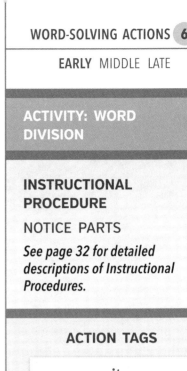

ACTIVITY: WORD DIVISION

INSTRUCTIONAL PROCEDURE

NOTICE PARTS

See page 32 for detailed descriptions of Instructional Procedures.

ACTION TAGS

write

cut

trade

put together again

read and define

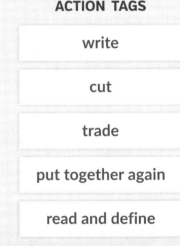

Apply

Write the following words on chart paper or on the whiteboard: *review, misread, dishonest, safely, breakable, unwise, kindness, thoughtful, dislike, cheerful.* Have students choose five words to cut apart and trade with a partner. Make sure they choose some words with prefixes and some words with suffixes.

Share

Have students read to a partner the words they reassembled and tell what each word means.

Assess

■ Observe students' ability to break longer words into word parts and to use the word parts to decode and determine meaning.

■ Give students a few additional words, such as *disagree, unclean, banker,* and *colorful.* Have them break them into word parts and then tell what the words mean.

■ You may wish to use Word-Solving Actions Assessment B, C, E, or F.

Word-Solving Actions: Recognize and Use Word Parts to Solve an Unknown Word and Understand Its Meaning

Connect Learning Across Contexts

Shared Reading You may wish to use the following Shared Reading title from *Fountas & Pinnell Classroom™* to point out words with affixes.

SR *From Flower to Honey* by June Schwartz

Guided Reading Observe students' ability to take apart longer words as they read texts. Notice how efficiently students approach them and whether they use word parts appropriately.

Shared Writing As students write new words, have them think about the individual word parts. Guide students to spell one part at a time in order to spell the longer word.

Independent Writing As students write new words, have them say each word part by itself before writing it.

Extend Learning

Repeat this lesson with different words. Increase the challenge by including words with both prefixes and suffixes.

▶ Connect with Home

Send home students' cut-apart words. Have students work with family members to assemble them and read them aloud.

Use Alphabetical Order to Locate Information About Words in a Variety of Reference Tools

Plan

▶ Consider Your Students

By third grade, students know the alphabet and have worked with alphabetical order in a variety of ways (e.g., putting names in order), but they may not be fluent using letter order in more sophisticated ways. Use this lesson to help students understand the fundamental process of putting words in alphabetical order as well as the use of the alphabet as an organizing tool. You can use the words provided in this lesson or create your own list of words.

▶ Working with English Language Learners

Students' levels of familiarity with alphabetical order will depend on their previous experiences, not only with written English but also with print in their own languages. Remember that students' home languages may not be represented in writing with the Western alphabet. Give students plenty of opportunities to put simple words in order before moving to secondary levels of organization (using second or third letters). As always, it is best to create lists of words that students can read and understand.

UNDERSTAND THE PRINCIPLE

The alphabet is a powerful tool for organizing and accessing information. Most reference tools use alphabetical order as the organizing structure. Becoming familiar with and fluent in using alphabetical order will help students find information more quickly and free their attention for learning. Sometimes alphabetical order is referred to as "*ABC* order."

YOU WILL NEED

PWS Ready Resources
- ▶ Alphabet Strips
- ▶ WSA 7 Pocket-Chart Cards

Online Resources
- ▶ WSA 7 Action Tags
- ▶ WSA 7 Word Cards
- ▶ WSA 7 List Sheets

Other Materials
- ▶ pocket chart
- ▶ student dictionaries

Generative Lesson

A generative lesson has a simple structure that you can use to present similar content or concepts. Use this lesson structure to teach students to use alphabetical order to locate information about words in a variety of reference tools.

EXPLAIN THE PRINCIPLE

Common reference tools with information about words include glossaries, dictionaries, and thesauruses.

Information in most reference tools is arranged in alphabetical order.

Use alphabetical order to find information in a glossary, dictionary, or other reference tool.

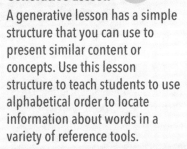

Comprehensive Phonics, Spelling, and Word Study Guide

Refer to:
page **81**, row **38**

ACTIVITY: ALPHABETICAL ORDER

INSTRUCTIONAL PROCEDURE

SAY AND SORT

See page 32 for detailed descriptions of Instructional Procedures.

EXPLAIN THE PRINCIPLE

Common reference tools with information about words include glossaries, dictionaries, and thesauruses.

Information in most reference tools is arranged in alphabetical order.

Use alphabetical order to find information in a glossary, dictionary, or other reference tool.

Comprehensive Phonics, Spelling, and Word Study Guide

Refer to: page **81**, row **38**

Teach

abcdefghijklmnopqrstuvwxyz

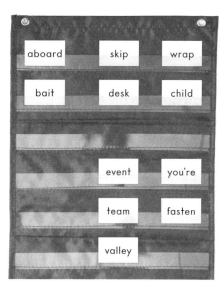

1. Place the words *after, because, could, from,* and *isn't* in alphabetical order in a pocket chart. *What do you notice about the way these words are organized?* Students may notice that the words are listed in alphabetical order. *One way you can organize words is in alphabetical order.*

2. *What are some things that are organized in alphabetical order?* • Students may note that class name lists, books in libraries, and words in dictionaries and glossaries are all organized alphabetically.

3. Tell students they will practice alphabetizing some words. Remove the initial cards from the pocket and place *aboard, bait, child, desk, event, fasten, skip, team, valley, wrap,* and *you're* randomly on the right-hand side of the chart. *How can we start to put these words into alphabetical order? Which word would you put first?* • Students may point out that *aboard* should come first because *a* is the first letter of the alphabet. Allow them to continue sharing their thought processes as they organize the words.

4. *Now I have some additional words to put into our list of words in alphabetical order.* Place *cloud, yellow, ask, bring, from, house, ride, home, were, into, like,* and *new* on the chart in random order.

5. *Suppose we wanted to put the word* cloud *on our list. Where does it belong?* Let students decide where to put *cloud* and discuss how they determined where to place it. Listen for observations such as:

    "*Child* and *cloud* both begin with the letter *c,* so you have to look at the second letter of the word. C*loud* comes after *child* because *i* comes after *h* in the alphabet."

    Continue to add new words to the list, helping students learn how to use the first letters and then the second letters when the words begin with the same letter.

6. Invite students to share and, if possible, to demonstrate how they would use their knowledge of alphabetical order to find a word in a dictionary or glossary.

7. Tell students that they will put words in alphabetical order, or *ABC* order. Explain that they will have twenty word cards to put in order and that then they will write the words on a list sheet.

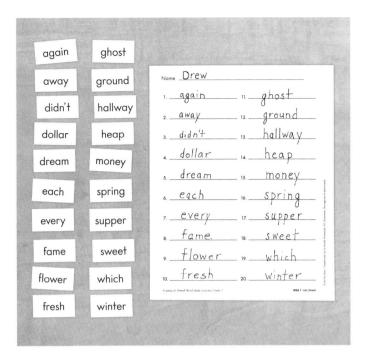

ACTIVITY: ALPHABETICAL ORDER

INSTRUCTIONAL PROCEDURE

SAY AND SORT

See page 32 for detailed descriptions of Instructional Procedures.

ACTION TAGS

read words

place in order

check

write list

Apply

- Give students twenty words on cards to put into alphabetical order. If they are new to this process, it is especially helpful for students to move the cards around as they compare words.

- After the words are in order, a partner uses a student dictionary to check the order. Then each student writes the twenty words in alphabetical order on a list sheet.

Share

Have students share their word lists with a different partner.

Assess

- Give students a list of words, such as *apple, bee, bet, elephant, fear,* and *fox.* Observe how quickly and accurately they can put the words in alphabetical order and whether they can alphabetize to the second letter.

- Have students find words in a student dictionary. Observe whether they are able to use alphabetical order to find words efficiently.

Connect Learning Across Contexts

Shared Reading You may wish to use the following Shared Reading title from *Fountas & Pinnell Classroom*™ to point out the use of alphabetical order in a glossary.

SR *Exploring Underground* by Louis Petrone

Guided Reading When students are reading books with indexes or glossaries, point out how they are organized in alphabetical order. Have students practice using them.

Shared Writing As you write together, have students use alphabetical order to locate words in dictionaries and thesauruses.

Independent Writing Help children use alphabetized word lists or simple dictionaries as tools for locating words.

Extend Learning

- Give students lists of words that start with the same letter and require them to notice the second, third, or even fourth letters of words. You can easily construct these lists by using a student dictionary and focusing on one letter (e.g., *machine, mad, made, magic, magical, magnet, make, mammal, man, mane, mango, many, map, mark, market, mask, math, maze, meal, mean, meat, medicine, meeting, men, meow, messy, met, might, mine, mist, mistake, model, moist, monkey, more, mud, musk, my, mystery*). If students can easily alphabetize a list such as this one, they will not need much more practice.

- Let students choose sets of words (e.g., number words, color words, animal words), and see how quickly they can alphabetize them. Use a timer to add interest.

- You may want to help students develop some systematic ways of using searching tools on electronic devices.

▶ **Connect with Home**

Have students construct lists of "home words" (family and pet names, rooms, toys and other possessions), alphabetize them, and then bring their alphabetized lists to share.

Use Alphabetical Order to Locate Information About Words in a Variety of Reference Tools

Plan

▶ Consider Your Students

Earlier in elementary school, students have used simple dictionaries and glossaries. Use this lesson when students are ready to begin using longer, more comprehensive dictionaries and need to become efficient with finding specific words or entries.

▶ Working with English Language Learners

The dictionary is an important tool for English language learners as they acquire new words and need to check their meanings. However, more understanding is needed to make dictionary work valuable. As examples of guide words and for the words students are locating, be sure to use words that students know how to spell (at least the first three or four letters) so that they can focus their attention on how a dictionary works. You may wish to begin with a dictionary designed for English learners.

YOU WILL NEED

PWS Ready Resources
- ▶ **WSA 8** Pocket-Chart Cards
- ▶ **WSA 8** Pocket-Chart Cards (long)

Online Resources
- ▶ **WSA 8** Action Tags
- ▶ **WSA 8** Word Cards
- ▶ **WSA 8** Three-Way Sorts

Other Materials
- ▶ pocket chart
- ▶ student dictionaries

Generative Lesson ✓

A generative lesson has a simple structure that you can use to present similar content or concepts. Use this lesson structure to teach students to use alphabetical order to locate information about words in a variety of reference tools.

UNDERSTAND THE PRINCIPLE

The alphabet is a powerful tool for organizing and accessing information. Most reference tools use alphabetical order as the organizing structure. Becoming familiar with and fluent in using alphabetical order will help students find information more quickly and free their attention for learning. Sometimes alphabetical order is referred to as "*ABC* order." To help users find specific information more efficiently within large, printed reference tools, organizational aids called *guide words* are provided at the tops of pages. The first guide word on a page represents the first entry that begins on that page; the second guide word represents the last entry on that page. By scanning just the guide words, a user knows which words will fall alphabetically on a page.

EXPLAIN THE PRINCIPLE

Use alphabetical order to find information in a glossary, dictionary, or other reference tool.

Words that appear at the top of a page in some printed reference tools identify the first and last words on that page. They are guide words.

Guide words make it easier to find a word quickly in an alphabetized reference tool.

Comprehensive Phonics, Spelling, and Word Study Guide

Refer to: page **81**, row **38**

ACTIVITY: WORD SORT

INSTRUCTIONAL PROCEDURE

SAY AND SORT

See page 32 for detailed descriptions of Instructional Procedures.

EXPLAIN THE PRINCIPLE

Use alphabetical order to find information in a glossary, dictionary, or other reference tool.

Words that appear at the top of a page in some printed reference tools identify the first and last words on that page. They are guide words.

Guide words make it easier to find a word quickly in an alphabetized reference tool.

Comprehensive Phonics, Spelling, and Word Study Guide

Refer to: page **81**, row **38**

Teach

1. Distribute dictionaries to students. If you do not have a dictionary for every student, partners or small groups can share a dictionary. Invite students to share what they already know about dictionaries. *What kind of information can you find in a dictionary?* • *What have you noticed about how words are organized in a dictionary?*

2. Select a page in the dictionary, and ask students to turn to it. Build on their comments as you invite them to notice and think about the guide words. *What do you notice about this guide word?* • *What do you notice about this guide word?* • Allow time for students to notice the guide words and make connections to the first and last words on the page. *The two words at the very top of the page tell you the first word entry on the page and the last word entry on the page. The two words are called* guide words.

3. *How do guide words help when looking for information?* • *Guide words make it easier to find a word quickly in an alphabetized reference tool, such as a dictionary.*

4. At the top of a pocket chart, display the three pairs of guide words. *Imagine that these are guide words on three different pages of a dictionary.* Have students read the guide words with you.

5. Display the word cards, and have students read the words with you. *Imagine that these are words that you want to look up in the dictionary.* Ask students to place each word below the correct pair of guide words. After the words are sorted, have students place the words in alphabetical order.

6. Tell students that today they will sort word cards according to guide words on a three-way sort. After the words are sorted, students place the words in alphabetical order.

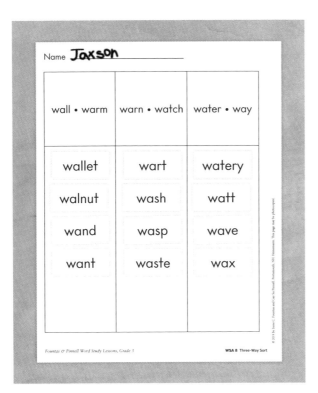

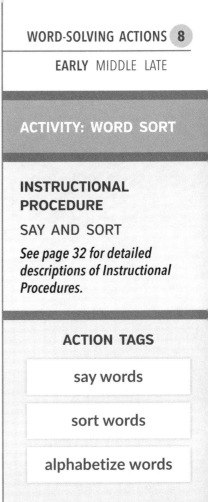

INSTRUCTIONAL PROCEDURE

SAY AND SORT

See page 32 for detailed descriptions of Instructional Procedures.

ACTION TAGS

say words

sort words

alphabetize words

Apply

■ Have students say each word and then sort the words according to the three pairs of guide words on the three-way sort. Remind students to place the words in alphabetical order after they complete the sort.

■ You may wish to have students glue the word cards to the three-way sort.

Share

Encourage students to share their sorts and talk about what they learned about using alphabetized reference tools such as a dictionary.

Assess

Observe students using a dictionary. Notice their use of guide words and their ability to find words alphabetically.

Connect Learning Across Contexts

Shared Reading You may wish to use the following Shared Reading title from *Fountas & Pinnell Classroom*™ to point out the use of alphabetical order in a glossary.

SR *Trapped in Tar* by Hannah Cales

Guided Reading When reading informational texts, call students' attention to glossaries and indexes. Have students identify the guide words. Help students use the guide words to locate information quickly.

Shared Writing As you construct pieces of writing, model pausing to check the spelling of words. Ask students to look up the words in the dictionary and tell the guide words that helped them find the correct page.

Independent Writing Ask students to proofread their independent writing to be sure they have correctly spelled each word. Prompt them to use a dictionary when they are unsure of a word's spelling. Remind them to use guide words to help them locate a word more quickly.

Extend Learning

- Expand this lesson by using a collection of challenging words and asking students to play Twenty Questions. One student says, *I am thinking of a word.* Students ask questions such as: *Is it in the first part of the dictionary? Is it in the middle of the dictionary? Is it in the last part of the dictionary?* Then they ask whether the word starts with a certain letter, and so on. Students finally ask whether the word is between certain guide words, and then they guess the word. The challenge is for the first student to keep a word secret for all twenty questions. The student who guesses the word then chooses another word and play resumes.

- Have small groups work with several different kinds of dictionaries.

▶ Connect with Home

Send home dictionaries for students to practice looking up words with family members.

Use a Dictionary to Solve and Find Information About Words

Plan

▶ Consider Your Students

Use this lesson once students are quick and flexible at putting words in alphabetical order as well as finding words that are in order. They should also have previous experience using guide words to locate words in a dictionary (Word-Solving Actions 8). You may want to create a large reference chart that shows an entry from your classroom dictionary with labels that explain the kinds of information each entry provides about a word.

▶ Working with English Language Learners

The dictionary is an important tool for English language learners as they acquire new words and need to check their meanings. In the beginning, work with simple entries and known words. Be sure that students understand (with your help) not only the specific word you are locating but also the words in the definition. Since entries represent a new type of text, read them aloud to students as many times as needed. You may want to "unpack" an entry by making the format more accessible (e.g., creating a list out of the alternative definitions). You may wish to begin with a dictionary designed for English learners.

UNDERSTAND THE PRINCIPLE

Even though searchable dictionaries are available electronically, students need a basic understanding of how dictionaries "work." Students who have the ability to notice visual features of words and understand the concept of alphabetical order can use a dictionary effectively to learn more about words. It is important for students to know the types of information that dictionaries generally provide about words. With this knowledge, students will understand why a dictionary is such a powerful tool and will begin to use it with greater independence to explore words and expand their vocabularies.

YOU WILL NEED

Online Resources
- ▶ WSA 9 Dictionary Entry
- ▶ WSA 9 Action Tags
- ▶ WSA 9 Word Cards
- ▶ WSA 9 Two-Way Sorts

Other Materials
- ▶ dictionaries

✓ Generative Lesson
A generative lesson has a simple structure that you can use to present similar content or concepts. Use this lesson structure to teach students to use a variety of types of dictionaries.

EXPLAIN THE PRINCIPLE

A dictionary is a book or digital tool that contains information about the words of a language or of some special subject.

A dictionary entry gives different types of information about a word, such as a word's spelling, syllables, pronunciation, meaning or meanings, as well as its history.

Entries in a dictionary are arranged in alphabetical order.

Comprehensive Phonics, Spelling, and Word Study Guide

Refer to: page **81**, row **40**

ACTIVITY: DICTIONARY ENTRY

INSTRUCTIONAL PROCEDURE

NOTICE PARTS

See page 32 for detailed descriptions of Instructional Procedures.

EXPLAIN THE PRINCIPLE

A dictionary is a book or digital tool that contains information about the words of a language or of some special subject.

A dictionary entry gives different types of information about a word, such as a word's spelling, syllables, pronunciation, meaning or meanings, as well as its history.

Entries in a dictionary are arranged in alphabetical order.

Comprehensive Phonics, Spelling, and Word Study Guide

Refer to:
page **81**, row **40**

Teach

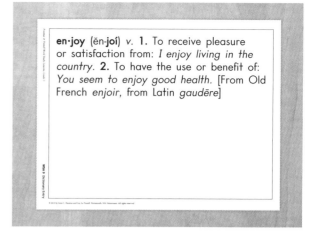

en·joy (ĕn-**joi**) *v.* **1.** To receive pleasure or satisfaction from: *I enjoy living in the country.* **2.** To have the use or benefit of: *You seem to enjoy good health.* [From Old French *enjoir,* from Latin *gaudēre*]

1. Invite students to share what they already know about dictionaries. Build on their comments to explain the principle. *A dictionary is a book or digital tool that contains information about the words of a language or of some special subject.*

2. Distribute dictionaries to students. If you do not have a dictionary for every student, partners or small groups can share a dictionary. Select a word entry that includes all of the features you wish to teach. Alternatively, you can project or distribute copies of the dictionary entry provided in Online Resources.

3. Read the entry to students. *What do you notice about the entry?* ● Build on students' observations to teach specific features. You may wish to choose from the following features and modify the language to reflect the style of the entry from which you are teaching.

   ■ entry word: *An entry word shows how a word is spelled. Entry words are listed in alphabetical order and printed in bold.*

   ■ syllables: *Entry words that have more than one syllable are divided into syllables (usually by dots).*

   ■ pronunciation: *The pronunciation of the word is in parentheses. Letters, sometimes with special symbols, stand for sounds. These are explained in the pronunciation key at the beginning of the dictionary (and, in some dictionaries, on every other page).*

   ■ definition: *The definition of a word tells what the word means. If a word has several meanings, each definition is numbered.*

   ■ word history: *Some entries include a history of the word in brackets. The history often lists the languages from which the word originates and may break the word into word roots and affixes, each with its own meaning.*

4. Ask students to turn to additional entries. Encourage them to compare features and to discuss new features that they notice. Prompt students to think about why the features may be helpful and how they will use them. *Why might it be important to read all of the definitions of a word?* ● *How might you use the history of a word?*

5. Tell students that today they will choose three words from a set of word cards, look up each word in a dictionary, and use a two-way sort to write a definition and a sentence with the word.

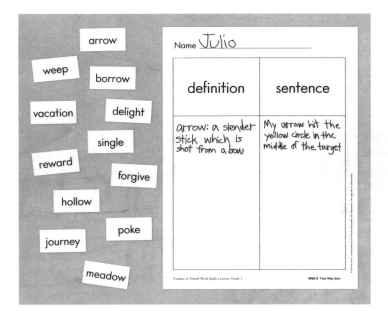

ACTIVITY: DICTIONARY WORK

INSTRUCTIONAL PROCEDURE

NOTICE PARTS

See page 32 for detailed descriptions of Instructional Procedures.

ACTION TAGS

say words

choose three words

write definition

write sentence

Apply

Have students say each word on the word cards and then choose three words to look up in a dictionary. Students write a definition of the word in the first column and a sentence using the word in the second column.

Share

Encourage students to share some of the definitions and sentences that they wrote.

Assess

Observe students using a dictionary. Notice their ability to find words alphabetically and their use of various features of word entries.

Connect Learning Across Contexts

Shared Reading You may wish to use the following Shared Reading title from *Fountas & Pinnell Classroom*™ to point out words about which students may find more information in a dictionary.

SR *Exploring Underground* by Louis Petrone

Guided Reading Discuss the meanings of new words that students encounter in a text. Have students occasionally check the dictionary when a meaning is unclear. During word work, you may wish to model using a dictionary with a small group of students who need more experience.

Shared Writing Have students occasionally look up in the dictionary the meanings of words that you wish to use in a piece of writing. Discuss which definition of a word you are using.

Independent Writing Ask students to proofread their independent writing to be sure they have correctly spelled each word. Prompt them to use a dictionary when they are unsure of a word's spelling.

Extend Learning

- You may wish to show an online dictionary and compare its features with those in a print dictionary.

- Repeat the lesson with additional entry words, or teach additional features of an entry, such as:

  parts of speech: *A word's part of speech is listed as an abbreviation near the beginning of the entry or of each definition. For example,* n *stands for "noun," and* v *stands for "verb."*

  example sentences: *Some entries include example sentences that show how a particular meaning is indicated in context.*

  usage labels: *Some entries include usage labels, such as old, slang, or informal. These labels identify forms or meanings that are limited in some way.*

- Have students compare meanings of a word that has more than one definition. Students can construct sentences with the word, and other students can identify the precise definition that is used.

▶ Connect with Home

Send home dictionaries for students to practice looking up words with family members.

Use a Study Routine to Spell a Word: Choose, Write, Build, Mix, Fix, Mix (Partner Study 1)

Plan

▶ Consider Your Students

This lesson will be most effective if students have a real need to learn the spelling of new words: e.g., they wish to include such a word in a piece of writing that they will share with an audience. You may wish to include a few words with which most students in your classroom need more experience in order to spell accurately.

The words in the lesson come from each student's specific spelling needs as evidenced in his writing. It is suggested that each student have a word study folder containing a list of "words to learn," and that you add priority words to students' lists when you review their writing. A high-frequency word list can be used as a class pretest, and misspelled items can be highlighted for selection on the weekly list. You might assign a few additional words–exemplars from lesson principles you teach.

You can pair this routine with many different lessons to help reinforce new principles. For example, after students learn a new vowel combination or letter pattern, you may wish to have them use the routine to solidify their learning. It is very important to work with students until they have habituated the routine and can use it efficiently. As students become accustomed to the routine, you may find it helpful to set a timer to encourage them to perform the routine quickly. It is also a suggested routine for the weekly Partner Study System (formerly Buddy Study–see *Word Matters*).

▶ Working with English Language Learners

It is important that the words English language learners choose are meaningful to them. Avoid confusing words that they find difficult to pronounce. High-frequency words they do not yet know are always appropriate. Choose, Write, Build, Mix, Fix, Mix is a simple technique to use, but it takes practice to perform efficiently.

UNDERSTAND THE PRINCIPLE

The tactile experience of building, breaking apart, and rebuilding words using magnetic letters or letter cards and then engaging the motor skills of forming the letters in sequence reinforces students' understanding of word parts and patterns. The process is an effective part of a routine to learn and retain in memory the spelling of new words.

YOU WILL NEED

Online Resources
- ▶ **WSA 10** Action Tags
- ▶ **WSA 10** Words to Learn

Other Materials
- ▶ index cards
- ▶ magnetic letters

EXPLAIN THE PRINCIPLE

Several routines can help in spelling words.

One routine for spelling words is Choose, Write, Build, Mix, Fix, Mix.

Comprehensive Phonics, Spelling, and Word Study Guide

Refer to: page **82**, row **50**

ACTIVITY: MAGNETIC LETTERS

INSTRUCTIONAL PROCEDURE

MAKE WORDS

See page 32 for detailed descriptions of Instructional Procedures.

EXPLAIN THE PRINCIPLE

Several routines can help in spelling words.

One routine for spelling words is Choose, Write, Build, Mix, Fix, Mix.

Comprehensive Phonics, Spelling, and Word Study Guide

Refer to:
page **82**, row **50**

Teach

1. Tell students that today they are going to learn a routine that will help them learn how to spell new words.

2. Invite students to choose three to five words that they would like to learn to spell accurately, such as words that they are attempting to use in independent writing, or words from their "words to learn" list or from their word study notebooks. In addition, have them choose three to five words from lesson principles you are teaching (or assign the words). Ask students to write each word carefully and clearly on an index card.

3. Explain that you will circulate around the classroom to check the spelling of the words on students' index cards. *If the word on your card is spelled correctly, I'll place a small checkmark in the corner of your card.*

4. *Next, you will build each word three times with magnetic letters. Each time you build a word, compare the spelling letter by letter to the word on your card. Say the names of the letters aloud, in order, as you check them.*

5. Select a word that a student chooses, and demonstrate building the word with magnetic letters and checking it letter by letter with the word on the index card. Then mix the letters, and quickly build and check the word two more times.

famous
treasure
proud
minute
evening
country ✓

Apply

- Have students choose the specified number of words they would like to learn from their "words to learn" list, and have them make a list on an index card. Give the class three to five additional words from recent lessons. Circulate around the room to review spellings. If the words are spelled accurately, place a small checkmark in the corner as a signal to students that they can rely on the spellings as they build and rebuild the words.

- After students have finished building the words with magnetic letters, they place their index cards in a pocket of their word study folders for future reference as they use additional study routines.

Share

Ask students to share some new words that they are learning to spell correctly. Encourage them to tell how the routine of building and checking the words several times is helping them.

Assess

- Notice whether students are building words accurately and quickly.

- Review pieces of writing over several weeks to determine whether students are using the routine to gain control of conventional spellings.

- You may wish to use Word-Solving Actions Assessment B, D, or F.

ACTIVITY: MAGNETIC LETTERS

INSTRUCTIONAL PROCEDURE

MAKE WORDS

See page 32 for detailed descriptions of Instructional Procedures.

ACTION TAGS

| choose word |
| write word |
| build word |
| mix letters |
| fix word |
| mix letters |

Word-Solving Actions: Use a Study Routine to Spell a Word:
Choose, Write, Build, Mix, Fix, Mix (Partner Study 1)

Connect Learning Across Contexts

Shared Reading You may wish to use the following Shared Reading title from *Fountas & Pinnell Classroom*™ to point out words that students may wish to learn to spell accurately.

SR *Saving Cranes* by Brenda Iasevoli

Guided Reading Draw students' attention to words they are learning to spell that occur in the texts they are reading.

Shared Writing As you construct pieces of writing, ask students to spell words that they have been learning while using the study routine.

Independent Writing As you review students' writing, point out words that students have recently learned to spell correctly. Remind them that they can check the spelling by referring to their index cards. Encourage students to add to their list of new words to learn and keep this list in their word study folder.

Extend Learning

Repeat the lesson regularly so that students are in the habit of using the routine to increase their repertoire of known words.

▶ **Connect with Home**

Have students take home their index cards and sets of letter cards. Encourage them to build and check the words at home with family members.

YOU WILL NEED

Online Resources
- **WSA 11** Action Tags
- **WSA 11** Look, Say, Cover, Write, Check Sheets

Other Materials
- folders for Partner Study

Plan

▶ Consider Your Students

In this lesson, you teach students another routine for learning to spell words. Students continue to use the words that they began learning in WSA 10. They will refer to the index cards that they created in that lesson. It is very important to work with students until they have habituated the routine and can use it efficiently. You can pair this routine with many different lessons to help reinforce new principles.

▶ Working with English Language Learners

Look, Say, Cover, Write, Check is a simple technique to use, but it takes practice to perform efficiently. Work with a small group of English language learners to be sure they are engaging in the steps in order and with precision. Demonstrate the routine as often as necessary.

UNDERSTAND THE PRINCIPLE

To remember the spellings of words, students need to examine words closely, take time to notice the features that make them different from every other word, and then test their memory of those features. They are studying how words look. The deliberate moves in Look, Say, Cover, Write, Check form a study routine for remembering and checking spellings that students can use to learn new words thoroughly and efficiently. This "slowed-down" way of considering a word ultimately becomes automatic.

EXPLAIN THE PRINCIPLE

Several routines can help in spelling words.

Another routine for spelling words is Look, Say, Cover, Write, Check.

Comprehensive Phonics, Spelling, and Word Study Guide

Refer to: page **82**, row **50**

EARLY MIDDLE LATE

INSTRUCTIONAL PROCEDURE

MAKE WORDS

See page 32 for detailed descriptions of Instructional Procedures.

EXPLAIN THE PRINCIPLE

Several routines can help in spelling words.

Another routine for spelling words is Look, Say, Cover, Write, Check.

Comprehensive Phonics, Spelling, and Word Study Guide

Refer to:
page **82**, row **50**

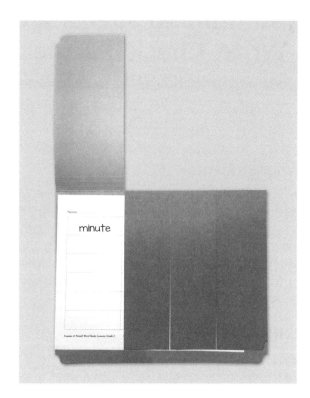

Teach

1. Tell students that today they are going to learn another routine that will help them study and spell new words correctly.

2. Briefly review the Choose, Write, Build, Mix, Fix, Mix routine. *You chose words, wrote them on a card, and built them with magnetic letters. You are going to continue to study those same words today.*

3. Display a Look, Say, Cover, Write, Check sheet in a precut file folder. Open all of the flaps.

4. Select a word that a student wrote on an index card. *You are going to choose a word that you are learning and write it in the first column.* Demonstrate writing the word on the sheet.

5. Explain the routine, and demonstrate each step. *Look carefully at the word. Say the word to yourself. Cover the word with the flap, and remember how it looks. Write the word again in the second column. Check your spelling letter by letter with the word in the first column.* Tell students to notice any mistakes and to think about how to write the word correctly.

6. Repeat the routine for the third column.

7. You may wish to repeat the routine with a second word and have students say each step.

8. Tell students that they will use this routine to continue learning the words they wrote on their index cards.

ACTIVITY: LOOK, SAY, COVER, WRITE, CHECK SHEET

INSTRUCTIONAL PROCEDURE

NOTICE PARTS

See page 32 for detailed descriptions of Instructional Procedures.

ACTION TAGS

look at word

say word

cover word

write word

check word

Apply

- Have students use the Look, Say, Cover, Write, Check routine and sheets to continue learning the words on their index cards.

- If students notice that a word is still misspelled in the last column of the sheet, you may wish to have them highlight on the index card the part of the word they need to remember. You may also want them to build the word several times with letter cards or magnetic letters and check it each time letter by letter with the word on the card.

Share

Ask students to share some new words that they are learning to spell accurately. Encourage them to tell how the routine of writing and checking the words several times is helping them.

Assess

- Notice whether students are writing the words accurately and quickly.

- Review pieces of writing over several weeks to determine whether students are using the routine to gain control of conventional spellings.

Connect Learning Across Contexts

Shared Reading You may wish to use the following Shared Reading title from *Fountas & Pinnell Classroom*™ to point out words that students may wish to learn to spell accurately.

SR *Wolf Pack* by Annette Bay Pimentel

Guided Reading Draw students' attention to words they are learning to spell that occur in the texts they are reading.

Shared Writing As you construct pieces of writing, ask students to spell words that they have been learning using the study routine.

Independent Writing Ask students to proofread their independent writing to be sure they have correctly spelled the words they have been learning.

Extend Learning

Repeat the lesson regularly so that students are in the habit of using the routine to increase their repertoire of known words.

▶ **Connect with Home**

Have students take their index cards home to practice writing the words with family members.

Use Known Words to Spell an Unknown Word (Partner Study 3)

Plan

▶ Consider Your Students

This lesson will be most effective if students have a need to learn the spelling of new words: e.g., a piece of writing that will be shared with an audience. Because students need to "overlearn" the techniques and routines for learning new words, you will probably find it beneficial to teach this lesson several times throughout the school year. You can add this lesson onto a lesson about any other principle.

▶ Working with English Language Learners

Making connections requires English language learners to notice features of the words they are studying and to link them with other words they know. This action helps them form personal word networks. Work with students in small groups to be sure they understand the concept of making connections, and remind them that they can transfer features of words they know to words they don't know yet.

UNDERSTAND THE PRINCIPLE

Students need to develop a network of knowledge about language. Effective word solvers rely on principles, strategies, and patterns that help them generate new knowledge: i.e., they use their current knowledge of words to learn new words. By establishing the habit of looking for patterns and making connections among words by how they look, how they sound, and what they mean, students form powerful categories of words rather than learning each word separately.

YOU WILL NEED

Online Resources
- ▶ **WSA 12** Action Tags
- ▶ **WSA 12** Make Connections Sheets

Other Materials
- ▶ blank chart paper

EXPLAIN THE PRINCIPLE

Use words you know to spell words you don't know.

Comprehensive Phonics, Spelling, and Word Study Guide

Refer to: page **82**, row **44**

ACTIVITY: CONNECTIONS BETWEEN WORDS

INSTRUCTIONAL PROCEDURE

NOTICE PARTS

See page 32 for detailed descriptions of Instructional Procedures.

EXPLAIN THE PRINCIPLE

Use words you know to spell words you don't know.

Comprehensive Phonics, Spelling, and Word Study Guide

Refer to: page **82**, row **44**

---

flight

fly	light
flew	night
floor	fight
flower	might

Teach

1. Tell students that today they are going to try a way to learn to spell new words.

2. Invite students to say words that they would like to learn how to spell. Select a word that will allow you to illustrate the principle clearly, e.g., *flight.*

3. *You can use parts of words you know to help you spell a word that you don't know. Think about the sounds that you hear at the beginning of* flight. *What words do you know that begin like* flight? • On chart paper, list the words in a column.

4. *Think about the sounds that you hear at the end of* flight. *What words do you know that end like* flight? • List the words in a second column.

5. Guide students to use the words on the chart as you spell the new word. *The word* fly *helps me spell the beginning of* flight, *f, l. The word* light *helps me spell the end of the word,* i, g h. t.

6. Repeat the procedure with another word that students would like to learn to spell.

7. Reinforce the principle. *As you just did, you can use parts of words you know to spell words you don't know.*

8. Display a make connections sheet, and point to the boxes at the top of the first page. Tell students that they will write in the boxes six words that they are learning to spell. Explain that they will write each word again in a box in the make connections section. Below each word they are learning, they will try to think of three words that begin like the word and three words that end like the word.

Fountas & Pinnell Word Study Lessons, Grade 3

WSA 12 Make Connections, a

ACTIVITY: MAKE CONNECTIONS SHEET

INSTRUCTIONAL PROCEDURE

NOTICE PARTS

See page 32 for detailed descriptions of Instructional Procedures.

ACTION TAGS

write six words

make connections to other words

write words

Apply

- You may wish to check the spelling of the six words that students write in the boxes.

- You may also wish to have students work with a partner to brainstorm words that begin and end like the words they are learning to spell.

Share

- Have students share connections that they have made. Listen for language that indicates that students are applying the strategy:

    "The word *shine* starts like the word *sheep*."

    "The words *shine* and *line* end with the same three letters."

- You may wish to post a chart that lists the kinds of connections students have learned how to make: e.g., start the same, end the same. As you teach and as students discover other connections, you can add them to the chart.

Assess

Review pieces of writing over several weeks to determine whether students are using the strategy to gain control of conventional spellings.

Word-Solving Actions: Use Known Words to Spell an Unknown Word (Partner Study 3)

Connect Learning Across Contexts

Shared Reading You may wish to use the following Shared Reading title from *Fountas & Pinnell Classroom™* to help students make connections among words while reading.

> SR *From Buds to Bananas* by Betty Riggs

Guided Reading Help the students solve new words by connecting them to words they already know.

Shared Writing When the students want to write a new word, prompt them to think of words they know that begin or end the same way.

Independent Writing Guide students to spell a new word by making connections to a similar word that they already know how to spell.

Extend Learning

Repeat the lesson to reinforce the understanding. Teach students how to make other types of connections among words, such as words with the same middle sound, words that rhyme, or words with the same consonant clusters.

▶ Connect with Home

Have students take their make connections sheets home to share with family members. Encourage them to think of more connections and then to share those with the class.

Plan

▶ Consider Your Students

Students need to think about how words sound and how they look. Letter boxes are a tool that helps students think about the letters and sounds in sequence and that provides a scaffold for writing. You may use your own word lists and increase or decrease the number of words each student is asked to spell, as appropriate. When students are checking to see if their spelling of a word looks right, encourage them to think about whether the word is one they may have seen before in a book, around the classroom, or at home. Suggest that they think about whether the spelling of the word they produced has the right letters in the right order. Ask them if the word sounds like another word they know. You may also encourage them to think about letter-sound relationships that they know.

▶ Working with English Language Learners

Noticing and remembering how words look will help English language learners' spelling skills. If students are not spelling words accurately, the words may be too difficult. Notice the errors students make, and use that information as you choose new spelling words.

UNDERSTAND THE PRINCIPLE

Ultimately, spellers must call to mind all of the features of a word and produce it in writing. This process needs to be fluent, automatic, and largely unconscious so that the writer can keep the meaning of the message in mind while constructing, and perhaps reconstructing, the spelling of the word. It is useful for spellers trying to write new words to attempt a spelling and then to check to see if the spelling looks right.

YOU WILL NEED

PWS Ready Resources
- ▶ Letter Boxes

Online Resources
- ▶ **WSA 13** Action Tags
- ▶ **WSA 13** Word Lists
- ▶ **WSA 13** Letter Boxes
- ▶ **WSA 13** List Sheets

Other Materials
- ▶ blank chart paper

EXPLAIN THE PRINCIPLE

Try writing a word, and see if the spelling looks right.

Comprehensive Phonics, Spelling, and Word Study Guide

Refer to: page **82**, row **43**

ACTIVITY: LETTER BOXES

INSTRUCTIONAL PROCEDURE

HEAR, SAY, AND WRITE: LETTER BOXES

See page 32 for detailed descriptions of Instructional Procedures.

EXPLAIN THE PRINCIPLE

Try writing a word, and see if the spelling looks right.

Comprehensive Phonics, Spelling, and Word Study Guide

Refer to: page **82**, row **43**

Teach

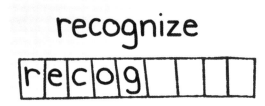

1. Tell students that today they will work together to spell new words and to check their work.

2. *You have been reading and writing many words. You can spell some words quickly. Other words are new to you, and you may not be sure how to spell them.* Draw five letter boxes. Say a familiar word such as *river,* and invite a student to spell it as you write the word in the boxes or on chart paper. *I wrote the word river with one letter in each box. Does the spelling look right?* • *What do you notice about the way it looks?* • If the spelling is right, move on to another word.

3. Draw nine letter boxes. Say a less familiar word such as *recognize,* and invite a student to think about how to spell it. Then write the word in the boxes or on the chart. *I wrote the word recognize with one letter in each box. Does the spelling look right?* • *To check the spelling, let's start by counting the number of letters.*

4. Run your finger under the boxes so the students can think about the letters with you. *What is the first letter in this word?* • *The first letter is r. What sound does the letter r stand for?* • *The letter r stands for /r/. What is the next letter?* • *What sound does the letter e stand for here?* • *The letter e stands for /e/.* Model blending the sounds of *r* and *e* together. Continue through each letter of the word. Help students recognize that the final *e* represents no sound in this word.

5. *Does it look like* recognize? • *Are all of the letters right?* • *Are the letters in the right order?* • *Are there any missing letters?* • *Are there any letters that should be taken away?*

6. Reinforce the principle. *Because you have seen so many words in books and inside and outside the classroom, sometimes you can tell when the spelling of a word looks right. When you're not sure about the spelling of a word, it's a good idea to try writing it, and see if the spelling looks right.*

7. Tell students that they will work with a partner to say and write words. Explain that one student says a word from a word list and tells the partner the number of letters. After finding the row of letter boxes with the correct number of letters, the partner says the word slowly and attempts to spell the word using the letter boxes. After working together to check that the spelling is right, the partner writes the word again on a list sheet. Students then switch roles.

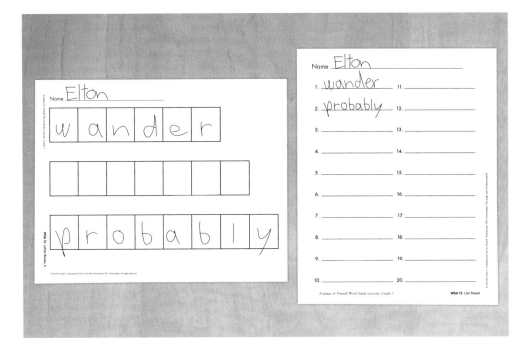

ACTIVITY: LETTER BOXES
AND LIST SHEET

INSTRUCTIONAL PROCEDURE

HEAR, SAY, AND WRITE: LETTER BOXES

See page 32 for detailed descriptions of Instructional Procedures.

ACTION TAGS

person 1
say word
tell number of letters
person 2
say word slowly
choose letter boxes
spell word
check spelling
write word

Apply

Have students work in pairs. Remind them to listen to each word and the number of letters it has, and then choose the row of letter boxes that has the same number of letters. Partners can work together to check the spelling of each word before the speller writes it on the list sheet.

Share

Have a few students share thoughts about the spelling of the words they attempted to write.

Assess

■ Notice the accuracy of students' spelling in their independent writing.

■ Observe students' attempts at spelling unknown words, and note their ability to see if the spelling looks right.

■ You may wish to use Word-Solving Actions Assessment D or F.

Word-Solving Actions: Attempt to Spell an Unknown Word (Partner Study 4)

Connect Learning Across Contexts

Shared Reading You may wish to use the following Shared Reading title from *Fountas & Pinnell Classroom™* to point out words that students may wish to learn to spell accurately.

SR *Tiny but Fierce* by Cheri Colburn

Guided Reading During word work, help students look more closely at features of words they find difficult. Students can work with magnetic letters, small whiteboards, or steno pads to write words quickly and then circle features that are important to notice.

Shared Writing As you construct a piece of writing, have students check a word to see if the spelling looks right.

Independent Writing Encourage students to try writing new words and checking to see if the spelling looks right.

Extend Learning

Repeat the lesson with additional sets of unknown words.

▶ ## Connect with Home

Invite students to take word lists home to share with family members. Tell family members to encourage students to try to spell other simple words when they are writing at home.

Glossary

abbreviation Shortened form of a word that uses some of the letters: e.g., *Mr., etc., NY*.

accented syllable A syllable that is given emphasis in pronunciation. See also *syllable, stress*.

adjective suffix A suffix put at the end of a word root or base word to form an adjective. See also *suffix*.

adverb suffix A suffix put at the end of a word root or base word to form an adverb. See also *suffix*.

affix A letter or group of letters added to the beginning or ending of a base or root word to change its meaning or function (a *prefix* or a *suffix*).

alphabet book / ABC book A book that helps children develop the concept and sequence of the alphabet by pairing alphabet letters with pictures of people, animals, or objects with labels related to the letters.

alphabet linking chart A chart containing uppercase and lowercase letters of the alphabet paired with pictures representing words beginning with each letter (*a, apple*).

alphabetic principle The concept that there is a relationship between the spoken sounds in oral language and the graphic forms in written language.

analogy The resemblance of a known word to an unknown word that helps you solve the unknown word's meaning. Often an analogy shows the relationship between two pairs of words.

antonym A word that has the opposite meaning from another word: e.g., *cold* versus *hot*.

assessment A means for gathering information or data that reveals what learners control, partially control, or do not yet control consistently.

automaticity apid, accurate, fluent word decoding without conscious effort or attention.

base word A word in its simplest form, which can be modified by adding affixes: e.g., *read; reread, reading*. A base word has meaning, can stand on its own, and is easily apparent in the language. Compare to *word root*.

behavior An observable action.

blend To combine sounds or word parts.

capitalization The use of capital letters, usually the first letter in a word, as a convention of written language (for example, for proper names and to begin sentences).

closed syllable A syllable that ends in a consonant: e.g., *lem*-on.

comparative ending A suffix (e.g., *-er, -est*) put at the end of a base word to show comparison between or among two or more things.

compound word A word made of two or more smaller words or morphemes: e.g., *playground*. The meaning of a compound word can be a combination of the meanings of the words it is made of or can be unrelated to the meanings of the combined units.

concept book A book organized to develop an understanding of an abstract or generic idea or categorization.

concept word A word that represents an abstract idea or name. Categories of concept words include color names, number words, days of the week, months of the year, seasons, and so on.

consonant A speech sound made by partial or complete closure of the airflow that causes friction at one or more points in the breath channel. The consonant sounds are represented by the letters *b, c, d, f, g, h, j, k, l, m, n, p, qu, r, s, t, v, w, y,* and *z.*

consonant blend Two or more consonant letters that often appear together in words and represent sounds that are smoothly joined, although each of the sounds can be heard in the word: e.g., *tr*im.

consonant cluster A sequence of two or three consonant letters: e.g., *tr*im, *ch*air.

consonant cluster linking chart A chart of common consonant clusters paired with pictures representing words beginning with each: e.g., *bl block.*

consonant digraph Two consonant letters that appear together and represent a single sound that is different from the sound of either letter: e.g., sh*ell.*

contraction A shortened form of one or more words. A letter or letters are left out, and an apostrophe takes the place of the missing letter or letters.

cursive A form of handwriting in which letters are connected.

decoding Using letter-sound relationships to translate a word from a series of symbols to a unit of meaning.

dialect A regional variety of a language. In most languages, including English and Spanish, dialects are mutually intelligible; the differences are actually minor.

diction Clear pronunciation and enunciation in speech.

directionality The orientation of print (in the English language, from left to right).

distinctive letter features Visual features that make each letter of the alphabet different from every other letter.

early literacy concepts Very early understandings related to how written language or print is organized and used—how it works.

English language learner A person whose native language is not English and who is acquiring English as an additional language.

figurative language Language that compares two objects or ideas to allow the reader to see something more clearly or understand something in a new way. An element of a writer's style, figurative language changes or goes beyond literal meaning.

fluency In reading, this term names the ability to read continuous text with good momentum, phrasing, appropriate pausing, intonation, and stress. In word solving, this term names the ability to solve words with speed, accuracy, and flexibility.

grammar Complex rules by which people can generate an unlimited number of phrases, sentences, and longer texts in that language. Conventional grammar refers to the accepted grammatical conventions in a society.

grapheme A letter or cluster of letters representing a single sound, or phoneme: e.g., *a, eigh, ay*.

graphophonic relationship The relationship between the oral sounds of the language and the written letters or clusters of letters. See also *semantic system, syntactic system*.

have a try To write a word, notice that it doesn't look quite right, try it two or three other ways, and decide which construction looks right; to make an attempt and self-check.

high-frequency words Words that occur often in the spoken and written language.

homograph One of two or more words spelled alike but different in meaning, derivation, or pronunciation: e.g., the *bat* flew away, he swung the *bat*; take a *bow*, *bow* and arrow.

homonym One of two or more words spelled and pronounced alike but different in meaning: e.g., we had *quail* for dinner; I would *quail* in fear. A homonym is a type of homograph.

homophone One of two or more words pronounced alike but different in spelling and meaning: e.g., *meat, meet; bear, bare*.

idiom A phrase with meaning that cannot be derived from the conjoined meanings of its elements: e.g., *raining cats and dogs*.

inflectional ending A suffix added to a base word to show tense, plurality, possession, or comparison: e.g., dark-*er*.

interactive read-aloud A teaching context in which students are actively listening and responding to an oral reading of a text.

interactive writing A teaching context in which the teacher and students cooperatively plan, compose, and write a group text; the teacher acts as a scribe but invites individual students to contribute some writing for letters or words that have high instructional value.

intonation The rise and fall in pitch of the voice in speech to convey meaning.

letter combination Two or more letters that appear together and represent vowel sounds in words: e.g., *ea* in *meat*, *igh* in *sight*.

letter knowledge The ability to recognize and label the graphic symbols of language.

letters Graphic symbols representing the sounds in a language. Each letter has particular distinctive features and may be identified by letter name or sound.

letter-sound relationships The correspondence of letter(s) and sound(s) in written or spoken language.

lexicon Words that make up language.

long vowel The elongated vowel sound that is the same as the name of the vowel. It is sometimes represented by two or more letters: e.g., *ca*ke, *ei*ght, m*ai*l. Another term for long vowel is *lax vowel*.

lowercase letter A small letter form that is usually different from its corresponding capital or uppercase form.

morpheme The smallest unit of meaning in a language. Morphemes may be free or bound. For example, *run* is a unit of meaning that can stand alone (a free morpheme). In *runs* and *running*, the added *-s* and *-ing* are also units of meaning. They cannot stand alone but add meaning to the free morpheme. The *-s* and *-ing* are examples of bound morphemes.

morphemic strategies Ways of solving words by discovering meaning through the combination of significant word parts or morphemes: e.g., *happy, happiest; run, runner, running*.

morphological system Rules by which morphemes (building blocks of vocabulary) fit together into meaningful words, phrases, and sentences.

morphology The combination of morphemes (building blocks of meaning) to form words; the rules by which words are formed from free and bound morphemes—for example, root words, prefixes, and suffixes.

multiple-meaning word A word that means something different depending on the way it is used: e.g., *run—home run, run in your stocking, run down the street, a run of bad luck.*

multisyllable word A word that contains more than one syllable.

noun suffix A suffix put at the end of a word root or base word to form a noun.

onomatopoeia The representation of sound with words.

onset In a syllable, the part (consonant, consonant cluster, or consonant digraph) that comes before the vowel: e.g., the *cr* in *cream*. See also *rime*.

onset-rime segmentation The identification and separation of the onset

(first part) and rime (last part, containing the vowel) in a word: e.g., *dr-ip*.

open syllable A syllable that ends in a vowel sound: e.g., *ho*-tel.

orthographic awareness The knowledge of the visual features of written language, including distinctive features of letters as well as spelling patterns in words.

orthography The representation of the sounds of a language with the proper letters according to standard usage (spelling).

phoneme The smallest unit of sound in spoken language. There are forty-four units of speech sounds in English.

phoneme addition To add a beginning or ending sound to a word: e.g., /h/ + *and*; *an* + /t/.

phoneme blending To identify individual sounds and then to put them together smoothly to make a word: e.g., /k//a//t/ = *cat*.

phoneme deletion To omit a beginning, middle, or ending sound of a word: e.g., /k//a//s//k/ - /k/ = *ask*.

phoneme-grapheme correspondence The relationship between the sounds (phonemes) and letters (graphemes) of a language.

phoneme isolation The identification of an individual sound—beginning, middle, or end—in a word.

phoneme manipulation The movement of sounds from one place in a word to another.

phoneme reversal The exchange of the first and last sounds of a word to make a different word.

phoneme substitution The replacement of the beginning, middle, or ending sound of a word with a new sound.

phonemic (or phoneme) awareness The ability to hear individual sounds in words and to identify particular sounds.

phonemic strategies Ways of solving words that use how words sound and relationships between letters and letter clusters and phonemes in those words.

phonetics The scientific study of speech sounds—how the sounds are made vocally and the relation of speech sounds to the total language process.

phonics The knowledge of letter-sound relationships and how they are used in reading and writing. Teaching phonics refers to helping children acquire this body of knowledge about the oral and written language systems; additionally, teaching phonics helps children use phonics knowledge as part of a reading and writing process. Phonics instruction uses a small portion of the body of knowledge that makes up phonetics.

phonogram A phonetic element represented by graphic characters or symbols. In word recognition, words containing a graphic sequence composed of a vowel grapheme and an ending consonant grapheme (such as *an* or *it*) are sometimes called a word family.

phonological awareness The awareness of words, rhyming words, onsets and rimes, syllables, and individual sounds (phonemes).

phonological system The sounds of the language and how they work together in ways that are meaningful to the speakers of the language.

plural Of, relating to, or constituting more than one.

possessive Grammatical form used to show ownership: e.g., *John's, his.*

prefix A group of letters placed in front of a base word to change its meaning: e.g., *pre*plan.

principle In phonics, a generalization or a sound-spelling relationship that is predictable.

punctuation Marks used in written text to clarify meaning and separate structural units. The comma and the period are common punctuation marks.

***r*-controlled vowel sound** The modified or *r*-influenced sound of a vowel when it is followed by *r* in a syllable: e.g., *hurt.*

related words Words that are related because of sound, spelling, category, or meaning. See also *synonym, antonym, homophone, homograph, analogy.*

rhyme The repetition of vowel and consonant sounds in the stressed syllables of words in verse, especially at the ends of lines.

rime In a syllable, the ending part containing the letters that represent the vowel sound and the consonant letters that follow: i.e., dr-*eam.* See also *onset.*

root See *word root.*

schwa The sound of the middle vowel in an unstressed syllable (the *e* in *happen* and the sound between the *k* and *l* in *freckle*).

segment To divide into parts: e.g., *to/ma/to.*

semantic system The system by which speakers of a language communicate meaning through language. See also *graphophonic relationship, syntactic system.*

sentence A group of words that expresses a complete thought.

sets and subsets In relation to concept words, words that represent big ideas or items and words that represent related smaller ideas or items.

shared reading An instructional context in which the teacher involves a group of students in the reading of a particular big book or other enlarged text in order to introduce aspects of literacy (such as print conventions), develop reading strategies (such as decoding or predicting), and teach vocabulary.

shared writing An instructional context in which the teacher involves a group of students in the composing of a coherent text together. The teacher writes an enlarged text while scaffolding children's language and ideas.

short vowel A brief-duration sound represented by a vowel letter: e.g, the /a/ in *cat*.

silent *e* The final *e* in a spelling pattern that usually signals a long vowel sound in the word and that does not represent a sound itself: e.g., *make*.

solving words (as a strategic action) Using a range of strategies to take words apart and understand their meaning(s).

spelling patterns Beginning letters (onsets) and common phonograms (rimes), which form the basis for the English syllable. Knowing these patterns, a student can build countless words.

stress The emphasis given to some syllables or words in pronunciation. See also *accented syllable*.

suffix A group of letters added at the end of a base word or word root to change its function or meaning: e.g., hand*ful*, hope*less*.

syllabication The division of words into syllables.

syllable A minimal unit of sequential speech sounds composed of a vowel sound or a consonant-vowel combination. A syllable always contains a vowel or vowel-like speech sound: e.g., *pen/ny*.

synonym One of two or more words that have different sounds but the same meaning: e.g., *high, tall*.

syntactic awareness The knowledge of grammatical patterns or structures.

syntactic system Rules that govern the ways in which morphemes and words work together in sentence patterns. This system is not the same as proper grammar, which refers to the accepted grammatical conventions. See also *graphophonic relationship, semantic system*.

syntax The way sentences are formed with words and phrases and the grammatical rules that govern their formation.

uppercase letter A large letter form that is usually different from its corresponding lowercase form. Another term for *uppercase letter* is *capital letter*.

visual strategies Ways of solving words that use knowledge of how words look, including the clusters and patterns of the letters in words.

vocabulary Words and their meanings. See also *word meaning/vocabulary*.

vowel A speech sound or phoneme made without stoppage of or friction in the airflow. The vowel sounds are represented by *a, e, i, o, u,* and sometimes *y.*

vowel combination See *letter combination.*

word A unit of meaning in language.

word analysis To break apart words into parts or individual sounds in order to parse them.

word boundaries The white space that appears before the first letter and after the last letter of a word and that defines the letter or letters as a word. It is important for young readers to learn to recognize word boundaries.

word-by-word matching Usually applied to a beginning reader's ability to match one spoken word with one printed word while reading. Younger readers learn by pointing. In older readers, the eyes take over the process.

word family A term often used to designate words that are connected by phonograms or rimes (e.g., *hot, not, pot, shot*). A word family can also be a series of words connected by meaning (e.g., *baseless, baseline, baseboard*).

word meaning/vocabulary *Word meaning* refers to the commonly accepted meaning of a word in oral or written language. *Vocabulary* often refers to the words one knows in oral or written language.

word structure The parts that make up a word.

words (as a text characteristic) Decodability of words in a text; phonetic and structural features of words.

word-solving actions The strategies a reader uses to recognize words and understand their meaning(s).

References

Adams, M.J. 1990. Beginning to Read: Thinking and Learning about Print. Cambridge, MA: MIT Press.

Allington, R. 1991. Children who find learning to read difficult: School responses to diversity. In E.H. Hiebert, ed. *Literacy for a Diverse Society: Perspectives, practices, and policies.* New York: Teachers College Press.

Armbruster, B.B., F., Lehr, and J. Osborn. 2001. *Put Reading First: The Research Building Blocks for Teaching Children to Read: Kindergarten Through Grade 3.* Jessup, MD: National Institute for Literacy.

Ball, E.W., and B.A. Blachman. 1991. Does phoneme awareness training in kindergarten make a difference in early world recognition and developmental spelling? *Reading Research Quarterly* 26 (1):49–66.

Biemiller, A. 1970. The development of the use of graphic and contextual information as children learn to read. *Reading Research Quarterly* 6:75–96.

Blachman, B. 1984. The relationships of rapid naming ability and language analysis skills to kindergarten and first-grade reading achievement. *Journal of Educational Psychology* 76:610–622.

Blanchard, J.S. 1980. Preliminary investigation of transfer between single-word decoding ability and contextual reading comprehension of poor readers in grade six. *Perceptual and Motor Skills* 51:1271–1281.

Bradley, L., and P.E. Bryant. 1983. Categorizing sounds and learning to read—a causal connection. *Nature* 301:419–421.

Bryant, P.E., M. MacLean, L.L. Bradley, and J. Crossland. 1990. Rhyme and alliteration, phoneme detection, and learning to read. *Developmental Psychology* 26(3):429–438.

———. 1989. Nursery rhymes, phonological skills and reading. *Journal of Child Language* 16:407–428.

Ceprano, M.A. 1980. A review of selected research on methods of teaching sight words. *The Reading Teacher* 35:314–322.

Chall, J.S. 1989. Learning to read: The great debate. 20 years later. *Phi Delta Kappan* 70:521–538.

Clay, M.M. 2001. *Change over Time in Children's Literacy Development.* Portsmouth, NH: Heinemann.

———. 1998. *By Different Paths to Common Outcomes.* York, ME: Stenhouse Publishers.

———. 1991. *Becoming Literate: The Construction of Inner Control.* Portsmouth, NH: Heinemann.

Daneman, M. 1991. Individual difference in reading skills. In R. Barr, M.L. Kamil, P. Mosenthal, and P.D. Pearson, eds. *Handbook of Reading Research* 2:512–538. New York: Longman.

Ehri, L.C. 1991. Development of the ability to read words. In R. Barr, M.L. Kamil, P. Mosenthal, and P.D. Pearson, eds. *Handbook of Reading Research* 2:383–417. New York: Longman.

Ehri, L.C., and S. McCormick. 1998. Phases of word learning: Implications for instruction with delayed and disabled readers. *Reading and Writing Quarterly* 20:163–179.

Fountas, I.C., and G.S. Pinnell. 2019. *Fountas & Pinnell Classroom™*. Portsmouth, NH: Heinemann.

———. 2019. *Fountas & Pinnell Classroom™ Guided Reading Collection, Grade 3*. Portsmouth, NH: Heinemann.

———. 2019. *Fountas & Pinnell Classroom™ Independent Reading Collection, Grade 3*. Portsmouth, NH: Heinemann.

———. 2019. *Fountas & Pinnell Classroom™ Interactive Read-Aloud Collection, Grade 3*. Portsmouth, NH: Heinemann.

———. 2019. *Fountas & Pinnell Classroom™ Shared Reading Collection, Grade 3*. Portsmouth, NH: Heinemann.

———. 2019. *The Reading Minilessons Book, Grade 3*. Portsmouth, NH: Heinemann.

———. 2017. *Guided Reading: Responsive Teaching Across the Grades*, 2d ed. Portsmouth, NH: Heinemann.

———. 2017. *The Fountas & Pinnell Literacy Continuum: A Tool for Assessment, Planning, and Teaching*, Expanded Edition. Portsmouth, NH: Heinemann.

———. 2017. *The Fountas & Pinnell Comprehensive Phonics, Spelling, and Word Study Guide*. Portsmouth, NH: Heinemann.

———. 2014. *Fountas & Pinnell Select Collection, Grade 3*. Portsmouth, NH: Heinemann.

———. 1999. *Voices on Word Matters: Learning about Phonics and Spelling in the Literacy Classroom*. Portsmouth, NH: Heinemann.

———. 1998. *Word Matters: Teaching Phonics and Spelling in the Reading/Writing Classroom*. Portsmouth, NH: Heinemann.

Fox, B., and K.D. Routh. 1984. Phonemic analysis and synthesis as word attack skills: Revisited. *Journal of Educational Psychology* 76:1059–1064.

Hohn, W., and L. Ehri. 1983. Do alphabet letters help prereaders acquire phonemic segmentation skill? *Journal of Educational Psychology* 75:752–762.

Holdaway, D. 1984. *The Foundations of Literacy*. Portsmouth, NH: Heinemann.

Hundley, S., and D. Powell. 1999. In *Voices on Word Matters*, eds I.C. Fountas and G.S. Pinnell. 159–164. Portsmouth, NH: Heinemann.

Juel, C. 1988. Learning to read and write: A longitudinal study of 54 children from first through fourth grades. *Journal of Educational Psychology* 80:437–447.

Juel, C., P.L. Griffith, and P.B. Gough. 1986. Acquisition of literacy: A longitudinal study of children in first and second grade. *Journal of Educational Psychology* 78:243–255.

Lesgold, A.M., L.B. Resnick, and K. Hammond. 1985. In learning to read: A longitudinal study of word skill development in two curricula, eds. G.E. MacKinnon and T.G. Walker.

MacKinnon, G.E., and T. Gary Waller. 1985. *Reading Research: Advances in Theory and Practice.* 4:107–138. New York: Academic Press.

Liberman, I., D. Shankweile, and A. Liberman. 1985. *The Alphabetic Principle and Learning to Read.* U.S. Department of Health and Human Services. Reprinted with permission from The University of Michigan Press by the National Institute of Child Health and Human Development. Adapted from Phonology and the problems of learning to read and write. *Remedial and Special Education* 6:8–17.

Liberman, I.Y., D. Shankweiler, F.W. Fischer, and B. Carter. 1974. Explicit syllable and phoneme segmentation in the young child. *Journal of Experimental Child Psychology* 18:201–212.

Lundberg, I., J. Frost, and O.P. Petersen. 1988. Effects of an extensive program for stimulating phonological awareness in preschool children. *Reading Research Quarterly* 23:263–284.

McCarrier, A.M., G.S. Pinnell, and I.C. Fountas. 2000. *Interactive Writing: How Language and Literacy Come Together.* Portsmouth, NH: Heinemann.

Moats, L.C. 2000. *Speech to Print: Language Essentials for Teachers.* Baltimore: Brookes Publishing.

Nagy, W.E., R.C. Anderson, M. Schommer, J. Scott, and A. Stallman. 1989. Morphological families in the internal lexicon. *Reading Research Quarterly* 24:262–282.

National Institute of Child Health and Human Development. 2001. Report of the National Reading Panel: "Teaching Children to Read: An Evidence-Based Assessment of the Scientific Research Literature on Reading and Its Implications for Reading Instruction." *Reports of the Subgroups.* Washington, DC: National Institutes of Health.

New Standards Primary Literacy Committee. 1999. *Reading and Writing: Grade by Grade.* Washington, DC: National Center on Education and the Economy and the University of Pittsburgh.

Perfetti, C.A., I. Beck, L. Bell, and C. Hughes. 1987. Children's reading and the development of phonological awareness. *Merrill-Palmer Quarterly* 33:283–319.

Pinnell, G.S., J. Pikulski, K.K. Wixson, et al. 1995. *Listening to Children Read Aloud:* Data from NAEP's Integrated Reading Performance Record (IRPR) at Grade 4. Report No. 23-FR-04, prepared by the Educational Testing Service. Washington, DC: Office of Educational Research and Improvement, U.S. Department of Education.

Pressley, M. 1998. *Reading Instruction That Works: The Case for Balanced Teaching.* New York: The Guilford Press.

Read, C. 1971. Pre-school children's knowledge of English phonology. *Harvard Educational Review* 41:1–34.

Snow, C.E., M.S. Burns, and P. Griffin, eds. 1998. *Preventing Reading Difficulties in Young Children.* Washington, DC: Committee on the Prevention of Reading Difficulties in Young Children, Commission on Behavioral and Social Sciences and Education, National Research Council.

Treiman, R. 1985. Onsets and rimes as units of spoken syllables: Evidence from children. *Journal of Experimental Child Psychology* 39:161–181.

Vellutino, F.R., and M.B. Denckla. 1991. Cognitive and neuropsychological foundations of word identification in poor and normally developing readers. In R. Barr, M.L. Kamil, P. Mosenthal, and P.D. Pearson, eds. *Handbook of Reading Research* 2:571–608. New York: Longman.

Vellutino, F.R., and D.B. Scanlon. 1987. Phonological coding, phonological awareness, and reading ability: Evidence from longitudinal and experimental study. *Merrill-Palmer Quarterly* 33:321–363.

Vellutino, F.R., D.M. Scanlon, E.R. Sipay, et al. 1996. Cognitive profiles of difficult-to-remediate and readily remediated poor readers: Early intervention as a vehicle for distinguishing between cognitive and experiential deficits as basic causes of specific reading disability. *Journal of Educational Psychology* 88:601–638.